新 GRE

阅读制胜法则

——多层结构法

陈虎平 ➡ 编著

群言出版社
Qunyan Press

图书在版编目(CIP)数据

GRE阅读制胜法则：多层结构法 / 陈虎平编著 .—
北京：群言出版社，2012（2015.4重印）
　ISBN 978-7-80256-352-0

　Ⅰ . ①G… 　Ⅱ . ①陈… 　Ⅲ . ①GRE—阅读教学—自学参
考资料 　Ⅳ . ①H319.4

中国版本图书馆CIP数据核字（2012）第148091号

责任编辑　张　茜
封面设计　大愚设计+赵文康
出版发行　群言出版社(Qunyan Press)

地　　址　北京市东城区东厂胡同北巷1号（100006）
网　　站　www.qypublish.com
电子信箱　bj62605588@163.com　qunyancbs@126.com
总 编 办　010-62605588　65265404　65138815
发 行 部　010-62605019　62263345　65220236
经　　销　全国新华书店
读者服务　010-62418641　65265404　65263345
法律顾问　北京市君泰律师事务所

印　　刷　北京鑫海达印刷有限公司
版　　次　2012年8月第1版　2015年4月第7次印刷
开　　本　880×1230　　1/16
印　　张　17.75
字　　数　370千字
书　　号　ISBN 978-7-80256-352-0
定　　价　42.00元

给 努力求知的优秀青年

序言

本项关于GRE文章阅读的研究目的在于揭示英文学术文章内在的独立的构成规律，并提出GRE阅读的结构化解决方案。本书透过GRE文章，分析以之为代表的学术论证，为有志攻克GRE阅读的优秀青年提供一些有益的信息，也为我们阅读与理解任何英文学术文章打开一扇窗。由于本书的方法并不依赖GRE文章本身，因此，书中所说的逻辑结构的阅读方法以及思维方式，对于准备GMAT、LSAT、TOEFL、SAT的学术阅读部分也是有帮助的；另外，不参加这些考试、但想学会如何阅读学术论文和著作的读者朋友，应该也能从中得到一些启发。

英文学术文章以严谨论证著称，GRE更是各类题材的学术文章的浓缩版。GRE阅读文章取材于学术期刊与杂志，多数题目都针对学术推理本身而不是专业背景知识，因此需要有特别的准备方法，本书称之为"结构化阅读法"。在结构上，GRE文章比普通学术文章更加紧凑，阅读的难度也因此增大，即便能够熟读本专业英文教科书和论文的人，也会在理解GRE文章逻辑思路方面有一定困难。此外，由于涉及的学科极为广泛，所以阅读GRE文章还有一个额外的好处：对各门学科知识的论证思路，都可以有一定程度的理解；为将来从事本学科的研究工作以及广泛阅读多个学科的科研著作或畅销书籍打下坚实的基础。

本书的第1章介绍GRE阅读的学习方法，讲明考试要求、训练材料、多层分解的分析方法、刻意练习的训练方法，还会将结构化的阅读与自然阅读法进行对比分析。第2章是全书的核心。该章分别从文章、段落、句子3个层次，对GRE阅读文章进行细致的多层结构的演绎分析。其中关于段落和句子的分析，还会举例说明。该章难度颇高，也许需要多读几遍；但考生或读者在真正掌握以后，相信会有实质收获。该章也会简要说明单词的问题。第3章讨论GRE阅读题目，分成10种题型，多数题型都会举例说明；这一章还探讨如何定位和甄别选项。第4章是6套GRE阅读的模拟练习题，其中文章选编自各种学术作品，题目则由作者编写。每个练习都有自然科学、生命科学、社会科学、人文学科文章各1篇，同时加上1~2道逻辑单题，尽可能贴近实际考试。读者可按照提示做题。第5章是上述6套练习题的详细解析，分为结构分析和题目分析。读者可以在做完任何一个练习之后，仔细阅读，了解文章结构分析的方法和做题的技巧。第6章在做题的基础之上进行多层分解的单项训练，包括文章结构、段落论点、长句分析、题型、题干、选项等6个方面的集中训练，通过这些训练，读者可以真正掌握考试所要求的各个层次的技巧。最后的第7章试图将本书倡导的结构化的逻辑阅读方法延伸到更多体裁的文章，并简要说明逻辑方法在商业与社会中的应用。

本书在结构分析方面涵盖了论点的所有论证方式，也涵盖了论点及论点之间的所有可能的关系。鉴于考试现场的时间压力极高，仔细阅读每个单词显然并不可行，于是需要特定的方法来提取信息，本书所倡导的结构或逻辑提取的方法，就是为此而来。在开始训练时，试图按照结构思维来分析文章、提取核心，显然会拖慢速度，这就好比在网球训练的起步阶段，按照教练说的步骤练习，打球的动作会比平常慢；但经过一段时间的训练以后，就能慢慢掌握各种逻辑结构和解题方法，到后来再经过更多文章和题目的练习，就能融会贯通，所有方法不在当前意识中，而变成大脑的自动反应，这样，速度就提高了。如果不按特定的方法，只是多读，很可能到后来会有很大的阅读瓶颈，再也过不了。

本书的主要立场是，阅读要从结构出发，而不只是从单词出发。单词是可见的，但逻辑是眼睛看不见、需要大脑去思考的。由于GRE阅读主要考查逻辑关系，所以，我们一定不能只是关注眼睛可见的单词，而是也要思考和把握那些不可见的逻辑关系。阅读不只是认识单词的问题。以为认识所有单词就能读懂文章，就好比以为认识所有砖块，就懂得建筑的结构和功能。阅读要求的能力在眼睛可见的单词之外，也就是逻辑。本书所谈的逻辑，是狭义的。所谓逻辑，是指从一个前提、公理或论点出发，经过一系列推理步骤，得到一个结论或者支持初始论点的推理过程。也就是说，我们研究的逻辑结构是，主题（**Topic Words**）与各个论点（**Key Words**）、论点与论点之间（kw1–kw2）、论点（kw）与论据（a b c / x y z）之间、论据与论据（a–b, x–y）之间的关系。这些结构分析以及由此产生的结构阅读的方法，对于准备GMAT、LSAT、TOEFL阅读以及SAT阅读非文学部分，通常也是适用的。事实上，对于任何想要学习和掌握阅读分析类的文字的读者来说，这些方法也许都会有所帮助。

本书的另一个重点是目标的多层分解的训练方法。一个复杂的技能常有各个部分组成，阅读技能就是如此。只是随机搜索训练的方法，得到的常常是迎合个人偏好的做法，对于高难度的问题通常无效，随机学习的效率是很低的。靠单纯的大量做题，希望反复练习之后有所体悟，有时可以找出一些模式和规律，有时又感到迷惑，常在迷惑与有所悟之间徘徊，所以，这个方法的效率也不算高。毕竟，用于准备GRE阅读的时间通常只有200–400个小时，依然是有限的；如果别人已经发明了轮子，你不需要再发明一个，尤其考虑到自己发明的概率较低，而且自己还有很多别的事要处理，这都需要时间。对于像阅读这样的技能，模仿和学习已经被承认的主流方法，往往效率较高。本书提供的训练方法是，将一个看似模糊的大目标(阅读技能)分解成为清晰的、可以操作的小目标(文章结构、段落结构、句子结构、题型解法、题干定位、选项甄别)，针对每个小目标进行训练，最终组合起来，形成完整的、有效的整体技能，并通过更多训练，达到自动反应的程度，再上考场，就能毫不慌张、马到成功。

本书也提供了6套完整的GRE阅读模拟训练题，这对于当前可用的GRE阅读材料较少的局面，也许会有一定的补助。考生做了这些训练，相信会对GRE所要求的技能有更好的理解。

本书能够完成和出版，我要感谢的人很多。感谢我的同事们，与这些同事在一起共事是愉快的，而且他们很优秀，我从他们那里学到很多。人都有拖延症吧？我也有，所以我要特别感谢那些督促我写书的同事和朋友。感谢新东方大愚文化的编辑们做了细致的编辑工作，让本书快速出版。最重要的，感谢这么多年以来，尤其是2007年以来，所有在课堂内外支持我、鼓励我的学员朋友们，是你们的求知和求学的热情，让我看到了另一个自己，让我开心，让我知道我的工作有时真的有些价值。

我教GRE阅读已有10年。十年会磨一剑吗？这本书，尤其是其中的第2章，可以看做我对这段长期的教学经历的一个交代。希望读者会喜欢它，会觉得它有用，会用其中的思维方法阅读文章、思考问题、学习新知。我很乐意听到关于本书的各种反馈意见。读者如愿意与我分享阅读感受或有商榷和指正意见，可通过我的实名新浪微博或人人网公共主页与我联系。

祝阅读快乐！祝你们快乐！

陈虎平

于北京

目录

本书缩略语

缩略语	英文表达	意义
TS	main idea, thesis	Topic Sentence或Thesis，文章主题句，常在首段或转折句处。TS不是所有文章都有，它包含TW在内。其变形形式为TS' / TS''，指在前引出或在后说明主题句的句子。一些短文章仅有一个论点的，TS = KW。通常，一篇GRE文章包含2-3个论点，因此，TS = KW1 + KW2（+ KW3）。
TW/tw	topic, subject（matter）	Topic Words 主题词，不区分大小写。文章所讨论的对象，常为一个名词词组。其变形形式为TW'，指帮助引出TW的句子，常在首句或第二句。
KW/kw	main idea, major points	Key Words 关键词，不区分大小写。仅指作者的某个分论点或不同人物提出的观点、解释、理论、模型、假说、方案的核心词或其所在的句子，通常在段首句，有时也在转折句中提到。有时有KW'，表示引出论点的句子，但其本身并无内容，如There is another theory；或者表示论点的重述句。
AW/aw	attitude, tone	Attitude Words 态度句，多为负评价句，常由however, but, yet等词引导给出。AW - 表示态度为负评价；AW + 表示态度为正评价。不区分大小写。
a/b/c x/y/z u/v/w o/p/q i/j	supporting ideas, minor points, evidence, argument, reasoning, etc.	Evidence or argument 证据，跟在KW/AW之后的证据或论据。一个观点的多个论据常用连续几个字母表示。不同观点的论据则选用不同的连续字母表示。其中i/j，除表示论点或态度之后的论据以外，也用于表示在主题句之后的说明性内容。有时还用a'，指的是证据a的再次或补充说明。
e	example, instance, illustration	Example 举例，专指举例的句子，多为单独句子，有时是长句的后半句。举例属于证据，但因结构和考法特殊，经常专门表示。
~kw/~x but kw/x	concession, refutation	让步转折。~kw表示针对某一观点/kw的让步或取非，~x或~小写字母（如~a），表示针对某个证据（x或a）的让步。But kw/x表示针对该让步的转折。让步和转折往往同时出现。
CS/cs	conclusion, summary	Conclusion Sentence 结论句。在文章较短末段给出的总结句。有时也用cs指在某个段落末尾给出的该段核心的总结句，这时cs = kw。

GRE 阅读的学习方法论

本章内容

材料与考试要求 ◎

技能训练的方法论 ◎

结构张力与阅读方法 ◎

本章首先介绍GRE阅读考试的要求，然后说明训练的方法，特别是需要多加练习的三层结构关系，最后讨论GRE文章取材的来源和特点，并分析自然阅读方法与本书提出的结构化阅读法的差别。前两部分比较容易，最后一部分涉及思维和方法，相对困难，但可以帮助考生更快地转变阅读习惯，将自己从传统的认单词、读句子的自然阅读状态，转变到抓结构、记核心的结构化阅读状态。

第一节　材料与考试要求

1.1　GRE文章是浓缩的学术英文

从长度上看，GRE阅读的文章有3种：长文章，约450字，出4道题；短文章，约160字，出2-4道题；短文章，约120字，出1-2道题。任意一个Verbal Section里面，阅读文章都有4篇，分别涉及自然科学(natural sciences)、生命科学(biological sciences)、社会科学(social sciences)、人文学科(humanities)这四大学科，每个学科门类通常各占1篇。这4篇文章合计配有8-9道阅读题。此外，还有1-2道逻辑单题，往往涉及非学术的生活和社会话题。合起来，一个Verbal Section的阅读题为10道。在一个Section之内，除了10道填空题之外，常见的阅读文章组合有两种：

	Section（含长文）	Section（纯短文）
长 450 ± 20字	1篇，4题	0篇，0题
短 160 ± 20字	1篇，2-3题	1篇，3-4题
短 120 ± 20字	2篇，1-2题	3篇，1-2题
逻辑 40-80字	1篇，1题	1-2篇，1题
总计	4 + 1篇，10题	4 + (2-1)篇，10题

考试时如果加试数学，则只有2个Verbal Section，通常这两种阅读组合会分别出现；如果加试Verbal，则有3个Verbal Section，通常2个Section没有长文，1个Section有长文。这并非绝对，完全可能2个或3个Verbal Section都只有短文，没有长文，或者其中2个都出现长文；但通常来说，会有长文Section和纯短文Section。

除多数逻辑题外，GRE阅读文章都取材于学术期刊和著作，因此属于学术英文。学术英文与生活英文、媒体英文、商业英文都不同。生活英文，涉及生活中的具体场景，多为口语和对话，掌握之后比较简单。媒体英文，以报道事实为主，主要叙述新闻事件各个当事人的观点、说法、态度等，并做简要的分析。商业英文主要用于商业交流，与生活英文接近，但用词准确、有话直说、减少歧义，只要学会基本格式，也是容易明白的。这三者的一个共同点是，语言所讨论的对象往往就在眼前，多数时候，讲者和听者或读者都聚焦到同一个人际空间。与此不同，学术英文则往往讨论一些抽象的话题或与此相关的作品、研究和活动，而非具体生活的场景，或者偶然发生的新奇事件，或者具体的商业活动。其中内容往往是非人身的，作者与读者并不针对同一个人际交往环境。在这种情况下，阅读材料带给人的陌生感是很强烈的。因为讨论的对象陌生，所以就不能借助共同生活的场景，而要借助逻辑，才能完成有效沟通。于是，学术文章的命题往往通过论点和论据展开，作者论点作为一种关系到非人身对象的论断，要得到陌生读者认可，需要一些论据以合乎逻辑的方式来支撑。但是，逻辑的视角又不是读者和正常人类天生就习惯的，可以自动领会的。人习惯的是生活和社会的事情，而非抽象的逻辑关系。报纸上的新闻，谁跟谁怎么样了，这个国家与那个国家如何了，马上就能点燃我们的兴趣。与此不同，某个文艺作品的解读争议、移民的途径和理由分析、岩石的构成及其形成原理，这些内容却往往让人退避三舍，其中的推理过程也让人难以亲近。所以，阅读学术文章的第一个障碍就是题材的陌生和逻辑的疏离。

GRE文章与正常的学术英文也有差别。正常学术论文也许有8000字，篇幅足够，论证充分，论据较多，有些甚至用图表和图片展示来辅助论证，一目了然。但是，这样的学术文章经测试专家压缩、改编后，变为大约450字、160字或120字的GRE文章。这意味着，GRE文章的信息高度浓缩，证据省略较多，论点和观点的数目也减少了。于是，论点的过渡会更快出现，逻辑推理的过程显得急促甚至扭曲，所以有时比初始的学术英文更难理解。可以设想，专家都需要8000字才能看懂的内容，让非专业的考生在短时间内看450多字就做题，显然不是要检查考生对文中专业知识的理解程度，而是针对别的方面。总之，学术文章的丰富论据更容易让读者信服其所支持的论点，并主要照顾专业读者的需求，而GRE文章则因为考试设计的篇幅限制，着重考查逻辑推理本身，而非论据是否成立、论点是否得到有效支持等只有学术专家才会关注的问题。

但无论如何，GRE与学术英文共有的特点是，它们都有严密的逻辑推理结构。证据可以压缩、观点可以减少，但逻辑推理的过程却不会因此而改变。这个推理过程就是：**论点与论点的关系，论点与论据的关系，论据与论据的关系**。当然，GRE阅读也要求词汇、句法等能力，但这也是填空要考查的内容。阅读最主要、最独特的地方，还是考查考生在论点–论据上的逻辑推理能力；从逻辑对应到语言层面，则是考查句子之间、段落之间的关系、以及部分句子尤其是长句难句的语义理解。只有以逻辑推理为考查对象的考试，才能有助于衡量GRE考生是否为进入研究院的学习和研究做了足够的认知和心智准备。

1.2 材料的选择

既然GRE阅读考查的主要是论点–论据方面的逻辑分析能力而不是考查广义上的、缺乏定义的所谓"阅读理解能力"，正确阅读备考资料就显得特别重要。这些资料需要满足这些标准：逻辑严密、结构复杂、句子繁难。

新闻报刊、商业、演讲、文学等方面的英文作品不太适合作为GRE阅读的备考资料。新闻报纸的英文反映社会生活中的新事，词汇的含义与具体的社会语境有关，非母语的英文阅读者往往不易明白。商业英文的内容往往过于直白。演讲的文字较口语化，同时有情感诉求，这在学术文章中罕见。文学作品叙述故事情节，人物在其中轮番登场，与逻辑推理关系较小。所有这些英文文字都对提高我们的阅读能力有好处，但这个好处是模糊的、不确定的，与GRE没有直接关系。

注重分析推理的作品是比较适合的材料。比如，《经济学人》杂志(*Economist*)，其中有很多篇目是对世界各地政治和经济的分析。更好的是《科学美国人》杂志(*Scientific American*)，其中的文章多由专家和专业记者撰写，多数文章逻辑层次清晰，有些甚至也很复杂，适合作为GRE文章的改编材料。一些非文学类的畅销书也可作为阅读材料，例如英美科学家编写的面向大众的科普著作。美国大学的教科书也可参考。当然，所有这些面向大众或学生群体的文章的逻辑结构还是太直接了，比GRE阅读考试中逻辑扭曲、层次复杂的文章难度低。所以，可以用它们来熟悉背景，克服对陌生题材的恐惧感，但是，不可以直接以它们代替GRE阅读文章的训练。不仅简单的分析文字不太适合作为备考资料，过难或专业内容过多的文章也不够好。专业期刊上刊登的学术论文和学术专著，一句之内如果出现太多专业术语，需要太多背景知识，外行通常难以把握。同理，数学公式较多的文献也不适合。GRE文章中从来没有数学公式。

最好的材料永远是GRE的阅读真题和高度仿真的模拟题。ETS出的新版《GRE考试官方指南》(*The Official Guide to the GRE Revised General Test*，简称GRE OG)和官方提供的备考软件(PowerPrep II)，都是非常有用的。对GRE阅读来说，从GRE历年真题改编的"新GRE阅读36套"可以作为主要的备考资料，如果要做好逻辑单题，从1990年代的GRE真题中抽选的"新GRE阅读逻辑10套"也是重要的资料(以上两个资料请考生在网上自行搜索下载)。如果考生做了一些GRE真题以后，对符合GRE考试标准的文章有了一定判断能力，则部分机构出的模拟题也可作为参考。本书所提供的GRE阅读模拟真题，尽量仿真，忠实反映GRE阅读的考试思路和难度，也希望能给考生提供一些有用的训练材料。GMAT(商学院入学考试)的文章难度与GRE高度接近，可以作为参考资料。但是，GMAT文章有一些是商业和经济题材，GRE中很少涉及，故要略去这一部分，仅仅选择其中的科学、人文和非经济题材的社科文章。相比之下，LSAT(法学院入学考试)与GRE的文章相似度比较低。LSAT阅读文章全为长文章，其中部分可以作为GRE长文章的训练材料，但没有短文章。想体会最高难度英文阅读的朋友，可以按照LSAT考试时间的要求（35分钟4篇长文章27道题），做做LSAT阅读，体会一下醉生梦死的阅读感觉。看过一些LSAT文章之后，也许就不会觉得GRE长文章的阅读难度很高了。但时间紧迫的考生，没有必要去看LSAT文章，甚至也不必看GMAT的文章，而是专注于GRE考试的文章就足够了。

不适用	
演讲 / 文学类	Fiction：例如 *Harry Potter, Twilight, Pride and Prejudice, Little Prince*，属于叙事(narrative)文体，与逻辑论证的 GRE 文章不同
新闻 / 商业类	ft.com, wsj.com, newsweek.com, yahoo.com
中等材料	
大众杂志	*Economist*：陈述各方立场，分析论证较为简单 *Scientific American*：题材上佳，但结构比 GRE 简单
英文教科书	Textbooks：面向大学生读者，写作直白、清晰，结构层次复杂度低于 GRE
科普	Nonfiction：面向大众的科普文章，有口语表达及较多设问，与 GRE 文章有差别
论文 / 专业期刊专著	Papers, Periodicals, Monographs：有些文章术语繁多，过于艰深，但许多文字分析的段落符合 GRE 论证的风格
TOEFL / SAT	逻辑清晰，但结构层次复杂度不及 GRE；句子较短，平均 20–25 个单词
好材料	
LSAT	难度高于 GRE；均为 450 字左右长文章，平均句子长度 30–35 个单词；无短文章，故材料不够丰富
GMAT	非经济和商业类的文章，150–350 字，3–4 题
GRE 模拟题	美国部分机构模拟题，本书模拟题
GRE	OG (*Official Guide*), PPII (PowerPrep II), 新 GRE 阅读 36 套，新 GRE 阅读逻辑 10 套等

GRE文章的取材来自一些学术文献，有的朋友如果有时间，可以看看其中部分文章，感受一下学术分析文章的气息，体会GRE阅读文章的源头。准备时间紧迫的朋友，不必做这件事。下面是一份期刊列表，其中的一些文章或许会成为GRE文章的来源（*Passonneau et al*, 2002）。考生不必都去看这些期刊的文章，但至少可以感受一下。

African American Review

American Journal of Economics and Sociology

American Scholar

Art Journal

Astronomy

BioScience

Black American Literature Forum

Business Horizons

Commentary

Discover

Feminist Studies

Journal of American Ethnic History

Journal of Black Studies

Journal of Social History

The Nation

Science News

Scientific American

Sloan Management Review

Smithsonian

Technology Review

Wilson Quarterly

Women's Review of Books

1.3 阅读速度与正确率

GRE文章的阅读速度要求极高。通常，中国大学英语的四六级考试，速度达到80–100字/分钟就可以了，但是GRE的正常速度要求是150–160字/分钟。如要取得高分，则正确率应在70%左右，也就是10道题对7题，错3题以内。（LSAT阅读的要求更高，达到180–200字/分钟，正确率需达到80%以上。）

	Section(含长文)	Section(纯短文)	考试要求
长 450 ± 20字	1篇，4题	0篇，0题	450words/2.5–3min, 1min/question
短 160 ± 20字	1篇，2–3题	1篇，3–4题	160words/1min, 1min/question
短 120 ± 20字	2篇，1–2题	3篇，1–2题	120words/50seconds, 1min/question
逻辑 40–80字	1篇，1题	1–2篇，1题	1–1.5min
总计	4+1篇，10题	4+(2–1)篇，10题	17 ± 1 min; 正确率7/10

如何达到这么高的水平呢？一个自然的想法是多读。似乎只要读得多了，速度就会自然快起来。这种观点永远不会错，因为多读总是对的。谁会否认多读对于阅读的重要性呢？就像谁会否认多游对游泳的重要性？但是，一个总是对的想法，通常没有用。奇怪吗？因为它不包含多少信息量，无法提供具体的步骤、策略，从而让我们做到它——如果目标本身不明确或不量化，这个目标就是无意义的。多读是对的，但多少算多？我们需要一个大致的量。

而且，读得越多，速度就会越快吗？没有证据表明，多读就一定会读快。常见的情况是，有的人阅读中文小说的速度数十年如一日的快，但一开始就不曾多读。读*Harry Potter*的中学生，速度一开始就很快，后来因为有很多思考，也许反而慢下来。还有人读学术书籍，读了很多年，速度还是一样。当然有多读之后就变快的，但这两件事同时发生并不直接表明它们存在因果关系（coincidence is not causation）。

事实上，多读就是希望通过广泛阅读碰巧掌握阅读方法，而这其实是一种随机搜索（random search）。多读之后，百炼成精，当然是可能的。但这个步骤也许只对少数人有效，而且可以确定，这些少数人，应该不是多读而已，而是在读的过程中不断有些发现、不断评估进度、找出难点、克服障碍，持之以恒，才能成为阅读达人。问题是能够做到这点的人很少，或者说，通过多读而找到正确的学术文章阅读方法的概率是小的，其效率也是低的。多读不是不好，但是，life is short。我们要的是效率，在合理的一段时间内达到目标。

既然多读不一定能够取得效果，一个进一步的想法就是精读，再与泛读结合。泛读练速度，精读练理解。对吗？但到底什么是精读和泛读？泛读的做法似乎成了泛泛而读，读很多材料来训练阅读能力。读很多材料当然是对的，但问题是多少算多。我们需要一个粗略的量或者大致的范围。让我们把泛读量化，给出一个替代的可操作的方案。对想学好学术英文阅读的朋友，我们建议，读各个学科的材料，从四大学科门类（natural sciences, biological sciences, social sciences, humanities）中选取至少20个子学科的材料，每份材料读20页×800字左右，就能完成泛读的目标——读得多而广、克服对英文阅读的畏惧心理。（一个容易获得的材料选择库是Oxford: A Very Short Introduction的系列书籍。）对准备GRE的考生，我们建议，读GRE真题文章以及GRE的模拟文章就可以了，因为题材够广泛，而且，100篇左右的量，每一大类题材都有25–30篇，如果能够集中一段时间读某一类文章，比如花2天共10个小时集中阅读文学评论和历史题材的文章。这样，就能克服对题材的畏惧心理。

常见的精读做法是，认识单词、查出生词、弄懂句子语法、理解意思。这里，前三项还是可操作的，但"理解意思"就不知如何处理了。理解什么意思？理解到什么程度？什么叫理解？这些概念缺乏定义，不具有可操作性。更进一步的，精读的做法还包括翻译每个句子，查找背景知识，掌握专业内容，人们认为这样就能弄懂原文。翻译句子，是从英文译成中文，好的翻译对于中英文双语自如应用当然有作用，但是，我们学习学术英文的目的是直接从英文去理解内容，而不是把它翻译成中文。翻译一开始也许是必要的，但翻译了5–10万字的时候，也许其作用就丧失了，到最后，不是在学英文，而是在研究中文如何表达英文的意思去了。对于学习翻译的人，翻译永远重要，但对于只是想掌握英文阅读的人来说，翻译只是其中的一小步。对于GRE考生而言，翻译当然是最不重要的事情之一，因为考试的时间压力极大，现场是没有办法通过翻译来理解文章和做题的。而且，查找背景知识的做法也有争议性。查到多少才算够？通常的做法是查查文章里的人名和事件的发生背景，比如看看wikipedia里的相关内容。这样做对理解文章有直接帮助吗？如果有一篇文章讨论海豹的觅食策略，知道海豹的大小、种类、演化历史，对于理解文章本身有无帮助？背景知识的查找往往枝蔓太多，容易让读者游离于文章主旨之外。如果有人看到海豹的觅食文章，大谈特谈一番海豹的种类、样子、生活地域或者Discovery关于海豹的影片，然后人们以为这是知识渊博，甚至他还谈到人类捕杀小海豹来获取毛皮是罪恶，没有买卖就没有伤害，然后人们认为这人充满正义，那么，我们真是无言以对了。残害海豹来获取毛皮，在今天人类已经吃饱穿暖的时代，当然是一种令人心痛的事，但是，这与文章的主旨海豹觅食有何关系？甚至海豹的演化历史和类别，有时也与海豹的觅食策略无关。把话题蔓延当做知识渊博，把情绪铺张当做道德文章，这些都是典型的类属错误。谈事实的，不要带入情感。谈这个事情的，不要扯到其他事情。所以，精读听起来是认真的，但是，做起来却很模糊，无从下手。认真的做法永远必要，但需要量化和可操作性。

既然多读、精读和泛读这些常见的"做法"并不自动保证阅读速度和理解精确程度，那么什么样的方法可以做到既能快速阅读，又能掌握文章核心信息呢？下面会看到，我们的替代方案是**特定内容的精读**，或说**结构化阅读**，高度重视文章整体结构、段落核心、句间关系、长句主干、逻辑提示词汇，在做题之前忽视具体论据和推理，不做翻译、不查背景、不查专业名词。也就是说，通过学术文章的逻辑结构和相应的有取有舍、有详有略的阅读方法，提高阅读速度，而不是通过快速移动眼球来提高速度。有人也许会说，考试时间非常紧张，哪里有时间来关注逻辑结构呢？好像关注逻辑结构挺花时间似的。看单词、一字一句理解、拼凑意思，这是最耗时的，而且理解得也不清不楚；一边在扫描单词、一边就在想上下句的逻辑联系，通过逻辑联系来选择性地记忆核心词，这是阅读最快的方法，而且还能读得相当清楚。开始训练时，分析20-30篇文章的逻辑结构，是很花时间的，训练到一定程度，就能将逻辑结构变成自动反应，这个阶段，速度就自然提高了。再强调一遍：与我们的直觉相反，速度提高的方法不是通过眼睛快点看，而是通过似乎在阅读速度之外的结构思维训练！懂得了建筑物的结构，才能迅速浏览完这个建筑，找出关键的柱梁结构和功能用途；把每面墙、每块砖看一遍，浏览建筑物的时间是会很长很长的，而且走马观花、随机扫描，也不知道重点。文章的阅读同理。

在备考GRE时，还有一个常见的说法是，做题时间短或读得速度快，做题正确率下降，做题时间长或读得慢一些，正确率就上升。这种相关性成立吗？很少有人验证这一点。当然会有一些人"觉得"看文章的时间长了，做题就容易对，这种情况也确实会出现。但总是如此吗？1个练习5篇文章10道题，30分钟做完，正确率只有4/10，而压缩时间以后，正确率可能还是一样。在初始阶段，正确率与做题时间可能无关。

	时间（min）	正确率
Exercise 1	30	4/10
Exercise 2	25	4/10

但在训练的瓶颈期，一旦卡时间训练，正确率的确会随做题时间减少而降低。

	时间（min）	正确率
Exercise 3	25	5/10
Exercise 4	20	3/10
Exercise 5	28	5/10

这时，降低文章阅读速度并非正确做法，因为，增加练习的时间，将一个练习的时间卡在28分钟而不是25分钟，也许还是只能10道题对5道（如Exercise 5）。找出真正的原因至关重要。也许，在回头检查时我们发现，当时我们面对好些题目的答案就是在两个选项之间犹豫，然后自己选了错的那个。所以，正确率不一定是因为阅读过快造成，而是对选项的分辨还不够仔细。要改变的不是阅读速度，而是做题技巧。这时，就要针对这个难点进行专门训练：选20-30道错题，找出第一次做题时错误的原因。集中训练以后，对选项的陷阱设计会更敏感，以后做题的时候准确度会相应提升，而判断选项所花的时间反而可能减少，从而整个练习所花的时间也会随之减少（如Exercise 6）。在做过更多卡时间训练以后，时间减少，正确率反而提高（如Exercise 7）。

	时间（min）	正确率
Exercise 4	20	3/10
Exercise 6	20	5/10
Exercise 7	18	6/10

不能指望多读就自然提高阅读速度。我们必须通过特定的训练方法，抓住文章和段落的核心词，抓住常考的特殊形式的句子，快速略过证据和细节的描述，这样阅读速度就能提高。然后，在做题的时候快速把握题干，反应基本解法。在看选项时，小心GRE选项的常见设计陷阱，加快甄别速度，这样，就能在阅读和做题速度都很高的情况下，同时保证正确率。

第二节　技能训练的方法论

GRE阅读的训练一定要注意方法，尽量避免用常见的一些模糊概念，妨碍自己认识真正的学习目标。用跑步来做比喻。一个人跑100m，每次跑得慢的时候，姿势都很好看，呼吸都很平稳，似乎这个方法是对的了，而一旦上场比赛，跑步动作就会变形，大喘气，腿抽筋。问：怎么训练来备战100m比赛？答：慢慢跑，跑多了就好了。对这个答案我们还满意吗？类似的，一个人在没有时间压力的情况下读GRE阅读或学术文章，好些读得挺懂，但一旦开始做计时训练，做起题来，就做不完或心慌意乱，或能做完但错误百出，这说明什么问题？多读并不是阅读成功的充分条件。就像学跑100m比赛必须分项分解训练腿部肌肉、摆臂动作、起跑、中途跑等等，同样，学习GRE阅读也需要分解训练文章、段落、句子、题干、选项等多个方面的内容。而多读、精读、泛读、降速阅读保正确率这些做法，都不是最有效的。

2.1　多层分解

大凡困难的事情，往往不是只有一个因素造成，而是由多个因素共同作用的。这些因素往往不是彼此干扰而是相对独立，也就是说它们在不同层次上起作用，这是我们所说的**多因素分层作用**的理论。多数智能都是如此，例如生物体对外部环境的认知和反应能力，总是由神经细胞、神经回路、自动反应模式等等构成。学术英文的阅读技能也是如此，它需要多个技能模块同时协调作用，才能帮助使用者将文章信息迅速分析出来。阅读技能本身是一个过于宽泛的概念，非分解不足以识别和掌握。

所以，学习一项技能通常需要多个方面的训练。学术英文的阅读技能比一般技能的难度更高，涉及多个方面的能力模块。如果学习者自己独自摸索，那会很难找到方法。也许找到一个技能模块容易，但要找出全部，同时融会贯通，难度极高。假定学好GRE阅读（包括读文章和做对题）需要5个因素：文章、段落、句子、题干、选项；假定一个能力很强的学习者（High Competency: H）掌握每个因素的概率是80%，又假定这5个因素的学习是独立事件，则该学习者自己独自学好GRE阅读的概率（Probability: P，经四舍五入，下同）是：

$$P_H = 80\% * 80\% * 80\% * 80\% * 80\% = 33\%$$

如果正常能力的学习者掌握这5个因素的概率分别是50%，则普通学习者（Medium: M）独自学好GRE阅读的概率是：

$$P_M = 50\% * 50\% * 50\% * 50\% * 50\% = 3\%$$

如果经过一段时间努力，有些方面掌握得强，能做好其中3个方面的概率均为80%，而有些方面掌握得弱，能做好其中2个方面的概率均只有50%，则努力学习者（Diligent: D）独自学好GRE阅读的概率是：

$$P_D = 80\% * 80\% * 80\% * 50\% * 50\% = 13\%$$

任何一个技能模块的缺失，都足以让多因素构成的总技能的学习功亏一篑。如果技能模块或者因素增多，则学成的概率通常会更小。从这个概率分析想到，阅读技能的分解训练是十分必要的。我们需要通过有效率的、经过精心设计的训练过程，降低失败的概率，提高成功的可能。如果只是自己独自学习，其效果相当于随机搜索，那么冥思苦想或偶有所得的那些阅读体悟甚至方法，往往是诱人的陷阱，至多只是平地的小坡，与真正的结构思维指导下的阅读方法的山顶，距离遥远。如果已经搜索到了经过验证有效的方法，就要紧紧跟随，而不要再自创一套，创新的感觉固然美好，但多数只是幻觉。我们相信，备考时间有限的考生，跟随特定的、已经确立的训练方法和步骤，有更大的机会在合理的较短时间内快速掌握GRE阅读方法。

要将阅读方法这种常见但却空泛的字眼分解为可操作、可练习的多个技能，其实并不容易。在更广泛的意义上，这属于认知的分解问题，或者**认知的多层还原**。在这方面，笔者从认知科学获得很大启发。一个人的认知能力常常有多个层次，分析它的过程就是向下的还原过程，还原出的每个层次必须是可观察的、可识别的，一直到最低层，它作为一个最小认知模块，并不是向下分解的终极，而只是一个大家接受的出发点，可以在此暂时停步。换个角度来说，从最低层开始的向上建构，或者各个层次之间的组合，也必须是可行的、可操作的，而不是胡拼乱凑的。将这种观念应用到阅读上，我们就需要把阅读的认知能力分解为若干个层面，最后的分层必须是可识别的训练单位，可以由此开始进行密集的专门训练，以逐步建立各个层次的阅读技能，并最终掌握阅读的分层系统的所有方面，完成阅读技能的飞跃。

通常对阅读能力分解的看法是：阅读嘛，无非是认识单词、读懂长句。但这只是讲到一些层面而已，如何训练，训练到何种地步，没有说，而且，这种分解是否完整，也有疑问。要知道，学好100m跑，不是只有摆臂和步长。又如，通常的文章分类为议论文、说明文等，但这样的分类单位难以观察和操作。与这些不同，本书的文章分类规则都是由可操作的变量构成，可以有针对性地进行训练。每个层次也有各自的独立规则，这意味着，各个层次之间的规则不会相互干涉。更重要的是，一个层次的训练不必以另一个层次的掌握为前提，**我们可以从任何一个层次开始进行集中训练**。

关于GRE学术文章的阅读和做题技能，我们细分为6个层面，每个层面都可以单独训练，直到掌握为止。再通过计时训练来组合各个阶段或层面的能力，我们就能最终突破GRE的阅读。这些层次划分也许只是关于阅读技能的一些粗糙的模型，但是，有一个粗糙的模型在手，总比完全没有模型、纯靠感觉和体悟甚至幻觉要好得多。笔者也希望有心的读者，在了解、应用和掌握这些模型以后，能够修正、改进这个结构分析的多层分解模型。下面简要介绍这6个层面，更详细的分析请见后面的章节。

2.2 文章分析的三个层面

很显然，GRE文章由4个层次构成。

文章 — 段落 — 句子 — 单词短语
Passage — Paragraph — Sentence — Words & Phrases

其中，单词短语是文章分析的最底层，不作为独立的文章分析单位。按照每个层次分解的可观察、可操作的原则，我们可以将文章的3个层次进行再分解，每个层次各自又有3-4个子层次，每个层次以及子层次的规则相对独立，可以单独分析。我们要求最后分解的子层次必须是可以观察和操作的训练对象。下图就是本书关于文章结构分析的全面概括。在这里我们先做简单介绍，后面章节会再做详细说明。

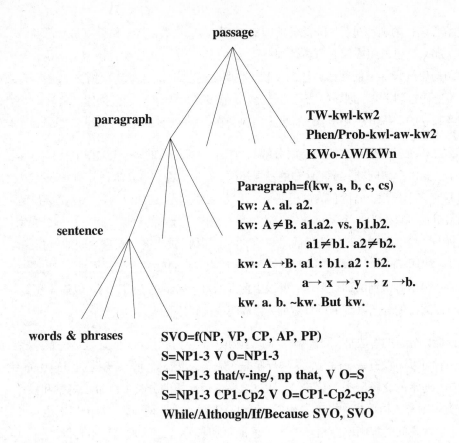

passage

TW-kwl-kw2
Phen/Prob-kwl-aw-kw2
KWo-AW/KWn

paragraph

Paragraph=f(kw, a, b, c, cs)
kw: A. al. a2.
kw: A≠B. a1.a2. vs. b1.b2.
  a1≠b1. a2≠b2.
kw: A→B. a1 : b1. a2 : b2.
  a→ x → y → z →b.
kw. a. b. ~kw. But kw.

sentence

words & phrases

SVO=f(NP, VP, CP, AP, PP)
S=NP1-3 V O=NP1-3
S=NP1-3 that/v-ing/, np that, V O=S
S=NP1-3 CP1-Cp2 V O=CP1-Cp2-cp3
While/Although/If/Because SVO, SVO

2.2.1 文章

按照构成观点的数量及其关系，文章结构可以分为3类，每一类结构都涉及主题（Topic Words = TW或 Topic Sentence = TS）与各个论点（Key Words = kw）的关系、以及论点之间的关系（kw–kw），一些论点会有评价态度（AW=Attitude Words），任何论点或分论点之后都可以有让步语气提出替代论点（~kw），然后转折回到原论点（kw）。

1. 论点说明或评述类

TW — KW1 — KW2
主题或总论点 — 分论点1 — 分论点2

2. 现象解释或问题解决类

Phen/Prob — kw1 —   aw   — kw2
Phenomenon or Problem = TW — 解释1 — （负）评价句 — 解释2

3. 新老观点对比类

KWo — AW / KWn
old view = 老观点 — 态度句（常为负评价或转折句）/ new view = 新观点

2.2.2 段落

普通段落（Paragraph）由首句论点（kw）和中间证据（a/b/c）以及末句可能出现的结论句（cs）构成，因此段落可看成这些要素之间的组合或函数关系（f=function）。论点与中间证据之间是总分关系，或kw a b c，是论点分析的主要对象：

$$Paragraph = f(kw, a, b, c, cs)$$

按照论点特征以及中间证据之间的关系，一个论点的展开结构或段落结构可以分为3大类。

1. 论点描述一个单独的事物(以A 表示)的性质、特征，或给A以态度评价，或说明和描述A做了什么事。这时证据之间有并列结构，a1, a2代表证据。

$$kw: A.\ a1.\ a2.$$

2. 论点涉及两个对等事物之间的关系，如果关系为对比关系，则有对比结构，可以先讲一个事物，讲完后经对比关联词引导，再讲与之不同的另一个事物。

$$kw: A \neq B.\ a1.\ a2.\ vs.\ b1.\ b2.$$

也可以从两个方面分别对比，是为总分+并列套对比结构。

$$kw: A \neq B.\ a1 \neq b1.\ a2 \neq b2.$$

3. 论点涉及两个对等事物之间的关系，如果关系为因果关系，则有因果结构。其中一种是平行因果(parallel causation)，这时两个因果证据并列出现。

$$kw: A \rightarrow B.\ a1 : b1.\ a2 : b2.$$

另一种是序列或串行因果(serial causation)，或说机制(mechanism)，这时出现连续动作作为证据。

$$kw: A \rightarrow B.\ a \rightarrow x \rightarrow y \rightarrow z \rightarrow b.$$

针对以上任何一种结构，都可以在中间证据之内出现让步(concession)转折(refutation)的间接、辅助论者，而且常考。让步内容是对段落论点的取非(~kw)，有时也是对直接支持的论据(如x)的取非(~x)，转折则会回到论点(But kw)。

$$kw.\ a.\ b.\ \sim kw.\ But\ kw.$$

有些段落，特别是现在新GRE的短文章，往往给出2个论点，省略各自的一些论据。这些段落的结构可以写成：

$$Paragraph = kw1.\ a.\ b.\ kw2.\ x.\ y.$$

也有少数段落，先给出现象、事实、数据或实验情况(i, j)，然后给出假说，再展开其推理过程：

$$i.\ j.\ kw.\ a.\ b.\ c.$$

● 2.2.3 句子

按照语法的基本单位，通常是由NP(Noun Phrase = 名词短语)、VP(Verb Phrase，谓语结构)构成。其中也许包含AP(Adjective Phrase = 形容词短语)和PP(Preposition Phrase = 介词短语)等语言成分。这些语言成分再加上从句成分(Clause Phrase = CP)，可以形成十分复杂的句型。因此，一个由主谓宾(S=subject, V=verb, O=object)构成的句子，可以看做句子构成要素之间的组合或函数关系(f=function)：

$$Sentence = SVO = f(NP, VP, CP, AP, PP)$$

由于句子分析占文章整体理解的比重较小，并非结构分析的主要内容，所以，我们留到"句子/Sentence"分析的章节再做详细论述。

以上分析的原理是，文章结构的每个层面都可以看做一个总分结构。这三层总分结构就是：从总论点到分论点，从论点到论据，从主干到修饰。**在逻辑上**，这就是从一般到特殊(from general to particular)，属于演绎推理(deduction)。演绎推理说起来很玄，但操作起来也没那么复杂。文章三层结构的推理，就是演绎推理在主题、论点、主干三个层次的体现。与演绎推理相对的是归纳推理 (induction)，从特殊到一般(from particular to general)。例如，这个男人不好。那个男人不好。所以，(所有)男人都不是好东西。归纳推理往往是不可靠的（如这个例子），虽然它对于启发我们做出猜想、提出一般论点或者假说有很大的帮助。下面我们简单说一点推理方式对于阅读方法的影响，更详细的阅读方法讨论请见后面的章节。

在英文阅读上，归纳推理表现为"总结"的思维。有人会希望在读懂论据以后"总结"论点。但这其实是不可能的。因为是论点(kw)在约束、管理论据(a, b, c)，而不是论据本身导致论点。论据是从属性的、可替换的、可增减的。论点之后列出的a, b, c的论据只是全体可能论据的一部分。同时，所有论据的加总也不是论点，它们并不是在同一个层次上：论点展开为论据，或者得到论据支持。所以，通过总结所有看到的论据然后理解论点，这是方法上的错误。论点是要直接理解的，无非是描述一个事物或说明两个事物之间的关系（通常是对比关系和因果关系）。论据只能辅助理解，不能直接代替论点。

$$kw = f(a, b, c, d, e, \dots)$$
$$a + b + c \nrightarrow kw$$

既然做不到所希望的总结，实际的阅读操作就变成抓住一些单词、部分句子，随机组合，得出文章的中心大意。在为此组合或总结做出辩护时，还可能会进一步深入到作者的文风、成长环境、人生经历、社会观察等等方面，穿凿附会一通，头头是道，很渊博的。

但是，如果有了演绎推理，或者有了三层总分结构的思维，那么，在实际阅读中，我们从论点所在的句子，主要是从论点句的主干，确立它的核心以后，也许就能从逻辑上演绎出、或者说预期到后面论据之间的关系、甚至论据的部分内容。因为总分结构要求分的论据不可超越总的论点，在接着阅读每个论据时，会想到**论据重现论点核心，论据向论点收敛**，于是在首句论点和第2、3句的论据之间，会出现逻辑等价词(logical equivalents)，甚至是直接的字典同义词(synonyms)。这样，通过总分结构或论点-论据的演绎推理，我们就能管理我们在阅读中间证据时的注意力，将焦点放在论据与首句论点的同义词对应的关系上，而不是论据本身的全部单词，避免从某些单词开始发散联想。类似的，**论点向主题收敛**。在长文章的首段首句会出现文章主题(TW)，在第2、3段首句往往会出现重现该主题词的内容，因为这些首句会对首段主题进行具体说明。这样，各段首句往往出现相互呼应的词汇，这样，可以反复强化文章主题，并通过各段首句的内容差异来识别各自段落的论点的核心词，同时，也避免在看文章某一段时，认为这一段与另一段完全无关，甚至脱离文章主题。同样，对句子而言，**修饰向主干收敛**。一个长句的分词结构、定语从句，尤其是并列的修饰，可以在某种意义上，被看做支持和说明句子主干(SVO)的证据，这样，修饰与主干的词汇应该逻辑等价，甚至是同义词。如果在主干或修饰中发现生词，就能通过逻辑关系，从已知单词推断未知单词的意思，避免自己记忆或想象生词的意思。综上所述，**逻辑**上的总分结构，应用到**语言**上就是逻辑等价词、从已知推未知单词。这样，我们就能明白，在实际阅读时语言上需要注意什么，防止思维发散，从某些自己觉得重要的单词开始浮想联翩。

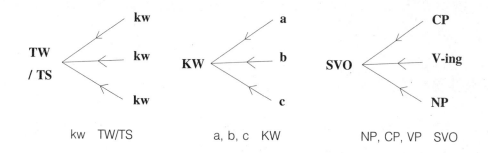

kw TW/TS   a, b, c KW   NP, CP, VP SVO

2.3 解题能力的三个层面

题目由题干与选项组成：

题干 + 选项
Question + Answer Choices

其中，题干的判断又可分为两个方面，一是题干信息的提取和回文定位，一是从题干判断题型并找出相应解法。于是，解题能力就可分为三个可操作的层次，每一层又可细分为很多小的可训练的技巧。

解题	题干定位	快速提取发问对象（常在concerning, about, regarding, of 之后） 依据结构或其他定位词，快速定位
	题型解法	核心题（可细分为主题、结构、态度题） 信息题 定点题（可细分为细节、列举、取非、作用、选择句子等题型） 逻辑单题
	选项分辨	5个选项，3个排除，2个对照 正确答案特征 错误答案特征

在做过一定量的题目比如50道题以后，我们建议考生针对这3个层次，分别进行集中训练，这样就能同时提高解题速度和正确率。详细的训练分解目标，请见后面相关章节的分析。

想提高解题速度和准确率吗？解题速度取决于多个因素，不是单凭多读或读懂就能解决的。事实上，解题速度与定位有关，而定位涉及文章结构的把握，题干的词汇往往会给出文章某个观点的核心词，只有把握好结构，才能迅速找到相应的论点及其论据的位置，这是不能单凭记忆的，在现场时间高度紧张的情况下，记忆通常是不太可靠的。结构分析是提高解题定位速度的非常隐蔽的前提，考生通常会忽略这一点，以为文章读得慢点、记的内容多点，这样在看题时就有印象，就可以直接看选项，这样就做快了，甚至有的时候不回文章定位确认，看到一个选项，好像在印象中，是原文说过的，于是就选了，甚至都还没有把后面的选项看一眼。唉呀，恭喜！这样就做错了！这个思维看似挺合乎逻辑的，但很不幸，不是所有合乎逻辑的说法都是正确的。在GRE阅读做题方面，有很多实际的做题结果表明，看得慢点，多记内容，这样并不能保证题目做得正确，当然更没法帮助提高阅读和解题速度了。一定是通过对结构核心、常考句子进行反复训练、识别、熟悉，同时又对题目题型、解法、选项特征等进行反复训练、识别、熟悉以后，才有可能同时提高解题速度和准确率。

这就是训练的含义了：**就复杂目标进行分解小目标练习，才能掌握整个完整的技巧**。在嘴上说的好目标，不是说说就可以达到，而是要通过分层的步骤才能达到。

2.4 训练步骤与刻意练习

在找到正确的训练框架以后，就要按照步骤逐步进行分项的集中训练。我们认为可以在200个小时以内完成GRE阅读的准备，达到考试要求，这200个小时的训练可以分成3个阶段：

阶段	时间	训练内容
第1阶段： 初步	50小时	掌握3-4类文章结构、段落结构、长句结构，把握9-10类题型及解法。 做24-30篇左右不同题材、不同结构的文章，速度控制在120-150字/分钟，每道题控制在1-1.5题/分钟，做5-6遍。 进行多角度分解训练，如集中时间训练10篇长文章、40个段落结构、30-50个长句、100个题干、300个选项等。
第2阶段： 进阶	100小时	中间训练阶段是最枯燥的，目标在于熟练掌握阅读方法，从主动思考练到自动反应。 卡时间做40-50篇文章，做3-4遍，第1遍计时，第2遍写出逻辑结构，第3遍找出所有题目对应原文位置、识别出题点，第4遍集中分析所有选项错误或重做文章。 阅读速度稳定在150-160字/分钟，正确率从30%逐渐进步到60%。 针对弱项进行2-4小时的集中训练，如集中训练某类常错题型、集中分析某类阅读困难的段落结构、集中阅读某类题材的文章等。
第3阶段： 冲刺	50-100小时	结合套题练习。 做10套完整的VERBAL题，与填空一起做，要求速度提升到160-180字/分钟，正确率接近70-80%。 在做完2-3套题以后，就对其中的8-10篇阅读文章进行集中训练。 针对弱项进行训练。

在第1阶段，可以直接利用本书提供的GRE阅读模拟题6个练习；在第2阶段，则用"新GRE阅读36套"或类似的材料进行练习；在第3阶段，可用ETS官方出的套题，尤其是PowerPrep II，加上一些模拟的套题来进行训练。多读文章当然可以，但我们要给它一个限定的量。我们认为，100篇文章×3-4遍就足以掌握GRE文章的逻辑结构的精髓。一旦掌握了文章的逻辑结构和逻辑思维，其他新的文章都类似，我们并不需要更多文章。巩固、提高之类，也早已在3-4遍滚动循环的训练中达到了。同时，这3-4遍也不是单纯地看文章、做题目、对答案而已，而是必须针对特定的阅读技能和做题方法进行练习。

有效训练的主要方法是**刻意练习**（deliberate practice）。按照Ericsson对专家和天才的研究，这些人的才能并不一定是因为天分，而是因为刻苦的、持久的训练才具备的。

"The journey to truly superior performance is neither for the faint of heart nor for the impatient. The development of genuine expertise requires struggle, sacrifice, and honest, often painful self-assessment. There are no shortcuts. It will take you at least a decade to achieve expertise, and you will need to invest that time wisely, by engaging in "deliberate" practice—practice that focuses on tasks beyond your current level of competence and

通往真正卓越的成绩的道路不是为心智虚弱或没有耐心的人准备的。发展真正的专家技能，需要艰苦的拼搏、牺牲、诚实，往往还有痛苦的自我评估。这里没有捷径。你至少要花十年时间，才能获得专家技能，你需要明智地投入时间，这就是说，你需要进行"刻意"练习——你要**在超出你当前的能力水准和舒适水平的任务上**

comfort. You will need a well-informed coach not only to guide you through deliberate practice but also to help you learn how to coach yourself."

"When most people practice, they focus on the things they already know how to do. Deliberate practice is different. It entails considerable, specific, and sustained efforts to do something you can't do well—or even at all. Research across domains shows that it is only by working at what you can't do that you turn into the expert you want to become." (Ericsson *et al*, 2007, *Harvard Business Review*)

集中练习。你也需要一个通晓方法的教练，不仅指导你进行刻意练习，而且还帮你学会如何自己训练自己。

多数人在练习时，只是集中在那些他们已经知道如何做的事情上。刻意练习则不同，它意味着要花费大量的、特定的、持久的努力，去练习一些你还不能做得很好甚至完全**不会做**的事情。多个领域的研究都表明，只有练习你还不会做的事，你才会变成你想成为的专家。

幸运的是，GRE阅读能力并非顶尖的专业技能，我们不需要10年才能掌握。但训练的原理相似。要在尽可能短的时间之内练好GRE阅读，对平常没有接受大量的学术和非虚构类英文阅读训练的多数读者来说，我们需要做到以下几点：

1. 卡时间集中训练200小时

这200个小时必须非常有效地利用，而不是单纯坐在那里看200小时阅读文章而已。**整个训练**应该集中在20–40天完成，并分3个阶段（如上）。如果在第2和第3阶段发现有些项目没有掌握，就需要进行3–6个小时的专门的集中训练。**每天训练**也要集中时间，只有集中时间才能集中精神。在开始训练阶段，不要每天只读1个小时阅读；经常转换学习项目会导致效率低下。按照经验，如果一天之内转换研究的对象太多，每次转换都要花上15分钟，则转换的时间成本是相当大的。在做练习时最好将手机静音、装包或关闭；最好在图书馆、自习室、教室、公共学习场所练习，而不是在家、在宿舍里练习。

阅读要么不做训练，要么就集中训练，例如每天做4–6个小时或更多，也就是说，上午/下午/晚上的3个时间段的其中至少两个都要进行阅读训练。不要每天只做1个小时阅读！！！美其名曰增加语感，其实获得的都是挫折感。基础英语学习可以做这样的事，但这对GRE这样高难度的逻辑严密的英文阅读无效。而且，连续多看阅读的好处是获得文章结构、题目类型的"数据"，有了数据，才能进行模式分析。每天只是看一点文章，量太小了，样本太少，很难从中找到可归纳的模式。**练习的量之所以重要，除了熟练以外，还因为它提供模式**。因此，3天的阅读训练可以是这样：

	周一	周二	周三
上午	GRE 阅读	专业课	GRE阅读
下午	专业课	GRE阅读	GRE阅读
晚上	GRE阅读	GRE阅读	GRE阅读

每次训练也要卡时间。多少分钟读完文章，多少分钟做完题目，正确率如何，都尽量记录在案。这样，获得自己做题的客观数据，而不是自己想象的情况。考生可参考下图的示范，自己制作表格，记录下自己阅读每篇文章的时间和做题的时间。

	开始	结束	题目	文章	做题
p.3.1, S2	11:10:00	11:12:15	11:14:45	2′15″	2′30″
p.4.2 , L4	11:15:30	11:19:20	11:27:00	3′50″	7′40″
p.6.3, S1	11:28:00	11:29:30	11:31:00	1′30″	1′30″

（S2: Short Passage, 2 Questions; L4: Long Passage, 4 Questions; p.3.1 = page 3 passage 1其余类推; 开始和结束分别指读一篇文章开始和结束的时间，用于计算读每篇文章时间；也可以直接记下读一篇文章的时间）

2. 目标分解、即时反馈

阅读的训练目标要明确，不能只是做题、对答案、做题、对答案，这样看起来也花了不少时间，但没有多大提高，因为除了速度与正确率以外，没有达到这些量化标准的小的可行步骤。反复这样做，只能重复这个正确率，并不会提高它，学习时间长了，会感到疲倦，还可能引发情绪挫折、心情烦躁等不良反应，甚而诱发怀疑自己、怀疑人生的貌似深刻、其实无力的思想病状。想想高中时候自己或同学在做题方面可能存在的低效率行为，避免类似的事情在GRE备考上重演。

正确的高效率做法是，除了针对做题速度、阅读速度进行专门的卡时间练习以外，还要按照阅读所要求的能力进行多层分解，然后针对每个能力层次进行训练。对GRE阅读来说，就是按照前面6个层次的能力**分解训练**。而且，每过一段时间，就要**提高训练难度**，或者提高速度和正确率要求，或者不断找到自己感到陌生的地方和角度，专门训练，这样总能找到可学的东西，避免简单重复导致的学习疲劳。这要求我们把目标分解到可以操作的、甚至可以量度的程度。如开尔文（Kelvin）所说，"如果你没有量度它，你就不能提高它"。（"If you cannot measure it, you cannot improve it."）只有形成可量化的目标，才知道如何评估自己的进度，并针对目标与现状之间的差距，给出**即时反馈**，对照训练要求，改进不足，消除错误。

3. 在学习区练习

专家技能的研究者将学习分为3个区域：舒适区、学习区、恐慌区（comfort, stretch, panic zone）（另可参考《哪来的天才》/*Talent is Overrated*，《1万小时天才理论》/*The Talent Code*两本精彩的著作）。舒适区是已经掌握的内容，比如查单词、查背景、甚至翻译句子等相对轻松、不费脑力的工作；学习区是有难度的、还没有完全掌握的内容；恐慌区则是超出当前学习能力的内容。

我们不需要一步登天，马上学会150-160字/分钟，甚至180-200字/分钟读文章，3天达到考试要求，这不现实，也没必要，有些时候甚至是懒惰的借口，因为3天学不好，于是就证明了自己学不好，于是可以不去学；没有什么高难度技能是3天就能学好的。我们也不需要在已经学会的技能方面继续磨时间，比如，因为专业名词对于GRE阅读不重要，就不必每天对着字典查生词。不要只是重复做题对答案，或者翻译已经看过几遍的文章，对于那些已经熟悉的内容，再做额外训练不大必要；事实上，在已经会的项目上做更多训练，边际收益递减，它们本身也不费脑力，只是简单重复，没有实质技能的提高。我们需要的是在学习区练习。每过一个阶段，比如20小时，就要专门训练新的、自己还没能完全掌握的内容，并每天评估自己学习的进度。

Deliberate Practice

舒适区	学习区	恐慌区
查单词	Core, Function	180–200w/min
查背景	计时段落速读	正确率 90%
翻译	长句分析	长篇学术论文
读文章做题	分题型训练	
	陌生题材训练	

以下列出几个常见的学习瓶颈，需要在第2和第3阶段的进阶和冲刺训练中进行专门练习，同时也给出了粗略的量化指标。

陌生题材	文科同学可集中读选自理科题材的GRE文章，如连续10篇遗传学，5篇气候学；理科同学可集中读文科题材文章，如连续10篇文学评论，5篇历史研究等
长句	集中2个小时读30–50个长句，在20秒内抓出主干，找出从句
段落	集中读理科文章的连续动作或机制段落，或读文科文章的对比段落，30–40秒内找出核心
整体结构	集中看长文各段首句或短文的首句、转折句和中间的观点句，写出所有kw及其关系图
题型	分题型训练，比如10道信息题，20道逻辑题，10道作用题(In order to)，找出共同解法
选项差异	集中看自己做错或蒙对的题目20道，找出错误原因和出题者常用的陷阱

只有通过反复的刻意练习，才能将每个技能熟练掌握，烂熟于心，最后达到**自动反应**的境界。就像上球场比赛时，球员是不大可能还有时间考虑如何上网拦截、如何抽底线，一切动作都在极短时间内完成。但这熟练到似乎不用思考的动作，都是平常在教练指导下刻意练习的结果。同样的，真正上考场和做模拟测试时，或将来读学术英文时，是没有时间在脑子里反应逻辑结构是什么、关联词是什么的，一切都应该已经练习到自动反应的程度，才能达到最高效率。在做题的时候，也没有时间想这是什么题型，有什么解法，如何定位，等等，一切当前的注意力都是这些做法的结果，不再去想中间步骤。这需要大量的练习。练习吧！

例如，我们建议，在阅读训练的那几天，要么不读，一读就读8–12篇文章，先单篇或4–5篇集中计时做题，然后再做2–3遍分析。这样，这8–12篇文章每篇至少读3遍，而且在1–2天内完成：

第一遍	**卡时间读文章做题**，然后对答案，检查错误。
第二遍	不是重复看文章和做题！按后文给出的示范，分析**core+function**。下笔写出文章和段落的核心词(core)、每句的功能作用(function)，甚至写出提示主题、论点、论据、态度、结论的提示词(cues)。
第三遍	找出所有题目在原文中的对应句子，按后文给出的示范，写出**考位分析**。

也就是说，每一遍都有不同的关注点，每一遍都能练习与阅读和做题技能相关的不同侧面。

第三节　结构张力与阅读方法

本节首先讨论GRE文章的取材，分析什么文章不适合作为GRE文章来源，GRE文章有什么结构特征，然后探讨传统的、人们习以为常的自然阅读方法，或者单词+句子+随机总结的方法，指出其不足以应对逻辑结构井然的学术文章，最后说明结构化阅读方法是如何获得的。本节后面的内容相对艰深，读者可多读几遍，或先跳过不读，在训练一些GRE式的文章以后再看，慢慢体会自然阅读方法与本书倡导的结构阅读方法之间的差别。

3.1　GRE文章结构的张力

几乎所有分析性的、非虚构类的作品都有相对严密的逻辑结构，我们的结构分析方法适用于这些文章。但GRE的阅读文章到底与这些文章有何分别？出题人是如何从这些文章原料中筛选、改编成GRE文章的？我们先来考虑什么样的分析类、非虚构类文章不适合作为GRE文章。鉴于**GRE阅读要公平地测试几乎所有学科背景的本科生的学术英文阅读和逻辑把握能力，同时又要制造一定难度以区分考生水平**，GRE阅读会尽量避免文化敏感、专业词汇过多或依赖背景知识、平铺直叙过于直白的文章。

1. 文化敏感：种族歧视、性别歧视、情绪敏感。尽量避免种族歧视的字眼，没有白人文化优越的任何论述，以避免引起现场考生不快，影响答题。也杜绝出现针对女性或男性的贬义词，避免可能引起与女性或男性相关的负面感受的内容。类似abortion, amputated, depressed, addicted等可能引起任何考生不快的词汇，也都不会出现。这个容易理解，就不举例了。

2. 专业词汇过多或依赖背景知识：如果一篇文章的每个句子都包含3–5个甚至更多专业术语，需要专业知识才能解读，则有这个专业背景的考生就能获得优势，其他多数考生则会因此处于劣势。这显然违背公平原则。结果是，所有GRE句子内的专业名词都很少，或者整篇文章只有1–2个，并不影响对文章整体结构的把握和对句子基本意思的理解。当然，普通动词、形容词和抽象名词并不属于专业名词（technical terms）。考生如果觉得它们都是生词，就要加强单词了；通常，对于GRE阅读来说，词汇量达到8000左右是必需的。下面是一个专业词汇过多导致非专业读者不可读的例子，我们以黑体标出每句的专业词汇：

Alpha（α）**amylase**（**4-α-d-glucan glucanohydrolase, EC 3.2.1.1**）is classified as family 13 of the **glycosyi hydrolases** and is responsible for the **hydrolysis** of the **α-1,4 glycoside** bonds in **glycogen** and **starch**, and related **polysaccharides** and **oligosaccharides** containing three or more $(1 \rightarrow 4)$-α-**linked D-glucose** units. The main function of the digested and assimilated products is to supply energy to the organism. **Alpha amylase** is produced as a **zymogen granule** by **pancreatic acinar** cells, and their presence is considered to be an indicator of the **exocrine pancreas** maturation in fish larvae.

（Source: G. Joan Holt, ed. 2011, *Larval Fish Nutrition*）

不是只有理科文章才会出现专业术语，有些文科文章也会在一句之内包含多个看似认识、但意义特殊的专业词汇，所有没有背景知识的人也不太能够看懂。只有当我们既掌握逻辑思维、又具备必需的背景信息时，才能读好这些文章。下面是文科文章的例子，专业词汇同样以黑体标出：

The **recursive** nature of **frames** deflects the seeming paradox that the **frame**, as a whole, represents a concept, but its elements, or **nodes**, are themselves concepts. This is not an **atomistic** form of analysis; there may be no ground floor or ultimate **conceptual repertoire** at which the **chain of frames** terminates. Similarly, there may be no single, unique way of drawing a frame for any given concept; there may be several equally defensible **representations** of a given concept or **conceptual structure**. A particular **frame representation** should be judged by its **empirical adequacy** as a **representation** of the behavior of a **linguistic community**, and beyond that it should be judged by its effectiveness as a problem-solving tool. Philosophers who expect the universe to divide into a single unique set of **natural kinds** may be displeased with this. However, to the extent that their belief in such **natural kinds** is alleged to be based on the actual use of language by nonphilosophers, including scientists, it is unfounded. There are no ultimate **natural kinds** in Wittgenstein's account of languages structured by **games** and **family resemblance** or in Kuhn's account of **concept acquisition** by learned relations of similarity and dissimilarity.

（Source: H. Andersen, P. Barker, X. Chen 2006, *The Cognitive Structure of Scientific Revolutions, p.45*）

3. 平铺直叙、过于直白。教科书上的许多英文段落往往简洁明了，不适合作为GRE阅读文章。其他说明性的文字，因为没有可取的论证扭曲，也不适合。只有经过逻辑扭曲的改造以后才行。

"The core is the innermost of the Earth's layers. **It is** a sphere with a radius of about 3470 kilometers and **is composed largely of** iron and nickel. The outer core is molten because of the high temperature in that region. Near its center, the core's temperature is about 6000℃, as hot as the Sun's surface. The pressure is greater than 1 million times that of the Earth's atmosphere at sea level. The extreme pressure overwhelms the temperature effect and compresses the inner core to a solid."

（Source: Thompson and Turk, *Introduction to physiological geography,* pp. 21–22）

该段多数句子的谓语动词都是is，全是属性描述，每个句子都很短，10–15个单词，而且各句之间基本是并列关系，逻辑过于直接，不适合作为GRE文章。

真正的GRE文章往往从讨论抽象事物或事情的学术分析类文章压缩、改编而来，并制造一定难度以区分考生水平。制造难度主要通过扭曲论证结构与增加逻辑层次来实现。一项研究对GRE文章的取材的逻辑扭曲标准做了相当直接的说明。

"Reading comprehension passages generally rely on some kind of tension to give them difficulty. A discussion or argument that develops in a linear fashion toward a conclusion is usually too simple to support challenging items. The requisite tension can take various forms: a conflict between different or opposing arguments about something, an unexpected finding that challenges previously established ways of understanding

"阅读理解文章通常依赖于某种张力以获得难度。一个讨论或论证，如果只是以线性方式展开，达到一个结论，则它通常是太简单了，不足以构成有挑战的阅读文本。阅读理解文章必须体现结构的张力，这可以采取多种形式：不同或对立论点的冲突，意想不到的发现——挑战以前确立的理解方

something, a disagreement about what evidence is relevant to the solution of a particular problem, etc. But disagreement or contrast or opposition is not in itself enough to provide the tension: a passage that merely states or describes opposing positions, without discussing in much detail the reasoning behind them, will not support very many or very complex items. For example, instead of saying that Brown believed X and Smith believed Y, a passage might tell us that Brown, heavily influenced by such-and-such school of thought, tended to assume A, and therefore believed X. Smith, on the other hand, had access to information that Brown did not have, namely B and C, and this information led Smith to conclude Y. However, Smith interpreted B in such a way that it seemed logical to conclude Y, when in fact this interpretation was ill founded. The more interdependent details, the more logical twists and turns, the better. Naturally, a passage containing this kind of density can only be created from a source that provides the requisite information, and such sources are not easy to find."

（Source: Passonneau *et al.* 2002）

式，关于什么论据与某个问题的解决相关存在意见分歧，等等。但是，分歧或对比或对立本身并不足以提供结构的张力：一篇文章如果只是陈述或描述对立的立场，而不详细讨论对立立场背后的推理，也不能作为复杂的阅读文本。例如，一篇文章不是说Brown相信X而Smith相信Y，而是告诉我们，Brown深受某个思想学派的影响，倾向于假定A，因而相信X。另一方面，Smith则有途径获得Brown当时没有的信息，即B和C，这一信息导致Smith做出结论Y。但是，Smith在解读B时，说从B推出结论Y合乎逻辑，但其实这一解读理据不足。简言之，相互依赖的细节越多，逻辑的曲折越多，这文章就越好。很自然的，包含这种复杂论证的文章只能来自提供这类必需信息的源文章，而这样的源文章并不容易找到。"

　　这就是说，增加文章结构的张力（structural tensions），使得文章不是直接总分+并列论点结束，而是出现更多不同的、对立的观点，而且不同观点之间反复辩难，或者在同一个观点之内既有支持论据，也有反对的证据。结合以上内容，我们认为，增加GRE文章结构张力和逻辑扭曲的主要方法包括：

增加论点　　长文1段即有1个论点，2-3段就有2-3个论点，有的段落甚至本身就有2个论点或1个论点1个态度。短文章则尽量在一段之内包含2-3个观点或态度，每个观点或态度之后可跟随1-2句证据。但论点也不可太多，因为论点的堆积不能反映逻辑过程，每个论点内部最好都包含一些论据。通常而言，GRE阅读文章的论点（包括态度句及其论据）为2-3个。于是，可以从只有1个观点的结构：TW-kw-a-b-c-d-e-cs，变成复杂的结构：TW-kw1-a-kw2-x-y-kw3-u-v-cs。这样可以既保证不会超出现场考试所能把握的水平，同时又能制造一定难度，符合难度适中的原则。

对比/让步　　单纯列举的几句话并列在一起，逻辑关系太直白。如果在论点的论证和展开过程中加入让步，则论证的直线推理就会因为出现限制性内容而被扭曲；加入对比，推理也会被撑开一个新的空间，有别的对象挤进来，从而增加难度。也就是说，从原来的kw. a. b. c.的简单论证，变成 kw. a. b. ~kw. But kw. 或者 kw. a. b1≠b2. ~c, but c.

结构嵌套　　在一个单独的论点之内，同时写入两个左右的论证，比如并列套对比，某个并列的论据部分，其中出现对比内容；或者对比套机制，对比的其中一个部分，写出连续的因果动作。我们把这些都可以称为结构嵌套。如果段落有2个论点，某个论点之内又有结构嵌套，那就更复杂了。

增加长句　　通常GRE句子平均有25-30个单词。但为增加难度，有的短文章只有4-5句，有的长文章段落只有2句，每句话有35~40个单词甚至更多。增加句子长度的方法主要是增加从句（尤其是以although/ while/ whereas引导的从句）、分词结构、有从句和分词结构修饰的同位语、将可以写成一个简单句的内容压缩成长名词短语等等。

这样，就将GRE文章的逻辑张力和结构扭曲的特点直接变成可观察的过程了。我们已经知道，GRE文章是学术英文文章的浓缩版。学术英文文章的特点是什么？怎么分析这些特点？如果只是列举几点，如严谨、深刻、艰深之类，我们是不知道什么意思的。我们的概念必须是可观察、可操作的概念单位，才能指引实际阅读的步骤和程序。所以，分析学术英文的逻辑结构，一定要具体化甚至量化。**本书在提出主要概念时，都要尽量做到可量度、可观察、可操作，拒绝那些虽然常见但却模糊、缺乏定义的概念**。只有这样，才能让尽可能多的读者，毫无偏差地接收、认可、进而实行其中的观念，而不是看了之后似乎钦佩和敬仰，但却无所得。

从最简单的可以观察的语言单位来看，日常英文的特点是相对简单的。单词容易、多用短句、逻辑直接；有的日常英文还是叙事，使用第一人称、加入作者的情绪化表达。还有一些长篇叙事的回忆录或传记之类，都不是逻辑论证。与此不同，学术英文为了说服读者，不是诉诸情绪、权威，而是诉诸语言的逻辑。语言的逻辑包含着论点与论据，呈现出来就是一个又一个的论点与论点的关系、论点与论据的关系、论据与论据的关系等层次。因此，关于GRE文章的一个基本公理是：**学术文章是有逻辑结构的**。如果在看一篇GRE文章时，觉得文风散漫、观点不明，那么，我们应仔细想想是谁的问题，然后针对这类自己一时难以弄懂的文章，反复练习，直到把握这种从前陌生的结构为止。**GRE文章的另一个公理是：逻辑结构是可调整的**。我们看到的文章虽然逻辑严密、结构井然，但并不一定是唯一可行的逻辑论证，甚至在少数情况下还不是最佳的。我们从结构的角度处理文章，不只是识别结构、看完文章之后归纳结构，而是带着一套逻辑结构的预期，处理文章内容，找出重要的核心，略读次要的证据，这种预期结构的阅读可以称为**结构化阅读**（**Structuralized Reading**）。下文将讨论结构化阅读与自然阅读思维之间的差别，说明为什么我们要约束自然习惯，转向新的阅读思维，也进一步解释为什么我们要对文章进行多层的结构分析。

3.2 传统的自然阅读法

按人们习惯的阅读方法，读学术英文，就是从单词出发，明白单词意思，进而明白短语内容、句子语法，再到段落大意。这种常见做法，可以称为自然阅读法，其实质是通过认识单词，尤其是生词以及专业名词，来理解短语和句子，进而理解段落和整篇文章。这种方法的一个必然推理是，阅读之所以不好，是因为单词量不够，如果单词量大，阅读自然好，因此阅读的好坏取决于**单词**。支持这个观察的事实是：总是在学术文章中遇到不认识的单词，所以学术文章才读不懂。但是，GRE阅读常考的逻辑关系以及学术英文的内容，重心并不在生词尤其专业名词上。此外，没有生词的学术文章，即便并不要求专业背景知识，如果阅读者没有足够严谨的逻辑思维，还是不一定能够读懂的。请试读以下段落。

In general, the more constrained the information that the outputs of perceptual systems are assumed to encode — the shallower their outputs, the more plausible it is that the computations that effect the encoding are encapsulated. If, for example, the visual analysis system can report only upon the shapes and colors of things （all higher-level integrations being post-perceptual） it is correspondingly plausible that all the information that system exploits may be represented internal to it. By contrast, if the visual system can deliver news about protons （as a psychologized version of the

Hanson story would suggest), then the likelihood that visual analysis is informationally encapsulated is negligible. Chat about protons surely implies free access to quite a lot of what I have been calling 'background knowledge'.

（Source: Jerry A. Fodor, 1983, *The Modularity of Mind*, p. 87）

　　该段没有专业名词，也基本没有生词（encapsulated的意思是"封装"），但是不容易读懂或抓住中心。为什么？因为它有相对复杂的结构关系，而这并不反映在生词层面。自然阅读法试图通过认识每个单词以后，拼出段落中心意思；如果单词之间的联系不是读者所熟悉的，那么，中心意思就无处寻了。在自然阅读的思维中有一个基本假设：懂得所有单词，就能读懂内容，或者，文章大意是所有单词的总和。以建筑做比方，单词好比建筑物的砖块，人们习惯的阅读方法似乎认为，认识所有砖块，就了解建筑物的结构。这显然是荒谬的，因为建筑物的结构不在砖块这一层次，而是在承重墙、柱架结构、外围结构等层面。另一方面，不认识一些专业名词，是否就不能读懂文章？这问题类似于，抽掉建筑物的几块砖，是否影响我们欣赏整个建筑？多数时候不会。当然，我们是要认识一些单词的，但是，单词不需要全部认识，认识95%就可以了；即便单词全部认识，也能对应成中文，但还是不一定能读懂。因为文章的中心在于它的逻辑结构，而这并不表现在单词这个最低层次上，而是属于更高的层次。学术论文的逻辑原则，不是在单词和翻译这种肤浅的层面上反映的。

　　自然阅读法的另外一个推论是，单词即使足够，句子不理解也不行，因此需要读懂**句子**，为此就要恶补英文语法，尤其要集中训练长难句。这种想法是，只要长难句弄懂了，以后读文章就能读懂了。长难句分析当然是重要的，它的主要作用在于克服长句阅读的心理恐惧。但人们常常把长难句分析变成语法分析，结果长句的语法是清楚了，该句的核心意思却还不清楚。诚然，由while, whereas, although等词所引导的句子，句子本身的核心就在其对比中，而且，一些简单句的核心也在于它的主干或主谓宾（SVO），但是，对长句来说，它们的核心意思却不是孤立表达于该句本身。事实上，并不存在一个唯一判断标准，来确定到底什么语法成分决定了句子最重要的信息。相反，长句的核心是在一个语境中即在上下句的相互联系中，因此是在写作者的意图中，不只是在句子的语法中，而这个意图就是文章的逻辑线索和结构图像。如果认为懂得句子，尤其是长句、难句，就可以直接读懂文章，那就相当于，看了一座建筑物的所有墙面，我们都懂得了整个建筑的结构。当然，一些墙对于理解建筑物的结构是必需的，但不是所有墙都如此，非承重墙就不是，普通家居内部的隔墙就是可随意拆卸的，看看还没有完工的楼房我们就知道了，里面空空如也，还没有基于生活功能需求隔出房间。而且，重要的还不只是承重墙以及剪力墙，还有承重墙-剪力墙得以稳定的更大型的力学结构，通常由钢筋混凝土浇筑的柱和梁，而柱和梁又立在特定的地基之上。对应到阅读文章，承重墙-剪力墙相当于作为论点和态度的句子，非承重墙或隔墙则是论据。掌握特定的、作为论点和态度的句子对于把握文章重要；更重要的还有这些论点和态度句之间的关系，而这不会表达在句子的语法中。想想吧，我们显然不会认为，知道砖块和隔墙，我们就能懂得建筑物；同样的，不能因为我们知道单词和句子，就以为我们知道了整篇文章！

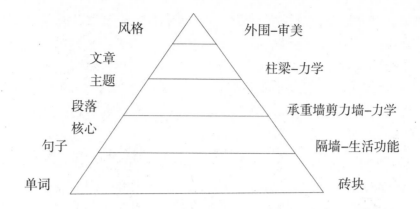

按照自然阅读法，在懂得单词和句子以后，读者会从文中挑选自己主观上觉得重要的句子，总结之后得到段落的大意和文章的主旨。很好奇不同读者如何会得到相同的大意和主旨，但似乎这个问题被归之于阅读者的文化背景、思想倾向、意识形态等等因素，由于后者很难研究，于是这个方法也就似乎没有得到反驳，于是就这样成立了。难道谁能说阅读不是这样吗？

鉴于自然阅读的习惯是单词 + 句子 + 随机总结，在此方法下衍生出来的阅读训练规则就是，**多读**就能练好阅读，这是自然阅读法的第3个看法。多读的说法听起来当然不错；问题在于效率。考生需要在很短的时间之内训练出解题能力，为此需要训练对解题常考逻辑关系的理解。除了时间的限制，多读作为一种解决方案的缺陷还在于，也许多读是从来解决不了核心问题的。这个结论令人震惊，但却是事实。考虑两种情况：1. 读了50篇GRE文章，答案都记住了，文章的翻译也看了，背景知识也查了，花了很多心思去记忆；2. 读了20篇GRE文章，文章的句子之间的逻辑关系都分析清楚了，甚至可以跟考友讲明白。哪种情况下，考生更容易在GRE考试中取得好成绩？答案不会令掌握学术英文思维的人惊讶：第二种。为什么呢？GRE阅读是以英文为基础的学术逻辑考试，不是以专业背景为噱头的歧视非此专业考生的考试。背景知识与文章翻译统统是不必要的，虽然翻译若干篇可以让译者本人确定自己的确是明白了一些，但多做无益。主张多读的朋友要仔细了：多读永远正确，但我们需要知道的是自己读的时候以什么为重心。学术文章阅读的重点是体现于上下句和上下段的逻辑推理，而不是每个孤立的句子内部的孤立的生词或专业名词。如果只是勤查背景知识，就只能模糊掌握这篇文章，这些知识不能应用和推广到别的题材。所以，勤奋是勤奋了，时间也花了，但效果却未见得就好。事实上，在错误的道路上奔跑，勤奋得令人崩溃。

自然阅读法的第4个常见说法是**多记**，记住的文章信息越多，做题就做得越好。这也是一个符合直觉的错误策略：一篇文章所有单词的总和也不等于是文章的核心信息；同时，多记的想法是很好，但人其实在短时间内是记不住所有单词的。George Miller（1956）在他著名的论文"The Magic Number Seven"中谈到，人在短时记忆（short memory）中能够记忆的信息单位是有限的，约在7 ± 2个。就我们阅读GRE而言，50″– 60″能够记忆的信息十分有限。但为什么人会觉得自己记住很多东西呢？这是一种心理幻觉。通常，人在1–2分钟内阅读一篇文章以后记住的只是认知敏感的词汇，比如生词，或者最后几个词，或者自己随机挑选的觉得重要的词汇。但这些多数时候都不是文章的重心，也不是GRE考试的重点。此外，如果记忆的维度增多，记忆的精确度就会下降：既想记住生词、又想记住几个观点、还想记住某些人名，这到最后也许一个也记不清楚。我们必须找到一个方法，记住有限的、重要的核心词和常考语言的位置，而不是试图把所有东西都记住。

自然阅读法的第5个也是最后一个误区是**读懂**。有时读者恰好熟悉所读篇目的基本背景，结果就会带着自己的知识去对应和理解，有时甚至不惜以自己掌握的既有知识来扭曲文章中的逻辑链条。阅读考查的是作者写了一些什么和怎么写的，而不是读者认为某个问题是怎么样的。因此，读者在阅读学术文章时，不能先行带入自己的知识。读得越懂，在做题时还可能越不仔细，放弃回原文定位，错题反而比那些没有读懂的文章的错题更多，这也就并不奇怪了。读懂这个概念，每个人似乎都有不同的理解，因为缺乏一个公共的评价方法，所以，这个概念不如不用。

总体来看，人们太习惯于从单词、句子中寻找含义，进而猜测文章意思，这种从下而上的自然阅读思维，也不是没有来由的。他们似乎要把单词和句子等同于人类社会的个体和小群体，对个体和小群体的细节和故事决不放过，而对小群体之间的关系和社会趋势等却不做分析。因为人的智能只是适应于局部小群体的社会智能，关心个人的八卦和群体的敌我关系，是人的心理常态，分析群体的目标函数和互动关系，构造社会趋势的模型，则需要人为的刻意的努力，不是习惯所能自动做到。从人的社会智能到其他认知任务，就会发生这种认知迁移。于是，在理解学术文章，尤其是其浓缩版GRE文章时，人们常常是在随机拼凑。他们仔细地读每个句子和每个单词，但由于缺乏客观标准，无法决定哪些是重要的，于是一个也不放过，生词还要查字典，然后随机抽选一些单词，拼凑出文章意思，或者按照自己对作者的动机和目标的揣测，得出所谓的中心大意。想想高中语文阅读吧！但是，文章分析是寻找秩序，而不是随机拼凑。阅读是寻找文本逻辑的过程，不是寻找微言大义、寻章摘句的游戏。逻辑结构不是眼睛看出来的，眼睛看到的只是单词、句子，看不到句子之间的关系，更不用说论点之间的关系，甚至有时连单词和短语之间的关系也看不出来。单词和句子是具体的事物，而关系是抽象的设想。**逻辑结构是脑子想出来的**，心眼可以"看"到，肉眼却看不到。

如今，多数关于GRE阅读方法的讨论也基本上都会重视逻辑结构，但对逻辑结构的内在含义，却人见人殊，意见纷呈。一种常见的说法是，读完了文章以后，总结出文章的主要内容，这就是逻辑结构了。按照这种观点，读了一个段落以后，也要总结出该段的主要内容，也就是逻辑结构了。这种观点有很多问题。第一，不清楚它的"总结"是什么意思。"总结"的意思可以有很多：归纳、找出中心思想、概括重点内容、记住关键信息，等等。其中每个意思都必须要有可操作的具体流程，读者自己在阅读任何题材的学术文章时，才能遵循高度固定的、但数量有限的规则，读好每篇文章。如果读不同的文章时，读者都必须采用不同的"总结"，采用不同的做法，那么，这种每次都要调整的方法就太偶然、太特殊了，不存在模式和规则，缺乏稳定性，而这正是它本身意义不明、操作不便的显著后果。

第二，看不出这种读完"总结"的方法如何可以适用于长句或者学术论文。检验一个方法的经验规则是看它能否应用于所有层次。如果这种方法能够向外推广到论文和著作层面或向内推广到句子层面，那就是很强大的方法。试着将应用层次向句子、尤其是长句推进，这种"总结"方法也许会说，读过一个长达50字的句子以后，总结出该句的主要内容。什么？这种说法没有提供任何信息。如果"总结"是指长句的语法分析，那么，语法书就足够了；如果"总结"是指长句的内容理解，那么，鉴于每个长句的内容不同，我们很难由这种方法明白这个"总结"可以怎样操作。

总结毫无疑问是必要的，但问题在于，我们需要在读GRE文章的时候总结什么。不过，即使总结什么的问题解决了，"总结"也不一定意味着是好的阅读方法。这有两个原因。一，"总结"在中文中往往是指读完以后才回顾并提炼，因此，这种方法暗示着，在阅读的先后顺序操作上，必须先读完所有内容，包括所有单词和短语甚至语法分析，才能提炼文章内容，而这几乎必然带来阅读时间长的问题，因此无法应对高强度、时间压力奇大的GRE阅读。二，"总结"还假定了，文章全部单词的总和可以单独地为文章的主要论证思路提供线索，这个假定是中文文字向学术英文的一种错误映射的结果，同时加上翻译的迷思，使得阅读者在读英文学术文章时把重点放在了生词而不是逻辑思路上，甚至将阅读过程变成查阅字典的过程。有的观点以为，既然背诵名篇能够掌握中文语感，背诵英文的典型文章也能自动掌握英文逻辑思路，但这是一个虽然流行、但却严重不当的类比。背诵当然是必要的，但是由于中文的语流模式与英文的论证过程有着相当的差别，所以，单纯的背诵不能达到目标。当然，如果从逻辑思路的角度去记忆和背诵整篇文章，的确可以帮助大脑迅速建立一个框架意识，从这个角度来说，按照特定的方法背诵GRE阅读文章也是有益的。即便如此，这种有逻辑的记忆也必须以事先扎实细致的分析过若干篇文章为前提。否则无从理解所背诵文章的基本线索是怎样的，背诵就会成为死记硬背，过段时间就全忘了。想想自己高中背过的英文课文吧！它们的命运怎样了？

一篇英文学术文章的单词的总和，或者，如果翻译过来就是所有翻译内容的总和，并不自动等于这篇文章的逻辑信息。事实上，许多逻辑信息在文章的单词的字典或者翻译意义之外；单纯通过"总结"、其实是"加总"单词的含义，在有的情况下，无论如何也得不到文章的逻辑线索。逻辑结构，虽然不是在绝对的意义上但确实在相当程度上独立于文章单词的字面含义；逻辑思路并不等于文章单词字典或翻译意义的算术加总。在这里，整体并不等于部分之和，因为这个文章整体是由各个部分分层建构的，而不是一层就完成了。因此，从单词、句子的细碎处、特殊处进行总结归纳的思维，对于具有逻辑结构的学术文章是不适用的。看来，我们需要一种新的思维，来获得文章的逻辑结构和核心内容。这种方法就是从演绎推理出发的结构化阅读。

3.3 结构化阅读法

结构化阅读（Structuralized Reading）的方法不同于自然阅读法。将自然阅读法的5个观念一一取非就是结构化阅读法的基本立场：认识单词不等于理解文章；读懂长句不等于把握逻辑结构；多读不足以把握文章逻辑，把握文章甚至不必以篇数取胜；阅读文章记忆的标靶要集中于少数目标；"读懂"往往带来理解偏差。虽然自然阅读法是人类认知配置的基本阅读"方法"，一时很难消除，也由于中国的学术传统中缺乏处理科学推理的思维方式，再加上以往中文阅读纠缠于字词本身的传统，更增加了改变视角的难度；但是，掌握了结构逻辑分析的方法，好处是巨大的，受益是终生的，值得所有优秀的青年学子尝试。

GRE结构化阅读法解决的主要问题是掌握学术文章中的逻辑思路。逻辑思路不会直接在文章中用实际意义的词汇、尤其生词来表达，而是用一些基本的套路词，以及学术推理的常用词汇，这些词汇在几乎任何一篇文章中都是存在的。这一主张适应于GRE、GMAT、LSAT的考试文章，也许在经过一定调整后，也适应于所有英文学术文章。

与通常从单词基础、到句子理解、再到段落和文章的中心大意的猜测和回忆这样的从下到上的阅读路径相反，结构化阅读是从上到下的取向。这种方法从文章的整体和写作意图出发，以演绎的方式，推断和推测段落的结构关系，再从段落的首句，按照总分结构的思维，推断和推测段内若干句子的逻辑关系和词汇提炼的核心，再到段内的中间句子层面，仅仅看重那些由对比和让步转折等语言形式写成的句子。

这种思路与通常的阅读"方法"的对立，不是它存在的原因，而是它本身的一个副产品。结构法之所以先从文章整体出发，是因为学术文章的主题是先行的。作者先有了写作的基本图像，然后才展开写作。阅读者虽然不能像写作者本人那么清楚，但是至少可以按图索骥，找到文章的核心路线图。自然阅读法好像一个人闯进了单词的密林，然后陷在了沼泽地。结构阅读法好像一个人带着地图和指南针走进了有时明亮有时幽深的树林，沿着最直的道路前进，顺利抵达终点，然后向树林外的人讲述旅途的精彩。明亮的地带是结构性的句子，包括首末句、转折句和态度句，幽深的地带是专业细节句子，尤其是那些专属于某个学科的纯证据描述，甚至包括专业名词以及在中间句子出现的哪怕是不认识的动词和形容词。

怎么得到文章的结构呢？文章结构不是从单词的归纳得来，而是预先断定的写作模式。或者，逻辑结构不是归纳的结果，而是演绎的假设。在分析GRE阅读的学术文章时，我们似乎武断地假定文章存在相对稳定的写作结构，然后将此结构强加于所要阅读的文章之上。90%的文章都符合这些模式中的这种或那种，10%的文章是其中的若干种的变化组合。所以，这种方法是读者先形成对于学术文章的逻辑结构方面的一套假说，然后将此假说应用于具体文章的事实。为什么是结构化(structuralized)阅读而不只是阅读结构(structure)呢？因为我们所面对的阅读文章的结构并不是静态的、自然存在的、可从单词直接看出的，而是要靠我们自己的头脑思考，主动猜测得出的，是认定文章有结构、相应的将自己关于结构的一套假说应用于文章之上，然后在阅读某篇文章时指定文章结构的过程。所谓主动阅读(active reading)与被动阅读(passive reading)的差别，从这个角度来理解，才可以操作、甚至量化。当然，考生准备时只要能够识别固定的一些结构就可以；结构化的思维方式，不经过长时间的训练难以获得。

结构化阅读的发现过程本身也符合科学方法的原则。首先，随机找出若干GRE真题的阅读文章，然后，分析是否可以归为几种模式，这是从现象观察到假说提出的过程，接着，将这些有限的模式应用于更多的文章，验证是否适用，如果不是，则根据例外情况来修正最初的结构假说。我们在研究足够多量的文章以后发现，GRE, GMAT, LSAT阅读真题的文章都符合这里提出的结构化假说。所以，我们一开始似乎是在武断地决定文章以及段落分别存在某几种结构模式，但然后我们的推测得到了验证，假说(hypothesis)变成了关于学术英文的逻辑结构的理论(theory)。这是从数据到模式、再到更多数据验证的分析过程。"文章分析的三个层面"就是这样一个多层结构假说。

通常人们认为模式是八股，但这个明显带有贬义的词实际上是指，文章的中心主题是为了证明一个意识形态的命题，为此采用特定的起承转合式的写作程序、甚至语言表达形式。写作遵循一定程序，并不必然意味着成为八股；一个合理的操作流程，可以极大地提升沟通的效率。而语言表达方面的重复，当然对于任何文章都是不好的，尤其是当其中的语句空洞无物的时候。但在现代学术英文当中，主题都是活生生的事实，推理是严格的钢铁般的逻辑，不存在八股的问题。有时人们也会说模式就是套路。套路词当然是存在的，而套路本身只是文章的建造框架，文章本身的核心词毕竟还是与套路词有差别的，虽然它们往往与套路词同时出现在一个句子中。所以，模式不只是套路，而是还要包括核心词汇，这些词汇往往出现在段落首句的论点中。

在文章层面，结构模式的核心词通常不是不同文章各自不同的专业术语，也不只是那些表示起承转合的词汇，比如however, but, on the other hand, alternative，而是起承转合词加上相互关联的核心词，有时还是前面没有出现过的新词。通过这些词汇，读者很容易分辨和判断作者的主旨和意图，对文章后续内容形成特定的预期，然后按照这个预期去管理自己的阅读注意力。在段落层面，模式则体现为特定的论点构成方式，这些构成方式本身也有它确定的词汇，通过它们读者也能预期段内的写作方式，并按照这些段落写作的模式提取核心信息，而不是企图认识每个单词，归纳段落中心大意。中心大意不是归纳出来的，而是直接断定会出现在首句或转折句的；在多数时候，中心大意的判断甚至不以读完整段所有句子为前提，而是直接从特定的句子得出。再用建筑的比喻，当我们明白建筑物的柱、梁、承重墙和剪力墙，我们就知道了它背后的力学结构，也读懂了这个建筑物的结构，至于隔墙之类或类似文章论据的东西，留给每个房子里的人或作者自己去鼓捣就行了。

结构化阅读法有两个方面。第一个方面是从数据到模式以形成结构假说，这是研究的过程，以上已经描述；第二个方面是从结构假说然后演绎出具体逻辑关系，这是考生学习的过程。考生不必重复研究者发现这套方法的过程，只需要学会如何应用结构化阅读就可以了。

高效率的准备程序是从分析开始，到应用结束。考生只要先了解关于结构化阅读的抽象理论，应用这些理论实际分析20篇真题文章，写出每篇文章句子之间的关系，就能掌握整套方法。由于文章、段落、句子的结构模式分别只有3-5种，考生在分析了20篇文章、60多个段落、250个句子以后，每种结构也许会分别重复5次、15次、50次或更多。重复是重要的，积累必要的阅读量是分析的第一步，这是数据搜集的步骤，没有数据也就不会存在模式。但只有量还是不够的：正如只有数据，没有数据分析的架构，数据只是一堆分散的、毫无意义的数字而已；同样，只是读过很多文章段落和句子，没有分析结构的框架，那些文章段落和句子就依然是分散的、缺乏联系的碎片，没有组织，难以进入长期记忆，过了几天就会忘记。所以，分析框架和必要的阅读的量，两者缺一不可。在做过这20篇文章及其中的段落句子之间的关系的细致扎实的分析以后，考生就基本上明白了结构模式是怎样一回事，接下来就可以应用这些抽象的、但是依然可以操作的理论，去分析任何新的GRE文章了。

由于结构化阅读遵循的是学术研究的思维模式，如果考生完全不了解学术方法，在学习学术英文的逻辑结构时会有观念上的不适应，因为这种方法本身违背直觉，甚至有些考生会对分析逻辑结构有抵触情绪，因为从前受到错误的阅读方法的误导。一个常见的疑问是：难道这些模式就是学术文章的所有模式？难道就没有文章不存在模式吗？或者，模式是死的，文章是活的，万一遇到的文章不符合这些模式怎么办？对这些问题，我相信不仅是一个备考的问题，而且是思维方式的转换问题。把这些问题换一个面目会更好理解它们的实质：物体的运动真的存在规律吗？难道就没有什么东西不符合这些规律？确实，石头飞滚，苹果落地，导弹发射，飞船离开地球，行星的运动，这个世界的物理对象丰富多彩，但是，如此多变的现象却都符合牛顿力学的基本原则。从几条有限的假说出发，就能推演出人类所看到的几乎所有宏观物理对象的具体运动，这是科学的假说演绎法的威力。我们希望，结构化阅读中提供的模式也能模仿物理学的这种伟大创造，为变化万千的英文学术文章提供一个统一的操作程序，指引写作者写出结构井然的文章，指引阅读者读出文章的逻辑意义。逻辑结构也许不是变来变去的，因此并不那么活泛，但是，学术英文的逻辑结构是生存法则，不符合这些原则的学术文章都在学术交往中慢慢被淘汰了。而即便这些逻辑结构只有有限的几种模式，它们所能容纳的文章的题材、依据它们所能写出的文章，也是浩如烟海、丰富多彩、精彩绝伦。事实上，读懂逻辑线索才是真正读懂学术文章。如果连论证的过程都不明白，只是认识几个单词，然后按照自己的偶然感受揣测作者的意图，那么，说读懂是说笑了。

以上两节主要讨论了通常理解的阅读方法与把握逻辑结构为主的阅读法的区别，并由此指出，学习GRE阅读主要是学习以英文为基础的逻辑分析。由于阅读考题通常聚焦于段落之间、句子之间的逻辑关系，所以，学术英文的逻辑结构的理解，对于快速提高GRE阅读的解题能力极为重要。考生在有了基础的6000-8000词汇量和基本的长句阅读经验以后，就应把复习准备的主要精力，80%的精力，放在分析逻辑结构以及依据逻辑结构解题的重点上。

我们相信，为了理解GRE阅读文章的逻辑思维，多了解一些学术文章的基本写作方法是必要的。英文维基百科（wikipedia）里关于scientific method以及scientific revolution的条目，非常值得一读。如果有任何关于科学方法论（scientific method）的课程都值得去听，任何讨论critical thinking的书籍也值得去读（比如Moore and Parker写的Critical Thinking一书第9版的chapter 2, two kinds of reasoning, chapter 11, causal explanation）。最后，牛津出版的写作指南（*Oxford Essential Guide to Writing*）的第3部分专门讨论段落的写作模式，对于分析阅读学术类文章也有极大的帮助。我认为，以上3类材料是掌握学术英文分析的必要基础，对于从未接触过学术逻辑思维的考生也许是特别有益的，有时间的考生多看一点吧！

一位网友在看过自然阅读法与结构化阅读法的文章以后，画了一张图来总结：

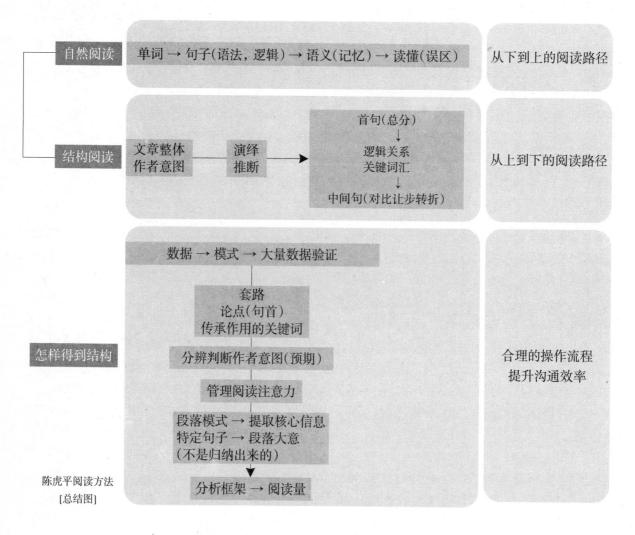

陈虎平阅读方法
[总结图]

（Source: http://blog.sina.com.cn/s/blog_497114370100pz89.html ）

随遇而安，随波逐流，顺其自然，率性而为，看似自由，其实处处掣肘。率性，其实只是任性；看起来很高超，其实处处被偶然事件所决定。没有实力的自由都是假的。

GRE 学术文章的多层结构分析

本章内容

Passage 文章 ◎

Paragraph 段落 ◎

Sentence 句子 ◎

Words & Phrases 单词和短语 ◎

Online Reading: Minimal Solution 阅读现场：最简方案 ◎

阅读与写作不同。阅读的主要目的是分析作者的论证思路，而不是看清楚所有的论据、单词，甚至修辞方法，或者思考自己对作者讨论的话题有什么看法。与此不同，写作是要表达自己的观点，必须自己组织论点，寻找证据，懂得证据的内容。另一方面，阅读与写作也可以在一定程度上相互配合。阅读可以帮助写作。好的文章是一个模范，可以模仿。但是，在模仿时，我们要记住模仿什么。模仿GRE或英文学术文章的框架结构、论证方法或论点展开方法、句子的构造，这是可以的。单纯模仿单词和句子，会忽略学术英文的核心逻辑。另外，好的写作书也能帮助阅读，因为其中讲述了文章的组织技巧。当然，要将写作书中的技巧应用到有时间压力的阅读中，需要做一些调整。

GRE学术文章有层层独立的逻辑结构原则。要读好文章，就要学会分析其中的结构模式，以后再读类似的结构时就能快速进行模式识别(pattern recognition)，有时甚至还能提前预期结构(anticipate structure)，这样可以提高速度。简要来说，在文章层次上，要抓住主题词或主题句(如有)，这是极度常考的内容。在段落或论点层次上，要抓住首句的论点，或者中间由关联词引出的态度句或新论点句。对于对比关系的论据，要抓住对比的反义词；对于因果关系的论据，要抓住原因和结果。如果有连续3-4个并列成分或并列证据，只要注意位置，不必当时理解和记住内容，等考到题目时再回文定位。在句子或论据层次上，除了各段首句、末句结论句（如有）、转折句、态度句的内容重要以外，中间句子内部出现对比、比较、让步转折、首次大写或举例的地方，都要留意其位置，因为可能出题，但不必将全部内容记住，因为短时间阅读文章后人的记忆容量有限，我们只能选择性地记忆。

从结构角度来处理文章，也与人们习惯的自然阅读不同。自然阅读的实质是一种随机阅读过程(random reading process)。在这种阅读过程中，读者在所阅读的文本中挑选一些词汇作为自己主观理解的重点，比如记住生词(recognize new words)、记住最后几个词(remember the last words)、或随机挑选一些自己觉得重要的词汇（random selection of words)。由于没有一个客观标准，因此读任意一篇文章时，读者的选词标准会受到词汇量、知识背景、临时信息、甚至阅读心情的影响。甚至在不同时间读同一篇以论证为主的学术文章时，会有完全不同的感受。与此不同，结构化的阅读的实质是一种有设计的阅读过程（designed reading process)，它的焦点在于对文章和段落信息进行逻辑提取(logical extraction)。提取什么信息和依据什么标准，这是我们要探讨的内容。

本章会从文章、段落、句子三个层次分别分析其中的逻辑构造，并相应地给出阅读重点，最后会简要说明单词在阅读中的地位。本章的多层结构分析是本书方法论的重点，我们会把三层逻辑结构图的内容逐层展开，详细说明。

从学术方法论看，从上层到下层，都是从一般假设到特殊实例的假说-演绎推理(hypothetico-deductive reasoning)，而从下层到上层，却是从多到一、从特殊到一般的过程，但不是归纳，而是特殊向一般的还原过程（reduction)，为特殊的、具体的事物找到它的一般原则。文章分析的三层结构，从演绎推理来说，是从文章-主题到段落-论点、再到句子-论据，从还原角度来说，则是为众多单词的一个有秩序的集合即文章，找出了其中各层的独立原则。这是解释复杂现象的多层还原方法在语篇理解和话语分析中的应用。

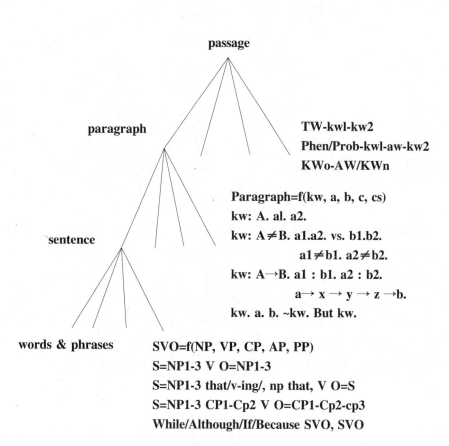

passage

paragraph

TW-kwl-kw2
Phen/Prob-kwl-aw-kw2
KWo-AW/KWn

Paragraph=f(kw, a, b, c, cs)
kw: A. al. a2.
kw: A≠B. a1.a2. vs. b1.b2.
      a1≠b1. a2≠b2.
kw: A→B. a1 : b1. a2 : b2.
      a→ x → y → z →b.
kw. a. b. ~kw. But kw.

sentence

words & phrases

SVO=f(NP, VP, CP, AP, PP)
S=NP1-3 V O=NP1-3
S=NP1-3 that/v-ing/, np that, V O=S
S=NP1-3 CP1-Cp2 V O=CP1-Cp2-cp3
While/Although/If/Because SVO, SVO

第一节　Passage 文章

TW-kwl-kw2
Phen/Prob-kwl-aw-kw2
KWo-AW/KWn

一篇文章（Passage），尤其是3-4段的文章，是主题（TW = Topic Words）或总论点（Thesis = TS = Topic Sentence）和各个观点（subtheses, different views = kw1, kw2）的组合或函数关系（f=function）。所以，我们有：

$$Passage = f\,(\,TW/TS,\ kw1,\ kw2\,)$$

从开头看，文章通常会引入一个话题。在学术文章中，不同的话题会有不同的论述模式。不是说，相同的话题一定用同样的方式论证，但如果80％情况下都如此，则论证模式的作用就很明显了：它能帮助我们快速猜测文章后面的模块大致是什么。下面我们从演绎法来设想文章的可能情况，为它做一个穷尽无遗的逻辑分类。有的文章，只有作者一个人的观点或评价，他要么提出自己的论点（Thesis = TS = Topic Sentence），要么评论近期研究或作品（recent study/work = TW）。然后，分成几个角度展开，有几个分论点（kw1, kw2）。通篇文章只有作者一个人讲话；被评论的对象不说话，它们只是文艺作品、历史研究等。于是，我们有GRE文章的**单观点结构**（小写字母a b, x y等为各观点的证据，每个符号代表一个句子，可以增减）：

TW/TS. i. j.

KW1. a. b. c.

KW2. x. y. z.

KW3. u. v. w.

有的文章，多个人讨论同一个主题（TW），例如某个现象（Phen.）、问题（Prob.）、或争论的话题（TW），出现多个观点（kw1, kw2, kw3），每个观点作者给出的态度评价（AW=attitude words）通常也会不同，而正评价观点（或者就是作者本人观点）往往在最后出现。事实上，学术论文，尤其是作为标准的科学论文，通常一开始会简要介绍论文的主题、研究的目的（Introduction），然后就会对既有的研究流派和方法做出文献评论（Literature Review），这些评论有赞有弹，常常以批评为主，因为如果以前的观点很对，就没有必要再做新研究了。之后就是作者本人的研究方法和思路（Author's Method）以及提出的假说或模型（Hypothesis or Model），然后就会有大量的实验数据或其他类型的证据来支持（Data or Experiment），到最后会有一些数据的讨论、分析，或者还有对未来研究的展望，或者说明目前研究存在的不足，以及还需要解决的问题（Discussion, Analysis）。通常，一篇学术论文可以分为5节（也可以将I与II合为一节）：

Paper

I　Introduction

II　Literature Review

III　Method and Hypothesis

IV Data

V Analysis and Discussion

　　将这种学术文章的Introduction简化后写出TW，单独写出或写在第一句的某个论点中，又从Literature Review截取1–2个既有观点，给予负评价，再把后面作者本人观点、数据和讨论的部分压缩成1–2段新的观点或作者观点，这样就可以得到GRE阅读文章的**多观点结构**：

2个观点	3个观点
[TW] KW1. a. b.	[TW] KW1. a. b.
AW-. x. y.	AW-. x. y.
KW2. u. v. w.	KW2. u. v.
	AW-. p. q.
	KW3. i. j. k.

　　有时，多个观点是递进解释或说明一个问题的，一个比另一个更好，能够解释更多事实，解释力（explanatory power）更强，或者能够更全面地解决问题，解决效果（problem-solving efficacy）更好。有时，多个观点，主要是两派观点，是完全对立的，一个排斥另外一个，这时，就有过去与现在、多数与少数的观点之间的对比关系，文章的重心在观点之间的对立，而不是解释同一个现象或问题。

　　我们可以把以上的演绎分类画图如下：

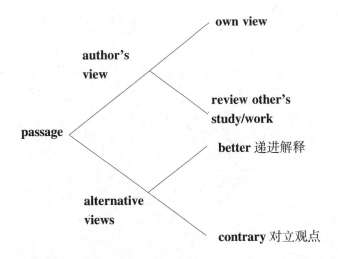

　　不是每个演绎结构都能有用，单纯构造体系，虽然有时也可以作为思维训练的一个步骤，但常常流于空泛，徒增思维深刻的外表，没有实际的用场。好的演绎结构的分类必须变成可操作、可观察、甚至可量度的项目，这样才会获得公共的认可和接纳，帮助人们组织和加工信息。这就好比，一个演绎的学术体系，必须要能推出可验证的假说，这些假说还可以验证于经验性的事实，变成原则上可证伪、但现在未曾被证伪的理论，这样才有解释力，才能帮助我们认识和组织该理论所覆盖的现象、事实和行为。下面，我们就把这个演绎分类的项目具体化。

1.1 A General Structure of Passage 文章结构图

对于单观点结构，首段或前3句直接给出有态度或判断的论点的，可称为**论点说明型**文章，该论点就是文章主题；对开始没有给出论点，只是给出中性的评论对象，如出现人名+书名、人物+近期研究、人物+作品的，可称为**评述型**文章。这两种文章的结构相同，只是开始有点差别，一个常有作者判断或态度句（论点说明），一个没有态度，只有中性的作品和研究（评述）。

对于多观点结构，首段或前3句给出中性的现象或问题，后文给出2-3个解释或解决方案的，称为**现象解释**和**问题解决型**文章，现象解释和问题解决的结构高度相似，差别只在于首句给出的是现象还是问题，可归为一类，这种文章里，某个解释或方案比其他的更好，是观点递进。首段或前3句给出关于主题的判断和意见，通常是老观点或大众意见，后文给出反驳意见和新观点的，称为**新老对比型**文章。这种文章里，观点之间通常完全对立，非此即彼。首段给出作者的判断和意见，后文才出现对立观点的情况，极为罕见；如果出现，往往只是把替代理论与自己观点进行对照，突出自己的观点，故这种情况可以略去。

以上分类方法源于杨继的杰出创造，他从考试要求出发讨论文章套路，最早系统说明了GRE/GMAT长文章的结构模式，解决了主题题、结构题的定位问题。本书将这种偶然发现的文章模式与学术论文的结构对接，从演绎的角度对文章进行系统的完备的分类，这样就可以从长文章推广到短文章，从**考试类**的文章推广到所有450字长度的**分析类**文章或学术文章的3-4段话。下面给出GRE文章的结构模式总图，横行为3大类结构（细分为6种情况），纵列分4项，"开篇套路词"和"全文结构"说明文章结构，"AW"（态度）与"TS & CS"（主题句/结论句）说明核心。

	开篇套路词/cues	全文结构 / TW, KW	态度/AW	TS & CS
现象解释 （多个解释） Phen. –KW –AW	phenomenon, fact, behavior; what causes, why	TW=Phen. 1st explanation=kw1 But aw- 2nd interpretation=kw2+	前负后正 （80%情况）	explain/answer+ TW → 首段首/末句 有时TS=TW+KW+ CS: 少见
问题解决 （多个解决） Prob. –KW –AW	problem, difficulty, puzzle, question	TW=Prob. Solution 1=kw1 But aw- New method=kw2	前负后正	
唯一解释 （少见）	TW=Phen. / Prob.	Author's expl. =TS	唯一解释+	
新老对比 Old – New KW	has been, traditionally, until recently, long, once; ［ however, recently ］ frequently, widely, many, most, usually, dominant, common ［ however, now ］	KWo（含TW） However, aw- KWn	老：否定或次要 新：正评价	TS: 反驳或新观点 → however/recent句 → 二段段首或一段后半部分 CS: 少见

论点说明 TS-KW	is, remain, prove + adj. can, may, should, must attitude words: +, –;	Thesis / TW subthesis 1 = kw1 subthesis 2 = kw2 （Conclusion）	论点说明，态度 不定	TS = Thesis → 首 段某句，多为首末句 CS: 末句/较短末段
评述 TW-KW	recent study（人名+书名/人 物+研究）		评述文章多混合 评价	无TS CS: 综合各个 KW→各个意群首句

1.2 Phen./Prob. –KW –AW 现象解释/问题解决

标志　首句给出一个现象、社会事实、问题、困难等（e.g., a distinct animal behavior, a mysterious phenomenon, there has been a puzzle, difficulty, Why, What causes...?），后文会给出若干解释或解决方案，通常会有评价。

结构　前负后正。主题之后有多个解释/方案，内容不同。2个解释，则第2个对。3个解释则前两个错，第3个对。文章、段落重点的主题、态度、论点等内容，以下划线划出，是阅读时需要主动把握的内容。（少数时候，文章只有一个解释：如果是他人的解释，则后面通常会提出态度评价，这时类似于评述型文章；如果是作者自己的解释，则会展开几个方面的证据来说明，尤其常见的是给出验证假说的实验和推理，这时类似于论点说明型文章。）

Long Passage	Short Passage	Variant /变体
phen/prob. i. j.	**phen/prob.**	TW. kw. kw1. a. b. kw2. x. y.
kw. a. b. / kw.	**kw1.**	一个解释，自己证明，类似论点说明
aw–. x. y.	**aw-. x.**	TW. kw. a. b. kw' = testing. x. y.（7句）
kw+. u. v. w.	**kw2+. u. v.**	先数据/TW，后假说/kw，再验证/kw'
4个模块，11–15句	7句	也可记为：i. j. kw. a. b. kw'. x. y.
		有时还会有让步性的替代观点/~kw：
		i. j. kw. a. b. ~kw. x. But kw. a'. b'.

态度　如有多个观点，前面观点常为负评价，负评价有两种，一种完全否定，一种部分否定，后者更为多见。

主题　找到文章首句或首段的现象或问题，文章主要关注点在于解释现象或解决问题。少数情况下，例如只有作者一个人的观点，没有其他观点，可用现象加上最后正评价观点(KW+)作为主题。

▶ 例1 ◀

As XXX, YYY, and others observed long ago, all species appear to...	TW, 观察到的是现象
one school of thought proposes...	kw1, 人物常有观点
This...has its uses, but it can cause problems...	aw+, -, 混合评价，但主要为负评价
...we may think of...as...	kw2, 作者观点和判断，为正评价

（左边为**提示词/cues**，右边为**说明**，其中TW, kw, aw等符号表示提示词所在句子的功能，如kw表示该句是论点所在的句子。下同。）

► 例 2 ◄

Paradoxically, ...has been one of the last to develop.	TW, 提出悖论或问题, 即为主题
Different explanations of this paradox have been suggested.	kw', 暗示不同解释, 但尚未提出
One is...; but we might ask why...	kw1, aw-, 第一个解释, 随即负评价
It has also been proposed that...	kw2, 第二个解释, 无态度提示

► 例 3 ◄

There is some dispute about...	TW, 关于某问题的争议
Some biologists argue that...are responsible for...	kw1, 人物常有观点, responsible for暗示因果关系
Yet the results of...experiments cast doubt on these hypotheses.	aw-, 实验质疑上文假说
More probable is...	kw2+, 更可能的观点出现

► 例 4 ◄

Why...should body temperature...rise?	TW, 提出主题, 问体温升高的原因
It has long been known that...	kw1, 已知观点, 在理科中常作背景
...first suggested a relationship between...and...	kw1', 已知观点的因果关系
...were used to test this hypothesis	kw2, 检验假说的实验, 可看做观点
...reported that	x, 检验报告的内容
	(一个解释及其验证, 没有前负后正)

► 例 5 ◄

...	TW, 开头有某些事实提出
Two reasons for this...seem obvious.	kw', 作者本人将会给出两个理由
First, ...	kw1, 第一个理由, 相当于分论点
Second, ...	kw2, 第二个理由, 相当于分论点
	(作者解释分别展开, 无他人解释)

1.3 Old-New KW 新老观点对比

标志　首句给出过去时间的老观点(e.g., traditionally, it was once believed that)，或大众看法(定义为老观点)(A widely accepted view, it has been generally believed that)，后文有however / yet / but引导的反驳句出现，之后提出新观点。

结构　新老对比。老观点在先，然后反驳或者直接给出新观点，新老观点内容对立，如一个说高，一个说低；一个说增加，一个则讲减少；一个说有巨大影响，一个则说只有很小影响，等等。

Long Passage	Short Passage	Variant /变体
KWo. a. **AW-. x. y.** **KWn. u. v. w. p. q.** 3个模块，11–15句	**KWo. AW-. x.** **KWn. u. v. p. q.** 8句	KWo. AW- = KWn. u. v. p. q. 6句，有时负评价就是新观点 KWo. i. j. TW. KW1. a. b. KW2. x. y. 老观点有时仅作为背景

态度　前负后正。老观点负评价，负评价有两种，一种完全否定，一种部分否定，后者更为多见。有时老观点作为背景，后文也有But转换给出真正主题，这种文章不属于新老观点型。

主题　反驳意见和新观点/TS＝AW- + KWn。它们有时不同，都可作为主题答案。注意，主题不是首句老观点。

▶ **例 6** ◀

Biologists have long maintained that... But the recent discovery of...undermines the attempt...	KWo, 长久以来的观点是老观点 AW-, 近期发现摧毁老观点，该句可能同时给出新观点

▶ **例 7** ◀

Present-day...usually envision their discipline as an endeavor... The basis for this view, however, lies in a serious misinterpretation The idea..., turns out, on close examination, to be...	KWo, 通常的看法被定义为老观点 AW-, however转折句加负评价词 KWn, 肯定性动词短语给出新观点

▶ **例 8** ◀

It is frequently assumed that...has a revolutionary effect on... Historians...now seriously question this assumption of transforming power.	KWo, 频繁假设被看做老观点，认为X对Y具有革命性作用 AW-/KWn, 质疑上文假设是负评价句，同时可能就是新观点，认为X对Y不具有革命性或根本性作用

▶ **例 9** ◀

Traditionally, ...has been viewed as a...process marked by random events... However, a number of features...	KWo, 传统观点为老观点，has been为过去观点的暗示 KWn, 转折句既暗示与老观点对立，又给出新观点；老观点说random，新观点说新特征，可视为不随机

▶ **例 10** ◀

The common belief of some linguists... Many linguists are deaf to those instances...	KWo, 一些人的常见信念，即老观点 AW-, deaf在此表示负评价

► 例 11 ◄

Many critics of XXX's novel...see its second part as... However, any interpretation...is bound to be... unconvincing.	KWo, 多数人的观点被看做老观点 AW-, 转折句的否定词给出负评价

Context 铺垫结构

请注意，不是所有老观点在文章首句都一定会遭到反驳。在少数时候（约25%的情况），老观点在前文只是作为铺垫和背景，后文会以此为前提，提出新的观察或研究，文章重点依然在后面的新观点，但它与老观点的关系不是对立，而是增补。我们可称之为"铺垫结构"，它相当于文章的引子或背景（introduction or context，以下简写为Intro），这种情况常见于理科文章。通常无法直接从提示词直接判断老观点是作为反驳对象还是作为已知背景，在这方面，逻辑就无能为力了，只能借助内容把握。

► 例 12 ◄

...is well established... However, ...properties have been known for a century.	Intro, 已经根深蒂固的观念和认识 TW, 与通常所知不同的另一个观点

► 例 13 ◄

It has long been known that... The contribution of the recent model is to show that...	KWo, 已知观点，可作背景或被反驳 KWn, 近期模型的贡献，未反驳前文

1.4 TS/TW-KW 论点说明/评述

标志 论点说明文章：首句给出判断句，常为系表结构（e.g., remain the standard, appear to be discouraging）、情态动词（e.g., must, should）、态度句（e.g., A series of highly suggestive essays, A misconception is that），或者其他可以表示作者观点或判断的句子。

评述文章：首句给出近期研究、作品、著作、流派等（e.g., recent historians have argued that, XXX's work YYY, a new design, a recent music movement），少数时候过去的作品也行，没有与之对立的新作品

结构 总分 + 并列。首段或首句给出总的主题，后文分角度并列展开2-3个分论点，并分别给予论据支持。

Long Passage	Short Passage	Variant /变体
TS/TW. i. j.	**TS/TW.**	TW. i. AW-. kw1-. a. kw2-. x. kw3-.
kw1+/-. a. b. c.	**kw1+/-. a.**	负评论，批评一个作品或研究，但无新观点出现
kw2-/+. x. y. z.	**kw2-/+. x.**	TW. i. kw1. kw2. ~kw2. But kw2.
kw3-/+. u. v. w.	**kw3-/+. u. v.**	某个分论点后有让步转折
(CS)		
4个模块，11-15句	6句	

态度　　论点说明型文章作者态度完全自由，没有规律。评述型文章也如此，不过经常对他人作品给出正和负的混合评价，由于任一评价本身即为分论点，两个论点之间常由转折关联词连接（e.g., however, nevertheless, on the other hand）

主题　　首段或首句论点。如末段或末尾有结论，也可作为主题。如果都没有，就综合主题词和所有分论点。

● 论点说明

▶ 例 14 ◀

| Scholars often fail to see that... | KW/TS, 首句态度 = 作者判断 |

▶ 例 15 ◀

| Because of its accuracy in..., the...method remains the most important tool in... | KW/TS, 首句正评价=作者观点，既有 most important, accuracy，也有 remain 系动词表判断句 |

▶ 例 16 ◀

| ...finds can still contribute much to the study of... | KW/TS, 情态动词 can 表判断句，contribute to/贡献表示态度，且通常通过时间对比展开 |

▶ 例 17 ◀

| The evolution of...was due...to the interaction between... | KW/TS, 首句直接给出因果命题(due to)，非他人观点，属作者判断 |

▶ 例 18 ◀

| The complications, ..., are now thought to result from the lack of... | KW/TS, 虽有被动语态，但为现在观点，作者通常同意，且有因果关系 |

● 评述

▶ 例 19 ◀

| In a recent study, XXX examines two central questions concerning...: ...and...? | TW, 人物及近期研究，标准的评论对象，后文依次说明问题(KW1, 2) |

▶ 例 20 ◀

| Currently, there are two models of... | TW, 近期或当前研究，评论对象，这里有两个模型同时被评论 |

▶ 例 21 ◀

| XXX's masterly writings on...reveal... | TW, 人物及其著作，这种评述模式在文学、历史题材文章中尤其明显 |

▶ 例 22 ◀

At least so argues XXX in his...study of...	TW，人物及其研究，评述对象
XXX does present a quantity of examples, ...	KW1，第一个方面
Although these observations are true, XXX overestimates their importance by concluding from them that...	KW2，让步转折给出混合评价，同时引出第二个方面，给负评价

以上文章的分类，并不是绝对的，少数文章处于灰色地带，可从属于两类，例如有些给出负评论的文章，也可以看做新老观点型文章，不影响主题的判断。事实上，不需要在阅读每篇文章的时候都进行分类。分类的目的，以理解主题、观点和态度为限，不必拘泥于每篇文章的类别归属。但是，通过这里的分类模型，掌握多数文章的主题、观点和态度的位置和内容，这对于快速理解文章依然是重要的。

主题、结构或态度通常会在题目中考查。除了新老观点的主题在转折句或新观点（But/However/Yet句），其他文章的主题都在首段前三句（现象解释，主题=Phen./Prob.，论点说明，主题=首句TW/TS）。任何文章如果没有主题句，可以综合各个分论点、解释、或理论以及态度句（KW1，KW2，AW1，AW2），作为主题题答案（main idea = KW1 + KW2 + AW1 + AW2）。

我们把表现文章主题、论点、态度的句子称为**结构性句子**，它们的位置在**首末句、转折句、态度句、过渡句**。

首末句是指段落首尾。段首句在90%情况下给出该段核心，只在少数情况下可能出现让步转折，或者，首段首句偶尔出现铺垫内容。一个论点或段落通常以论据结束，但少数时候（如20%的情况）会有总结，这时总结的引导词可以是：thus, then, hence, therefore, as a result, as a consequence, in summary, in general, together, these factors, the point is that等，不用引导词直接给出结论也是可以的。

转折句指由转折关联词引出、而且表示负评价的句子。转折关联词包括however, but, yet, nevertheless, nonetheless，这些词不是每次出现都表示负评价，而是只有在别人观点之后才表示负评价。负评价内容由具体的否定词来提示，如fail to, cast doubt on, cannot fully explain, little explanatory value。转折句在段首或段中。

态度句往往为负评价转折句，如But this genetic theory cannot fully explain，这时，与转折句等价。可以把负评价态度句看做论点的变形形式，它后面可以跟随证据来支撑，写成公式就是：AW-. x. y. 正评价多数时候只是作为一个单词在有核心的句子中间出现，如A more compelling explanation is that；正评价偶尔也会单独成句，如This theory is correct because... 。

过渡句是指不在首末句和转折句、而在段中引出新的观点或态度的句子，如An alternative model supposes that，这时alternative就引出不同的或替代的论点，这样的句子与首句一样重要，因此要读如首句。表示并列论点的过渡句词汇很多，例如，another theory, a more convincing hypothesis；表示对比和转折的过渡句也有很多，例如，alternatively, a new theory, an opposing view。短文章以及长文章的某些段落，往往会有多个论点或转折句，这时，核心内容不只在首末句、转折句、态度句，也可以在段中的过渡句中出现。我们要高度重视这些小词提示核心的作用。

1.5 Short Passage and Long Passage 短文章与长文章

从以上结构图可以看出，长短文章在结构上是相似的，都有同样多的TW（唯一一个）、KW（2–3个）、AW（多个观点时，别人观点常为负评价）。所以，它们的差异不在结构本身，而在于中间展开证据的多少，证据多，为长文章，证据少，为短文章。

短文章有3点值得注意：1. 多数120字的短文章的句子都比较短，每句20–25个单词，这样在1个110–130词的段落之内，就能写5–6个句子。考试的重点是句子之间的逻辑关系、论据对论点的支持或反对的关系。2. 文学评论和人文学科的短文章，有时会出现含有多层从句和修饰的长句。这样，句子之内的对比、让步、并列从句或分词结构，就会成为考点。3. 160字的短文章的句子数也就在3–8句之间，通常是5–6句，这样，既可以用多句构造复杂的逻辑关系，也可以写入1–2个长句。

与此对应，长文章的篇幅常为450字左右，可以写15个句子甚至更多，每个句子平均25–30个单词。由于篇幅足够，但观点（KW）并不增多，也只有2–3个，所以每个观点后面的证据都可以写3–4句，可以相对充分地展开。在读长文章时，重点不在段落中间的证据，而是在首末句、转折句和过渡句。中间证据皆可略读或快速处理，不求甚解，待做题时，看到题干内容后，通过各段首句的结构信息定位相应段落及中间句子，找到定位句后再考虑答案；那些没有在做题时定位过的中间细节句，读过永远忘记就好了。

我们把这些内容概括为两点：

1. 长短文章结构相似，差别只在证据多少，长文证据多，短文证据少，但它们的TW KW AW 数目通常一样；

2. 长文各段核心常常就在各段首末句、转折句，短文核心在首末句、转折句和有论点提示 词处。

当我们已经明白文章的主题、观点、态度在哪些句子中时，我们就要知道它们各自是什么。态度（AW）的正负当然最容易判断。主题（TW）多数时候也容易看出，在短文多句或长文各段首句重复出现的往往就是主题，而主题多数时候也是一个中性的话题。比较困难的是观点（KW）的核心词，更困难的是观点后的证据核心的把握，这是下一节"Paragraph 段落"部分所要分析和处理的内容。

第二节　Paragraph 段落

Paragraph=f(kw, a, b, c, cs)

kw: A. a1. a2.

kw: A≠B. a1. a2. vs. b1. b2.

　　　　　　a1≠b1. a2≠b2

kw: A→B. a1 : b1. a2 : b2.

　　　　　　a → x → y → z → b.

kw. a. b. ~kw. But kw.

段落是论点与论据的组合，可记为Paragraph = f（kw, a, b, c, cs），其中 f 为function/函数，段落是论点与论据之间的关系构造的，有时也包括末尾的结论。**论点之后常有论据，论据重现论点核心**。本节主要讨论段落分析，它分为两个层面，一个是论点核心的提取，相对容易，一个是充分展开的论据的核心内容的提取，相对困难。对于一个GRE段落，要么有一个论点及其论据(kw. a. b. c.)，要么有2-3个论点(kw1. a. b. c. kw2/aw. x. y. z.)，但无论如何，kw a b c是段落的基本分析单位。正常学术文章的段落多数与这里分析的一致，少数会有变化，也许写得没有GRE段落那么清晰，但基本的逻辑思路不变，因此这里的结构分析，适用于所有分析性文字。最基本的一点是，一个段落如有论点，则要么论点在先，要么论据在先；通常是先论点后论据，有些时候也会先事实再解释，或说先论据后论点。我们重点讨论先论点后论据的结构（kw a b c），对先论据后论点的结构(i. j. kw.)会简略处理。

kw a b c总分结构的语言意义。对于所有论点及其论据的内容，抓住论点都是最重要的，其后的论据通常都可略读。在略读时，可以尝试找出中间证据与首句论点的对应词汇。为什么会有对应词汇呢？因为从结构上来说，首句与中间句是总分结构，这种抽象的结构在语言上必须有所体现，才能说明论据从属论点，论点约束论据。因为总分结构要求分的论据不可超越总的论点，在接着阅读每个论据时，要想到**论据重现论点核心**，**论据向论点收敛**，于是从语言上看，在首句论点和2/3句的论据之间，会出现逻辑等价词(logical equivalents)，甚至是直接对应的字典同义词(synonyms)。有时，通过这种前后照应，我们可以从已知单词推出未知生词；而且，即便中间有内容读不懂，只要明白它一定只能从属于首句，就不用担心其中可能出现偏离内容，避免误读段落核心和论点。

段首句	中间句
kw	a b c
view	evidence
main idea	supporting ideas
1st句	2nd, 3rd, 4th句
kw/核心词	**kw的同义词或逻辑等价词**
总	分
论点	论据/证据
观点	细节

除此以外，段落首尾经常相互呼应。推而广之，如果文章有多个段落，则各段首句也经常呼应，甚至上段末尾下段首句也会前后呼应。这样，文章和段落紧密衔接、结构紧凑。

kw: 论点及其论证效度。一个论点，要么重点讨论一个事物，要么讨论两个、至多三个事物之间的关系。一个论点如果讨论3-5个事物的关系，通常是太笨重了，不容易论证，不如化为几个小论点一一论证，集合起来与大论点等价。因此，就单个论点而言，它通常讨论1-2个事物。这里，我们没有使用归纳的方法，而是直接使用演绎推理，这样在逻辑上相对完备，而不是经验搜集的偶然组合。每类论点或首句常有特定的展开方式。采用这种而不是那种展开方式，通常由论点的内容来决定。特定论点需要特定论证，我们可以用论证效度来评估论据对论点的支撑关系。效度不是个人任意的判断，而是学术共同体所认可的论证标准，约束多数学术文章作者的写作思维。讨论一个事物的理由、特征、态度评价的论点，通常以并列论据展开；讨论两个事物之间的关系的论点，通常有两种，一种是对比，以对比证据展开，一种是因果，以平行和序列的因果证据展开。

先事实后解释、先数据后假说的分总关系: i. j. kw. a. b。少数GRE段落会先事实、现象、数据、观察、实验或行为，然后在段中提出解释、假说、模型、猜想或理论。在现象解释文章中会出现先现象后解释、先事实后假说，从结构上看，就是先分后总。同时，有些段落的实验数据较多，也会采取这种论证方式。这两种情况都可记为：i. j. kw. a. b. 在GRE文章的来源即学术文章中，这种情况并不少见。当然，先事实再假说的内容以后，还是会有证据/a. b. 来支撑或验证这个假说，这时，这些论据仍然会按照因果机制、对比、并列等方式来展开。

2.1　A General Structure of Paragraph　段落结构图

在下文的段落结构图中，"首句线索词"为段首句给出的提示，"句间关联词"为段中论证的细节各句之间可能出现的关联词，"把握重点"告诉我们要提取的论据的核心是什么，"考题"暗示通常针对特定的论据可能会出的题目。在大约50%的情况下，中间论据都是并列展开，通常不需要现场掌握内容，只要记住位置就可以，到时考题再通过论点核心词定位回来；但也有一些时候，中间论据是以对比或因果关系展开，考题的频率很高，因此要提取这些证据的主要信息。

	首句线索词与句间关联词	把握重点 （100-120字 → 2-3字）	考题
并列 Juxtaposition / parallelism	首句描述一个事物kw: A has NPs / is adj. / does sth. (a1. a2.) 中间for example, for instance; 或者In addition, Moreover, also **another**, furthermore	并列所属的大主题=kw 并列找**并列** （2-3个并列, 找并列词; 3-5个并列, 位置>内容）	1. in order to → 首句 2. 列举 → 并列内容
因果 Causation	首句A causes/correlates with B. 中间并列因果 parallel causation A → B(a1 → b1. a2 → b2)	首句：因果找**双方**	1. 因果双方; 尤其数量因果 （正或负相关: A increases as B increases/declines）
机制 Mechanism	首句或有process, procedure 中间连续动词serial causation A → B(A → x → y → z → B)	首末句：机制找**末句**	2. 细节 → 结果 → 末句 常考列举法; 连续动作取非

对比 Contrast & Comparison 对象对比	首句 differ, contrast, more than A ≠ B.（a1 a2 vs. b1 b2） A ≠ B.（a1≠b1. a2 ≠ b2） On the contrary, however, on the other hand, different, In contrast, alternative, other	有无对比或程度对比 对比找**反义**	细节取非 → 对比内容(谁和谁 比, 比的什么) → A vs. B → 相互取非, 反义词
时间对比	首句change, contribute, further early vs. recently/new/now most, typical vs. recent/new	同上	同上
*让步[转折] Concession [Refutation]	Granted, ... [However, ...] one may argue that.... [But...] （kw. a. b. c. ~kw, but kw）	转折或一对反义词 （anticipate objections）	1. 细节取非 → 答案出现对比词 2. 常考含有态度让步转折

在大致找出论点核心之后，可以猜测后文如何展开论据，如果论据展开相对充分，有2-4句，也要提取重点。通常，并列展开的论据不太重要；对比或因果展开的论据的某些内容重要，常会出题。

2.2　kw: A. a1. a2. 并列

2.2.1 并列论点的判断及核心

讨论一个事物的论点，要么给态度，要么不给态度，在没有态度的情况下，也许是说该事物的**性质**、**理由**、**作为**等等。无论哪种情况，都可以使用举例、并列等方式来论证。这时，核心就是作者关于这个事物所给出的性质、理由、态度等，一般就在宾语或表语位置，因为主语常常是这个事物。令这个事物为A，则一个论点只讨论一个事物的情况，可以表示为A has NP / A is adj. / A is sth. / A does sth. / A is not adj. / A didn't do sth.（NP=noun phrase, sth.=something）。判断的方法是，首句的论点常有名词复数（NPs）或态度词（aw），总之不涉及多个对等事物。

▶ 例子 ◀

A has NP / A is adj. / A is sth. / A does sth. / A is not adj. / A didn't do sth.

Black Fiction does leave **some** aesthetic **questions** open.（questions为名词复数，后文会并列展开问题）

The kind of intelligence favored by the interplay of increasingly smarter catchers and increasingly keener escapers is defined by **attention**—that aspect of mind carrying consciousness forward from one moment to the next.（句子主干为"某种智能是注意力"，无对比及因果关系，重心为attention，后文会并列展开，但真实文章的下句内容讲到过程，出现例外）

Many critics of Emily Brontë's novel *Wuthering Heights* **see its second part as** a counterpoint that comments on, if it does not reverse, the first part, where a "romantic" reading receives more confirmation.（谓语动词see...as... 非对比和因果关系，批评家认为第二部分在评论第一部分，后文会并列展开这种看法的证据）

The implication of the papyrus **administered a severe shock** to the vast majority of classical scholars, who had confidently asserted that not only the role of the chorus but also language, metrics, and characterization all pointed to an early date. （谓语动词为造成震惊：administer shock，讲莎草纸的含义，后文会并列展开）

It has been known for many decades that the appearance of sunspots **is roughly periodic**, with an average cycle of eleven years. （太阳黑子是周期性的，一个事物的性质描述，后文会并列展开周期的行为或影响）

To impose some order on this kaleidoscope of patterns, one school of thought proposes **dividing populations into two groups**. （two groups为名词复数，后文会分别说明）

However, cortical locus, in itself, **turned out to have little explanatory value**. （负评价句，后文或许会说明little value的证据）

There are, however, **certain difficulties** with this interpretation. （负评价句，且difficulties为名词复数，后文并列展开）

Scholars often fail to see that music played an important role in the preservation of African culture in the United States. （谓语动词fail to see，表示对学者的负评价，后文展开说明他们失误在何处）

The basis for this view, however, **lies in a serious misinterpretation** of the past, a projection of modern concerns onto past events. （宾语名词misinterpretation表示负评价，后文如果有证据，会并列展开）

● 2.2.2 并列论点的论据展开

论点首句或段首句描述一个事物的，后文一般并列展开，举例是并列的特例。如果不容易判断kw句是否描述一个单独事物，则可通过排除法：凡是论点没有两个事物的因果和对比关系的，都可认为是描述一个事物，后文如有证据，都会并列展开。论点及其并列结构可记为 kw: A. a1. a2. 这里a1, a2表示论点核心词A的论据。

第一种并列的形式是举例，在中间句可用关联词，for example, for instance, in the case of, say, illustrated by。这容易理解，不必举例。

第二种形式是正常并列，中间各句之间偶尔使用并列关联词，如also, another, In addition, Moreover, Furthermore, Similarly。首先，并列内容描述一个事物的特征或原因：

A has some features. For example, feature 1. In addition, feature 2. **=> kw. a. b.**
A has some causes. One cause is...Another cause is... **=> kw. a. b.**

学术论文的篇幅足够，有时会将某事物的性质穷举并列表（tables），这种情况在GRE考试文章中不会出现。

其次，并列内容描述一个事物的性质，常有形容词出现。可记为kw: A is adj. a1. a2. 例如，讲一项研究是有说服力的，然后从几个方面展开说明。

This hypothesis is convincing. It successfully explains...Further evidence comes from... **=> kw/aw. x. y.**

含有态度的词汇，往往都是对一个事物进行评价，因此，后文都是并列展开，这就是说，态度句的论证一定是并列展开的，此时，中间证据一定会与首句态度保持一致。可记为aw. x. y.，其中负评价及其证据十分常见，且经常出题，可进一步记作：aw-. x-. y-. 如：

The A theory cannot fully explain...evidence shows that...not A. A also fails to explain... **=> aw-. x-. y-.**

这样的证据也可以在负评价句本身以从句或介词短语形式出现，如：

Something cannot be the result of A because...and because... **=> aw-: x1, x2.**

再次，并列内容可以讲述一个事物的行为和动作，分开几点说明，通常没有特别明显的并列关联词。作为证据的句子，主语往往相同，描述该主语的若干动作。如：

Scientists studied A. They investigated...They found that... **=> kw. x. y.**

在GRE文章中，几乎100%都是总分结构，很少变化。与此不同，在正常学术文章中，结构的变化较多，虽然多数时候依然是先论点后论据、先假说后验证（实验证据以平行因果关系展开，见后），但有时也会出现先证据后论点、先观察后假说的情况。如：

The experimental evidence shows that...A similar result can be found in...A hypothesis is that... **=> x. y. kw.**

通常，GRE一个论点的并列内容不会超过2~3句，这时可适当把握并列内容，在证据中找并列词，是为"并列找并列"。但少数时候，并列内容可能多达4个，这时记住位置，比记住内容重要，是为"位置 > 内容"。并列结构通常考**列举题**，问原文提到过关于A的什么，如果并列内容3~4个，也许会问没有提到什么（mention A EXCEPT）。并列内容也可能考其中某个证据的**作用题**。证据的作用是为了说明论点，这时给出首句论点做答案就可以了。

以上所说的论点只讨论一个事物。当论点不只以一个事物为重心，而是以两个事物之间的关系为重点时，论点后面的证据就会有对比和因果展开的形式了。广义上，对比和因果的证据都可以并列，但既然这时重点不在并列，而在对比和因果本身，尤其是有些证据完全与并列无关，因此要独立出来讨论。

2.3 kw: A → B. 因果

2.3.1 因果论点的判断及核心

讨论**两个事物**的论点，这两个事物必须是对等的，处于同等地位和相同层次的，它们之间的关系主要有两种。一种是**因果**关系，kw: A → B，这时首句论点的核心是因与果，分别在表示因果联系的谓语动词的左边和右边的主语和宾语，简单来说就是，**因果找双方，双方在主宾**。判断的方法是，论点的谓语动词含有因果关系，如：

determine, cause, effect, is affected by, is due to, is responsible for, account for, explain, is attributed to, credit...with..., blame...for...

或者，论点含有任何可以表示动作关系的动词，如：

induce, elicit, facilitate, precipitate, speed up, improve, enhance, reduce, block, inhibit, suppress, prevent, remove, lower（v.）

或者，论点含有因果关系的前提条件即相关关系，如：

correlate with, relate...to..., have to do with, vary with, coincide with, is coupled with, is accompanied by, parallel, relationship between...and..., link, connection

以及表示两个事物之间数量关系的词汇，如：

is proportional to; the higher, the higher; the more, the lower; A increases when B decreases; A increases when B increases; absence of the high level...may be explained by...; A falls when B rises

▶ 例 ◀

A → B

The evolution of intelligence among early large mammals of the grasslands **was due** in great measure **to** the interaction between two ecologically synchronized groups of these animals, the hunting carnivores and the herbivores that they hunted. （互动造成智能演化，后文可讲互动如何造成的连续动作，或讲智能的内容）

However, a number of **features** that are characteristic of wind-pollinated plants **reduce pollen waste.** （特征减少花粉损失，后文可讲这个、那个特征，以这种或那种方式减少损失）

It is frequently assumed that the mechanization of work **has a** revolutionary **effect on** the lives of the people who operate the new machines and on the society into which the machines have been introduced. （机械化影响人和社会，后文可以平行因果展开，这种工业技术影响人，那种工业技术又影响人）

Other data from the Vostok core show that methane gas also **correlates closely with** temperature and carbon dioxide. （m=methane气体与温度和二氧化碳相关，后文可讲数量因果关系，谁增加，谁也增加或减少）

Anaerobic glycolysis **is a process** in which energy is produced, without oxygen, through the breakdown of muscle glycogen into lactic acid and adenosine triphosphate（ATP）, the energy provider. （首句谈过程，后文也许继续展开其中详细步骤，以连续动作写出）

Because of its accuracy in outlining the Earth's subsurface, the seismic-reflection method **remains the most important tool in the search for** petroleum reserves. （s. method → search petroleum）（S. method可以帮助search petroleum，后文也许讲该方法如何去找石油储备的过程，连续动作或机制展开）

● 2.3.2 因果论点的论据展开

如果论点的重心在于两个事物之间的因果关系，则论据会用平行或序列的动作关系展开，前者是狭义的因果（causation, correlation），后者是广义的因果，我们称为机制（mechanism）或过程（process, procedure）。它常见于理科论点的论证。因果关系是科学研究的核心，它是逻辑命题的一种。逻辑命题本身并不自行成立。一个命题可以随意展开，其中一些展开前后自洽、能够回归原命题，称为逻辑收敛；在逻辑收敛的命题里，又只有少数分类展开的项目是可以数理验证的，这就是科学所研究的数理实证的命题。通常，只有一个命题里的项目定量化，才能判断它是否正确或符合事实。数理实证的命题多数都是数量因果，它将原因和结果量化，能够观察、操作、验证，这是判断"原因 → 结果"的关系是否正确的主要途径。至于那些不能定量的和数理实证的命题，在学术讨论中，我们应当保持沉默。

平行因果(parallel causation)首句给出**因果**或**相关**关系，中间证据平行讲述原因变化、结果变化的情况。可记为：$A \rightarrow B. a1 \rightarrow b1. a2 \rightarrow b2$。有些因果关系没有数量表述，有些则有。一个例子是，二氧化碳影响温度$(CO_2 \rightarrow t)$，CO_2 多时，温度高，另一方面，CO_2 少时，温度低，可记为：$CO_2 \rightarrow t. CO_2\uparrow: t\uparrow. CO_2\downarrow: t\downarrow.$。不是所有因果关系都能给出明显的数量关系，但在科学文章中十分常见，甚至多数时候还会根据两个变量(X, Y)的数据关系作图。可以认为，理科学术论文中的曲线图，多数都是因果关系$(X \rightarrow Y)$。

以数量来表达的因果关系包含相关性（correlation），相关性有正相关和负相关两种，通常取决于谓语动词是肯定还是否定；在展开的相关证据之间会使用对比关联词来联结，如however, By contrast，因为前后两句虽然结构平行，但内容相反。数量因果或者说相关性，几乎是必考的。

Positive correlation:　　　　$kw: A \rightarrow B. a\uparrow: b\uparrow. a\downarrow: b\downarrow.$

Negative correlation:　　　　$kw: A \rightarrow B. a\uparrow: b\downarrow. a\downarrow: b\uparrow.$

在把握因果关系时，考生需要尽量抓住因和果，它们通常在首句论点的主语和宾语，在中间证据中也会有重复。如果原因和结果都是专业名词，取其**首字母**，这样可以降低记忆负担。所以，**因果找双方，双方在主宾**。

序列因果(serial causation)首句给出因果关系，中间证据通过连续动作说明如何从原因到结果。这些动作通常有时间顺序，不可逆，不能颠倒位置。这与并列和对比关系都不同，后两者多数时候论述部分的位置是可以交换的。这时，可记为：$A \rightarrow B. a \rightarrow x \rightarrow y \rightarrow z \rightarrow b$。可以把这种序列因果关系称为**机制**(mechanism)、**过程**(process)等。同样的因果论点，二氧化碳影响温度$(co_2 \rightarrow t)$，可以不去讨论变量之间的数量关系，而是讲一个变量，如何通过影响局部气候、冰雪多少、反射度、其他温室气体、反馈循环等，最终导致温度变化。这就是机制。

$CO_2 \rightarrow t. CO_2 \rightarrow$ regional climate $\rightarrow$ ice $\rightarrow$ reflexivity $\rightarrow$ water vapor $\rightarrow$ feedback $\rightarrow$ temperature

在学术文章中，可能会有一些流程图或箭头图来表示工艺流程、形成过程、操作步骤等。在改编和压缩过的GRE阅读文章中，这些图当然都被省略了。但处理的思路相同。对于机制或过程，我们在现场阅读时，作为非专业读者，很难记住所有步骤和环节，它们可能多达8-10个甚至15-20个，GRE题目也不要求我们全部记住；只要抓住开头和末尾就可以了。如果考到中间细节，通过题干提供的核心词定位到相应的论点内容，再到证据或细节句里找到内容，在选项中找文字对应就可以了。于是我们得到，**机制找末句**。除了连续动作从原因出发做正向因果推理以外，还有可能会从结果出发做溯因推理，即$kw: A \rightarrow B. B \leftarrow x \leftarrow y \leftarrow z \leftarrow A$；在社科段落中，还有可能出现连续推理的情况，如，A暗示x，x要求y，y预设z，z表明B。也许因为这两种情况相对难以在短时间掌握，它们在限时考查的GRE文章中极少出现。

对于数量因果关系，原文如说A增加B减少，GRE考题往往**取非**一个变量，问情况是怎样的（问A减少会如何，答案是B增加）；对于连续动作的机制，GRE考题往往问其中一个**细节**怎样（直接找文字对应），或者将某个动作**取非**之后，会出现什么情况(答案是该动作之后的动作都不存在)。

2.4　kw: A≠B. 对比

● 2.4.1 对比论点的判断及核心

论点讨论两个事物之间的**对比**(不同)与**比较**(相同)的关系，可以记为kw: A=B, A≠B，这时首句论点的主语和宾语通常说明了谁和谁在比，谓语动词则表示比较关系，通常是对比关系，这是该句的核心。如果它能直接给出对比的内容，当然最好，但通常，对比的内容只会在后面的论据中才会出现。多数时候，论点句会有表示对比关系的词汇，如：

different from, differ, distinguish, distinct from, separation, contrast, conflict, dichotomy, rival, competitive, two different models, more than, less than, compared to

一些含有时间对比的词汇，本身即需要对比证据来展开，如：

change, alter, contribute, development, further, history

少数时候，论点句会有表示比较关系的词汇，如：

similar to, analogous to, counterpart, counterpoint

► 例 ◄

A ≠ B

The elements of intelligence and consciousness come together marvelously to produce **different** styles in predator and prey. (后文展开讲不同的风格)

We can distinguish **three different** realms of matter, three levels on the quantum ladder. (三个不同领域，展开说明)

Both Jewish law and canon law are **more uniform than** Islamic law. (more ... than ...，本句讲述J法、c法与I法的差别，后文会分别展开各个法律)

Modern archaeological finds can still **contribute** much **to** the study of ancient literature. (贡献通常通过时间对比展开，先讲以前如何、再讲现在有了考古发现之后如何)

Roger Rosenblatt's book *Black Fiction*, in attempting to apply literary rather than sociopolitical criteria to its subject, successfully **alters the approach** taken by most previous studies. (alter改变，意味着从前与现在的对比，后文先讲previous study，再讲R的研究方法)

◎ 2.4.2 对比论点的论据展开

如果论点的重心在于两个事物A与B之间的对比关系，则展开的模式有两种。第一种是先讲完一个事物，给出对比关联词，再讲第二个事物，可记为：A≠B.（a1. a2. vs. b1. b2.）。中间的对比关联词常常是, On the contrary, On the other hand, however, By contrast。对比关系常见于文科文章论点的论证。

第二种是先讲两个事物之间的第一个对比方面，然后并列讲出另一个方面，可记为：A ≠ B.（a1≠b1. a2≠b2.），表示对比的关联词在句内出现，如：while, whereas, unlike, rather than, differ from。这时并列不重要，重要的是句内的对比内容。

对比展开的论点，我们知道，谁和谁比，比的什么。比较的对象容易发现，通常在两句的主语，而比较的内容则通常在两句的宾语，有时也在谓语。将此提炼为一个口诀，我们有，**对比找反义，反义在宾语**。如果首句已经有对比的内容，则后面的证据也会同义重复或反义重复该内容。

少数情况下，论点说的不是表示不同的对比，而是表示相同的比较，论点句里出现similar to, analogous to等词，在中间句子中也用类似的词。这时就要在中间证据找同义词。它们可以记为：kw: A = B. a1. a2. = b1. b2。由于这种情况太少，而且容易掌握，通常忽略。

还有一种特殊情况，论点并无表示对比的词汇，但有表示时间的概念，如change, alter, contribute, development, further, history，这时后面常常是以时间对比展开，先讲过去或多数的情况，再讲近期或少数的情况，通过这种对比来证明改变、变化、贡献、发展。

关于对比内容，考题常问A不同于B的地方在哪里，答案是将B的性质和描述**取非**。这可写成一个模式：

原文：A ≠ B

题干：A? or A differs from B in that A?

答案：not B

2.5　~kw, but kw 让步转折

让步转折不是一个论点，也不一定含有态度，它是某个事实或其他论点与本段论点的**关系**。让步可以在任何位置出现，但通常不单独构成论据，而是作为辅助论证，表明作者考虑过不支持自己观点的**事实**、或与自己观点不同的**替代观点**，然后通过转折表明这个事实或替代观点不能动摇自己的观点，因此，它是一种以退为进的间接支持。论点后面会有论据的直接支持，如kw a b c。但读者也许会问：我见过好像与你的观点直接对立的事实，我听过好像与你的观点完全不同的观点，你怎么应对？这时，作者就可以通过让步转折，预先消除读者的疑虑，因此，让步是预期反对（anticipate objections）。让步的内容一定与论点不同甚至相反，记为~kw，而转折则必须回到论点，与论点内容同义重复或出现逻辑等价词，记为But kw，这里，but当然也可以用however, yet以及其他表示转折的词。这样，与直接支持的证据一起，一个含有让步转折的论证可以写为：kw. a. b. c. ~kw. But kw。在与kw的关系上，**让步找相反，转折找相似**。

让步转折可以放在任何一个位置，有时甚至可以放在首句。有人认为让步的内容是错的，是作者反对的。这是误解。让步不能脱离上下文来理解，不能单纯从**字句**上理解，而只能从它所代表的、作者也承认的事实或替代论点、从它与作者论点的**关系**来理解。让步的内容也是作者所同意的或承认存在的，但作者认为这个内容虽然存在且合理、且不支持自己的观点，但还不足以动摇自己的观点，而只能在部分程度上限制自己的观点，划定它的使用条件、缩小它的适用范围，但自己的观点却并不因此受损。因为几乎任何一个观点都有适用范围，通过让步转折锁定这个范围，并不是退缩，而恰好是强化。一个没有自我划界的观点，不是好观点；一个勇敢的作者，是应该多写让步的。

让步: fact or alternative theory

1. not support, not undermine kw

2. qualify kw（限制论点）

让步转折可以写成两句，也可以写在一句之内，有时让步甚至用非常简单的短语表示。下面列举了让步的一些提示词汇。

although, though, while; despite, in spite of + NP; as adj. as it is	［主句转折］
did/does（助动词）, may be, may seem, might seem, there might be, there is some evidence	［But］
of course, certainly; undoubtedly, no doubt, no problem	［But］
It is true that, to be sure, Granted; this is not to deny	［But］
无上述提示词而突然出现的相反态度或内容为让步	［But］

让步转折至少包含**对比**，同时还有**主次**之分，让步次要，转折主要；在阅读时，让步转折的重点是转折，它会有与论点相似的逻辑等价词或同义重复词。不是所有让步都重要，但含有态度的让步转折重要，常常会出现在考题中。

2.6　kw-kw 多观点段落

我们知道，综合论点的三种可能形式，一个论点的论证结构可以画成如下的图：

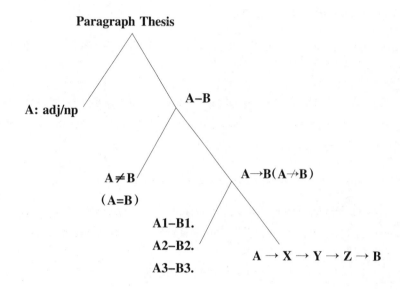

有些段落不只一个论点，而是有2个论点或1个论点1个态度（有论证支持的态度都可算作论点），这点在新GRE的短文中尤其常见。对这样的段落，段落分析本身就涉及论点之间的关系。可以给出一个一般的分析框架：

kw1. a. b. kw2. x. y.（kw2可以是一个aw-）

对任何一个论点，论据支持的方法如前所述，有并列、因果、对比、让步转折等模式。唯一需要补充的是引出第二个观点(kw2)的方法，它不在首句这个位置出现，而是在中间句，这时可能需要使用过渡词。视第二观点与第一观点的关系，可有两种情况：

对比或转折观点	however, but, yet, By contrast, alternative, on the other hand, opposing view, a more compelling explanation...;
并列观点	another theory, In addition, Similarly...

对于这些提示不同观点的句子，要读如首句，因为它与首句的地位和功能完全相同。如果在其中再加入让步的变化，2个观点的段落还可以写成：

kw1. a. ~kw1. But kw1. kw2. x. y. ~y, y'/ kw2.

这是说，在一段之内增加观点、或者增加让步转折，都可以加大段内结构的难度。可以认为这是观点的组合结构。如果在任意一个观点之内加入嵌套结构，比如并列套对比、并列套机制、对比套机制，等等，段落就可以写得十分复杂：

kw1. a. b. b1 vs. b2. kw2. x. y. y1 → y2 → y3.

观点的组合与论证的嵌套，是制造段落逻辑难度和结构紧张(tensions)的重要手段。看的时候，应该分别抓出论点核心以及各种论证结构的核心。

2.7 Linking Words 关联词

关联词是把握段落以至文章结构的钥匙。通过它们，可以快速而且准确地判断论据之间的关系，相应地找出核心内容。下面分别说明几种关联词的用法。

并列关联词，如 In addition, another, 要求大主题与作者态度都一致。内容一致、但态度不同的地方，也不能使用并列关联词。

因果关系直接以类似determine, cause, correlate的动词表示，没有关联词。通常所说的thus, then, hence, therefore, as a result, as a consequence, 并不表示这里定义的变量之间的因果关系，而是常见于段落末句，引出结论(cs)，其功能类似于 In general, In sum。

对比关联词，如on the contrary, however, 前后是同等层次的对比内容。

一些特殊的对比关联词，可以称为转折关联词，不仅表示两个观点之间的对比关系，而且确定后者否定前者，有态度的不同。如nevertheless, nonetheless, 纯粹表示对比或转折。但however, but, yet, 用法则比较多样。

However, but, yet 的作用
0. 表示对比，可用on the contrary等替换；
1. 在别人观点之后，表示否定，如however + fail to；
2. 转换主题：前1-3句背景+Yet新主题；转换态度：并列内容, but另一并列内容；
3. 其他。递进: a b c / Many factors, but X; 让步转折: true, but; 否定肯定: not ... but ...

<小结>

综上所述，在看一个论点及其展开的论据(如有)的时候，重点是把握2-3个词。如果一个论点或一个单观点段落有100-120字，我们不必认识所有单词，翻译每个单词，甚至记住每个单词，而是要提炼2-3个词。提炼什么词呢？提炼的标准是什么？不是我们觉得生僻或敏感的词，而是从段落结构角度来看比较重要的词。按照上文的分析，我们总结出段落论据展开结构的常考信息的20字口诀：

对比找反义；因果找双方；机制找末句；并列找并列

当首句、中间证据出现类似differ, contrast, more than, on the contrary, on the other hand的词汇时，对比找反义。当首句、中间证据出现类似cause, responsible for, correlate with以及连续动作的词汇时，因果找双方，机制找末句，这时机制是广义的因果关系。当中间出现举例或2-3个内容并列时，可注意位置，如果有3-4个内容连续并列，更要注意位置，因为常考列举题。技巧性比较强的还是对比和因果关系，而且它们通常也集中于特定的文章题材。按我们的经验，我们有：文科讲对比，理科讲因果。

当然，任何时候，首句、有结论的末句、转折句都是重点。

2.8　Examples 段落结构练习

鉴于GRE文章是学术文章的浓缩版，我们直接从学术文章中举一些例子。这些例子通过在学术文章中搜索关键词得到，其中一些是：on the contrary, on the other hand, however, differ, in addition, another, moreover, for example, for instance, cause, correlate, vary with, coincide。这些例子有的偏难，有的做了微调。

提示： 读者可以自己先读一遍（1–2分钟）；之后看右边解释，看完后再读一遍文章，重点关注我们加的黑体和斜体字，看看能否从中提取段落核心（5–8分钟）。段落核心词、以及证据重现论点核心的词（core）以黑体表示，结构和逻辑的提示词（cues）以斜体表示，少数提示词可兼任核心词，以**斜黑体**表示。文章右边是简要解释，其中符号的意思，如不清楚，请复习本书开头的"缩略语"表。在看文章时，要借助提示词，尽量记住核心词，并将它在证据中的对应词读如同义词，即论据重现论点核心，常有逻辑等价词，在右边解释中以等号=表示。这样的阅读就能聚焦核心，而不是随机提取、发散联想、魂游万里。

● 2.8.1 并列 kw: A. a1. a2.

2.8.1.1 举例 kw. e.

► 例 1 ◄

Voluntary actions don't just spring up from nowhere, then, but are **learned**, sometimes with great effort. *Indeed*, the notion that voluntary actions are **modifiable** through **experiencing** their consequences is a key facet of the definition of action rather than mere movement. *In studies of action in animals, for instance*, this is the main way in which voluntariness is identified. *A nonhuman primate* reaching for a banana might **learn** to reach differently depending on whether the banana is attained or not, and this **malleability** is the hallmark of apparent willfulness of action in all those creatures who can't otherwise report on their sense of will. *In human beings and other animals*, actions that are **not sensitive to rewards and punishments** may be thought of as **involuntary** and normally are not believed to be subject to willful control.

（Daniel Wegner, *The Illusion of Conscious Will*, p.33）

1st: kw = learned，一个事物的性质

2nd: a, evidence; 也可看做观点重述
（indeed: 顺承提示词）; modifiable, experiencing = learned

3rd: e, example

4th: e', specific case, 例子的深化
learn, malleability = learned（逻辑等价）

5th: b, 双重否定: 对经验和后果不敏感，则非有意志行为。
（rewards, punishment = learned）
（~x : ~y = x : y）

全段: kw. a. e. e'. b.
（注: 1st表示文中第一句话，2nd表示文中第二句话，其余类推。下同。）

► 例 2 ◄

Our **autoappraisers** are **powerful**, **scanning** continuously, out of our conscious awareness, watching out for the themes and variations of the events that have been relevant to our survival. To use a computer metaphor, the **automatic appraising** mechanisms are **searching** our environment for anything that resembles what is stored in our emotion alert database, which is

1st: kw: 一个事物 + 形容词 = 判断句
可举例或给出并列证据

2nd: e, 比喻，类比是广义的举例
automatic appraising = autoappraise
scanning = searching

written in part by our biology, through natural selection, and in part by our individual experience.

（from Paul Ekman, *Emotions Revealed*）

全段：kw. e.

2.8.1.2 普通并列 kw. a. b.

► 例 3 ◄

There were *many ways* by which the [medieval] city **raised the small sums** needed to discharge its many petty debts. The town, like the parish, sometimes **possessed property**, which it let at a **rental**. There was an **income** from market **tolls** and from the **rent** of stalls in the marketplace. Then, *too*, the **administration** of justice was made into a source of **income** for the town. Few offenses could not be redeemed by the payment of **a fine**. *And if in a particular year* obligations looked as if they would exceed income, it was always possible to levy a **tax** on every "head" or every home. Among the obligation of the urban community was, in England at least, a **payment of taxes** to the crown. **A lump sum** was usually imposed and was paid by the city and recouped from the community's varied tax income.

（Norman Pounds, *The Medieval City*, p.117）

1st: kw = ways, raise sums

2nd: a, evidence; 自有地产的租金 property, rental = sums（逻辑等价）

3rd: b, evidence; income, toll = sums

4th: c, evidence; income = sums

5th: c', 续写上句证据, fine = sums

6th: d, evidence; And提示并列, tax=sums

7th: d1, 续写上句证据 tax = tax

8th: d2, 续写证据 lump sum = tax

全段：kw. a. b. c. c'. d. d1. d2.

该段结构较直接，似TOEFL文章或英文教科书文章，难度低于GRE。

► 例 4 ◄

As human wills clash in the everyday struggle for survival and realization as they see it, people attempt to persuade（or force）others to **accept their view** of who should have opportunities and who is exposed to those opportunities. *Some* will reason from **religion**, others from **natural law**, **economic efficiency**, process, etc. *The* law and economics *movement* has attempted to find a guide to court decisions that rests on economic theory. *One proposed test is that* the cheapest avoider of a cost should bear it. *But as one* of the reformed originators of the law and economics movement *suggests*, "who is the cheapest avoider of a cost, depends on the **valuations** put on acts, activities, and **beliefs** by the whole of our law and not on some objective or scientific notion". He insists that efficiency must ask the prior moral question of **whose interests** should count.

（A. Allan Schmid, *Conflict and Cooperation*, p.87）

1st: kw: accept their view/wills 观念与意志，后文具体说明

2nd: a, b, c, 句内并列证据

3rd: e, 特定例子，基于经济理论 economic = a view

4th: e1, 检验例子的方法

5th: e2, 对该做法的反驳 valuations, beliefs = views 论据重现论点核心

6th: e2', 继续反驳 interest, moral = views 间接证明各人观念或利益的冲突

全段：kw. a,b,c. e. e1. vs. e2. e2'.

► **例 5** ◄

In a situation like this, where the distribution of available alternatives is unknown, there is no way to return to previous options, and it is hard to switch to another option once a committed choice has been made, a good *approach* is to search with an '**aspiration level**': a minimum threshold of apparent mate value for saying 'yes' to the current potential mate. Aspiration-level search *is a simple* heuristic *method* that Herbert Simon （1990） called *satisficing*. In particular, satisficing search *can be divided into* **two phases**: *In the first phase*, potential mates are just looked at **without a selection** being made, so that the searcher can **gather information** about the available range of mate values. *For example*, this would include young adolescents being keenly interested in **observing and evaluating individuals** of the opposite sex, but being 'too shy' to actually court them—because they're **still learning** who's worth courting. This information is used to **set an aspiration level**—the minimum mate value that the searcher will try to get in further search. *The second phase then* consists of looking at additional potential mates, until one is found who **exceeds the aspiration level** set in phase 1. **Search is stopped** at that point and that individual is pursued: one gets a 'crush' on him or her and invests substantial mating effort in attracting his or her romantic attention. Once the aspiration level is set, the length of the second search phase is out of the searcher's control—it depends on the more or less random sequence of mates encountered from the mating market.

（Penke et al., in *Mating Intelligence*, p.44）

1ˢᵗ: kw: search with an aspiration level

2ⁿᵈ: kw': satisficing, 进一步定义

3ʳᵈ: kw'': kw1, two phase 为提示词 兼核心词, kw1 = gather info; 展开第一阶段

4ᵗʰ: a, 举例, observe, evaluate, still learning = gather info

5ᵗʰ: b, 继续说明

6ᵗʰ: kw2: x, 第二阶段

7ᵗʰ: y, 步骤的继续说明

8ᵗʰ: z, 细节

全段: kw. kw'. kw1. a. b. kw2: x. y. z. 两阶段为并列关系, 为方便用kw1, kw2表示, 因为它们是分别展开的。

2.8.1.3 态度及其证据 aw. x. y.

► **例 6** ◄

Apostatic **selection** is an elegant theory, *but until recently*, empirical support has been only ***fragmentary and indirect***, primarily because experimental evolutionary ecology is an ***exceedingly difficult undertaking***. When predators and prey are brought into the laboratory, the **simplified environment interferes** with normal population cycles. *And* when evolutionary effects are sought in the field, **limited experimental control reduces one's ability** to make causal inferences. *Although there*

1ˢᵗ: kw/aw-: 态度句=判断句=kw
A. selection, fragmentary support
专业名词取首字母Apostatic = A.

2ⁿᵈ: a, 第一个理由, 简化环境

3ʳᵈ: b, 第二个理由, 实验控制有限, 降低能力

4ᵗʰ: ~b, b', 让步转折, 给出证据, 有例

are many documented instances of apparently stable polymorphisms *and a fair amount of field experimentation* indicating that predators tend to feed preferentially on more common morphs, it has proven **impossible to isolate the role of predation** in the production and maintenance of prey polymorphism. *What has been* **needed** *is a method* for studying the detection of cryptic prey that allows the isolation of the many variables that can affect the decisions of a predator, including recent experience, and then allows predation to feed back onto the prey population.

（Alan C. Kamil and Alan B. Bond, in *Cognitive Animal*, p.144）

子和实验，但很难隔离捕食因素

5th: c, needed暗示目前还没有

全段：aw-. a. b. ~b, b'. c.
负评价及其并列证据，很常用。

● 2.8.2 因果 kw: A → B

2.8.2.1 平行因果 kw: A → B. a1 → b1. a2 → b2.

（公式里的A, B, a1, a2, b1, b2只是指原因和结果所在的主语和宾语，不同于表示中间证据句子的a, b, c。）

▶ 例 7 ◀

Archeology demonstrates the radical nature and consequences of the last event［**cultural** explosion］, but it says nothing about ***what prompted it***, and it is here that we face a conundrum. Arguably, the *most plausible* **cause** was a **genetic mutation** that *promoted* the fully **modern brain**. *This* mutation could *have originated in* a small east African population, and the evolutionary advantage it conferred would have *enabled* the population to **grow and expand**. This is because it *permitted* its possessors *to extract* far more energy from nature and to **invest it in society**. *It also allowed* human populations to **colonize new and challenging environments**. *Possibly the most critical aspect* of the neural change *was that it allowed* the kind of rapidly **spoken phonemic language** that is inseparable from culture as we know it today. This ability *not only facilitates communication, but at least equally important, it allows people to* ***conceive and model*** complex natural and social circumstances entirely within their minds.

（Richard G. Klein & Blake Edgar, *The Dawn of Human Culture*, p.24）

1st: tw: 提出本段问题，追问文化发展原因

2nd: kw=genetic mutation → culture cause = prompt, 因果论点出现

3rd: a, evidence, 中间地点是证据，讲一个好处: grow & expand

4th: b1, evidence, society=culture

5th: b2, also暗示并列, colonize new environments = culture

6th: c, 最高级讲最重要好处language = culture

7th: c1, c2, 句内并列communication, model natural and social circumstances = culture

全段：tw. kw. a. b1. b2. c. c1,2.
（如kw=g → c, 则a=g1 → c1. b,c类推）
平行因果，可作并列或因果例子

▶ **例 8** ◀

There is considerable evidence that much of the **circuitry** used **in carrying out an action** *is* also ***involved*** when people **simulate** their own **actions** or those of others. *Some of this evidence comes from* reaction time experiments, like those described in chapter 7. *For example*, if subjects are asked to imagine walking to targets at various distances, the elapsed times to the **imagined** goal are **similar to** those for **actually** walking. *Another experiment* exploited the fact that the right hand is controlled by the left side of the brain. Subjects were asked whether they would use an overhand or underhand grip to grasp a cylindrical object, presented briefly to either the left or right visual field. Although no motion was involved, the choice of a right-handed **posture was much faster when** the left side of the brain **saw** the picture. *There are also various clinical reports* that patients with specific **motor deficits** show similar **problems in imagination** tasks.

(Jerome A. Feldman, *From Molecules to Metaphor*, p.215)

1st: kw: circuitry in action → simulate involve暗示相关，模仿行为用到执行回路，kw: action–s(imulate)

2nd: a, evidence

3rd: a', example, imagined = simulate, actually = action(逻辑等价)

4th: b, 另一个实验证据

5th: b1, 实验内容

6th: b2, 续, 看图想象, 引动作姿势 posture = action, saw = simulate

7th: c, 从相关性的另一面讲证据, 运动能力不足, 想象任务有困难 ($x\downarrow : y\downarrow <=> x\uparrow y\uparrow$)

全段: kw. a. a'. b. b1. b2. c.
2nd=action$\uparrow$: s$\uparrow$, 7th=action$\downarrow$: s$\downarrow$

▶ **例 9** ◀

Though these rather basic reward and punishment mechanisms have the potential to strongly guide behavior even in complex social decision-making tasks, these prediction error **signals** can be greatly ***modulated by* top-down processes**, such as **declarative information** previously learned about a partner. *For example*, in another recent TG study（Delgado *et al.*, 2005）, players were provided with brief **personality sketches** of their partners prior to game play. Some partners were described in **morally positive** terms（for example, by noting how they had recently rescued a person from a fire）and some partners were described in **morally negative** terms（by describing an unsavory act they had committed）. Results demonstrated reduced caudate activity ***in response to*** actions of the morally **positive or negative** partners, though responses to morally **neutral** players **remained unchanged**. *This suggests that* **prior social knowledge** about a partner can ***reduce the amount*** of trial-by-trial learning, demonstrating both **top-down** and bottom-up ***influences on*** the neural basis of **social cooperation**.

(Sanfey and Dorris 2009, in Glimcher *et al.*, ed., *Neuroeconomics*, p.77)

1st: kw: be modulated by, 因果 原因: top-down, 结果: behavior

2nd: e, 举例证明personal sketch = info = top-down

3rd: a1, a2, 句内并列morally ... terms = personal sketch

4th: b1, b2, 相关性, 正负描述对应合作反应增减; 中性则无变化（moral → action. b1= m+ → a+. m- → a-; b2= $m^0 → a^0$（0表示中立和不变）

5th: cs, this引导末句总结, 先证据后总结, top-down → cooperation; social knowledge = moral = top-down

全段: kw. e. a1,2. b1,2. cs.
b1,2句/4th句为相关性论证核心。

2.8.2.2 机制：kw: A → B. a → x → y → z → b.

► **例 10** ◄

Dolphin **echolocation** is one of the most sophisticated cognitive **processes** that have been studied. *When a dolphin uses* its biological sonar to recognize objects, its brain *performs* the equivalent of some extraordinarily complex computations. *These* computations *transform* one-dimensional sound waves *arriving at* each of the dolphin's two ears into representations of objects and their features in the dolphin's environment. *The process* by which this transformation occurs is the focus of our interest. （Herbert L. Roitblat, in *Cognitive Animal*, pp.183-4）	1st: kw: process提示讲连续动作 2nd: x, 过程开始 3rd: y, 过程的延续 4th: cs', 类似结论，强调主题（看各句斜体可知连续动作） 全段：kw. x. → y. cs'.

（说明：学术文章除了连续动作以外，还会出现连续推理，GRE考试目前还没有出现这种情况。）

► **例 11** ◄

Such examples provide overwhelming *empirical support for the existence of* the **event structure metaphor**. And the *existence of that metaphor shows that* some common **abstract concepts**—TIME, STATE, CHANGE, CAUSATION, ACTION, PURPOSE, and MEANS—are conceptualized **via metaphor**. Since such concepts are at the very center of our conceptual systems, *the fact that they are conceptualized metaphorically shows that* **metaphorical** mappings are **linked to our core ideas**. Metaphors are often organized in **hierarchical structures**, in which more specific mappings in the hierarchy inherit the structures of the more general mappings. （Jerome A. Feldman, *From Molecules to Metaphor*, p.208）	1st: kw': a, 存在事件结构隐喻 2nd: b, 抽象概念也要用隐喻表达 3rd: c, 抽象概念与核心观念相连 4th: d, 隐喻的分层结构 全段：kw': a. → b. → c. → d.

● 2.8.3 对比 kw: A ≠ B

2.8.3.1 kw: A≠B. a1. a2. vs. b1. b2. or a1≠b1. a2 ≠ b2.

► **例 12** ◄

Although both **bats** and **dolphins** use echolocation, the characteristics of the medium in which their signals are emitted, the mechanisms by which the signals are produced, the type of signals, and the neurological apparatus they use to processes those signals **differ** substantially. Bat biosonar is adapted for use in **air**, *whereas* dolphin biosonar is adapted for use **underwater**. Bat biosonar signals are relatively **long** in duration	1st: kw: differ, 让步讲相同/both, kw: bat ≠ dolphin or b ≠ d 2nd: x, evidence: b1≠ d1, air≠ underwater 对比找反义 3rd: y1, evidence

（up to several milliseconds）, and contain both **narrow-band** constant-frequency and frequency-modulated components depending on the species. *By contrast*, the dolphin echolocation signal is very **broadband** and, as indicated, extremely **short**. Echoes typically range in duration from 50 to 200 ms.

（Herbert L. Roitblat, in *Cognitive Animal*, p.183）

4th: vs. y2, evidence 反义在宾语narrow $\neq$ broad; long $\neq$ short

y1$\neq$y2: b2$\neq$d2.

全段: kw. x$^{\neq}$. y1. $\neq$ y2.

or: kw: b$\neq$d. b1$\neq$d1. b2. vs d2.

▶ 例 13 ◀

A large number of studies have reported cognitive and behavioral ***differences* between men and women**, on average. *The general picture is that* as a group men are typically *stronger* at **non-verbal spatial** tasks and that as a group women are *stronger* at **verbal and social** tasks. Kimura（1999）summarizes *some of the major findings from the sex differences literature concerning* **motor** skills, **spatial and mathematical** ability and **verbal** skills. *In general, findings indicate that* on average men are *superior* at **targeting** and women at **fine motor skills**. Men tend to navigate using **spatial cues**; women rely more on **landmarks** and have a superior memory for object location. *The most reliable sex difference on* spatial *tasks is found in studies* of mental rotation（Linn and Petersen 1985）. *In* **math**ematics, men tend to be *stronger* at **problem solving and reasoning**, women stronger at **computation**（Geary 1996）. *With regard to* **verbal** *abilities*, women tend to have better **verbal memory**, spelling ability, and verbal fluency, *although* their vocabularies are not larger than those of men. Developmentally, *however*, a number of studies have reported **greater vocabularies** and **faster** rates of language acquisition in girls. *Sex differences in* **emotion** perception *have been revealed* on tasks where children are required to attribute subtle mental states to a person—for example, when interpreting the eye region of the face.

（Simon Baron-Cohen et al., *Prenatal Testosterone in Mind*, pp. 13–14）

1st: tw: difference m$\neq$ w 本段主题；展开方式常为mi$\neq$wi, mj$\neq$wj.

2nd: kw: m$\neq$w, general暗示论点m: non-v., spatial vs. w: v, social

3rd: kw': m$\neq$w, summarize, 总述

4th: a, targeting vs. fine skills

5th: b, spatial vs. landmarks

6th: b', evidence

7th: c, m$\neq$w, reason vs. compute

8th: d, less vs. better verbal; 让步~d

9th: d', 让步之后转折 w: greater

10th: e, m $\neq$w. mental attribution

全段: tw. kw. kw'. a.b.(b').c.d.(d').e.

1–3句总，4–10句分（并列对比）

2.8.3.2 比较 kw: A=B. a1. a2. = b1. b2.

▶ 例 14 ◀

One ***common feature*** of the two cases, one in England and one in Texas, is that *in each* the court was clearly conscious of the **wider implications** of its verdict. The **English** judges discussed the **potential loss of life** from bursting reservoirs, despite the fact that the actual accident being litigated killed

1st: kw. common, each暗示相同

England = Texas, E = T.

E1.E2. = T1.T2.

2nd: a1, E1, potential loss = wider implication

nobody. Presumably they *had in mind* catastrophes *earlier in the century* in which bursting dams had killed hundreds—in one American case thousands—of people and wanted to establish legal rules that would make such accidents less likely in the future. The **Texas** court based its result in part on the importance of reservoirs **for agriculture**, although the particular reservoir whose failure was being litigated contained, not water for irrigation, but salt water produced as a by-product of pumping oil. *Both* sets of judges were looking at the case from what I earlier described as a **forward-looking** perspective. They were determining *not merely* how to deal with a **particular** accident that had already happened *but* how **future** accidents would be dealt with, and thus affecting the incentives of the people whose future actions would determine how likely future accidents were to occur.

(David Friedman, *Law's Order*, pp. 200–201)

3rd: a2, E2, earlier = wider (=: 在此仅表示逻辑等价)

4th: b, T, agriculture = wider

5th: c, 说明相同, Ei = Ti. Forward-looking = wider

6th: d, 续写相同, Eii = Tii. particular vs. future = wider

全段: kw. a1. a2. b. c⁼. d⁼.

or: kw: E = T. E1.E2. T. Ei = Ti.

Eii = Tii.

◉ 2.8.4 让步转折 kw. a. b. ~kw. But kw.

▶ 例 15 ◀

Some might object that a **neurological** explanation *for* the explosion of **culture** after 50,000 years ago is **simplistic** biological determinism, a just-so story or a *deus ex* machina explanation for a paleontological paradox. The idea *admittedly fails* one important measure of a proper scientific hypothesis: it **cannot be tested or falsified** by experiment or by examination of relevant human fossils. Human brains had reached fully modern size many hundreds of thousands of years earlier, and skulls **reveal little** about the functioning of the brain underneath. There is **nothing** in the skulls of people from shortly before and after 50,000 years ago *to show that* a significant **neurological change** had occurred. The **neurological** *hypothesis* does, *however*, measure up to one important scientific standard: it is the simplest, most **parsimonious explanation** for the available archeological evidence. And that evidence, as incomplete and imperfect as it is, is what **we must rely** upon to reconstruct our evolutionary past.

(Richard G. Klein & Blake Edgar, *The Dawn of Human Culture*, pp. 24–25)

1st: aw-: x, or, ~kw, some might object, 预期反对, simplistic 表负评价

2nd: y, 续写反对意见, not testable

3rd: y1, 负面证据, 化石记录弱

4th: y2, 续写负面, 记录无法证明

5th: aw+: m, or, kw, 回到正面好处 Parsimonious = frugal

6th: n, 续写其作用

全段: aw-: x. y. y1. y2. aw+: m. n.

or: ~kw. x. y. y1. y2. kw: m. n.

● 2.8.5 多观点段落 kw1. a. b. kw2. x. y.

多个观点组合构成一个段落，既可对比，也可并列。通常对比关系比较重要，以下给出的是对比观点的例证。

► 例 16 ◄

It is generally assumed that an important method of socialization in all societies is **imitation of the parents** by the child. Verbal instruction is less likely to be important, because in many preindustrial societies children are given little or no explicit instruction—they are expected to learn the necessary skills and behaviors **by observation**. Young children *do* imitate their parents in all societies, *but* they *imitate many other people* as well: older siblings, nonfamily adults and children, and characters they see on television. *Rowe* (*1994*) *has pointed out that* it would *not* make evolutionary sense for children to *learn only from* their parents; it would mean, for example, that children might fail to pick up useful innovations unless the innovator happened to be their parent. Rowe *postulated* an innate adaptive mechanism that directs the child to **learn from any source**, not just parents—a learning mechanism that is "general with respect to informational source".

（J. Harris 1995, "Where Is the Child's Environment?"）

1st: KWo, 大众假设 = 老观点imitate parents

2nd: a, evidence, verbal < observation = imitation（逻辑等价）

3rd: KWo' = ~KWn, KWn. 让步转折 imitate parents vs. other people

4th: x, evidence, 中间人名及研究, 给出理由, not only from parents

5th: y = KWn, learn from any source

全段: KWo. a. ~KWn, KWn. x. y.

2个观点: 老观点 + 新观点

► 例 17 ◄

Expected utility *theory* inspired by Bernoulli *assumed that* people think in terms of levels of **wealth**. *But*, past **outcomes and reference** points matter. The **prospect** *theory* of Kahneman and Tversky （1979） noted in section 3.3.7 above *is based on observation that* "the carriers of decision utility are gains and losses **relative to a reference** level, which is often **the status quo**" （Kahneman 1999: 17）. *And* losses from that **status quo** are weighted more than equivalent sized gains. The status quo can shift over time and create a hedonic treadmill as noted above. Kahneman argues that the proper measure of well-being *should be* the objective reporting of good or bad at the **moment** something is **experienced** and **not** at the **point of decision** （decision utility looking forward） **or recalling** of the past. People can be made happier even if on a satisfaction treadmill.

（Allan Schmid, *Conflict and Cooperation*, p.56）

1st: kw1: expected utility

2nd: kw2: reference

3rd: kw2': x, prospect = reference = status quo（逻辑等价）理论及其观察证据

4th: y, evidence

5th: z, evidence

6th: cs, well-being: experienced vs. decision

7th: cs', happy = well-being

全段: kw1.vs kw2. kw2': x. y. z. cs. cs'.

两个对立观点

▶ **例 18** ◀

Nonetheless, it seemed likely that the [spot] **patterns** were again the result of a **competition** between a handful of basic processes: cell multiplication by division, cell migration (diffusion) in search of food, and cell clustering by chemotaxis once the local density of cells (and thus the local rate of chemoattractant formation) exceeds a certain threshold. *Eshel Ben-Jacob and colleagues from Tel Aviv University in Israel attempted to reproduce* the **spot patterns** in a **cellular automaton** *model* that captures these basic features of the bacteria's behaviour. *In essence, the model postulates* groups of bacterial cells that move *en masse*, consuming food, reproducing and emitting a chemoattractant if food becomes scarce. The model generates an expanding **ring of cells**, which cluster into **spots** behind the advancing front *when they* **attract** one another through chemotactic signalling. The spot patterns become aligned along **radial lines**, as in the experiments, if a *further component is added to the model*: a **repulsive** interaction between the bacterial clusters, resulting from their emission of a chemical signal that warns other clusters to stay away. Radial spots *then emerge from* a delicate balance between **attractive and repulsive interactions**. Whether real E. coli bacteria exude a **chemorepellent** of this sort is, *however,* **an open question**. At the same time, *Herbert Levine and Lev Tsimring at the University of California at San Diego proposed an* **alternative** *model* that included the same kinds of interactions but described the bacteria's motions using **reaction-diffusion** equations akin to those first studied by Ronald Fisher in the 1930s, *instead of* invoking discrete **cellular automata**. This model also generates **rings** that break up into clusters behind the advancing front of the colony.	1ˢᵗ: tw, spot patterns 来自竞争句内连续并列次要, 位置 > 内容
	2ⁿᵈ: kw1; automaton → pattern 人物及其模型, 提示kw
	3ʳᵈ: a, evidence, 模型的假设
	4ᵗʰ: b, evidence, 模型的结果attract: ring
	5ᵗʰ: c, evidence, 另一结果repulsive: radial
	6ᵗʰ: cs1, 相当于模型结论 interaction → spots
	7ᵗʰ: aw-, 质疑, repellent不清楚
	8ᵗʰ: kw2: 人物及其模型替代理论出现 diffusion vs. automata
	9ᵗʰ: x, 模型的结果 → rings

(Philip Ball, *The Self-Made Tapestry*, pp. 73–74)　　全段: tw. kw1. a. b. c. cs1. aw-. kw2.x.

2.9　**Paragraph–Passage–Paper–Monograph 段落–文章–论文–著作**

我们已经讨论了段落（Paragraph）的论点论证方式、文章的2-3个论点之间的组合方式，分析了主题与论点、论点与论据的两个层次的**总分**关系。就如后文关于句子尤其是长句分析的部分所会论述的，总分的观念还可以**向下**延伸到句子内部。那总分的思路能否**向上**拓展到论文以至学术专著的层面呢？完全可以！

GRE的短文（Short Passage）大约110–160字，有时只有一个论点加上几个证据，有时会写2–3个论点，各自有一点证据。GRE的长文（Long Passage）也只有2–3个论点，只不过各自的证据相对充分，于是文章变长，但毕竟它是限时测试的阅读文章，不会写出5–6个或更多论点，那样会超出考生现场把握的认知极限；所有人都不能短时间内看清楚的文章，大家都会做错题，这样就不能检验考生的相对水平，因此，即便是GRE长文章的复杂程度也是有限制的。它们通常都是由2–3个论点构成，以2个论点为例，则全文结构可以表达为：

TW. i. j. KW1. a. b. c. KW2. x. y. z.

一篇学术论文（Paper），可以写5000–8000字或更多，长度是GRE 450字长文章的10–20倍。怎么可以写这么长？因为有好多论点要说，有些内容是别人的观点、模型、假说，给证据说明，同时还给态度评价，一般是负评价，而评价也要给证据说明；多数内容则是自己的观点、实验和分析，总的观点之下有很多小的观点，每个都有证据支持，实验的流程和结果都要一一说明和报告，相当于好多个论点，最后的分析和讨论也会分成好几点，每个点分别用论据来支撑。做一个非常粗略的计算，一篇论文的总论点数是：别人的3–5个论点+3–5个负评价 + 自己的8–10个小论点 + 报告结果的8个小论点 + 分析和讨论的5–7个小论点= 35个小论点。每个小论点写成1段，150字左右，则论文如果有35段，总的字数大约就是35*150 = 5250字。

这种估计当然不精确，也不是基于数据统计，但它依然有意义，因为它给我们以启发：学术论文无非是**多层论点的组合**。写学术论文，就是想清楚说什么主题（Introduction, Topic），有几个大的方面（Section: Literature Review, Method, Result, Analysis），每个方面又分几个部分或几大论点（Part = several paragraphs: 别人的观点及评价、自己的观点），这些部分通常不会明确说出，但可以识别几大块内容；每个大部分又分几个小论点或段落来说明（Paragraph = kw, 别人观点的内容、评价、自己假说的内容的第一点、第二点、结果等），每个小论点都要有3–4个或更多论据（a b c; x y z; u v w）来支撑。读学术论文，不只是认单词，甚至重点都不在认单词、看语法、读句子，而是看有多少论点，论点如何得到论据支持；如果是专业读者，还要考虑论据是否真实，论据对论点的论证关系是否满足逻辑推理和科学实证的标准。说一个人掌握了一些学术知识，无非是说这个人有一些论点，而且这些论点都能得到真实数据的有效支持。

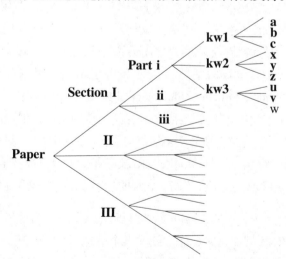

论文是主题–节–部分–段落–句子的四层总分结构或层级系统。仔细观察论文结构图，虽然我们并不知道如何写出论文的具体内容，但却知道怎样构造论文的总体架构，有了这种思维方式，就能管理自己看到的各种论据、事实、数据，将它们通过论点组织起来，然后再把各个论点通过论点之间的关系组织起来，构成一个整体的文章框架。各节之间是并列关系，因为都是作者想说的内容，虽然节的内部的一些段落的论点也许与另外一些段落的论点是对立关系。

以上已经说明如何从段落到文章，再从文章到论文，那么从论文到著作（Monograph, Book）又如何呢？有的著作就是8-10篇主题相关的论文汇集而成；有的论文集更是多个作者各写一篇论文，编成一本书；正常的著作的每一章（Chapter）相当于一篇论文，也分节，节下会有通常不会明说的几个部分，每个部分有几段，每段通常都有论点和论据。这样，书的结构无非是在论文的结构之上再加上一层总分。各章之间是并列的结构，都属于文章的平行的组成部分。有的书还会把各章组合成为若干部分（PartI, Part II, PartIII）或者各卷（Book I, Book II, Book III），它们之间都是并列关系。

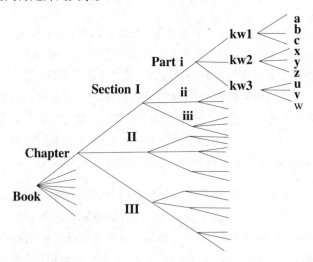

所以，一本学术著作，从结构的角度，从上往下，就是多层分解的结构：Book（Chapter［Section {Part[kw(abc)]}］）；从下往上看，著作则是论据、论点、部分、节、章层层组合的结果。多层分解其实也是多层还原，而且分解或还原的每个层次的规则基本相同，都是并列关系，到了句子、段落和小节这一层，也许会有对比关系。

一个事物，可以多层分解，每层的分解方式相似，每层的规律也都相似，这就类似于分形几何学讲的分形结构（fractals）。事实上，一个复杂事物，往往是由分层嵌套、层层独立的结构组成，比如海岸线的形状、树叶的结构、树的形状、细胞的分布、中国古代的郡县制度、西欧的封建制度、现代社会的官僚科层制、公司、电脑资源管理器的目录结构、电脑的结构、人类大脑皮层的层层叠加的结构，等等。Ray Jackendoff在他的伟大著作*Foundations of Language*（《语言的基础》）中，以分层结构的思维分析语言，将语言分为Spatial Structure, Semantic Structure, Syntatic Structure, Phonological Structure四个层次，每个层次再分几个小层，每个小层再分几个更小层，这给了本书作者巨大启发；我们这里谈的是语言推理的结构，也遵循类似的规则。请读者试想一下本章的整体结构。一篇复杂的文字如何构成？分层再分层，总分再总分而已。这种思维方式非人天生，要通过后天练习才能学会、掌握和应用。GRE文章是学习语言推理结构的第一步！由此我们可以上溯到论文和学术专著，为学习和吸收迷人、美好、壮观的学术知识，打开思维的大门。

不仅如此，以上关于段落、文章、论文、著作的结构分析，也可以用于自己的学术文字的写作。一个大的主题，如何论述清楚？分成几个方面讲吧！这些方面，再分成几个小的方面展开吧！这是总分套总分。一个论点，如何论述清楚？按照我们的结构分析方法可知，论点有因果关系的，以平行因果或序列因果的方式展开，甚至以层层推理的方式说明；论点有两个事物对比关系的，以对比的证据展开；不属于这两类的，统统以并列展开。任何时候都可以加入让步转折，考虑相反意见或者对自己观点不太有利的事实，批判地面对自己的观点。在学术和分析文字中，例子则只是点缀；分析类的作品，通常是不能单用例子来说理的，那样太单薄，没有推理的过程。要特别小心那些管中窥豹、一叶知秋、以小见大式的所谓文章，它们违背基本的统计原则，以小样本和个案来代替规律和平均值。除非例子经过精心组织、逐层推广以涵盖一般事实，否则不要只凭举例来说理。

第三节　Sentence 句子

本节分为两个部分，第一部分讨论长句的结构分析和信息提取，第二部分归纳GRE常考的作为中间证据的句子的语言特点。

句子是各种成分在一定关系下组合起来表达意义的整体，这些成分主要包括主语/S、谓语/V、宾语或表语/O；再做细分，则包括NP(noun phrase，名词短语)，VP(verb phrase，谓语结构，包括谓语动词V及其宾语NP，通常我们只分析谓语动词V)，CP(clause phrase，从句)，AP(adjective phrase，形容词短语)，PP(preposition phrase，介词短语)等等。句子是短语或成分之间的函数关系(f = function)，于是，一个句子可记为：

$$Sentence = SVO = f(NP, VP, CP, AP, PP)$$

对于分析句子结构来说，AP与PP相对次要，最重要的还是NP, VP, CP，下面会重点以它们为基础构造长句。

3.1　A General Structure of Long Sentence 长句分析

SVO=f(NP, VP, CP, AP, PP)
S=NP1-3 V O=NP1-3
S=NP1-3 that/v-ing/, np that, V O=S
S=NP1-3 CP1-Cp2 V O=CP1-Cp2-cp3
While/Although/If/Because SVO, SVO

GRE文章的长句通常被认为是难点。这是对的。但有人因此认为，只要读懂了长句，文章就能读懂，这却有点夸大了，因为长句的任意组合并不等于文章。句子之间的关系、论点之间的关系，在更大程度上决定了文章的结构和核心。事实上，有些作为证据的句子，无论长或短，在有些情况下读不太懂，也并不影响做题和对文章的理解。当然，也不能走向另一个极端，认为不读任何长句也可以把文章弄懂。长句毫无疑问是文章分析的一个重要层次，但其重要性是有限的。长难句分析的开创性工作属于杨鹏的《GRE&GMAT阅读难句教程》，该书从语法角度分析长难句，帮助考生克服长句阅读的语言障碍。本节将从不同的结构角度处理长句，帮助考生理解长句的意义。

长句如何构成？我们可以用**假说演绎法**来推导句子的结构。从上往下看，一个句子，要么有一个主谓宾(SVO)，这时，它的主语或宾语(S/O)可以有一层从句修饰(CP)或多层从句修饰(CP1-Cp2)；要么有多个主谓宾(以两个主谓宾的情况作为代表：SVO, SVO)，这时，各个主谓宾之间的关系要么是并列(SVO + SVO)，其中有正常并列的，如有when, if, because这些提示词表示并列，偶尔也有总分关系，如由冒号：表示(SVO: SVO)，可算作广义并列；要么是对立(SVO vs. SVO)，其中有纯对比，如有whereas, however这些提示词表示对比，也有让步转折的，如有although, though这些词表示让步。以上演绎结果可以总结如下：

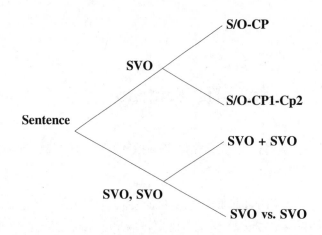

换个角度，我们可以从只有一个主谓宾的简单句开始，从下往上，逐步建构长句。长句在阅读时如何处理、如何提取信息？多数时候，长句的核心都在其主干中，而不在修饰成分，包括分词、同位语、修饰性的从句等。我们提出长句提炼的8字原则：**主干 > 修饰；主句 > 从句**。

主干与修饰之间有总分结构吗？对任意一个主谓宾的主语或宾语，都可以展开说明，主语或宾语的NP好比是总的小论点，而修饰它的从句、分词、同位语，尤其是并列的修饰成分，好比是分的小论据，这样，就有NP–CP结构；对CP结构应用同样的规则，其主语或宾语的Np好比中心，可以展开说明，也就是修饰它的更下一层的从句、分词、同位语，尤其是并列的修饰成分，这就是第二层从句，于是就有NP-CP1-Cp2。对任何一层修饰（CP），作为小论据，都会重现所修饰名词（NP）的核心词汇。这就是说，针对NP that Np' v Np''，通常会有v Np''= NP（逻辑等价）。这样我们就把总分结构的思维应用于句子的分析了，可以在修饰成分的词汇和主干词汇相互推导，如其中一部分为生词，则可从另一部分的熟词来猜测它的意思。在GRE填空中，这种方法从技巧的角度被称为同义重复，其根基是在总分的思维，有时并非词典同义词，而是逻辑等价词。但为简单起见，我们将之称为**名词与修饰同义重复**。这给我们一个很大的优势：当主干中出现不认识的单词时，我们可以从修饰内容的谓语部分来找对应词，反之亦然。

最基本的句子是主谓宾各自只有一个单词，SVO = NP V NP。至于NP V AP的主语–系动词–表语形容词结构，因为比较简单，这里不作分析。

3.1.1 LNP & Parallelism 长名词短语和并列成分

增加句子长度的第一个方法就是把主语和宾语都变成长名词短语（**Long Noun Phrase = LNP**）。

S = np1 of np2 in np3 V O = np1 of np2 in np3 over np4. => SVO = np1–3 V np1–4.

该句的主语和宾语有3–4个名词短语。只计算名词和动词的词数，主语有3个词，谓语是1个动词，宾语3–4个词，则这个句子有8个单词左右。对长名词短语，需要把握的核心通常在第一个名词np1。如果np1是抽象名词，如the view of, the discovery of, the fact of等，或有动词和形容词修饰的名词，如development, lack, scarcity，或数量词，如the number of, the amount of，则需要掌握第二个名词np2；简单来说就是，如果np1不是有实际意义的名词，就要找到np2，找到第一个有实际意义的名词。第3–4个名词往往都是限定范围的词汇，不太重要。于是，通常情况下，对于这个句子，把握的重点是：**np1 V np1**。

并列成分，只抓一个。有时，句子变长不是因为主语和宾语位置的长名词短语，而是因为这些位置出现连续并列，有时可称为parallelism(平行结构)。如果是主语并列、宾语并列，只抓其中一个就行，因为各个并列成分是等价的，没有哪个比另一个更重要或次要。有时甚至会出现谓语并列，这时抓住一个能够马上理解的谓语就行，可以相对忽略其他的谓语结构。

● 3.1.2 NP-CP 单层修饰

主语和宾语的任何一个名词都可以被从句(CP, that/which/who...)、分词结构(VP, v-ing/v-ed...)、同位语及其从句(NP+CP, np that...,)所修饰。由于分词结构可以转化为定语从句、同位语及其从句的修饰内容也包含从句，为求方便，我们把这些都称之为广义从句。这里，没有考虑纯粹的名词同位语、形容词短语或其他不包含动词的修饰，因为它们都比较简单。谓语动词通常没什么可修饰的。于是，我们得到：

$$S = np1\text{-}3 \begin{cases} \text{that/which/who...} \\ \text{v-ing/v-ed...,} \\ \text{, (with)np that...,} \end{cases} \quad V\ O=np1\text{-}4 \begin{cases} \text{that/which/who...} \\ \text{v-ing/v-ed...,} \\ \text{, (with)np that} \end{cases}$$

在这里，主语(S)和宾语(O)的修饰方法完全一样。这样，句子有1个主句和2个从句。主句约8个词，每个修饰的广义从句也可能有6-9甚至更多单词。粗略估计，整句有1个主句 + 2个广义从句 = 3个小句，每句6-9个词，整句就有25个词左右，正好是GRE阅读句子的平均长度。

显然，句子的主干比修饰的从句、分词、同位语及其从句都重要，因此，抓住主干的np1-4 V np1-4即可；再按照长名词短语的np1原则，则整个句子要把握的核心依然是：**np1 V np1**。

有时，句子的主语或宾语的第一个词是that, whether, why, how等引导的一个完整小句子，这些从句被称为主语从句或宾语从句。对于任何这样的从句，当然要单独分析其主干，而不能只是以主语或宾语的第一个词作为核心。如：

That np1 of np2 V np1 of np2 that...V that np1 of np2 V np1 of np2 which...

这时的重点就是三个句子的主干了。通常在这种情况下，各个主谓宾中，有一两个是最重要的，找出来并不困难，少数时候重点在主语从句的主干，多数时候则是宾语从句的主干。由于宾语从句比主语从句更常见，所以我们有一个口诀：**宾语从句，单独分析**。

● 3.1.3 NP-CP1-Cp2 多层修饰：从句的递归

句子的构造可以使用递归(recursion)或嵌套(nesting)方法，其中思维类似于文章结构分析中所说的多层分解。在句子上的递归和嵌套是说，任何一个广义从句(CP = clause phrase)里的主语和宾语的名词，又可以被从句、分词、同位语及其从句所修饰，这个下一层修饰的广义从句里的主语和宾语的名词，又可以被再下一层的广义从句所修饰，依次进行下去。Steven Pinker在他的杰作*Words and Rules*里画过这样一张图 (p. 9)，图里的S = sentence，相当于我们所说的广义从句/CP；NP = noun phrase；VP = verb phrase/谓语结构，VP = V + NP，而NP可被从句或新的句子/S修饰，于是VP = V + NP + S，这个新的S = NP + VP，VP = V+ NP + S，依此下去，层层递归：

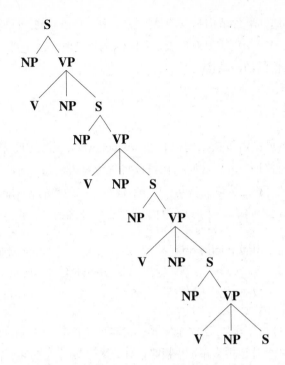

（Source: Steven Pinker, *Words and Rules*, p. 9）

但是，从句的递归可以直到无穷吗？没有那么长的句子。GRE最长的句子约88个单词。更重要的是，修饰内容如果是层层嵌套的广义从句，会很难理解。学术文章的句子并非越长越好，越难越好；学术句子写得长，通常是出于严密推理的考虑，而不是以故意让人读不懂为乐。尤其是，如果一个短语的修饰从句层次太深，人的天然认知水平很难跟进，读到第4层、第5层可能就迷失了，这样的句子并不便于学术沟通，因此往往很少出现。多数时候，主语的从句最多2-3层，宾语的从句可稍多，3-5层。在GRE的句子里，我们假定长句的主语的从句修饰有2层，宾语有3层，则我们可以构造一个包含6个广义从句(CP)的长句：

SVO = np1–3 CP1-Cp2 V np1–3 CP1-Cp2-cp3

将其中的广义从句展开，则有：

SVO = np1-3 that..., which..., V np1-3, which...and which..., v-ed..., np1 of np2 that...

该句的主语是长名词短语，np1-3, 后面有that从句，该从句里的名词再被which从句所修饰，然后是谓语动词V，接着就是宾语的长名词短语，np1-3，然后有并列的两个which从句，该从句的名词被分词v-ed修饰，分词结构里的名词再被同位语np1 of np2修饰，该同位语本身的名词被that从句修饰。已经很复杂了。估算这个句子的字数：1个主句，主语2个从句，宾语可算3个从句，则整句有6个小句子，每句6-9个单词，于是该句也许有50个单词。按照主干 > 修饰原则，所有从句，无论多层修饰还是单层修饰皆次要，则该句的把握核心依然是：**np1 V np1**。

这种分析，不是从语法着眼，而是聚焦句子的构造，这就给我们看长句时提供了一个关注焦点，管理了我们的注意力，让我们从每个单词的分散思考的状态，转变到专门针对主句主干的聚焦状态。当然，到此为止，我们只是以长名词短语、单层修饰、多层修饰构造了长句子。更长句子的构造还需要加入独立的主谓宾。

● 3.1.4 SVO, SVO 独立从句或多个主谓宾

很多长句含有好几个相对独立的主谓宾小句子。与作为修饰内容、从属于所修饰名词的that/which/who从句中的先行词在主句中充当一定成分不同，这些从句是完整的，由连词if/because/when/although/while/whereas等引导，这些连词本身并不充当句子成分，我们将这些从句定义为独立从句，或简单说成新的主谓宾。

独立从句与主句之间的关系有时是广义并列，最常见的就是正常并列或平行的关系，如：

SVO if/because/when SVO

如果每个主谓宾的主语和宾语都被1–3层从句修饰，则该句展开就可以写成：

np1–3 that...V np1–3, which..., v-ed..., np that...if/because/when np1–3 which..., V np1–3, which..., v-ed..., np that...

该句有2个主谓宾的句子，各自有1 + 3 = 4个广义从句，共有10个小句子，平均每个小句子8个单词，整句会有80个单词或更多。这时，把握的重点通常不在独立从句，因为if, because, when等表示条件、原因和时间的从句，多数时候只是说明主句动作发生的周边情况，并非句子核心。把握重点是主句主干，也就是主句的**np1 V np1**。

少数时候，广义并列的2–3个句子也会有总分关系，通常会有冒号作为提示，如：

SVO: SVO, SVO

这时，冒号前后是总分关系，最重要的是总的句子的主干，分的句子的主干也可关注，因为它好比是证据，会重复总的句子的内容，出现同义重复或者至少是逻辑等价的词汇。

独立从句与主句之间的关系有时可能是对比的，如：

Although/While/Whereas SVO, SVO

While, whereas通常表示对比；让步从句与主句之间至少也包含对比，属于广义对比。如果每个主语和宾语都被1–3层广义从句修饰，显然也可以写成：

Although/While/Whereas np1–3 that...**V np1–3** which..., v-ed..., np that..., **np1–3** that...**V np1–3**, which..., v-ing...

这时，按照对比关系出现时，**对比找反义**的技巧，就不能只是关注主句，还要考虑独立从句的内容。这样，我们就要分别抓出主句和独立从句的主干，于是要把握的核心就是：**np1 V np1 vs. np1 V np1**。由于对比反义的内容通常在两个分句的宾语，因此抓住各自从句的宾语，有时也包括谓语，是比较重要的：**np1 V np1 vs. np1 V np1**。事实上，含有对比或让步的句子，语义上的对比反义词比单纯的句子主干更重要。这一点可以推广，对含有**因果、机制、对比、让步的句子**，语义的核心词，即因果双方或对比内容，比各个分句的语法主干更重要，我们将这称为**语义压倒语法**。

句子还可以写得更长：加入更多独立的主谓宾，每个主谓宾的主语和宾语各自再给多层修饰。写长句不是写作的目的，写作的目的是严密而且清晰。但如果遇到这些句子，我们需要知道怎么快速处理得到核心。如：

SVO; SVO; SVO（3个句子并列；核心是各自主句的主干）

SVO: SVO; SVO; SVO（冒号前后是总分关系；最重要的是总的句子的主干）

Although SVO, SVO while SVO（2个层次的对比句子，可找两对反义词）

SVO if SVO; however, SVO because SVO, though SVO.（第1个SVO的主干和however之后的主句主干重要）

以上关于句子结构的分析，是应用**递归**、**组合**等方法，从下往上，从简单句逐步构造出复杂的长句，并指出相应的阅读重心，以管理我们阅读长句的注意力。

3.2 Examples 句子结构练习

提示

1. 左边是原句，读者先自己读一遍，想想核心是什么；然后再读右边，**黑体**表示句子核心，***斜黑体***表示广义从句（含有动词的修饰）中重复核心（核心等价）或反义重复的词；关于如何和为何找这些词，请见下面的"说明"。*斜体*表示第一层广义从句修饰引导词，<u>*划线斜体*</u>表示第二层，<u>**双划线斜体**</u>表示第三层；**从句修饰内容皆次要**。凡修饰内容均有斜体。此外，并列或对比的独立从句的先行词，如when, if, although, whereas，不作标识。

2. 句子的分析分3个层面：语法主干（所有句子）、语义核心（一些句子）、句内逻辑关系或上下句关系（少数句子）。一些仅凭主干还无法了解其意义的句子，配有译文。句子分析不是翻译；翻译其实并非必需。

3. 句子选自GRE-RC-36套的Exercise 13, 15, 23, 24, 25, 26。选择这些练习的句子并无特别原因，只是提供足够的句子。不必收集所有长句，长句不是读得越多就越好，否则边际收益会递减。精心练习30–50句最重要。

3.2.1 长名词短语和并列成分

1. But the recent discovery of detailed similarities in the skeletal structure of the flippers in all three groups undermines the attempt to explain away superficial resemblance as due to convergent evolution—the independent development of similarities between unrelated groups in response to similar environmental pressures.

But the recent **discovery of** detailed **similarities** in the skeletal structure of the flippers in all three groups **undermines the attempt** to explain away superficial resemblance as due to **convergent evolution**—the independent development of similarities between unrelated groups in *response* to similar environmental pressures.

【说明】

　　主语和宾语是长名词短语，抓np1。主语是np1-5，其中，np1 discovery，抽象名词，不够用，还要找np2 similarities，后面的in np3 of np4 in np5为范围限定，对该句本身的处理来说相对次要。谓语动词为undermine，= weaken, ruin，意为"摧毁，削弱"。宾语attempt后有不定式修饰，对于不定式要抓住动宾结构的核心词，在这里就是explain away（敷衍或草率解释）... as due to之后的名词convergent evolution。之后的破折号为具体说明，次要，其中的response与evolution在意义上相等，属逻辑等价词。核心内容可再简化：similarities undermine convergent evolution。（flipper: 鳍脚，脚蹼；superficial: 表面的；convergent: 趋同的，汇聚的）

2. They were fighting, albeit discreetly, to open the intellectual world to the new science and to liberate intellectual life from ecclesiastical philosophy and envisioned their work as contributing to the growth, not of philosophy, but of research in mathematics and physics.

They were fighting, albeit discreetly, to **open the intellectual world to the new science** and to liberate intellectual life from ecclesiastical philosophy and envisioned their work as *contributing to the growth*, not of philosophy, but *of* research in mathematics and *physics*.

【说明】

主语是they，两个谓语成分并列：were fighting, envisioned...as，由于并列，只抓一个，第一个就很好。在第一个谓语部分有连续动词，v1 to v2，多数时候，**连续动词取最后一个动词作为核心**，因为它紧跟宾语，决定动作的主要内容。同时，to open后面的to liberate则不重要，因为两者是并列的，这样也就很轻松地处理掉了ecclesiastical philosophy这种专业术语。中间有一个表示让步的插入成分，albeit = although，注意位置即可，若在考题中出现，可通过句子主干定位回来。第二个谓语与第一个并列，如果抓核心，则是contributing to the growth...of mathematics and physics，这里mathematics and physics = new science，与第一个谓语的核心open to the new science逻辑等价。它有两个动词，envisioned, contributing to，后者是前者的补足成分，当动词连续出现时，可取最后一个动词作为重点，因为它能清楚说明动作内容。(discreet = prudent, modest, not obtrusive：谨慎的；ecclesiastical：教会的；Ecclesiastes：圣经的传道书)

● 3.2.2 单层修饰

3. Friedrich Engels, however, predicted that women would be liberated from the "social, legal, and economic subordination" of the family by technological developments that made possible the recruitment of "the whole female sex into public industry."

Friedrich Engels, however, predicted *that* **women** would be **liberated** from the "social, legal, and economic subordination" of the family **by technological** developments *that* made possible the recruitment of "the whole female sex into public industry."

【说明】

主句的主语是人名，取最后一个大写字母，E；宾语是that引导的**宾语从句，单独分析其主干**。宾语从句的主语是women，谓语动词的主要词汇是liberated by；谓语动词右侧是广义宾语，宾语核心词为by后面的technological developments，development属抽象词，抓实际意义的technological；之后为that从句修饰，不算前面的宾语从句（predicted）that，这是该句的第一层修饰性的从句，不重要。因此句子核心只是：E说，women...be liberated by technological...；他认为技术发展可让女性从家庭中解放。（subordination：秩序ord-，之下sub- → 从属，附属；recruitment：招聘）

4. This is not because such an interpretation necessarily stiffens into a thesis (although rigidity in any interpretation of this or of any novel is always a danger), but because *Wuthering Heights* has recalcitrant elements of undeniable power that, ultimately, resist inclusion in an all-encompassing interpretation.

This is *not* because such an interpretation necessarily *stiffens into a thesis* (although rigidity in any interpretation of this or of any novel is always a danger), but **because** *Wuthering Heights* **has** recalcitrant **elements** of undeniable power *that*, ultimately, **resist inclusion in an** all-encompassing **interpretation**.

【说明】

主语是this，谓语动词是is，广义宾语是"not because, but because"形成的对比结构，重点在but because。把because看做一个宾语从句，单独分析主干，则其主语是一本斜体表示的书名，取首字母，*WH*；谓语动词是has；宾语是名词短语np1 of np2，抓np1，如果不认识recalcitrant，就看elements，之后是that引导的定语从句修饰，只有一层，为单层修饰，按照**名词与修饰同义重复**或逻辑等价原则，可以推出，resist inclusion = recalcitrant。于是，整句的核心意思是说：这是因为WH有一些要素，抵制包含在解释中。如果愿意，可以通过"not, but"的对比找前后两个分句的一对反义词，按**对比找反义、反义在宾语**的原则，这就是，not stiffen, but resist inclusion，意思是：不是因为僵化成一个论点，而是因为抵制在一个囊括一切的论点中。最后，该句括号里表让步的although属于补充说明，注意位置即可，不必当时理解，理解也很容易，rigidity = stiffen（注意：这些等号均属逻辑等价，并非语言等同）。（stiff = rigid, stubborn：僵硬的，不灵活的；recalcitrant = obstinately defiant, unruly, resistant：顽固的，不服从权威的，抵制的）

---

5. Metaphysics, philosophy's traditional core—considered as the most general description of how the heavens and the earth are put together—had been rendered almost completely meaningless by the spectacular progress of physics.

Metaphysics, philosophy's traditional core—*considered* as the most general description of how the heavens and the earth are put together—had been **rendered** almost completely **meaningless by** the spectacular progress of **physics**.

【说明】

主语是metaphysics，专业词汇取首字母M。之后有同位语，可以注意其中的时间词traditional，可能暗示下一句有关于recent的对比内容，该同位语被破折号里的过去分词considered所修饰，属于次要信息，这个广义从句之内的宾语含有how引导的名词性从句。谓语动词是been rendered，广义宾语（谓语动词右侧皆是）是meaningless，真正宾语是physics。本句简单，但依然要注意基本功训练，看到句子，别被专业内容吓倒，迅速找出核心即可。只要一句之内的专业词汇不太多，这样的处理方法就十分有效。全句的意思是：M被physics弄得无意义了。（metaphysics：形而上学，研究自然原理的学问；render = make, do：致使；spectacular：壮观的，惊人的）

---

6. Kant, however, by focusing philosophy on the problem of knowledge, managed to replace metaphysics with epistemology, and thus to transform the notion of philosophy as "queen of sciences" into the new notion of philosophy as a separate, foundational discipline: philosophy became "primary" no longer in the sense of "highest" but in the sense of "underlying".

Kant, however, by focusing philosophy on the problem of *knowledge*, managed to **replace** **metaphysics with** epistemology, and **thus to transform** the notion of philosophy as "queen of sciences" **into the new** notion of Philosophy as a separate, **foundational** discipline: philosophy became "primary" no longer in the sense of "highest" but in the sense of *"underlying"*.

【说明】

主语是专业人名，取首字母K；谓语动词为连续动词v1 to v2，抓第二个动词replace；广义宾语为专业名词，均取首字母，m vs. e。插入的方式状语by focusing on属于广义从句（有动词成分的修饰），作为单层修饰，它与谓语动作平行，故可推出focus on = replace with, knowledge = epistemology，于是前半句的意思是：K以e或knowledge取代m。后半句本为不定式的并列，但因为由thus连接，故为该句甚至全段结论，可再抓其动词和宾语，动词是transform/根本改变，宾语核心是new p(hilosophy)/新哲学，冒号之后为具体说明，用一个句子说明new p的特点，可以看做修饰性的广义从句，按照修饰与名词同义重复的原则，underlying = foundational。整个句子的意思是：K以e取代m，变成新的p，作为foundational的学科。(underlying = basic, fundamental：根本的，基础的；epistemology：认识论，知识理论)

7. Only in the case of the February Revolution do we lack a useful description of participants that might characterize it in the light of what social history has taught us about the process of revolutionary mobilization.

Only in the case of the February Revolution do **we lack a useful description** of participants *that* might characterize it in the light of *what* social history has taught us about the process of revolutionary mobilization.

【说明】

本句为only引出的倒装结构。主语是we，谓语动词是lack，宾语是useful description，倒装所强调的"二月革命"必须予以重视。宾语descrpition之后有that引导的单层修饰，该从句的广义宾语含有what引导的名词性从句。整句的意思是：只有在"二月革命"中，我们才缺乏有用描述。至于that从句，的确属于次要信息。(characterize：刻画(特征)；in the light of = according to, in the view of：按照；mobilization：动员)

8. It was not the change in office technology, but rather the separation of secretarial work, previously seen as an apprenticeship for beginning managers, from administrative work that in the 1880's created a new class of "dead-end" jobs, thenceforth considered "women's work."

It was *not the change in office technology*, **but** rather the **separation of secretarial work**, previously *seen* as an apprenticeship for beginning managers, from administrative work that in the 1880's **created** a new class of "**dead-end**" **jobs**, thenceforth *considered* "women's work."

【说明】

本句为强调句型，It was...that...，所强调部分为一个对比结构，not...but rather...，but之后是重点，也是句子主语，为一长名词短语np1 of np2, v-ed, from np3，中间被过去分词修饰seen as所隔断，是单层修饰，属于次要信息，抓np1, separation，为抽象名词，还要抓np2, secretarial work；谓语动词created；宾语核心词dead-end jobs (没前途的工作)，之后有分词considered修饰，也属于单层修饰。可以考虑not...but的对比，一对反义词是 technology vs. separation，不是技术原因，而是文秘工作分离的原因。整句的核心意思是：不是技术，而是文秘工作分离，创造了dead-end jobs。(apprenticeship：实习、见习工作；thenceforth：由此，于是，因此)

9. When nitrogen levels are low, however, specialized cells called heterocysts are produced which lack chlorophyll (necessary for photosynthesis) but which can fix nitrogen by converting nitrogen gas into a usable form.

When nitrogen levels are **low**, however, **specialized cells** called **heterocysts** are **produced** *which* **lack** chlorophyll (necessary for **photosynthesis**) *but which* can **fix** nitrogen by **converting** nitrogen gas into a usable form.

【说明】

包含有主句和独立的时间从句when。首先抓主句的主干，主语是specialized cells，特化细胞，后有分词

called引起的命名，专业名词取首字母h，然后是"which...but which"两个平行的单层修饰的定语从句，修饰主语cells或h。句子到这里，应该结束了。但是，规则总有例外：对理科文章的句子而言，数量概念始终重要，特别是当出现两个量对应的时候，很可能是数量因果＝相关。所以，when从句讲，n(itrogen)的水平或数量低(n↓)，主句讲h会产生，它缺少c(hlorophyll)，而photosynthesis需要c，故p此时也少(p↓)，但能固定n(itrogen)，n会开始增多。按**因果找双方**的原则可得：n↓：c↓：p↓，简化之后就是n↓：p↓。这个例子可以推广，只要句内出现两个概念之间的数量相关，则这一关系比任何句子成分都重要，因为有时特定的**语义会压倒语法**的重要性。另外，从上下句关系看，相关性的内容一般会谈到正反两个方面，故上一句或下一句也许会出现：n↑：p↑。

---

10. According to the model, that signal is generated as a negative Rossby wave, a wave of depressed, or negative, sea level, that moves westward parallel to the equator at 25 to 85 kilometers per day.

According to the model, **that signal** is **generated** as a negative **Rossby wave**, a wave of depressed, or negative, sea level, *that* moves westward parallel to the equator at 25 to 85 kilometers per day.

【说明】

本句简单，主语that signal，谓语动词generated，广义宾语R. wave，宾语后有同位语名词短语，还有that从句单层修饰，均次要，按**修饰与名词同义重复**原则，depressed＝negative。整句意思是：某信号产生，成为R. wave。（depressed：下压的，抑制的；parallel：平行的）

＊ 宾语从句，抽象词从句

11. The alternative explanation supposes that the Sun's large-scale magnetic field is a remnant of the field the Sun acquired when it formed, and is not sustained against decay.

The **alternative explanation** supposes *that* the Sun's large-scale **magnetic field** is a **remnant** of the field *the Sun* acquired <u>when</u> it formed, and is not sustained against **decay**.

【说明】

主语alternative explanation，谓语动词suppose，宾语为that引导的**宾语从句**，在此进行**单独分析**。在宾语从句中，主干是太阳的magnetic field/磁场，谓语动词is，宾语是remnant（残余，来自remain）；宾语之后其实有两层修饰（不算that宾语从句，单独计算），the Sun acquired为第一层，定语从句，省略了先行词that/which，之后有when从句的第二层修饰，但比较简单，不作重点分析，之后有并列的谓语结构，**并列成分同义重复**，于是可知，remnant＝not against decay＝decay。全句的意思是：替代理论认为，磁场是残余，会衰败。从上下句关系来看，本句提出alternative explanation，与前文已有的explanation对立，本句之后，可以展开替代理论(kw)的证据(x y z)。

---

12. They conclude that such dramatic technological innovations as the spinning jenny, the sewing machine, the typewriter, and the vacuum cleaner

They conclude *that* such **dramatic technological** innovations as the spinning jenny, the sewing machine, the typewriter, and the vacuum cleaner have **not** have not resulted in equally dramatic social changes in women's economic position or in the prevailing evaluation of women's work.

resulted in equally **dramatic social changes** in women's economic position or in the prevailing evaluation of women's work.

【说明】

典型的**宾语从句单独分析**的例子。They conclude that是主句的主谓宾。宾语从句的主语是dramatic technological innovations（剧烈的技术革新），其中有连续并列的举例成分，次要，谓语是否定性的动词not result in，宾语是长名词短语，np1 in np2 or in np3，抓np1，dramatic social changes。全句的意思是：剧烈的技术变革没有导致关于女性的剧烈社会变化。从上下句的结构关系来分析，可注意本句conclude提示论点核心，如放在段落前1–2句，为主题句（ts = kw），如放在段落末尾，为结论句（cs），任何情况下，中间证据均从属于它。（dramtic = striking, fundamental, revolutionary, transforming：戏剧性的，剧烈的，根本的）

13. Since 1953, many experimental attempts to synthesize the chemical constituents of life under "primitive Earth conditions" have demonstrated that a variety of the complex molecules currently making up living organisms could have been present in the early ocean and atmosphere, with only one limitation: such molecules are synthesized far less readily when oxygen-containing compounds dominate the atmosphere.

Since 1953, many experimental **attempts** to synthesize the **chemical constituents** of life under "primitive Earth conditions" have **demonstrated** *that* a variety of the **complex molecules** currently *making up* living organisms could have been **present** in the **early** ocean and atmosphere, with **only one limitation**: such **molecules** are synthesized far **less readily** *when* oxygen-containing compounds **dominate** the atmosphere.

【说明】

主句的主语是attempts，由不定式to synthesize修饰，可抓动宾结构的核心，即名词chemical constituents；谓语动词是demonstrate（证明、表明），之后是that**宾语从句，单独分析**，其主干是该句的真正中心。That宾语从句的主语是complex molecules，有现在分词v-ing修饰，次要，谓语内容为been present，在广义宾语中要注意early。句子到此为止的内容是说：一些研究表明，复杂分子在早期就存在。但规则都有少数例外，后面来了only引导的强调内容，冒号之后的句子还出现了广义数量词（less, dominate）、when等，暗示相关性，当氧主宰时（o↑），分子不容易合成（m↓）。**数量相关，语义压倒语法**，于是，整个句子的重心先从第一个主谓宾迁移到宾语从句的主谓宾，再迁移到only强调的数量相关。全句的核心意思是：研究表明，o↑：m↓（氧多：分子少）。最后，相关性的另一方面会在上句或下句提到：o↓：m↑（氧少：分子多）。

14. The common belief of some linguists that each language is a perfect vehicle for the thoughts of the nation speaking it is in some ways the exact counterpart of the conviction of the Manchester school of economics that supply and demand will regulate everything for the best.

The common **belief** of some **linguists** *that* each **language is** a **perfect** vehicle for the thoughts of the nation *speaking it* **is** in some ways the exact **counterpart** of the conviction of the Manchester school of economics *that* **supply** and **demand** will regulate everything for the **best**.

【说明】

该句的主语belief，宾语conviction，都是抽象名词，其后跟着的that从句恰好都是同位语从句（整句修饰一个名词，that不作从句成分），需要单独分析。不必追究从句的语法分类；我们只要知道，**抽象词的从句，单独分析**，例如the fact that, the theory that, the hypothesis that等，都需要将其后从句的主谓宾作为真正重点。本句主语是语言学家的信念belief，之后的从句讲"每种语言都完美（perfect）"，宾语the nation后面有很短的分词修饰speaking it。谓语动词is的主语不是it，而是前面的belief。宾语counterpart重要，意思是说虽然位置不同但功能、作用相同的人或物，该词的重点不在前缀counter的不同，而在相同，counterpart = similarity。宾语中含有M. school以及起修饰作用的that从句，其核心在"供应−需求法则达到最佳（best）"。整句的核心意思是：语言学家认为语言完美，类似于经济学者认为供求最佳。由于句内含有相同的比较，**比较找同义**，所以本句最核心的词是perfect = the best。从上下句的结构关系来考虑，本句common belief是大众意见，后文常有反驳；另外，本句自身内容为两者比较，如有证据展开，则应为l=e. l1=e1. l2=e2. (l=linguists, e=economist)。

● 3.2.3 多层修饰：从句的递归

15. Many critics of Emily Brontë's novel *Wuthering Heights* see its second part as a counterpoint that comments on, if it does not reverse, the first part, where a romantic reading receives more confirmation.

Many **critics** of Emily Brontë's novel *Wuthering Heights* **see** its **second part as a counterpoint** *that* **comments** on, *if* it does not reverse, **the first part**, *where* a romantic reading receives more confirmation.

【说明】

主语名词短语，np1 of np2's np3，重点是critics，谓语动词see...as = view...as = consider...as，宾语有直接宾语和间接宾语，核心是second part, counterpoint。宾语之后，给出了that从句第一层修饰，次要；其中还有插入成分if从句，与that comments on的从句平行，次要；而that从句的宾语名词the first part，又被where的第二层从句所修饰，也不重要。于是全句的意思就是：批评家认为WH（*Wuthering Heights*取首字母）的第二部分是counterpoint。如不理解，按照**修饰与名词同义重复**，可认为counterpoint = comment on，批评家认为第二部分是在评论第一部分。宾语counterpoint，就如counterpart一样，不是字面上的counter/相反，而是相似、对应。句子的结构可以表示为：NP1-3 V NP CP1（that），Cp1'（if），Cp2（where）。从上下句之间的关系来看，本句有many critics的观点，是大众意见，常被反驳和纠正，后文会出现负评价和新观点的内容。

16. The demarcation of philosophy from science was facilitated by the development in the early nineteenth century of a new notion, that philosophy's core interest should be epistemology, the general explanation of what it means to know something.

The **demarcation of p**hilosophy from science was **facilitated by the development** in the early nineteenth century of a **new notion**, *that* philosophy's core interest should be **epistemology**, the general explanation of *what* it means to **know** something.

【说明】

本句的结构分析可以有效克服生词恐惧所带来的理解障碍。主语长名词短语np1 of np2 from np3，np1为抽象名词demarcation = separation（划界、分离），还要抓实际意义的np2，意思是p（hilosophy）的分离；谓语动词facilitate = precipitate（加速、促进）；宾语为by之后的长名词短语np1 in np2 of np3，np1为development，再抓后面，结果是时间，可注意一下。然后是抽象词new notion，看它的同位语从句that的主谓宾可以发现，第一层修饰的that从句的主干是 "p's interest应该是epistemology"，假装不认识这个长单词，**专业名词取首字母e**，之后还有同位语np1 of np2修饰，其中的np2是一个what引导的名词性句子，可认为是第二层修饰，按照**修饰与名词同义重复**可知，know = epistemology。于是全句的意思是：p的分离在19世纪加速，新观念是p应当是e，研究认识。从上下文关系看，本句的development暗示后文如要展开证据，需采用时间对比结构，先讲过去的、传统的p，再讲新的、现代的p。

---

17. Hank Morgan, the hero of Mark Twain's *A Connecticut Yankee in King Arthur's Court*, is a nineteenth-century master mechanic who, mysteriously awakening in sixth-century Britain, launches what he hopes will be a peaceful revolution to transform Arthurian Britain into an industrialized modern democracy.

Hank **M**organ, the hero of Mark **T**wain's *A Connecticut Yankee in King Arthur's Court*, **is** a nineteenth-century master **mechanic** who, mysteriously *awakening* in sixth-century Britain, launches *what* he hopes will be a peaceful revolution to transform Arthurian Britain into an industrialized modern democracy.

【说明】

主语人名，**取姓氏大写首字母M**，它被同位语名词短语所修饰，中间有人名及书名，应是主要讨论对象（topic），人名取姓氏大写首字母T，书名取前三个单词的大写首字母ACY；谓语动词is；宾语的名词取mechanic。宾语之后有两层修饰：第一层是who从句，从句的主语（who）又被分词awakening再行修饰；从句中的宾语本身也是第二层修饰，是what引导的名词性从句，可看做宾语从句，最后还有to transform的不定式。整句的核心意思就是：M是一个杰出的机械师（master mechanic）。宾语后面的who...what...结构只是描述了M的作为，并不重要。

【译文】

Mark Twain的著作ACY一书的主人公Hank Morgan，是19世纪一位杰出的机械师，他在6世纪的英国神秘苏醒，发动了一场他所希望的和平革命，企图把亚瑟时代的英国转变为工业化的现代民主体制。

---

18. None of these translations to screen and stage, however, dramatize the anarchy at the conclusion of *A Connecticut Yankee*, which ends with the violent overthrow of Morgan's three-year-old progressive order and his return to the nineteenth century, where he apparently commits suicide after being labeled as lunatic for his incoherent babblings about drawbridges and battlements.

None of these **translations** to screen and stage, however, **dramatize the anarchy** at the conclusion of *A Connecticut Yankee, which* ends with the violent overthrow of Morgan's three-year-old progressive order and his return to the nineteenth century, *where* he apparently commits suicide after being *labeled* as lunatic for his incoherent babblings about drawbridges and battlements.

【说明】

主语np1 of np2 to np3，抓np1 of np2，none translations，谓语动词dramatize（戏剧表现），宾语是长名词短语np1 at np2 of np3，抓np1，anarchy（无政府，混乱状态）。宾语的ACY之后有2-3层修饰，which从句为第一层，它的宾语nineteenth century之后有where从句作第二层修饰，该从句里的after之后有分词修饰，可算做第三层，但这些**多层修饰皆次要**。句子的中心意思是：没有哪种改编形式，在戏剧上体现出混乱状态。（conclusion：结束，结论；lunatic：与lunar同根，疯子；incoherent：不连贯的，不合逻辑的；babble：胡言乱语，瞎说）

【译文】

以上屏幕和舞台的改编作品，没有哪部在戏剧上表现了ACY一书结尾的政治混乱状态。该书的结尾原本是，Morgan三年之久的进步秩序遭到暴力推翻，他重返19世纪，然后自杀了，因为他成天胡言乱语，瞎说什么吊桥啊，城垛啊，被人看做疯子。

* 多层修饰作为连续动作

19. These winds tend to create a feedback mechanism by driving the warmer surface water into a "pile" that blocks the normal upwelling of deeper, cold water in the east and further warms the eastern water, thus strengthening the wind still more.

These **winds** tend to **create a feedback** mechanism by *driving* the warmer surface water into a "pile" *that* blocks the normal upwelling of deeper, cold water in the east and further warms the eastern water, thus *strengthening* the **wind** still more.

【说明】

主语winds，谓语动词v1 to v2，抓v2 = create，宾语是feedback mechanism；方式状语by driving，与谓语动词平行，driving = create（逻辑等价，语境同义，非词典同义），其宾语为pile，之后有第一层修饰that定语从句，该从句有并列谓语动词block和warm，从句里的eastern water被分词strengthening所修饰，是第二层修饰。句子重点原本应该只是主谓宾winds create feedback，但这里起多层修饰作用的从句、分词等并不只是修饰和限定，而是为了引出连续动作的环节。就连续动作也就是机制或过程而言，抓住动作的首尾比较重要，于是重点就是：开始的动作环节winds，加上末尾的动作环节，strengthen the winds。这里，**语义压倒语法**，机制的核心比句法的核心重要。语义压倒语法的情况，一般发生在理科文章句子的机制、因果（尤其数量相关）和文科文章的对比句中。（feedback：反馈，output本身成为input；upwelling：上涌）

20. For example, the spiral arrangement of scale-bract complexes on ovule-bearing pine cones, where the female reproductive organs of conifers are located, is important to the production of airflow patterns that spiral over the cone's surfaces, thereby passing airborne pollen from one scale to the next.

For example, the **spiral arrangement** of scale-bract complexes on ovule-bearing pine cones, *where* the female reproductive organs of conifers are located, **is important to** the production of **airflow patterns** *that* spiral over the cone's surfaces, thereby *passing* airborne **pollen** from one scale to the next.

【说明】

本句的主语np1 of np2 on np3，超级长的名词短语，抓住np1 = spiral arrangement（螺旋形状），np2 on np3全是**专业名词，内容次要**，千万别去仔细想它们的意思！主语名词之后有where从句第一层修饰，也次要。谓语暗示因果关系is important to = is important for = is responsible for = cause = determine。宾语的核心实义词为airflow pattern，之后有that从句第一层修饰，之后再有分词passing进行第二层修饰。句子的重点，按照**主干>修饰**原则，原本是spiral arrangement is important to airflow patterns，但是该句的多层修饰其实是连续动作，按照**语义压倒语法**，故最后的动作环节pollen也重要。句子的核心意思是：螺旋形状产生气流模式，传递花粉（passing pollen）。从上下文来看，本句属于举例，例子的内容次要，试题中常考in order to，即作用题，这时答案不在例子本身，而在前后的论点或结论。

21. As rock interfaces are crossed, the elastic characteristics encountered generally change abruptly, which causes part of the energy to be reflected back to the surface, where it is recorded by seismic instruments.

As rock **interfaces are crossed**, the elastic **characteristics** *encountered* generally **change** abruptly, *which* causes part of the energy to be reflected back to the surface, *where* it is **recorded** by seismic instruments.

【说明】

从语法上看，开始有由As引导的时间从句，主句的主语为e. characteristics，之后被过去分词encountered修饰，谓语动词为change；之后有which从句修饰整个句子，从句里的宾语名词surface被where从句进行第二层修饰。本句的as从句、宾语部分的which从句、从句之后的where从句，主要在描述连续动作，**语义压倒语法**，机制找首尾，因此，句子的核心不能只找主谓宾（e[lastic]. characteristics change），还要考虑最开始和最末尾的动作环节（crossed, recorded）。整句的意思是：穿过界面，e特征改变，能量反射，被记录下来；简化之后就是：穿过界面……能量被记录（crossed, energy recorded）。

● 3.2.4 多个SVO

22. Since the Hawaiian Islands have never been connected to other land masses, the great variety of plants in Hawaii must be a result of the long-distance dispersal of seeds, a process that requires both a method of transport and an equivalence between the ecology of the source area and that of the recipient area.

Since the Hawaiian Islands have never been connected to other land masses, the great **variety** of plants in Hawaii must be a **result of** the long-distance **dispersal of seeds**, a process *that* requires both a method of transport and an equivalence between the ecology of the source area and that of the recipient area.

【说明】

本句为主句与Since从句广义并列（非让步、对比、转折即为广义并列），Since从句次要，抓住**主句主干**。主句主语variety = diversity，谓语动词暗示因果关系，be a result of = be caused by = be determined by = result from，宾语给出原因，dispersal of seeds（种子散播）。宾语之后有同位语修饰，process = dispersal，同位语被that从句修饰，从句内容相对次要，但注意并列宾语之一equivalence = similarity，说明相似，常会在考题中出现。全句的意思是：植物多样性来自种子传播。（recipient：接受的，来自动词receive，意为"接受"；另外，名词形式receiver，意为"接受者"）

23. The great variety of dynamic behaviors exhibited by different populations makes this task more difficult: some populations remain roughly constant from year to year; others exhibit regular cycles of abundance and scarcity; still others vary wildly, with outbreaks and crashes that are in some cases plainly correlated with the weather, and in other cases not.

The great **variety** of dynamic behaviors *exhibited by* different populations **makes** this task more **difficult**: **some** populations remain roughly **constant** from year to year; **others** exhibit **regular cycles** of abundance and scarcity; still **others vary wildly**, with *outbreaks and crashes that* are in some cases plainly correlated with the weather, and in other cases not.

【说明】

　　4个SVO。句子虽多，但每句都很简单。冒号通常表示具体说明，故冒号之前的第1个SVO是总，为句子的核心，冒号之后的3个并列SVO是分。所有SVO都抓主干。第1个句子的主语variety，后有分词exhibited by修饰，谓语部分有make difficult。第2、3、4个句子的主谓宾分别是，some remains constant, others exhibit regular cycles, others vary wildly。最后一个句子有补足成分，其中的名词被that从句修饰。从语义上看，**连续并列次要**，因此重点只在第1个句子主干上：行为多样，难以研究。

---

24. No matter how severely or unpredictably birth, death and migration rates may be fluctuating around their long-term averages, if there were no density-dependent effects, the population would, in the long run, either increase or decrease without bound (barring a miracle by which gains and losses canceled exactly).

No matter how severely or unpredictably birth, death and migration rates may be fluctuating around their long-term averages, if there were no density-dependent effects, the **population would**, in the long run, either increase or decrease **without bound** (*barring* a miracle *by which* gains and losses canceled exactly).

【说明】

　　2个条件从句与1个主句，主句主干为重点。No matter how是广义的条件从句，if也是条件从句，这两者都是独立从句，但不重要。主句的主语是population，谓语部分是由either...or连接的并列动词，可抓without bound(没有界限)作为核心。之后的括号属于具体说明，次要，其中的分词barring是第一层修饰，by which是第二层修饰。全句的意思是：在某种条件下(if)，种群的增减会毫无边界。抓住主干有时不能解决一切问题，需要结合上下句来确认该句的重心。（severe：严重的；fluctuate：波动；bar = block, prevent：阻止，阻拦；barring = excluding, except：除…之外）

【译文】

　　无论种群的生、死和迁徙比率沿着长期平均值波动得多么剧烈或不可预测，如果没有密度依赖的因素，种群在长期内也许会毫无边界地增长或减少(除非增减恰好相互抵消的奇迹出现)。

---

25. They correctly note that slavery stripped some cultural elements from Black people — their political and economic systems — but they underestimate the significance of music in sustaining other African cultural values.

They **correctly** note that **slavery stripped** some **cultural** elements from Black people — their political and economic systems — but **they underestimate** the significance of **music** in **sustaining** other African **cultural** values.

【说明】

　　包含由but引起的2个对比句子。从语法上看，第1句主谓宾，其中that宾语从句，单独分析。从句的主干简单：slavery stripped(脱掉、剥夺) cultural elements。第2句的主干也容易找到，即they underestimate music，宾语是长名词短语，np1 of np2 in v-ing，可找其中的实义名词以及动词作为重点。全句的意思是：他们正确地看到奴隶制剥夺黑人的文化，但却低估了音乐可以维系非洲文化。从语义上看，第1句有correctly正评价，第2句则有underestimate负评价，**态度始终重要**；除了作者评价不同，该句有让步转折的意味，由于让步转折=对比+主次(让步次要，转折主要)，包含对比，**对比找反义，反义在宾语**，于是得到 strip vs. sustain。

26. If anatomical similarity in the flippers resulted from similar environmental pressures, as posited by the convergent-evolution theory, one would expect walruses and seals, but not seals and sea lions, to have similar flippers.

If anatomical similarity in the flippers resulted from similar environmental pressures, *as posited by* the convergent-evolution theory, **one would expect walruses and seals**, but not seals and sea lions, to **have similar f**lippers.

【说明】

条件从句与主句广义并列。条件从句的主干是anatomical similarity resulted from similar environmental（结构相似是因为环境压力相似），其后有分词posited 修饰。主句的主谓语是one would expect，宾语相对复杂，**出现陌生物种名称，取首字母**。全句的意思是：在某种条件下（If，如果按环境压力理论即趋同演化/convergent-evolution理论），我们也许会期待这两种而非那两种动物有相似的f(lippers)。当然，单独看此句，即便有译文，也不容易明白意思，必须结合上下文或立足逻辑论证才能理解。本句故意假设一种理论是对的，然后推出由虚拟语气would引出的、与事实相反的结果，这其实是为了否定所假设的理论，说它不对。（anatomy：解剖学，解剖；posit = suppose, assume, presume：假定；convergent：趋同的，聚合的；flipper：鳍状肢，脚蹼）

【译文】

如果真像趋同演化所假定的那样，鳍脚的结构相似是由于环境压力相似，那我们也许就会期待，w和s，而不是s和s.l.，有类似的鳍脚。

27. This link between philosophical interests and scientific practice persisted until the nineteenth century, when decline in ecclesiastical power over scholarship and changes in the nature of science provoked the final separation of philosophy from both.

This link between philosophical interests and scientific practice **persisted until the nineteenth** century, when **decline** in ecclesiastical power over scholarship and changes in the nature of science **provoked** the final **separation of p**hilosophy from both.

【说明】

2个独立SVO，when之前的主句的主干是重点。主句的主语为长名词短语np1 between np2 and np3，抓np1 = link，谓语为persist until 19th century。然后有when时间**从句就近修饰**，从句的**主语并列，次要**，只抓一个，比如decline，即可，谓语provoke，宾语np1 of np2 from np3，抓住前两个，separation of p(hilosophy)。从语法主干来看，句子的意思是：p与其他学科的联系一直持续到19世纪，19世纪一些原因导致p与它们最终分离。句内有until暗示时间对比，**对比找反义，反义在宾语**，但这里，前一句没有实质性宾语，只能找主语link，后一句的宾语核心是separation，所以，从语义上看，全句的中心是**link vs. separation**，这比从语法上提炼的主干内容更加精炼。通常，**对比、让步、因果关系的句子，语义压倒主干**。（persist：持续，顽固坚持；ecclesiastical：教会的；scholarship：academic study/学术研究，学术品质，奖学金等；provoke：向前pro- + 发出声音vok- → 激发，挑衅）

28. Biologists have long maintained that two groups of pinnipeds, sea lions and walruses, are descended from a terrestrial bearlike animal, whereas the remaining group, seals, shares an ancestor with weasels.

Biologists have long maintained that **two groups** of **pinnipeds**, sea lions and walruses, are **descended from** a terrestrial **bearlike** animal, whereas the **remaining group**, seals, **shares an ancestor with** weasels.

【说明】

　　宾语从句that之后有2句对比，对比反义是重点。**宾语从句单独分析**，2句的主语和宾语都无修饰从句，容易找出，但最重要的地方在whereas暗示的对比，谁与谁比？2组p(innipeds)动物与另1组对比；比的什么？不在动词，动词是等价descended from = share ancestors with；对比找反义，反义在宾语，所以这对反义就是bearlike vs. weasels，祖先不同。句内因有**对比，语义比主干重要**。全句的意思是：2组p动物的祖先与另一组p的祖先是不同的。这句分析是否到此结束呢？从语法上、语义上是结束了，但句子是在语境和上下文中的句子，所以还需要想到，生物学者长久以来的观点(long maintained)作为老观点(KWo)，经常遭到反驳，可以预期后文会有负评价(AW-)以及新观点(KWn)出现。(descend：下降；descendant = offspring：后代，后裔；terrestrial：陆地的，地球的)

29. Although these observations are true, Pessen overestimates their importance by concluding from them that the undoubted progress toward inequality in the late eighteenth century continued in the Jacksonian period and that the United States was a class-ridden, plutocratic society even before industrialization.

Although these **observations are true**, Pessen **overestimates their importance** by concluding from them *that* the undoubted progress toward inequality in the late eighteenth century continued in the Jacksonian period *and that* the United States was a class-ridden, plutocratic society even before industrialization.

【说明】

　　让步转折关系的2个独立句子，含有态度。**让步转折=对比+主次**，故本句至少有对比，**对比找反义**，在此例中是态度相反：**true vs. overestimate**。让步句although的主谓宾简单，observations are true，略过。转折主句的主谓宾也容易，P overestimates importance，只是后面有by concluding方式状语与谓语动词平行，之后再有that...and that... 并列的宾语从句，**句内并列成分皆次要**。第1个that从句的主干是progress...inequality continued，主语是长名词短语np1 toward np2 in np3，取np1为progress，太抽象，np2为补充，inequality；第2个that从句的主干是U.S. was a class-... society，宾语出现生词，取其部分内容，如class-...society，阶级控制的社会，即有钱人统治的社会，就理解大意而言，不必认识plutocratic。全句的意思是：虽然上述观察很对，但P这个人高估了它们的重要性，提出了两个错误的结论。从分句之间的逻辑关系上看，并列宾语从句that...and that... 可看做主句overestimate负评价的并列证据。(progress：向前走 → 继续发展、继续恶化；ridden：harassed, oppressed；class-ridden = class-dominated, class-governed：阶级统治的；plutocratic：pluto-=wealth + -crat-=rule, govern → 财阀政治的)

30. Although in both kinds of animal, arousal stimulates the production of adrenaline and norepinephrine by the adrenal glands, the effect in herbivores is primarily fear, whereas in carnivores the effect is primarily aggression.

Although in both kinds of animal, **arousal stimulates** the production of **adrenaline and n**orepinephrine by the adrenal glands, the effect in **h**erbivores is primarily **fear**, whereas in **c**arnivores the effect is primarily **aggression**.

【说明】

　　让步转折加上对比，一共3个SVO，重点在转折句中的两个对比句里面的反义词。让步讲相同both，主句讲不同whereas。Although句的宾语是并列的**专业名词，次要，取首字母**，a(drenaline)，n(orepinephrine)，该句主干因此是arousal stimulates a and n。转折主句又有由whereas引出的对比句，谁与谁比？食草动物h与食肉动物c；比的什么？**对比找反义，反义在宾语，语义压倒语法**，句子的重心无非是fear vs. aggression。整句的意思是：虽然也有相同，但食草动物和食肉动物的效果不同，一个害怕，一个进攻。（arousal：来自arouse：唤醒，刺激，激励；herbivore：herb- = grass + -vore = eat → 食草动物；carnivore：carn- = meat + -vore = eat → 食肉动物）

---

31. Granted that the presence of these elements need not argue for an authorial awareness of novelistic construction comparable to that of Henry James, their presence does encourage attempts to unify the novel's heterogeneous parts.

Granted that the presence of **these elements** need **not argue** for an **authorial awareness of** novelistic **construction comparable to** that of Henry James, **their presence** does **encourage attempts** to **unify** the novel's heterogeneous parts.

【说明】

　　本句是让步转折句，包含2个SVO，重点在转折，让步为次重点。从句法上看，让步句Granted that的主语为these elements，谓语动词not argue，宾语较长，有比较成分出现；前半句的意思是：不必认为该作者对结构的意识可以与J相比。转折句省略but，主谓宾是presense encourage attempts，宾语之后有不定式to unify修饰，由于attempt为抽象词，需要抓不定式的核心，动词为其核心，故unify parts重要。这样，后半句的意思是：这些要素的存在，支持我们去统一小说各个部分。从语义上看，让步转折含有对比，**对比找反义**，Granted句有否定词not，暗示对比，一个说没有，另一个对比方面就会说有，于是，再结合对比找反义的原则，这对反义词就是：**not construction vs. unify**。前一句讲"结构意识不太够"，后一句讲"但依然有统一性"。

【译文】

　　即便这些要素的存在不必让我们认为，该作者对小说结构的意识可以与J相媲美，但它们的确鼓励我们去统一该小说的各个异质部分。

---

32. When, in the seventeenth century, Descartes and Hobbes rejected medieval philosophy, they did not think of themselves, as modern philosophers do, as proposing a new and better philosophy, but rather as furthering "the warfare between science and theology."

When, in the seventeenth century, Descartes and Hobbes rejected medieval philosophy, **they** did **not think of** themselves, *as* modern philosophers do, as proposing a **new** and better **philosophy, but** rather as furthering "the **warfare** between **science** and theology."

【说明】

　　从句与主句2个独立句子，重点在主句主干。When时间从句的主干简单，主语**专业人名取首字母**，D and H rejected medieval philosophy，前半句的意思是，两个人拒绝中世纪的哲学。这两个人多么伟大啊，但是，知道他们是谁，与我们把握句子核心意思有何关系呢？人物背景是不重要的。主句的主语依然是they，谓语动词为think of，广义宾语出现了not...but...对比，这时对比找反义，得到**new philosophy vs. science**（新哲学 vs. 科学）。这样，后半句的意思是，他们不是提出新的哲学，而是促进科学（从促进科学与神学之间的战争简化而得）。（medieval: medi-=middle + ev-=eve, time → 中世纪，与 ancient, modern, postmodern 相对；further(*v.*) = facilitate：促进）

【译文】

17世纪D和H拒绝中世纪的哲学时，他们并不像现代哲学家那样，认为他们在提出一种新的和更好的哲学，而是认为自己在促进"科学与神学之间的战争"。

---

33. Modern philosophers now trace that notion back at least to Descartes and Spinoza, but it was not explicitly articulated until the late eighteenth century, by Kant, and did not become built into the structure of academic institutions and the standard self-descriptions of philosophy professors until the late nineteenth century.

Modern philosophers now **trace** that notion back at least **to** Descartes **and** Spinoza, but **it was** not explicitly **articulated** until the late eighteenth century, **by Kant**, and did not become built into the structure of academic institutions and the standard self-descriptions of philosophy professors until the late nineteenth century.

【说明】

2个对比的SVO，由but引导，对比反义重要。从语法上看，前半句的核心是modern philosophers trace back to D and S，意思是：现代哲学家将此观念追溯到D与S；后半句有not...until...（直到…才），主干是it was articulated by K，后面and did not...until... 是**谓语并列，次要**，因为**凡并列成分皆次要**，这半句的意思是，它的系统说明是由K在18世纪晚期完成的。从语义上看，but表示对比，谁与谁比？现代哲学家与文章作者的观点相比；比的什么？**对比找反义，反义在宾语**。现代哲学家认为某种观念来自D. S.，作者认为它来自K，因此全句的核心就是：**D.S. vs. K**。只用宾语的大写字母，就能拎出整句的重点！这就是结构化阅读在句子理解方面的威力！（trace back to：追溯、回溯，相当于attribute to；notion = view, idea；articulate：系统说明；清楚发音）

【译文】

现代哲学家现在把这个观念至少追溯到D和S，但对这种观念的清楚阐明一直到18世纪晚期才由K完成；而且一直到19世纪晚期，该观念才成为学术体制和哲学教授的标准自我描述的内在部分。

---

34. Through their interpretations, which exert a continuing influence on our understanding of the revolutionary process, the impact of the events of June has been magnified, while, as an unintended consequence, the significance of the February insurrection has been diminished.

Through their interpretations, *which exert* a continuing influence on our understanding of the revolutionary process, the impact of the events of June has been **magnified**, while, as an unintended consequence, the significance of the February insurrection has been **diminished**.

【说明】

2个对比的SVO，对比反义重要。句子一开始是一个介词短语，其中名词被which从句修饰，都不重要。对比两个分句的主语和宾语各自都没有任何修饰，直接可以把握，语法上没有难度。问题是语义上的：while对比，对比找反义，反义在…宾语？两个分句没有宾语，那就找谓语动词好了，于是得到**J: magnified vs. F: diminished**。全句的意思是：6月事件的意义被放大，而2月起义的意义则被削减。（exert：施加作用；impact =

influence, significance，冲击、撞击，意义；insurrection = rebellion, revolt, revolution，起义）

35. Although the June insurrection of 1848 and the Paris Commune of 1871 would be considered watersheds of nineteenth-century French history by any standard, they also present the social historian with a signal advantage: these failed insurrections created a mass of invaluable documentation as a by-product of authorities' efforts to search out and punish the rebels.

Although the **June insurrection** of 1848 and the **Paris Commune** of 1871 would **be considered watersheds** of nineteenth-century French history by any standard, **they** also **present** the social historian with a signal **advantage**: these failed insurrections created a mass of **invaluable documentation** as a by-product of authorities' efforts to search out and punish the rebels.

【说明】

让步转折关系的2个SVO，重点在转折句，两个句子的主语或宾语都没有多少修饰成分。Although让步句的主干：J i and PC would be considered watersheds，前半句的意思是，一些革命被认为是19世纪法国历史的分水岭。转折主句省略but，其主干十分简单，说"它们也给历史学者提供优势"，冒号之后给出具体说明的一句话，相当于同位语从句，由于宾语advantage是抽象名词，需要从修饰它的从句中找对应，因为**修饰与名词同义重复**，于是有invaluable documentation = advantage。最后还有as a by-product**补足成分，次要**。从语义上看，**让步转折=对比+主次**，前后半句应有对比反义词，于是有watershed vs. advantage/invaluable document。在词义上看不出来对比；但推测句子所在的段落的语境，可以想到，分水岭的那些革命的档案记录也许通常是没有多大价值的，但此处谈论的这些档案却是非常宝贵的。整句的核心意思就是：一些失败的起义虽然是历史分水岭，但同时也给历史学者提供了大量无价的档案。

（watershed：分水岭，转折点；signal (*adj.*) = significant：显著的；insurrection = rebellion, revolt, revolution：起义；invaluable = priceless：无价的，宝贵的；authority = government：政府当局；rebel = insurgent, insurrectionist, mutineer：*n.* 反叛者，革命者；rebel：*adj.* 反叛的）

【译文】

虽然1848年6月起义和1871年巴黎公社无论从什么标准来看，都可以被看做19世纪法国历史的分水岭，但同时它们也给社会历史学者带来一个显著的优势：这些失败的起义创造了大量非常宝贵的档案，它们都是政府当局在努力搜寻和惩罚反叛者时所产生的副产品。

36. Fundamentally, however, the conditions under which women work have changed little since before the Industrial Revolution: the segregation of occupations by gender, lower pay for women as a group, jobs that require relatively low levels of skill and offer women little opportunity for advancement all persist, while women's household labor remains demanding.

Fundamentally, however, **the conditions** *under which* women work have **changed little** since before the Industrial Revolution: the segregation of occupations by gender, **lower pay** for women as a group, jobs *that* require relatively low levels of skill and offer women little opportunity for advancement **all persist**, while **women's household labor remains demanding**.

【说明】

3个SVO，总分+并列关系，重点在冒号之前的起总领作用的句子。第1个句子主干是conditions changed

little，主语conditions后有under which 从句修饰，次要。冒号之后有2个句子，由while表示两句的关系，都在具体说明change little的情况，出现了同义重复词汇（change little = persist, remains）。第2个SVO的主语为连续3个名词成分并列，其中第3个主语名词jobs之后有that从句修饰，该从句的2个谓语并列（require...and offer...），从3个并列主语中可以找出一个最简单的如lower pay作为主语的重点和代表，谓语是persist。第3个SVO由while引导，主干简单，women's household labor remains demanding。这里，while前后有对比，但不是在观点上相反，甚至不是在内容上对立，而只是在内容上一少一多，其实前后两句在结构上是并列关系。全句的主要意思因此就是，根本条件很少改变：低工资等依然存在，而家务劳动也依然繁重。

37. With respect to their reasons for immigrating, Cressy does not deny the frequently noted fact that some of the immigrants of the 1630's, most notably the organizers and clergy, advanced religious explanations for departure, but he finds that such explanations usually assumed primacy only in retrospect.

With respect to their reasons for immigrating, Cressy does **not deny** the frequently noted **fact** that **some** of the immigrants of the 1630's, most notably the organizers and clergy, advanced **religious explanations** for departure, **but** he finds that such explanations usually assumed **primacy only in retrospect**.

【说明】

2个SVO，让步转折的关系，重点在but之后。第1个句子的主干是C not deny the fact, the fact that为**抽象词从句，单独分析**，从句的主语主干是some immigrants advanced religious explanations。but转折之后的第2个SVO，有宾语从句，单独分析，该从句的主干是explanations assumed primacy only in retrospect，only为观点限定适用范围，一个观点的范围有限，犹如一个解释所能解释的现象范围有限，这是学术文章常用的隐蔽的负评价。从语义上看，让步转折含有对比，religious vs. only。一些人认为移民的原因是宗教，而C认为这种理由仅有（only）有限的价值。从上下文看，该句的转折仅仅限制宗教的作用，尚未提到替代理由。后面的句子也许会讲到的新的非宗教的解释，religious在内容上的反面是什么呢？religious = spiritual = metaphysical vs. secular = material = sociopolitical。

【译文】

关于他们移民的理由，C并没有否认一个经常提到的事实：一些17世纪30年代的移民者，最突出的是组织者和神职人员，提出宗教解释来说明移民（现象）。但是他发现，这样的解释通常只有在事后回顾的时候才占据主导地位。

（assume：占据，采取，承担，假定；primacy：来自primary，主要、首要；retrospect：retro- = back + -spect = see → 回顾）

38. Traditionally, pollination by wind has been viewed as a reproductive process marked by random events in which the vagaries of the wind are compensated for by the generation of vast quantities of pollen, so that the ultimate production of new seeds is assured at the expense of producing much more pollen than is actually used.

Traditionally, **pollination by wind** has **been viewed** as a reproductive **process** *marked by random* events *in which* the *vagaries* of the wind are compensated for by the generation of vast quantities of pollen, so that the ultimate production of **new seeds is assured** at the expense of **producing much more pollen** *than is* actually used.

【说明】

2个SVO，重点在so that之后。本句so that前后有2个相对独立的小句子；或者，在某种程度上，也可以认为so that是从属于in which从句的内容。我们按第一种方案处理。前半句的主干是wind pollination = w. p. has been viewed as a process，风媒传粉被看做一个繁殖过程，该句本身除了提出w.p.这个主题词，再无其他。宾语名词process之后有两层修饰，第一层修饰是分词marked by random events，其中的random说明了被修饰的繁殖过程的性质，由于被修饰名词本身只是process这样抽象的说法，故可在修饰内容中找新词作为核心，random；这之后再有in which 从句第二层修饰，其中的vagaries = random（events），**修饰与名词同义重复**。后半句由so that引出，表结果。该句主语核心为new seeds = reproductive，谓语为assured，广义宾语at the expense...中，有动宾结构以及句子比较，要单独分析，重点是produce more pollen，在内容上与上半句的generation of vast quantities of pollen等价。最后的比较than is actually used，在than is之间省略了the pollen。整句的意思是：风媒传粉被看做随机性较强的繁殖过程，新种子产生要靠大量花粉的产出。从上下文看，本句的"traditionally"和"has been"都暗示该句观点是老观点（KWo），后面的句子也许给出证据，然后再会有负评价（AW-）和新观点（KWn）出现，说风媒传粉的植物也许不用那么多花粉。（pollination：传粉，授粉；random：随机的；vagary（*n.*）= caprice, erratic or unpredictable action：异常，多变）

---

39. Because the potential hazards pollen grains are subject to as they are transported over long distances are enormous, wind-pollinated plants have, in the view above, compensated for the ensuing loss of pollen through happenstance by virtue of producing an amount of pollen that is one to three orders of magnitude greater than the amount produced by species pollinated by insects.

Because the potential **hazards** *pollen grains* are subject to *as* they are transported over long distances **are enormous**, **wind-p**ollinated **plants** have, in the view above, **compensated for** the ensuing **loss of pollen** through happenstance by virtue of **producing an amount of pollen** *that* is one to three orders of magnitude **greater** than the amount *produced by* species *pollinated by* insects.

【说明】

2个SVO，because从句和主句，主句是重点。第1个SVO由because引导，它的主语十分复杂，主语名词是hazards，其后没有介词连接，直接出现与之没有任何联系的名词pollen grains，在这两个名词之间省略了从句先行词that/which，原型是，np［that］np' v' np' v np，pollen grains为修饰hazards的从句中的主语。不仅如此，在从句之后还有一个as引导的时间从句作为第二层修饰，但**多层修饰皆次要**，于是该句的主干核心是hazards are enormous。后半句即第2个SVO，主干是w-p plants compensated for the loss of pollen，然后有by virtue of doing = by doing的方式状语，它与谓语动词compensated平行，因为它比语法上的谓语动词更直接，也可看做重点，于是producing an amount of pollen成为谓语部分的核心；宾语amount of pollen之后出现了多达3层的修饰，that从句为第1层，从句宾语的amount再被produced by第2层修饰，该修饰里的species再被pollinated by第3层修饰。其中，除了greater than这个对比因为常会出考题，可稍微注意以外，其他皆次要。全句的意思是：因为危险巨大，所以风媒传粉植物为补偿花粉损失，产生大量花粉。如果再简化为主句的核心，则是w-p plants ... producing an amount of pollen（风媒传粉植物产生大量花粉）。

（potential = possible：可能的，潜在的；grain：谷物，颗粒；be subject to：面对、遭受、受到…支配；enormous = huge, tremendous：巨大的，庞大的；pollinate：传粉、授粉；ensue：随之而来；ensuing = resulted, following：

随之而来的；happenstance = accidents：偶然事件；magnitude：数量；orders of magnitude：数量级）

【译文】

　　由于花粉颗粒在长距离传播的过程中所面临的危险十分巨大，所以按照上述观点，风媒植物为补偿因为偶然事件所带来的花粉损失，就要产生很多花粉，其花粉量会比昆虫传粉的植物所产生的花粉量多1~3个数量级。

---

40. However, these patterns cannot be viewed as an adaptation to wind pollination because the spiral arrangement occurs in a number of non-wind-pollinated plant lineages and is regarded as a characteristic of vascular plants, of which conifers are only one kind, as a whole.

However, **these patterns cannot be viewed as an adaptation** to wind pollination because the spiral arrangement occurs in a number of non-wind-pollinated plant lineages and is regarded as a characteristic of vascular plants, *of which* conifers are only one kind, as a whole.

【说明】

　　2个SVO，重点在because句之前的主句。第1个SVO的主干简单，these pattern cannot be viewed as an adaptation，意思是，这些模式不能被看做对风媒传粉的适应。第2个由because引导，且有并列谓语，都次要，第2个谓语的名词v(ascular) plants之后还有of which的从句修饰。对于该句，只需抓住主句的主干即可，because从句在读的时候仅需注意其位置，如果在考题中出现，可以通过主句的否定内容定位回来。从上下文看，本句是对前文给的内容的反驳或负评价。读者可看译文，然后想想，译文对理解句子意思有帮助吗？——似乎没多大帮助，心理安慰多于实际用处。句子分析，不只是翻译，主要还是抓住主干、联系上下文来理解其作用，揪住一个句子的单独的意思不放，尤其是其中的专业名词，这是走错路了。

【译文】

　　但是，这些模式不能被看做对风媒传粉的一种适应，因为这种螺旋形状出现于许多非风媒传粉的植物后裔，它被看做所有维管(vascular)植物的特征之一，松柏目植物(conifer)只是其中的一个类别而已。

---

41. In her recitals Duncan danced to the music of Beethoven, Wagner, and Gluck, among others, but, contrary to popular belief, she made no attempt to visualize or to interpret the music; rather, she simply relied on it to provide the inspiration for expressing inner feelings through movement.

In her recitals Duncan **danced to the music** of Beethoven, Wagner, and Gluck, among others, **but**, contrary to popular belief, **she made no attempt** to visualize or **to interpret** the music; rather, she simply relied on it to **provide the inspiration** for expressing inner feelings through movement.

【说明】

　　3个SVO，重点在but之后的rather句，各句内部的主语和宾语没有多少修饰成分，故相对简单。全句的意思是：D伴着音乐跳舞，但她并不试图解读音乐，而是依赖音乐提供舞动的灵感。(recital：独舞，朗诵，独唱；inspiration：灵感)

42. In order to understand the nature of the ecologist's investigation, we may think of the density-dependent effects on growth parameters as the "signal" ecologists are trying to isolate and interpret, one that tends to make the population increase from relatively low values or decrease from relatively high ones, while the density-independent effects act to produce "noise" in the population dynamics.

In order to understand the nature of the ecologist's investigation, **we may think of** the **density-dependent** effects on growth parameters as the **"signal"** *ecologists* are trying to isolate and interpret, *one that* tends to make the population increase from relatively low values or decrease from relatively high ones, while the **density-independent** effects act to produce **"noise"** in the population dynamics.

【说明】

2个SVO，由while连接。前一句的主干在in order to引导的介词短语（PP）之后：we may think of d-d effects as signal，宾语signal之后有貌似无关的名词ecologists，属于省略从句先行词（that/which）的从句的主语，中间的one that... 同位语及其从句，**就近修饰**它能修饰的第一个名词signal，与之前的that从句平行，两个平行的**修饰内容次要**。后面while句的主干很直接：d-i effects produce noise。该句的结构可以写成：PP, S V O-CP1-Cp2 vs. S V O。从语义上看，while暗示对比，**对比找反义，反义在宾语**，正好是signal vs. noise。全句的意思是，我们认为密度依赖因素是信号，认为密度独立因素是噪音。（parameter = factor：参数，变量；dynamics：动态，动态过程，动力学）

43. For populations that remain relatively constant, or that oscillate around repeated cycles, the signal can be fairly easily characterized and its effects described, even though the causative biological mechanism may remain unknown.

For populations *that* remain relatively constant, *or that* oscillate around repeated cycles, **the signal can be** fairly easily **characterized** and its effects described, even though the causative biological **mechanism may remain unknown**.

【说明】

本句包含主句与让步句，2个SVO，主句的主干重要，让步句注意位置。句子前面有介词短语，其中名词被并列的2个that从句修饰，皆次要。主句主干和让步句主干都很直接，没有过多的修饰成分。全句的意思是：对一些种群，信号容易刻画，即使生物机制也许未知。

* 比较句

44. The increase in the numbers of married women employed outside the home in the twentieth century had less to do with the mechanization of housework and an increase in leisure time for these women than it did with their own economic necessity and with high marriage rates that shrank the available pool of single women workers, previously, in many cases, the only women employers would hire.

The **increase in** the numbers of **married women** *employed* outside the home in the twentieth century had **less to do with the mechanization** of housework and an increase in leisure time for these women **than it did with** their own economic necessity and with **high marriage** rates *that* shrank the available pool of single women workers, previously, in many cases, the only women *employers* would hire.

【说明】

本句中，2个句子以比较级形式进行内容对比，重点在对比反义。第1个SVO的主语是长名词短语，np1 in np2 of np3，但np1，np2都属抽象名词，实义名词在np3，married women，抓住这个词，该名词之后有分词employed修饰；谓语动词have to do with = relate to = correlate with，暗示因果关系，而且还有否定词less；宾语为并列名词，可抓第一个名词mechanization。前半句意思是：就业的已婚女性增加，不大是因为机械化。后半句主语与前半句相同，谓语动词也相同，只是宾语不同，它的宾语依然是并列名词结构，可抓第1个或第2个名词，但由于第2个名词被that从句修饰，应属重点，故抓住high marriage rates，它被that从句第一层修饰，该从句里的宾语single women workers再被同位语the only women及其从句employers would hire修饰，该从句省略先行词that/which，**多层修饰皆次要**。后半句意思是：这更多是因为经济需要和高结婚率。从语义上看，由于出现less than比较，故重点在对比，**对比找反义，反义在宾语**，正好是：mechanization vs. marriage rates。

【译文】

20世纪在家庭之外就业的已婚女性数量增长，这不大是因为家务劳动机械化(mechanization)或这些女性休闲时间增长，而更多是因为她们自己的经济需要和高结婚率，高结婚率减少了单身女性工人的劳力资源库(pool)；而在20世纪以前，在多数情况下，这些单身女性是雇主所会雇用的唯一女性群体。

---

45. Just as economists were blind to the numerous cases in which the law of supply and demand left actual wants unsatisfied, so also many linguists are deaf to those instances in which the very nature of a language calls forth misunderstandings in everyday conversation, and in which, consequently, a word has to be modified or defined in order to present the idea intended by the speaker: "He took his stick — no, not John's, but his own."

Just as **economists were blind to** the numerous cases *in which* the law of supply and demand left actual wants **unsatisfied**, so also many **linguists are deaf to** those instances *in which* the very nature of a language calls forth **misunderstandings** in everyday conversation, *and in which*, consequently, a word has to be modified or defined in order to present the idea *intended* by the speaker: "He took his stick — no, not John's, but his own."

【说明】

本句共包含2个句子，比较相同，**比较找同义**，重点是同义词。前半句由just as引导，主干是economists were blind to cases，宾语名词cases之后有in which从句单层修饰，次要。后半句由so also引导，表相同，主干与前半句对称，linguists are deaf to instances，宾语名词instances之后有2个in which**并列从句修饰，次要**，第2个in which从句中的宾语被分词intended by修饰，该句之后还有冒号，给出1个句子作为**例子，次要**。全句的核心是：经济学者对一些情况视而不见，同样，语言学者也对一些例子充耳不闻。从语义上看，重点在同义词，这就是blind = deaf；由于宾语cases，instances是抽象词，如果要深入到宾语之后的in which从句内部，则可找到unsatisified = misunderstanding。

【译文】

经济学家对许多情况视而不见，即供应与需求的法则无法满足实际需要；与此相似，许多语言学者也对一些例子充耳不闻，在这些例子中，语言的本性会造成日常谈话的误解，因此，一个语词必须要修正或定义，才能表达说话人要说的意思，如"他拿了他的拐杖 ——不，不是约翰的，是他自己的。"

3.3 Frequently Asked Sentences 常考句子

我们已经知道，首句、转折句、态度句常会出考题。首句往往是论点、假说、模型、理论或观点的核心（kw），长文章的首段首句、一些短文章的首句往往就是整篇文章的主题句（TS），有时也会在末段或末句给出结论句（CS）。转折句往往会给出负评价（aw-）或者对立的观点（kw1 vs. **kw2**）。态度句通常以负评价句较为重要，由however, but, yet, nevertheless, although等引导给出。所以，TS, CS, kw, aw句都是常考内容，抓住它们不仅对文章整体结构把握、题干定位重要，而且对于解题也很重要。估计一个范围就是，2-3/10的题目都考首句、转折句和态度句的内容。此外，中间证据之间的对比、因果、并列尤其是连续并列等内容，也经常会出题，这又占2-3/10。这样，考文章、段落核心以及句子之间逻辑关系的题目就占了5-6/10，甚至更多。结构分析对于文章把握和解题的重要性，是不会被夸大的。

同时，中间证据句子的内容也会出考题。一种情况是，直接考句内的细节内容，我们称为纯**细节**题，或者说直接事实题，占1-3/10。只要通过题干的词汇找到相应的论点和论据，在选项中找到文字对应就可以了。另一种更常见的情况是，考中间证据句子内部出现的特殊表达，这些表达形式往往涉及句内和句间的逻辑关系，是GRE出题的重点，大约占3-5/10。GRE的出题主要不是针对某个细节进行专业考查，那不是GRE的任务；GRE的宗旨是为研究生院挑选出进行有效地批判思维、学术推理的人才。因此，GRE阅读的重心应该放在逻辑关系而非细节名词上。

我们将GRE常考的中间句子分为两类：

A. 大写词与专业名词

大写词在中间句首次出现时，通常表示它是举例。这时并不需要专业背景知识，只要提炼首字母（initial letters）就可以了。例如：

Hargrave and Geen: 取首字母H. G.
; say, Brahms or Schumann: 取首字母B. S.

除此之外，专业名词在中间首次出现，也很有可能是举例，例子的内容不重要，例子与前面论点的关系才重要。在任何情况下，中间句子首次出现的大写或专业名词，都容易出举例的作用题或in order to题型（见后面关于题型一章的分析）。例如：

, say, a hungry lizard...: 物种名，蜥蜴一词容易，可取首字母，也可直接记住
adrenaline and norepinephrine: 专业词汇，取首字母 a. n.；无论文章看多少遍，也无需知道中文译名
Lymnaea peregra: 斜体拉丁文物种名称，取首字母Lp
Anabaena: 斜体拉丁文物种名称，取首字母A.

现场阅读时，取首字母只是在大脑中进行，不必写在草稿纸上。记住它们的位置并不困难；即便忘了，考题时再定位，也不会很难。

B. 句子蕴含对比

句子内部**表示相同的**比较，可看做广义的对比范畴，虽然频率不高，但如果出现，也常常出考题，例如：

like, similar(=), as...as, comparable to

句子内部的**狭义对比**很多，文科文章的句子尤其如此，要注意这些句子，例如：

unlike(≠), rather than, more than(>), less...than..., different from, contrast, opposed to, comparable to; whereas, when...however..., while

部分时候，**时间对比**在一句之内或上下句之间出现时，也会出题，例如：

early, before, prior to, initially, originally;

later, recent, now, new;

until

一些语气很强、表示最高级、唯一性的词，我们称为**极端语言**，也常出题，例如：

only, first, most (*adj.*), the least

让步转折含有对比，属于广义对比的内容，可以在两句之间出现，也可以在一句之内出现，经常出题，尤其含有态度的让步转折，几乎必考，末句的让步转折，因为有总结的意味，也特别容易出题。关于让步转折的详细分析，请见本章第二节"Paragraph 段落"中"2.5 让步转折"。这里可以复习一下表示让步转折的部分词汇：

although, though, while; despite, in spite of + NP; as adj. as it is	[主句转折]
did/does(助动词), may be, may seem, might seem, there might be, there is some evidence	[But]
of course, certainly; undoubtedly, no doubt, no problem	[But]
It is true that, to be sure, Granted; this is not to deny	[But]

否定肯定的句型含有对比，少数时候，也会针对其中对比内容考题。例如：

not...but/instead/rather...

not to suggest...but...

请注意，否定肯定结构，不是…而是…，不是让步转折，而是分别表述一个话题的反面和正面，正面内容一定与前面的观点一致。因此，可以把该结构所在的整个意群表示为：kw. not a. but b/kw.

有时，只要有**否定词**，前后半句或前后两句就有可能出现对比，在文科文章中尤其如此，也容易出题。例如：

without, never, absent from, the lack of, far from, away from, not until

<小结>

以上相对零碎的内容可以简化为：**句内对比、让步，大写常考**。现场阅读时，注意这些句子的位置，甚至可将其中对比反义的内容找出来，做考题时定位起来就相对比较快速。我们不能对文章中的每个句子、每个单词都平等对待，而是要重点关注常考的位置。现场阅读文章的目的不是弄懂所有地方，而是为了做题，常考的就多关注，考得少的，就读快一些。事实上，在强大的时间压力下（150–160字/分），临时弄懂一篇自己专业之外的英文文章的所有内容，几乎是不可能的。考试的紧张感也会使这种看似美好的理想不可能实现。从文章的多层分析的理论角度看，认识单词、弄懂语法，无论速度快慢，也不能自动保证读懂文章；以为认识单词、看懂句子，文章就能看懂，那是幻觉。在现场，我们要做的不是读懂，而是迅速**识别结构、找出核心、抓住考点、定位做题**。

第四节　Words & Phrases 单词和短语

4.1　单词量8000–10000

虽然单词丰富并不能保证一定取得GRE阅读高分，但单词量肯定是阅读的一个必要条件。短语相对来说没有这么重要；在学术文章中，很少有短语是特别难的，这点与口语和日常对话相当不同。为简便起见，下面的分析均以单词来代替单词和短语。做一个粗略的估计，我们认为对于任何一篇GRE阅读文章，掌握95%左右的单词是必要的。一方面，动词(v.)、形容词(adj.)、抽象名词(n.)，认识得越多越好；另一方面，专业名词，例如物种名等，则不需要知道中文译名，取首字母即可。此外，在很多情况下，句子修饰成分里的内容即便有单词不认识、或者没看到，只要考题不涉及，也就不会影响做题。按粗略的估计，GRE阅读的词汇量需要8000以上，最好能到10000。这比中国大学英语4–6级要求的4000–5000的单词量高很多。所以，为了阅读，更不用说为了填空，都需要掌握很多单词。

是否应该先背单词再做阅读训练呢？不一定，甚至不是那么必要。先背单词再做阅读的一个假想结果是，等到单词背熟了，在阅读GRE文章的时候就没有任何生词。这种想法有点夸张，因为很难保证永远没有生词。但背一些单词，到看句子的时候顺一点，这是正常的。当然，单词并不是阅读所要求的唯一技能，阅读训练的中心是句子之间关系的训练，在有长句心理恐惧或理解障碍的情况下，还包括长句的训练。我们说，做任何训练，一定要明确训练的目标，最好是可观察、可量化的指标。因此，在单词方面，可以先看GRE的单词书1–2遍，然后就进行阅读训练。以后就是边做阅读或填空的训练，边背单词。单词的记忆不是一日之功，也不是一月之功。

在记单词时，除了直接背以字母顺序排列的单词书以外，还可以多看一些词根词源的书籍。粗略估计，80%左右的单词都有词根，然后加上前缀或后缀。词根书很重要。此外，还可以看一些同义词、反义词书，在这方面，Merriam-Webster出的*Synonyms and Antonyms*是比较好的，即*The Merriam-Webster's Synonyms and Antonyms*。

再强调一次：不能指望单词都记住了，文章就自然读懂了。文章并不只是单词的堆积，而主要是在论点与论据关系的层面上谈问题。解决这个问题，就需要做句子之间关系的分析、每个句子在文章中的作用(function)、论点与论据的核心内容(core)的分析。

GRE考试的单词释义标准是《韦氏大学词典》(*Merriam-Webster's Collegiate Dictionary*)，还有《美国传统词典》(*American Heritage Dictionary*)。阅读时，不必每个单词都用这两个字典查。也许80%的中文翻译是准确的，但也有一些英文单词在中文语境中难以找到对应，这时看英文释义就很有必要了。

4.2　特殊词汇

我们把一些对于GRE阅读比较重要的词汇称为特殊词汇，其中包含结构词或抽象词、态度词、关联词，它们多数都是属于提示文章主题、态度、观点、证据的词汇，因此也可以统称为提示词(cues)。

● 4.2.1 关联词

关联词(linking words)指那些提示句子之间和分句之间关系的词汇，多数表示并列、对比、让步转折等等。出现这些关联词时，相应的要寻找结构上的重心，例如对比找反义。详情可参见本章第二节"Paragraph 段落"里关于关联词的分析。

● 4.2.2 态度词

GRE阅读文章是学术文章的浓缩版，通常是作者给出态度，偶尔也会有一些人对另外一些人的研究或某个作品给出态度。鉴于是学术讨论，通常情况下，态度鲜明、公平、温和。所谓态度鲜明，就是不会模棱两可、模糊不清，对就对，错就错，部分对部分错，都会出现。当然，有些文章没有态度，平铺直叙，这是属于态度中立（neutral, objective），不算态度不鲜明。所谓态度公平，就是不会出现偏袒和偏见。最后，所谓态度温和，就是不会出现极端的语气，歌功颂德或者人身攻击的语言都不会出现在学术文章中。准确把握和理解态度词的含义，对于常考的态度题是重要的。下面针对文章和选项的态度词列举出一些例子，请读者理解其中词汇的态度褒贬色彩。

A. 文章中的态度词

负态度

aridly, disappointed, inadequacies, imprecise, unwarranted, premature, fanciful, fantastic, cavalier(*adj.*), discouraging, disproved, misleading, problematic, unpleasant shock, disagreement, danger, misplaced, omission, erroneously, unfortunately, unhappily, untenable, woefully, impractical, willy-nilly, dubious, not reliable=unreliable, unconvincing, unclear, weak, curiously, precipitously, naïve, puzzling, deficient, curse, bitter, careless, neglect, obscure, ignore, overlook, fail to, overestimate, underestimate, exaggerate, misinterpretation, reevaluation, question, critique, rush, would be, would have further strengthened; reexamine, reinterpret, reconsider, should be expanded, not the whole explanation, little explanatory value, negligible in significance, alone cannot explain..., consider only..., account for only..., based only on..., no reason to do..., be careful about doing..., be wary of..., revision, cannot, undermine, does not provide an adequate explanation, has its critics, make it difficult, prove difficult or impossible, unworthy of its author; awaits further study, undetermined, not yet explored, underexplored, remain to be answered, remain unresolved

正态度

valid, cogent, exciting, impressed with, support, rightly, enlightening, a way to answer, one way out of this dilemma, likely, benefits, pioneering, promising, make it possible, feasible, begin the process

B. 选项中的态度词

易对

正评价

admirable, accurate, valid, respectful, laudatory, concerned, interested, enthusiasm, hopeful, optimism, dispassionate, disinterested, objective, approval, tolerance, novel, fascinating, thorough, plausible, justified, verifiable, convincing, persuasive

负评价

inaccurate, disappointed, (deep) skepticism, disapproving, unpersuasive, pessimism, critical, biased/amused(possibly right), disagreement, unimaginative, reject, reservation, suspicious, skeptical; disparaging, condescending

易错

过正评价 superior

过负评价

shocked, apologetic, lighthearted, jocular, facetious, derision, ridicule, scornful, ironic, cynical, offensive, envious, indignation, angry, defiance, condemn, dogmatic, deprecating, hostility, stilted(= pompous + stiff), argumentative = contentious, pedantic, insincere, incredulity

模糊、不明确、矛盾心理

conciliatory, tender, ambivalence, uncertainty, unclear, ambiguous,

resigned

不关心 无所谓

indifference, detached

B' 态度选项中的限定词

易对限定词   qualified, guarded, limited,   incomplete, partially, tempered by,

易错限定词

reserved, moderate sharp, complete, categorical, strong, absolute unmitigated, unquestioning, unqualified, uncritical, relentless

● 4.2.3 结构词或抽象词

学术文章的一些词汇不是实指某个事物，而是表达一种抽象的概念，比如逻辑结构的概念、科学研究的环节等，这些词即便翻译成中文，如果我们没有关于文章结构的基本常识，也难以理解。下文列举一些重要的词汇，并做解释。以后在读到类似词汇时，可以快速把握其逻辑、结构上的含义，而不是觉得单词会翻译，然后就放过了。这个词表是在Passonneau *et al.* (2002)的基础上改编而成的。请读者尽量熟知这些词汇的结构含义。

according to	按照、依据；表顺承关系
admittedly	必须承认；常表让步
alternative	替代的；提示替代观点出现，其内容与前一观点相反
analogous, analogously	类似的/地；表相同比较
analysis, analyze	*n./v.* 分析；an analysis = a study
approach	研究方法；approach = view，提示观点
arguably	可认为是、也许是；表语气
argue, argument	*v.* 主张；提示观点 *n.* 论证、观点 = view
assume, assumption	*v./n.* 假设；表论点的基本前提，常在前1–2句中出现
basis	基础
belief	信念；可表观点；common belief = common view
categorize	分类
cause	*n.* 原因 *v.* 导致；表因果关系：a → b, =determine
compare, comparison	*v./n.* 比较；既可表相同，也可表不同
compatible	兼容的；一个观点与另一观点或事实相符
competing	相互竞争的；可表竞争的理论
concede, concession	*v.* 承认 *n.* 让步；常与核心相反: kw. ~kw. kw.
conceive, conceivably	*v.* 构思、设想 *adv.* 可设想地、或许
conclude, conclusion	*v./n.* 总结、结论；常出现在段落或论点末尾，重要
condition, conditional	*n.* 条件 *adj.* 以…为条件
consequence, consequently	*n.* 结果、后果 *adv.* 因此；常顺承或表示结论
consider, consideration	*v.* 考虑 *n.* 考虑因素；= factor
consistent	一致的；可表示论点与事实一致，为正评价
contrary, in contrast	相反、不同；表对比关系，常考
controversial	*adj.* 有争议的；可暗示负评价，也可为中性事实描述
controversy	*n.* 争议；暗示有不同的两个观点，= dispute, debate
converse, conversely	*adj.* 相反的 *adv.* 反过来；暗示有对比的观点
convincing	令人信服的；表正评价，同compelling
corollary	自然推论，必然推论；表顺承的推理结果
correlate with	与…相关；暗示因果关系，= vary with, have to do with
correspondingly	相应地；顺承关系，有时也表相似
counterpart	对应者；位置不同但功能相似，表相同
counterpoint	对应点；位置不同但作用互补，好似对立统一
counterproductive	反作用的；表负评价
critical, criticism	*adj.* 批评的、关键的 *n.* 批评；可表负评价或只是一个中性词
deduce, deduction	*v./n.* 演绎；从一般到特殊，到论点到论据的过程
define, definition	*v./n.* 界定，定义；表示一个术语的定义
demonstrate	证明、表明；表示从前提到结论的推理过程

design	设计
despite	虽然；表让步
determination, determine	*n.* 决心 *v.* 决定；常表因果关系，重要
difficulty	*n.* 困难，=problem；可表中性问题，或负评价
discover, discovery	*v./n.* 发现表事实，后有假说
discuss, discussion	*v./n.* 讨论；=study
disputable, dispute	*adj.* 可争辩的 *v.* 争议；=controversy, debate，表对立观点
distinct, distinguish	*adj.* 不同的 *v.* 区分；表对比
divide	*v.* 分开，(观点)分裂，=disagree, dispute
due to	因为、由于；表因果关系
empirical	经验性的；empirical study = science实证科学研究
entail	必然包含、逻辑蕴含；表示给出理论的推理
entity	实体；抽象名词，无特别含义
equally	同等地，平等地；表相同的比较
equivalence, equivalent	*adj.* 等价的 *n.* 等价者；表相同
establish	建立、确立；无特别含义
estimate	估计
evaluate, evaluation	*v./n.* 评价、评估；常用于评论型文章，后有态度
event	事件；抽象词，无其他含义，近于occurrence
evidence	证据；常在论点之后；表示用于支持或反对论点的论据
examination, examine	*n./v.* 考查、检查；=study, investigation
example, exemplify	*n.* 例子 *v.* 举例；表示并列的特例
except, exception	*prep.* 除非 *n.* 例外
exhibit	展示、显示；正常动词，表证据
exist	存在；有时 it is = it exists
experience	经验、经历
experiment	实验；常为证据，故有experimental evidence
explain, explanation	*v.* 解释 *n.* 解释、理论；表论点，=hypothesis
explicit	明显的、明示的；反义词为implicit
familiar	熟知的、熟悉的、常见的；常暗示现象
fail to	未能、无法做；否定含义，理论后出现表负评价
feasible	可行的；表正评价
granted	假定；引导让步语气，后有转折
guarantee	保证，担保；无特别的结构含义
hence	因此；表顺承，如在某句则表结论，= then, thus
hypothesis	*n.* 假说；近于model, theory, view，提示观点
hypothesize	*v.* 假设，= posit, presume；表示待检验的理论
idea	观点、理念；文科文章可表观点，=notion, view
identical	相同的、同一的；表相同的比较
illogical	不合逻辑的；表负评价

illustrate	*v.* 举例说明、具体说明；illustration近于example
impact	影响、冲击；有时表示结果，=effect
implication	含义；抽象名词，表示一个观点的隐含推理
implicit	暗示的、潜在的；反义词explicit
imply	暗示；常提示证据、推理，=suggest, indicate
incompatible	不兼容的；可表负评价，理论与事实或理论不符
inconsistent	不一致的，前后矛盾的；可表负评价
in addition	此外；表并列，= moreover, furthermore, also
in fact	事实上；表顺承，常为肯定陈述引导词，= indeed
in order to	为了；在句子之内表目的，无特别作用
in particular	特别是，尤其是；常给出重点
in response to	对…作出反应；表因果关系，= is due to
in the guise of	在…的伪装下；无特别作用
indeed	事实上；表顺承，常为肯定陈述引导词，= in fact
indicate	暗示；常提示证据，= imply, suggest, hint
indisputable	无可争辩的；可表正评价
induce, induction	*v.* 引发、诱发，表因果 *n.* 归纳，从特殊到一般
inextricably	无可逃脱地、难分难解地；强调语气，无特殊含义
infeasible	不可行的；可表负评价
infer	推理；如A>B推出B<A，逻辑保真，不是乱推
inform, informant	*v.* 告知 *n.* 知情人，被采访人
instead	相反，=rather；常与not配合，表否定肯定结构
intangible	无形的、不可触摸的；学术化词汇，无特别作用
interpret, interpretation	*v.* 解读、解释 *n.* 解释，= explanation, view
investigate, investigation	*v.* 调查 *n.* 研究、考查，= examination, survey
justification, justify	*n.* 辩护 *v.* 辩护、给出理由；可表论点成立的理由
knowledge	知识、知道；无特别作用
likelihood, likely	*n.* 可能性 *adj.* 可能的；常表正评价
limitation, limited	*n.* 局限 *adj.* 有限的；常表负评价
logical	逻辑的，合乎逻辑的；可表正评价
magnitude	量级；学术化词汇，无特别作用
maximize, maximum	*v.* 使最大化 *n.* 最大；反义词minimum
measure, measurement	*v.* 测量、衡量、评估 *n.* 量度
meanwhile	同时；该词连接对比的两个方面
method	方法；可引导观点和做法，=way, solution
minimize, minimum	*v.* 使最小化 *n.* 最小；反义词maximum
model	模型；可引导观点，= theory, mechanism
moreover	而且；表并列，= furthermore, in addition
nearly	接近、几乎；表程度
necessary	必要的、必需的、必然的；学术用词

negative, negatively	*adj.* 否定的 *adv.* 否定地，消极地；可用于negative correlation负相关
negligible	可忽略的、不重要的，= unimportant, insignificant
nevertheless	但是；表转折，=nonetheless, however
numerical	数量上的
notable	显著的、知名的；=noticeable, significant
notion	*n.* 概念，=idea；观点，= view, theory, contention
notwithstanding	尽管；表让步，=despite, in spite of
novel	*adj.* 新奇的、新颖的；= new, creative, fresh
observation, observe	*n./v.* 观察；常提示事实、现象，后文常有假说、解释
objection	*n.* 反对；= disapproval；来自object *n.* 对象 *v.* 反对
occurrence	*n.* 发生、事件；近于event, accident
on the other hand	另一方面；提示对比的另一方
optimum	最优；学术用词，无特别作用
otherwise	否则、原本；常表相反
ostensibly	明显地；可表程度，学术用词，无特别作用
outweigh	*v.* 超出
overestimate	高估；是负评价，反义词underestimate也是
paradigm	范例，样式；表一套理论框架，学术用词，无特别作用
particular	*adj.* 特别的，= specific；与general相对
particularly	*adv.* 特别地；= in particular，强调重点
parameter	参数；近于factor；学术用词
pattern	模式；近于regularity, mode，常表现象的特征
percent, percentage	百分比；表比例
permanently	恒久地、恒定地
pertinent	切合的；可表正评价
phase	阶段；可表时间过程的一段，= stage, time, period
phenomenon	现象；=fact, observation；后有假说、模型
positive, positively	肯定的/地；表正相关positive correlation
possibility	可能性；暗示另一种理论可能，可提示另一观点
possible	可能的；有时表正评价
potentially	潜在地、可能地；=possibly
predict	预测；假说之后可预测，可表用于验证的推理
previously	以前；常与recent形成时间对比
primarily, primary	*adv.* 主要地 *adj.* 主要的、第一的；无特别作用
probability, probable	*n.* 概率 *adj.* 可能的
probably	*adv.* 很可能、也许；近于perhaps, presumably
problem, problematic	*n.* 问题；可为中性词或负评价 *adj.* 有问题的；表负评价
process	过程；可暗示连续动作，= procedure, mechanism
propensity	倾向、取向；近于tendency, inclination
prove	证明；常为证据、实验证明某一假说、观点

rather	相反；not...rather...表否定肯定；rather than表对比
rationale	原理、理由；= reason, principle
reason, reasoning	n. 理由，= factor v. 推理 n. 推理，近于argument
recently	近来、最近；常与previously等形成时间对比
reduce	减少，= lower；reduce to X，还原，explain...by X
redundant	冗余的、备用的；如汽车备胎，近于backup
regardless of	无论、不管；不考虑某一因素或条件
relation	关系；理科文章中极重要，表相关correlation
relative, relatively	adj. 相对的 adv. 相对地；relative to 相对于，表比较
reliability	n. 可靠性；无特别作用 adj. reliable可靠的；表正评价
require, requirement	v. 要求 n. 要求；可表理论的前提和条件
research	研究；= study, attempt, endeavour, discussion
respective, respectively	adj. 分别的 adv. 分别地、各自地；无特别作用
result	n. 结果，= effect, impact v. 导致，= cause
reveal	揭示；可引导观点或事实的具体内容
rigorous, rigorously	adj. 严谨的 adv. 严谨地；正评价；与rigid（僵硬的）不同
riskier	更有风险的；可表比较，负评价
salient	显著的；近于ostensible, marked, pronounced
science	科学；在英文中仅指经验科学，empirical science
severe, severity	adj. 严重的 n. 严重性；表程度强，近于grave
significantly	显著地；近于considerably, notably
similarly	类似地；表并列或相同的比较
simultaneous	同时的
since	自从；因为，= because, for, as，表句内原因
specific, specifically	adj. 特定的，= particular，与general相对 adv. 特殊地
specify	v. 具体指定
speculate, speculative	v. 推测、投机、思辨 adj. 思辨的、推测的，vs. empirical
stable, stability	adj. 稳定的；可表正评价 n. 稳定性；表性质
still	依然；有时可表并列
stipulate	详细规定；近于require, dictate, mandate（that）
strengthen	加强、强化；可用于证据支持某一假说
strictly	严格地
structure, structured	n. 结构 adj. 有结构的，结构化的
study	n. 研究，= research, attempt, endeavour v. 研究
subsequent	后来的、随后的；近于consequent
substantially	实质地、显著地；表程度significantly, considerably
success	成功；successfully 成功地；表正评价
successive	相继的、连续的；近于consecutive
sufficient, sufficiently	充分的、足够的；充分地；可表正评价，= adequate
suggest	提出、暗示、表明；= indicate, imply

summarize	总结、概括；表结论，= conclude
suppose, supposition	*v.* 假设，= posit, assume *n.* 假设，近于assumption
susceptibility	易受影响；genetic susceptibility, 遗传易感性
susceptible	易受影响的；= responsive to, subject to, prone to
systematic	系统的；近于methodical
tangible	有形的、可接触的；常表示物质、经济方面
technique	技术；近于technology
temporarily	暂时地
theoretical, theory	*adj.* 理论性的 *n.* 理论，=view, hypothesis, model
therefore	因此；常在观点结束处表结论，=thus, hence
thus	因此；常表结论，=thus, therefore；或表顺承动作
tradeoff	此消彼长；表两个因素守恒，一个升、一个则降
traditional	传统的；=conventional；常与recent表时间对比
true	*adj.* 真的，用于理论表正评价；it is true, 表让步
truth	真实性，真相；truth of a theory表理论与事实相符，正评价
ultimately	最终；近于finally，表动作或并列的最后一项
unconditional	无条件的
undeniably	无可否认地；双重否定表程度，也可表让步
underestimate	低估；表负评价，反义词overestimate也是
understand, understanding	*v.* 理解 *n.* 知识，理解
undoubtedly	无疑；= no doubt，常引导让步语气，后有转折
unfamiliar	不熟悉的
uniformly	一致地、均匀地；uniform motion: 匀速运动
unique	特殊的、独一无二的；暗示对比，近于only
unless	除非，=if not
unquestionably	毫无疑问地；常表程度
unusual	不同寻常的；暗示对比
valid, validate, validity	*adj.* 有效的；表正评价 *v.* 证实 *n.* 有效性；中性词
variance, variation	变异、方差；变异，近于difference, variety
vary	*v.* 变化 = range；vary with = correlate with, relate to
weaken	削弱、弱化；可表反对，近于undermine, undercut
weigh	*v.* 衡量；= measure
widely	广泛地；widely accepted /common view, 常被否定
yield	*n.* (农业)收成 *v.* 产生，= produce

第五节　Online Reading: Minimal Solution 阅读现场：最简方案

练好GRE阅读，需要注意4个原则：

阅读训练四大原则

原则1：先读文章后看题目

除了少数只有1道题的文章以外，多数文章都要先读文章后看题目。与托福和其他英语考试不同，GRE的出题顺序与原文的行文顺序并不对应。很多题目考的不是句子的细节内容，而是句子之内、句子之间的逻辑关系，先读题目对于预测考题是没有多大作用的。而且，先看题干再读文章找题干考的内容的做法，听起来很美好，其实很难操作。读文章的时候，精力高度集中，很难忽然停下来仔细看某一句，因为那样很容易丧失整体的结构感。同时，差不多半数以上的考题都与文章、段落的整体结构、论点与论据之间的关系有关，先看题目对把握这个方面毫无帮助。所以，扎扎实实地分析文章的写作或逻辑结构模式，然后再做题，这几乎是唯一可行的途径。只要将结构分析训练好、题型分类熟悉好，速度和正确率就会逐渐上去。

原则2：题目 > 文章

就考试本身来说，题目永远比文章重要。不要花太多时间读文章。文章看得一定尽量快，要把主要的时间放在做题本身，因为最终是正确解题决定了分数。文章里面出现的生词，看过就算了，不用翻译、不用查背景知识。即便那些基础词汇，万一现场没有反应出来，只要做题的时候不考，也就不必纠缠。一切以做题为依归。

原则3：首句 > 中间

各段的首句通常都是重点。转折句相当于首句。一些由像alternative, another theory等引起的过渡句，即便不在首句，也要读如首句。换言之，提示论点、态度的句子，都比其后的证据、例子、推理过程重要。在读的时候，认真读、相对仔细读的，一定是这些句子，而不是中间的推理细节。

原则4：每篇文章反复训练三遍

文章一定要反复训练，第1遍是计时阅读和做题，第2遍分析文章结构，写出核心词（core）和作用词（function），第3遍分析所有题目考的文章位置，将句子找出，想想是如何出题的。这3遍的工作可以在1-2天的短时间内完成。

遵循这些原则，按照正确方法，进行阅读的集中训练以后，就能掌握阅读的结构分析的方法，快速提取文章的核心信息。

总结本章关于文章、段落、句子的3个层次的分析，我们可以得出，现场阅读的关注重点是：

文章：结构性句子：首末句，however yet but 句，态度句
段落：对比找反义；因果找双方；机制找末句；并列找并列
中间句：让步、对比、大写词与专业名词

从这三个角度提炼信息才是阅读的中心任务。GRE的阅读不是：认识生词、分析语法、翻译句子、记住每个单词、拼凑中心大意。

落实到现场阅读和做题，在看文章的时候，我们可以想想这几个问题：

- 几个论点，什么态度？首句/转折句/过渡句
  - — 略读证据、举例、具体推理步骤
  - — 不用完全精确把握结构核心词，抓住70%就行
  - — kw：**句子主干原则**（主干里面有核心）；**新词原则**（核心通常是主干词汇里以前没出现的词）
- 句子：
  - — 长句抓主干：np1 v np1
  - — 宾语从句，单独分析 argue that / demonstrate that
  - — 略读所有修饰，分词/从句/连续并列，甚至可能出题的让步语气despite, even though，仅注意其位置，考时通过结构和位置记忆定位，找出题点，在选项中找文字对应
- 论点的论据：
  - — 对比找反义　　这一条最重要，在文科文章常见：文科讲对比
  - — 因果找双方　　在理科文章中常见：理科讲因果
  - — 并列记位置　　不太重要，并列的内容很多，通常不需要仔细记忆，看过后记得大致位置即可

最简单的说法就是：

几个论点　　　　　　**什么态度**
长句抓主干　　　　　**对比找反义**

这就是结构化阅读法（Structuralized Reading）最精练的表达。

很多年前的假日，校园的人都走了，我在自习室或图书馆读书，累了在绿树成荫的校园游走。自那以后多年以来的假日，无不是与努力奋斗的同学们一起在教室度过。想念多年未见的烟雨迷蒙绿柳才黄的家乡的春天，想念满眼金黄等待收获的秋天的原野。假日的匆忙是为了日后的收获么？是的。静静守候属于你的季节。

GRE 题目的题型和解法

做题的时间、准确率、步骤

GRE阅读的速度是150–160words/min；做题的时间平均为1minute = 1'，有的题目相对容易，可30seconds = 30''完成，有的题目，比如无法定位某个句子的信息题，则可能花上1.5minutes = 1.5'。这是考试的速度要求，达到这个要求，就可以在17分钟（17'）左右完成所有文章的阅读和做题。为了取得理想的分数，正确率达到7/10 = 70%是相对合适的。

	Section（含长文）	Section（纯短文）	考试要求
长 450 ± 20字	1篇，4题	0篇，0题	450words/2.5–3min, 1min/question
短 160 ± 20字	1篇，2–3题	1篇，3–4题	160words/1min, 1min/question
短 120 ± 20字	2篇，1–2题	3篇，1–2题	120words/50seconds, 1min/question
逻辑 40–80字	1篇，1题	1–2篇，1题	1–1.5min
总计	4+1篇，10题	4+（2–1）篇，10题	17 ± 1 min; 正确率7/10

先读文章后看题干，看了题干以后，通常先不看选项，而是以题干所问内容，回原文定位，找到相应的句子，大概知道答案以后，再到选项中找预想答案的中心词。有它的同义词或等价词的选项可先保留，通常2–3个，作为候选。没有这些预想答案中心词的选项可直接排除，通常不必读完这些选项（choices）的所有词汇。这一点对于选项特别长的题目尤其有效，这时通常不可能将每个选项都看一遍，因为那已经相当于一篇短文章的阅读量了，考试现场没有那么多时间花在5个选项上。剩下的时间主要用来比较2个候选选项的差别、仔细看哪个与原文句子更加对应。这样，1'做题的时间分配基本如下：

1' = 60''

3–5''：读题干

5–10''：定位原文

40''：选项比较–原文对应

要能在如此短的时间之内**读完题干**、**定位原文**、**排除干扰选项**、**比较候选选项**，同时还保证正确率，这需要对题型解法、出题方式、结构模块、常考位置、选项设置等方面特别熟悉，才能熟能生巧。在前面的章节，我们分析了结构模块和常考句子，本章则主要分析题型、题干、选项这三个方面。考生在大概了解每个方面的模式和规律以后，就要通过大量的集中练习来掌握这些内容，将它们变成自动反应的神经回路。单纯做题，只做一次，不做题目的分解目标分析和训练，肯定是不够的。

在做题时，要尽量定位，切忌凭印象做题，一开始尤其要注意。因为如果是5个选项，通常有3个容易排除，还有2个选项差异细小，故意设计陷阱，它们多数成分都等价，只有1–2个词有差别。这时，必须对照原文。这一点对除了逻辑推理以外的所有题目都适用。只有到了训练的后期阶段，对题目出题方式已经了如指掌，才可以考虑在做部分题目时直接看选项，但也仅限于那些容易排除的选项，在比较其中2个相似选项时，依然要回原文定位确认。

第一节　题型与解法

按照从题干出发定位原文的情况，可以把GRE题目分为3大类，每一类又包含一些小类。

核心题　针对主题、结构、态度发问。细分为主题题、结构题、态度题。
信息题　针对全文或全段内容发问，无法从题干定位某个句子，选项分散对应原文。仅信息题一种。
定点题　针对某个特定句子发问，可分为细节题、列举题、取非题、作用题等。

考推理的逻辑题相对独立，常常针对一篇短小的文章出题，没有计算在内。另外一种考推理的类比题，针对文中某个句子出题，做题时不必牵涉文章的理解，我们也会单独分析。

从问法来看，新GRE阅读题有3种情况：

Select only one answer choice.

5选1的单选题。这种类型比例最高，一个Verbal Section除10道填空以外的10道阅读题中，大约有7–9道单选，占比是7–9/10。本身不是题型，只是问法。

Consider each of the three choices separately and select all that apply.

3选多的多选题。凡是只有3个选项的题目，就是多选题。题目上方通常会有如上所示的做题指引。多选题可以选3个，选2个，也可以选1个。要全部选中才能得分。约占1–2/10。本身不是题型，只是问法。

Select the sentence that ....

选择句子题。在计算机考试的界面上，鼠标点一下某句的任何一个单词，该句就会全部刷黑，这就等于做出答案了。选择句子题一般就是考句子的功能作用。由于它与作用题/in order to题型高度贴近，我们把它放在后面，与作用题一起讨论。

问法并不是最重要的。重要的始终是按定位分类的题型及其解法。下面我们分别说明，其中多数会举例；例子都是作者仿照从前考题的思路自己编写的。

1.1　核心题

出题比例2–3/10=20%–30%，问主题或态度或结构。定位到首段/首句、转折句的TS解题。对新老观点文章，主题在负评价和新观点，对其他类别文章，主题在长文首段某句、短文第1–3句或however/but/yet句。

● 1.1.1 主题题

主题题的题干容易分辨，常常出现表示主要观点、总结文章之类的词，例如：

Which of the following statements best **summarizes** the **main idea** of the passage?

Which of the following **titles** would best describe the content of the passage?

The author of the passage **is primarily concerned with** discussing

解法：有TS，定位TS；无TS，则找CS；无CS，则综合各个kw，即综合各个观点，包括表示态度的however句。

● 1.1.2 结构题

结构题问整篇文章或长文中某个段落的写作方式和主要目的，例如：

The **primary purpose** of the passage is to

Which of the following is the most accurate description of the **organization**?

Which of the following best describes the **organization of the last paragraph** of the passage?

解法：综合各段首句

特定的文章结构有特定的词汇与之对应。

现象解释前负后正: phenomenon-explanation(s) / theory(-ies)

新老观点相互对比: new / novel / alternative theory; correct / revise / challenge / dispute an old theory / a long-held belief / a widely accepted thesis

总分结构展开论点: general view / thesis-illustration / developed; evidence supports a theory

(＊评述: review / evaluate / summarize and evaluate / assess a recent study / a scholarly research / a new book)

● 1.1.3 态度题

最直接的判断方法是，选项为态度词。题干通常没有明显标志，虽然有时也会有一些表示态度的词出现，如author's attitude, drawback, weakness, value highly。一个完整的题干例子是：

It can be inferred from the passage that the author **considers** the theory discussed in the second paragraph **to be**

解法：定位到态度句。由于负评价常考，通常会定位however, but, yet转折句，或有类似fail to, underestimate, little value等表示负评价词汇的句子；有时，让步转折也会含有态度，可以定位；少数情况下，态度词可能是句内插入成分，如though skeptical, as excellent as it is。

有时原文的态度既有正评价、又有负评价，这时与之对应的是混合评价的选项。混合评价的选项的表示方法有两种：

1）but, though, without, while, despite，用转折或对比关联词连接，不能用and 连接。

2）限定词+态度词，如qualified *agreement*。起到类似限定作用的词汇有：tempered by, guarded, restrained, partially, critically, mild, limited，它们与不同态度的词汇组合在一起，可表示混合评价，如mild skepticism（温和的怀疑，有怀疑有赞同），guarded optimism（谨慎的乐观，有乐观有悲观），partially correct（部分正确，有正确有错误）。

关于态度词的一个相对详细的说明，请参考第二章第四节"Words & Phrases 单词和短语"一节关于"4.2 特殊词汇：态度词"的讨论。

1.2　信息题

出题比例1-2/10=10%-20%。发问对象涉及多句或全文内容，无法精确定位单独某个句子，选项分散对应原文各句，通常是段中的首末句的论点和结论句、让步、对比等句。

这种题目的题干通常是：

The passage supplies **information** that would answer which of the following questions?

也有可能出现部分词汇，但它们仅仅只是某段甚至全文的主题词，所以，依然要定位全文。

The author would be likely to agree with which of the following statements regarding political offense exception

（这里的political offense exception是全文的主题）

解法：题干全文定位＝无法精确定位某句 → **从选项找线索 带核心去排除**

先想出题目所问段落或全文的核心（在首末段/首末句、转折句），然后直接看选项，但不要定位每个选项内容，因为有2-3个选项很容易看出是错的。

a）核心排除 → 首末句排除（2-3个选项与主题无关、与结论相反、与态度相反）

b）2个再定位 → 剩下的选项以其中的名词或其他帮助定位的词汇（大写、时间、数字等）定位原文内容。

1.3　定点题

出题比例5-7/10=50%-70%。考查某句内容，不牵涉上下文。只要不是考主题、结构、态度和全文信息的，就是定点题。定位之后直接将原句改写即为正确答案。答案为原句的语言变换，有时加上逻辑变换。做题步骤：**题干分析—回文定位—预想答案—对照选项/在选项中找答案中心词**。定位后按照常出题的模式，想想答案中心词，然后带着中心词去看选项，快速排除包含完全没有中心词的同义词或反义词的2-3个选项，剩余2个选项，比较其差异，再以差异定位原文，仔细对照，确定答案。下面的例子都省去了定位过程，主要谈题干、选项与原文的对应。

尽量**不要先读选项**。因为不是通过选项定位，而是通过题干定位。甚至也不是看了选项之后就想一阵，每个选项都仔细想，现场是没有这么多时间的。此外，即使选项说的内容，在原文中有，但与题干没关系，也不能作为答案。

请注意，题干往往出现according to, infer, imply, suggest, indicate等词，在做题方面没有实质差别。连官方指南等材料都说，according to 问的是explicitly stated/明确表述，infer, imply, suggest, indicate问的是inference/推理，或者implicitly stated/暗示。但出题人使用的inference，仅指最基本的逻辑变换，例如A > B → B < A，在逻辑上保真、前后一致，不是我们的日常"推理"，比如我听说A → B，于是我说A → X，或者A → B → X，这些都不是逻辑保真的推理，而是错误。所以为了避免误解，我们可认为inference题不存在。所有题目都要找对应就可以了。那些逻辑单题，与这里的inference没关系。

● 1.3.1. 细节题

在10道阅读题里，细节题约占1–3/10。针对某一细节内容发问。这种题型和其他题型不一样，没有明显的判断词汇，虽然题干经常有according to, infer, suggest等词汇。细节题也可以用多选的问法出题，这时答案可以多选，也可以单选，做题方法一样。

解法：提炼题干名词，确定结构模块，定位原文意群或句子。意群指的是一个观点或态度及其证据的若干句子的整体。这时，答案就是定位句的**文字对应、同义改写**。这时答案通常不牵涉上下文，只是针对定位的句子本身，在选项中找文字对应，而文字对应最常见的情况就是同义词改写，甚至有时就是照抄多数词汇、少数词汇同义改写。

▶ 例 1 ◀

Most disruptions and interventions that occurred during the development of culture virtually have little effect on the landscape of culture of a nation since the mindset of people will only "absorb and ingest" those proven, steady facts and ideas accumulated in the long run, with transitory and capricious ideologies being sifted out.

Which of the following statements about landscapes of culture can be inferred from the passage?

(A) They are composed of the successive periods of cultural development.

(B) They are influenced by large changes in the cultural vicissitudes.

(C) They are slightly adapted each time as they are interpreted by people.

(D) They are not readily modified by interferences and disturbances as the culture develops.

(E) They are preserved in the libraries and museums that are immediately accessible to the people.

【说明】

本题考的是文化地形图的具体内容。题干有about X，提问对象就是X，infer不起实质作用，可忽略。答案仅对应原句的前半段，后半句的since从句没有发挥有效作用。

A. successive，相继的；原文无此状态，迅速排除。

B. large change，原文没有大或小的变化，因此排除。数量词可以优先判断。

C. slightly，轻微地，表程度；程度词属于广义数量词，原文没有，迅速排除。后面的each time也是无关数量。

D. 正确。对应关系见字体对应。Most disruptions and interventions that occurred during *the development of culture virtually* have **little effect** = They are **not readily modified** by interferences and disturbances as the *culture develops*. 其中，development = develop，词性从名词变成动词，**词性变换**是改写的常见形式；interference = intervention, disturbance = disruption，相当常见的**同义改写**。另外，effect = readily modified，有效果就是能够改变，无效果就是不易改变，依然等价。

E. 原文没有提到immediately这样的副词；accessible，可接近的、易理解的。

细节题的文字对应的解法对于任何题目都是合适的，比如，主题题的答案也必须与主题句的文字形成一一对应。下面这个例子所考的内容虽然也是原文的一个特定句子，但它同时就是文章的主题句(TS)。

► **例 2** ◄

In fact, the fruits of studies to link neuronal structures to consciousness and perception seem to be still bitter.

The passage is primarily concerned with discussing views of the

（A）anatomy of the neuronal structures

（B）ways in which neuronal transmitters function

（C）significance of various neuronal areas in mental activity

（D）mechanical foundations of sense perception

（E）physiological correlates of some kinds of psychological experiences

【说明】

原文本身有负评价，认为一些研究的成果苦涩，是一个总的看法和判断，等于文章或段落的主题。题干问is primarily concerned with，为主题题，与主题句对应。由于题干问的是观点在研究什么，则原句最重要的词是link。有这个中心词的选项候选，没有的先排除。

A. 只讲到解剖结构：anatomy，没有涉及原文所说的关系，link(关系)是两个事物之间的联系。

B. 选项里的neuronal transmitters与原文的neuronal structure不同。

C. 只谈到area问题，不是原文讲的关系。

D. 只讲了mechanical foundations，不是讲神经结构与知觉、意识的联系。

E. **正确**。这时，studies to <u>link</u> *neuronal structures* to **consciousness and perception** = *physiological* <u>correlates</u> of some kinds of **psychological experiences**。其中，neuronal structures，神经结构，属于广义的生理范畴，所以，physiological虽然不是同义词，但是**上义词改写**或抽象改写，可以接受。联系link = 相关correlate。

● **1.3.2 列举题**

在10道题中占0~1/10左右，出题频率不算低。只要能够定位，列举题属于送分题。可分两种：

连续列举 原文连续并列3-4个内容，如", , and"结构，或者"; ; and"结构，或者连续单句并列，问哪个有(或没有)提到: mention/cite/refer to/state（EXCEPT）。相对常见。

论据列举 原文存在并列证据，问"作者提到哪个是缺陷(weakness)或理由(reasons)"，答案为并列其中之一。

► **例 3** ◄

Civil rights activists should consider conferring material benefits on the disadvantageous group, enhancing the media exposure of the conditions of minority, promoting the realization of "equal work equal pay" principle, and urging government to open official positions to the minorities who are obviously qualified.

The passage mentions each of the following as an appropriate kind of civil rights activists' action EXCEPT

（A）assigning governmental jobs to a certain group of people

（B）encouraging equitable pay between minority and majority

（C）facilitating the accessibility of minority conditions to the people

（D）mandating the percentage goal of minority representation in a certain social organization

（E）ensuring that disadvantageous groups obtain benefits

【说明】

　　原文有连续逗号引起的并列成分，在读的时候，位置 > 内容，不需要记住每个项目。等到看考题时再定位。本题题干有mention...EXCEPT，考连续并列，appropriate = 原文should。既然问题要求找没有的，那些有的就不需要精确定位和改写，模糊的有就可以（下文解释依然作了详细说明）。重要的是找**精确的没有**。一个精确没有的内容，往往与原文的主题、态度**无关或相反**。从这个角度出发，可以提高对正确答案的敏感度。

A. 分配政府工作给某些人，原文有文字对应：urging government to **open** *official positions* to the minorities who are obviously qualified = **assigning** *governmental jobs* to a certain group of people. 除了同义改写以外，这里 还用a certain group这个抽象说法，改写了原文的一个具体群体minorities who are obviously qualified，可以称为**抽象改写**。

B. **promoting** the realization of "*equal work equal pay*" principle = **encouraging** *equitable pay* between minority and majority。原文的主题内容是讲minority与majority工资平等，虽然本句内容原文并没有直接提到，但在选项中出现了文章的主题词，因此无影响。

C. **facilitating** the accessibility of *minority conditions* to the people = **enhancing** the media exposure of *the conditions of minority*。人们可接近accessible，在这里就等价于媒体曝光和报道media exposure。

D. **正确**。选项说规定百分比目标mandating the percentage goal，但原文中没有percentage或类似的数量词。题干问的是EXCEPT，因此该选项是正确答案。

E. **ensuring** that *disadvantageous groups* obtain benefits = **conferring** material benefits on the *disadvantageous group*。这里，benefit = material benefit，由于原句是从文章中抽出的，所以全文谈的关于物质利益的主题在本句内没出现。其实，利益也多数就是物质利益。即便脱离上下文，也可以作出这个推断。

● 1.3.3 取非题

　　出题频率较高，10道题占大约1~2/10。这时题干往往出现 would...if, might...if 或 differ from 等词，需要取非原文明确表述的部分内容来作答案，因此称为取非题。由于通常都是通过定位原文某句来做题，其实也可归入细节题。取非的定义是增加或减去否定词not/little/never等。只有A无否定词的，取非就是NOT A；A也有否定词的，取非之后就只有A了。

A: NOT A

NOT A: NOT（NOT A）= A

1.3.3.1 态度取非

　　原文：负评价 = AW-，多在转折句或however/but/yet句，有时也作为插入成分出现。AW-前后常有条件或原因，可以称为负评价及证据，或者负评价及原因。属于常考内容。也可能会有正评价取非的。

　　题干：...would have been more convincing / would be more valid / would be improved / might be not useful if...

　　虚拟语气would与AW一起，暗示原文其实是该态度的反面。这可以看做态度的另一种考法。

　　解法：定位态度句、找出原因、取非原因或态度本身

　　写成公式就是（主要以AW-为例）：

　　原文：AW- because / if X 或AW-. X.

　　题干：would AW+ if... ?

　　答案：NOT X.

原则上，可能出现的情况是，原文是正评价AW+，题干以would AW- if... 给出，这时答案依然是取非条件或原因。正评价取非的情况在GRE中相对少见，常见的还是负评价取非。

▶ 例 4 ◀

To be a reliable source of information, the archaeological material must have retained the signal unaffected by the geographical and geological changes in the area.

It can be inferred that the signal found in the archaeological material would be less useful to archaeologists if it

（A）could not be deciphered by modern scientific means

（B）reflected a change in the surface of earth rather than a stable climatic history

（C）was written into the material as the material took shape

（D）also reflected the changes in geological and geographical conditions

（E）was not subject to geographical and geological changes

【说明】

这是正评价取非的例子。题干有would be less useful，而原文其实是正评价。通过题干的archaeological material定位，找到它的肯定判断，然后将支持这个判断的条件、原因或证据取非，或者直接将正评价取非。原句说，考古学材料必须保持信号(或讯息)不受地理和地址变化的影响。题干将原文的肯定语气must变成否定语气less useful，这时答案就应该把另外一部分取非，说它受到影响即可，也就是affected by changes。

A. 没有提到存在影响，无关，deciphered = decoded。

B. 动词reflect = affected by，但后面的对比rather than，原句没有。

C. 写进材料这些说法没提到。

D. 正确。动词reflect = affected by，取非了原文的unaffected by。其他地方一样。

must have retained the signal **unaffected by** the *geographical and geological changes* = **would** be **less useful** ... if ... **reflected** the changes in *geological and geographical conditions*

E. 干扰选项。不受影响not subject to，没有取非，完全等于原文，没考虑题干的虚拟语气。

▶ 例 5 ◀

The evidence of group selection does apparently exist in some species, but one must be cautious about attributing social reciprocity to group selection. For instance, the blood-sharing by regurgitation with relatives and even occasionally with non-relatives among vampire bats is critical for the survival of younger individuals in the group, thereby inadvertently making the species prosper. However, this kind of behavior cannot be viewed as being selected for the group itself because the

The passage implies that the assertion that the blood-sharing by regurgitation with relatives and even occasionally with non-relatives among vampire bats is an instance of group selection might be more convincing if which of the following were true?

（A）Such a behavior occurred among familiar non-relatives.

（B）Such a behavior occurred regardless of genetic relatedness and the possibility of reciprocity.

（C）Such a behavior could be proven to be conducive to reproductive success.

（D）The amount of blood regurgitated could be revealed to have increased over time.

frequency of the sharing behavior highly depends on the genetic relatedness of individual vampire bats and the benefactor only helps those individuals it makes acquaintance within a group, who then are expected to reciprocate.

（E）The cognitive development of vampire bats could be shown to be shaped by such a behavior.

【说明】

题干有 might be more convincing if ... true，虚拟语气 + 正评价词 convincing，说明原文其实是负评价；负评价取非题。因此**定位负评价及其原因或证据**。原文有3句，按先后顺序就是：负评价句（aw-）、举例（example=e.）、反驳及其并列原因（x, y），可以表示为：aw-. e. aw-: x, y.。第1句 be cautious about 为负评价，认为社会互惠(social reciprocity)不能归因于群选择(group selection)；但该句只有孤零零的负评价，没有原因或证据。第2句由 for instance 引导，给出一个例子，讲了一种蝙蝠分享血的行为。第3句用 however, cannot be viewed，否定对上述互惠行为的 group selection 解释，该句的负评价内容等于第1句：cannot be viewed as being selected for the group = cautious about attributing social reciprocity to group selection。该句还有 because 引导的2个原因。于是，答案就定位在第3句的 because，不必看第2句例子里的具体内容！第3句 not group selection because X and Y；题干问 might be convincing if? 则答案应该是 not X 或者 not Y。原文负评价及其原因，题干问如何变成正评价，答案就说取非原因。第3句在阅读时，只要记住负评价 not group selection，不必记住 because 的内容；考题时再通过题干的态度信息定位回来就可以。

A. familiar non-relatives = those individuals it makes acquaintance within a group（because 的后半句），直接对应，未取非原因。

B. 正确。 第3句 because 原因从句讲两点，一点是依赖基因关联(genetic relatedness)，一种是只帮那些回报互惠(reciprocate)的熟人，只有熟人才有互惠的可能性。本选项用 regardless of 将两者同时取非。对应的情况是：*cannot be viewed as* being selected for the group because...**depends on** the genetic relatedness...only helps those individuals it makes acquaintance = *might be more convincing* **if**...**regardless** of genetic relatedness and the possibility of reciprocity

C. 无关。这种行为于繁殖成功有益(conducive to: 有帮助、有作用)，没有取非 because 里的原因。

D. 血量增加，不属于 because 里的内容的取非，仍为无关选项。

E. 主语 vampire bats 的认知发展(cognitive development)在 because 从句中未提及。这不是逻辑支持或反对题，不可以出现原文没有的内容来搭桥或者给出他因。

1.3.3.2 观点取非

题干虽然没有态度词，但有 would、might 或 could 将原文某句部分内容取非，则答案将该句另一部分取非。写成公式就是：

原文：A : B
题干：would not A
答案：would not B。

这里，A 与 B 的顺序并不表明它们之间在推理上的位置。这种题型本身并不容易判断，只是借助虚拟语气词和题干内容与原文是否相反来大致确定。有些时候，即便题干有 would，也不一定要取非。

► **例 6** ◄

Between the early 1910's and the 1930's, the increasing economic development in the great Delta coincided with the growing tendency of decentralizing the power of policymaking among many-level organizations of government.

The author suggests that, compared to the economic growth rate during the 1920's, the speed of economic growth in the Delta **would have declined** if the power distribution of economic policymaking would

（A）become much smaller in all governmental bureaus

（B）become much smaller in some governmental bureaus but stronger in others

（C）gravitate toward a single center of governmental organization

（D）be centrifugal in some area invested by a certain governmental organization

（E）be centripetal in some industry regulated by a certain governmental organization

【说明】

题干以would引导，说到1920's经济增长速度下降，以**时间优先定位**，则原文说1910-1930's速度增加，构成取非。这样，答案应将原文另一部分相关内容取非。原文的意思是，经济发展（economic development）与政府决策权分散（decentralizing）的趋势增长同时发生（coincide），这里的同时发生也意味着相关性，parallel = vary with = relate to = correlate with。相关变量X与Y，一个变化，另一个也会变化。原文说，分权程度增加，经济发展速度增加；题干则问，怎样经济发展或许下降？答案当然是说各级政府分权程度减少。答案一定要出现这个中心词或它的同义或近义说法，即集权程度增加。

A. 政府结构变小，但没说各级政府之间分权程度问题。

B. 一些政府机构强，另一些弱，只能说明不平衡，不能说明权力分散。

C. **正确**。政府组织存在单一中心single center，恰好是decentralizing的取非。gravitate toward = move toward，引向、朝向。取非情况：increasing...coincided with the growing...decentralizing = would have declined if... toward a single center

D. 错误。centrifugal逃离中心、离心，decentralizing的同义词，分权增加，没有取非。

E. **干扰选项**。选项的centripetal朝向中心、向心，权力集中的表现，不是权力分散decentralizing。与原文意思相反，构成取非。但后面只讲政府所投资的某些地区或领域，而原文是许多层级的政府组织，选项不够精确。这是一个陷阱。选项设计经常有3个容易排除，如本题的A、B、D，2个候选，如C和E。这时必须仔细**比较选项差异**，与原文对照。

1.3.3.3 对比取非

对比取非题针对原文任意一个出现对比的句子出题。可以归入细节题。

原文有内容对比：different, distinction, compare, distinguish, unlike, not found, absent, first, the most; more/less，或者时间对比：early-later, traditionally-now, until recently-recent。

题干常有differ from, distinguish, compare, characteristic, feature 等词，都可暗示对比。

解法：原文A-B相反，问A，取非B；问B，取非A，答案常有否定词；或者，原文说A>B，答案说B<A。

▶ 例 7 ◀

The value of gene pool remains largely unexplored and unappreciated; unlike economic and cultural wealth, which we understand for they are indispensable parts of our everyday lives, genetic wealth is hidden from the popular perception.

It can be inferred from the passage that which of the following statement is true of economic and cultural wealth?

（A）Because we could assess the value of economic and cultural wealth, it is not hidden from the people.

（B）Just as the gene pool is a source of potential economic wealth, it is an unexplored source of cultural wealth as well.

（C）The relative ignorance of the value of gene pool is inevitable given a certain knowledge condition.

（D）Economic and cultural wealth are of less value than genetic wealth because they have been almost exhausted.

（E）Economic wealth and genetic wealth are interrelated in a way that economic wealth and cultural wealth are not.

【说明】

题干的infer没有实质价值，不能依据这个词就断定这是所谓推理题。题干所问economic and cultural wealth在原文中有明显对应。原文中它们同基因财富进行对比（unlike）。既然问的是经济和文化财富，则答案应将基因财富genetic wealth的性质取非，答案应出现中心词not hidden。

A. 正确。后半句有not hidden；前半句because表示理由说明，对应原文的which从句，从句修饰可以表示理由。于是：**which** *we understand* for they are indispensable parts...is hidden from the popular perception＝**Because** *we could assess the value,* ...it is **not** hidden from the people。（not为取非）

B. 拼凑的选项，把基因库gene pool与经济财富联系起来，已经错误，后面都不用再看，遇错即停，可节约一点时间。

C. 即便接受原文的说法，大众感觉不到基因财富，大致等于relative ignorance，后面说的不可避免inevitable所表达的语气也太强。

D. 经济和文化财富与基因财富的新比较，less value；原文仅谈到它们的价值有没有被人看到，没有说到它们各自的价值高低。

E. 拼凑的选项，主语中把经济财富和基因财富用相互关联（interrelated）拼在一起。

● 1.3.4 作用题

极度常考的题型，接近核心题的出现频率，10道题占1-3/10。针对原文任何内容，问其在语境中或上下文（context）的作用。在机考界面下，对所问的内容，原文常有黑体提示，定位容易。作用题不考所问句子或成分的内容，而是考句子成分、句子之间的关系。单词内容看得见，逻辑关系看不见，需要思考。GRE喜欢考逻辑关系！

题干：文中提到某个句子成分、句子、观点为了干什么。题干常用词：in order to, serve...function, is intended to. 由于经常包含in order to, 有时也称作用题是in order to题型。对于那些考举例的作用题，有时也称其为举例作用题。

解法：所问对象指向的**逻辑上一层**。答案多往前找，偶尔也在后文，因为句子之间的关系多为总分关系，问分的内容，在其逻辑上一层找总的内容，通常在前；少数情况下后文有总结的，在后。注意，逻辑上一层并非是语序的上一句。例如，对kw a b c，问b serves which of the following functions? 答案不是上一句的a，而是上一层的kw。

逻辑上一层

成分（np, v-ing, that） → 句子主干（SVO）

句子（a b c） → 论点（kw）

观点（kw） → 主题（TS/TW）

第1层，句子成分是为了说明句子主干；句子主干好比是总的论点，句子成分，尤其并列的修饰成分，是分的证据，分从属于总，于是成分的作用是为了说明主干。

第2层，普通句子作为证据，是分，为了说明论点，是总。论点包括可看做论点的态度。这样，一种态度的证据，其作用就是为了支持这种态度判断。

原文：aw-. x. y.

题干：mention x in order to?

答案：support aw-

如果问到由引导词like, say, illustrated by, such as, for example, for instance, in the case of等引起的句子之内的例子或整句的举例（e），是为了做什么，这时，答案也常有表示举例的动词，如illustrate, give an example of。

原文：kw: e. 或 kw. e.

题干：e serves to...

答案：illustrate/give an example of kw

最后第3层，文章有多个观点、假说、模型、理论、或解释，问其中一个是为了做什么，答案就是文章的主题。主题为总，各个论点为分。这种情况考得较少。

将以上的**三层总分结构**从上往下写，我们得到：

TW/TS — KW1 — KW2（x y[=svo {modifiers}]）

这里，以kw2及其证据x y为例说明论点与论据的总分关系；以任选的y来说明句子主干SVO与修饰成分modifiers的总分关系。从这里可以看出，为什么GRE常出in order to题型，因为它反映了文章内部的各个层次的典型逻辑关系。

上述三层总分关系还不足以涵盖所有可能的句子之间的关系。有时，作用题也会问到纯对比、让步等句子的功能。

对比的作用

原文：x vs. y

题干：x serves to?

答案：1. contrast with y, not y. 2. emphasize y.

对比的一个部分或要素x，其逻辑上一层是什么？是对比的大结构，因此就是与y对比。这个答案的奇怪之处在于，问的是x的作用，结果答案给出的内容是y，虽然是与y对比，contrast with y, not y。这时，答案可能不是往前找，而是往后找，找对比关联词however之后的内容作为重点！由于出现however的地方几乎总是至少含有对比的意思，所以，问到however前后句子的作用时，答案常常要找however对比结构的另一半作为答案。除此以外，提到一个对比方的目的也可以是为了突出另一个对比方，因此emphasize y也可以作为答案，这时就更奇怪了：提到x的目的，是为了突出y，答案连对比的词汇也可以没有的。这些都只能通过句子之间的逻辑关系才能理解。

当然，如果对比结构又同时从属于一个论点kw，则x和y都是论点的证据，问到x的作用，也可以说是为了证明kw，这时kw肯定含有对比，将其中的内容展开，还是x vs. y，即：kw. x. vs. y. 此时kw= x vs. y. 这样，contrast with y 就与kw句的内容等价。

让步的作用

原文：kw. a. b. ~x=~kw, x=but kw.

题干：~kw/~x serves to?

答案：1. qualify kw. 2. contrast with x. 3. strengthen kw indirectly; anticipate objection

让步的地位相对复杂，它既与转折构成对比+主次的关系，同时又起到限制、约束，但不是摧毁、削弱论点的作用(参见以第二章第二节中"~kw, but kw让步转折"部分的分析)。因此，让步(~kw = ~x)的逻辑上一层，既有前面的论点，即1. qualify kw，还有对比的大结构，因此让步作为对比的一个要素，其作用可以是为了与另一个要素对比，即2. contrast with x。而且，整个让步转折结构的写作，是为了以退为进，限定自己观点的适用范围，才会更有效地捍卫自己的观点（矛盾吗？矛盾吗？不矛盾哦！——没有什么观点是无限有效的；主动指出自己观点的边界，反而是自信的表现）。这时，就可以说让步的作用(function, role)是为了间接加强自己的观点，于是有3. strengthen kw indirectly。第3种答案形式在目前的GRE阅读考试中尚未出现，在LSAT中则有。无论在GRE、GMAT，还是LSAT中，最常用的让步答案还是1和2。

▶ 例 8 ◀

The development of written literature in ancient history was allegedly claimed to play a crucial role in enhancing the well-being of various social classes. But a close study of the history of ancient literature reveals that much of literature was primarily intended to justify the power monopoly of elites while manipulating and domesticating the rest of the society.

The word "allegedly" used in the author's discussion of the claim is intended to

(A) contrast with the plausibility of recent study of ancient literature

(B) emphasize the historical significance of the development of written literature

(C) show the high regard of the scholars towards the development of written literature

(D) indicate that the development of written literature did not necessarily contribute to the happiness of people

(E) suggest that the development of written literature should be interpreted in terms of the benefits of elites

【说明】

成分与主干的关系。题干包含is intended to，考一个单词allegedly的作用。这个副词来自alleged，意为"自称的、所谓的"，通常为负评价，表示宣称内容与事实不符，它在句中的作用是为了说明整个句子的负评价。答案应该反映这一点，因此written literature DID NOT play a crucial role in enhancing the well-being of various social classes，这个内容当然也等于But句里的说法：manipulating and domesticating the rest of the society。

A. 对比（contrast）的说法比较奇怪。所考的allegedly只是前一句的一个词，它的逻辑上一层并不涉及but句。选项中的plausibility来自plausible(合理的、貌似有理的)，单独使用时表示正评价。

B. 强调历史意义(historical significance)，是肯定语气，与原文的否定姿态不符。

C. high regard表示高度关注、高度尊重，为正面评价，与否定态度不符。

D. 正确。给出了负评价，not = allegedly, contribute to = play a crucial role, well-being of various social classes = the happiness of people。

E. 干扰选项。重复了the development of written literature，但其后谓语的说法：按精英利益来解读，这依然不对。这涉及But句的内容，是另一句的内容了。如果要以该选项作为答案，则原文中的内容应该是written literature维护精英利益的具体证据，而不是前一句作者关于书面文献看似能够帮助各个阶层的一个暗示性的负评价。

► **例 9** ◄

Receptivity to electronic waste on the community's part was still a consideration, but when there was enough profit involved, the local government would invite the electronic companies regardless of the community's receptivity. The policy is predicated, first, on the assumption that the cost of environmental suffer can be offset by the benefit of economic gain, and, second, on the belief that the risks of recycling and disposal of electronic trash can be minimized with adequate anti-exposure facilities.

The author mentions government's assumption and belief about the development of electronic industry in an area in order to account for why

（A）environmentalists would abandon their initial opponent position

（B）environmental preservation should be given away to economic development

（C）workers with full protection would not suffer from the electronic pollution

（D）governments sometimes attempt to develop economy without regard to the community's preference

（E）the community sometimes should consider the feasibility of economic development at the cost of the local environment

【说明】

论据与论点的关系。题干有in order to，问作者提到政府的假设和信念的作用、意图或功能。原文的第1句讲地方政府对电子垃圾的政策，第2句讲这个政策的假设和信念。第2句给出第1句中做法的理由。第2句是论据，本身包含first, second并列小证据；第1句是论点；2个句子可表示为：kw. a1, a2。第2句论据的作用是为了说明第1句的论点。第1句的中心是but之后、when从句之后的主句主干：local government invite the electronic companies regardless of the community's receptivity，末尾的regardless of为否定性短语，通常重要。在选项中找与此对应的内容。

A. 环保分子放弃最初的反对立场，这点原文没有提到。

B. 环境保护与经济发展的关系，没有直接讲地方政府的作为，不对应。

C. 工人(workers)，未涉及。

D. **正确**。governments sometimes *attempt to develop economy* <u>without regard to the community's preference</u> = the **local government** would *invite the electronic companies* <u>regardless of the community's receptivity</u>. 在这里，接受度(receptivity)与社区的偏好(preference)等价。

E. **干扰选项**。社区应当考虑(should consider)，涉及价值判断，第1句只在陈述政府作为，没有提到经济发展与地方环境保护孰先孰后。

▶ **例 10** ◀

Friedman has painstakingly shown that the investigators were qualified professionals with indubitable record of academic honesty and were unlikely to give distorted transcription of the informants. From a textual perspective, however, it is not the ethical integrity of the researchers that is the main issue but the linguistic, literal, and cultural integrity of the transcription they produce.

It can be inferred from the passage that the author's discussion of Friedman's work primarily serves which one of the following functions?

(A) It offers an example that deviates from the central theme in the study of the transcription.

(B) It emphasizes the academic honesty is indispensable for the study of the transcription after all.

(C) It introduces a new approach to the transcription that contrasts sharply with the traditional methods.

(D) It exposes the insufficiency of previous approaches to the analysis of the transcription.

(E) It stresses the significant role of textual integrity in interpreting the transcription.

【说明】

对比的作用。题干的infer from没有实质作用，可忽略；serve...functions表示此题考查功能、作用。文中F(=Friedman)的作品或工作，是第1句的内容。第2句有however，表示至少含有对比。当有however出现时，如果问其中一个对比要素的作用，答案就是为了与另一个要素进行对比，或者突出另一个要素。这样，答案不在第1句本身寻找，而是要跳到however句，将其主干内容作为答案的中心词：linguistic, literal, and cultural integrity of the transcription。从内容上看，第2句主要也是为了防止误解，因此提到第1句的功能就是为了突出和强调第2句的内容。

A. 提到F是为了举例说明他偏离记录稿(transcription)的中心主题吗？不是，是为了说明问题的真正重心在别的地方。

B. 学术诚实(academic honesty)不可或缺(indispensable = necessary)吗？不是，第2句的not部分明确否定这是道德问题(not the ethical integrity)。

C. 引入新方法(new approach)，明显是错的。这里没有新老对比，new vs. traditional的说法无对应。

D. 提到从前研究方法不充分(insufficiency)，属于负评价，原文中并没有态度的问题。第2句的not...but...是否定肯定结构，与态度没有直接关系。

E. **正确**。第1句的作用是为了强调第2句，stress可以反映这点；textual integrity = linguistic, literal integrity，反映了文中句子的内容，虽然没有包含cultural，但选项E本身的内容是对的，就可以了。

● 1.3.5 选择句子题

2011年8月以来的新GRE阅读考试引入了选择句子，要求考生在文章中选出一个句子，该句子表现了题干所问的功能。题干一般这样开始：Select the sentence that...。在机考时，只要鼠标点中所在句子的任意一个单词，整个句子、直到句号就会被刷黑。选择句子题一般考句子的功能，与上面所说的作用题高度接近，而这些作用及其对应的常见英文词汇如下：

主题	main idea, main purpose
观点	theory, hypothesis, view, suggestion, proposal
态度	attitude, tone
证据	evidence, support for, detail
对比	distinguish, distinction, contrast, comparison
让步	concession, qualify, qualification of
举例	example, illustration

题干通常会有2–3个结构要素，每个要素涉及1个句子，要做出正确答案，就要理解好几个句子的功能作用，而不只是单独某个句子而已。如：

Select the sentence that provides support for an answer to a question.

在该例子中，question为中性话题或主题，answer为一个观点或假说，provides support为证据。因此，要选的是一个观点的证据，而不是问题或对这个问题的回答或观点。

1.4 推理题

占10道题的1–2/10，通常1道题，少数时候2道题。2011年8月开始的新GRE考试引入逻辑题。这并非新生事物。1999年以前的老GRE都有逻辑部分，每个部分有3–6道逻辑单题；一直以来，在GRE阅读题中，不时会有针对文章某几句内容出的逻辑支持或反对题。最新的GRE考试只是重新恢复了这些题型，单独出题而已。逻辑推理题所依据的文章可以是学术的，但多数时候还是非学术的、日常生活的话题。内容理解通常不难；难点在于其中的逻辑过程。在目前考到的GRE逻辑推理中，又可以分为正常的逻辑题和类比题两类。逻辑推理题的最大特点是，因为要寻找新的逻辑支撑，正确答案可以出现原文没有的内容。而且，可能正确的情况不一定只有一种，而是可以有很多种，虽然5个选项只会给出其中一种作为正确答案。

● 1.4.1 逻辑题

在新GRE考试中通常单独针对50字左右的段落出题，而且只出一题。特定情况下，也会针对正常阅读文章中的某些句子出逻辑题。题干经常会有if true, would support / would weaken，或者其他的形式。在读文章时，要特别注意其中出现的since, because, if等表示命题之间的因果、条件关系的词汇，也要注意句子的谓语部分出现的表示相关和因果关系的词汇，例如correlate with, coincide with。原文的推理，我们以a → b代表，它可以表示原文的命题或句子a推出b，等于一个小论证argument；它也可以表示，a作为原因导致结果b，等于理论theory。逻辑题分为支持、反对、假设或弥补差异等小类。逻辑支持与反对最为常见。我们这里给出5个例子，加上后面章节的6套阅读模拟练习的每个练习都有1道逻辑单题，本书提供的逻辑题目已经有11题。更多的例子可以参考"新GRE阅读逻辑10套"。

1.4.1.1 逻辑反对

题干: if true, would weaken/undermine/cast doubt on a certain theory/argument in the passage

解法: i) **反对原因；反对关系**。如果原文说a → b；反对原因，就是说a不存在，或者说a不存在时也存在b；a不变时b还在变化，总之要说得与已有理论不同；反对关系，有时也被称为抬杠法，则是说a → b。

ii) **有他因**。原文是a → b；如果有其他因素如X存在，可以产生b，就提供了一个竞争原因，这时原来的原因会被一定程度上削弱，符合would weaken。

▶ 例 11 ◀

The opponent warns about the possibility that microorganisms with recombinant DNA might escape from the laboratory. Foreign to the nature, the newly-created microbes may inhabit humans and become fixed there, with unpredictable and irreversible consequences. Similarly, the new strains of microorganism that parasite on their new hosts living on natural environments may wreck havoc into the fragile ecological balance.

Which one of the following, if true, would cast the most doubt on the claim of critics of recombinant DNA technology?

(A) The newly-created microorganisms are unlikely to escape from laboratories due to the development of state-of-the-art safety devices.

(B) A newly-created microorganism accidentally escaping from a laboratory is successfully contained.

(C) A particular microorganism with newly inserted genes encounters its enemy species that devours it quickly.

(D) A number of microorganisms with newly inserted genes cannot survive outside the bodies of many animals.

(E) A particular human genetic disease has been treated by a kind of microorganism with recombinant DNA.

【说明】

这道题考一个论证。题干问如何质疑批评者的主张，the most doubt的最高级没有用处。原文反对者opponent = critics所反对的理由在第2、3句。要反对其主张，可以反对这个批评本身，也可以反对其任意一个论据。第1个理由是影响人类，第2个理由是破坏生态。在反对时，答案可以出现否定词not。

A. 不太可能逃出实验室，因为有了全新的安全措施；批评者被批评的重点是可能逃逸之后的负面效果，而不是逃逸而已。

B. 逃出的被成功遏止。这不是重点。

C. 正确。某个基因改变的微生物遇到天敌，被吃掉(devoured)了，这就不会造成重大破坏(wreak havoc)，正好与第2个理由的说法相反，因此就是质疑了批评者的反对意见。

D. 干扰选项。许多基因改变的微生物不能在动物身体之外生存。第1个理由说的是，inhabit, fixed；如果反对，应该是说，这些微生物不会居住在动物身体中。

E. 基因改变的微生物能够治好一种疾病，这是好事，但原文的批评者没有用与此相关的内容来给出反对理由。这依然是一个无关选项，与A、B类似。

1.4.1.2 逻辑支持

逻辑支持题比反对题更难，反对的方法单一，但支持的答案就很多。事实上，任何能够帮助推理过程成立的说法都可以构成对原文推理的支持。

题干：if true, would support/strengthen a certain theory/argument in the passage

解法：i）**支持论据；举例或重复；提供中间环节；取非反对论据**。如果原文说a→b，支持论据，的确有a存在；举例或重复，真的发现有a的时候也有b，或者a的某个变化引起了b的变化；提供中间环节，a会产生x，而x会导致b；取非反对论据，通常只对正常阅读文章的论点x与负评价态度aw-: m的结构出题，要支持x，可以以取非负评价的证据方式进行：if not m。

ii）**无他因**。对原文a→b的理论或论证，指出存在x→b时，则a→b的关系被质疑，其可能性降低。

▶ **例12** ◀

Whereas neither farmers nor the potential urban purchasers benefited from the restriction on the free alienation of rural lands delineated in the Rural Land Act, there was one group that would benefit: the bureaucrats who implement and administer the incomplete property rights system of land.

Which of the following, if true, would support the author's assertion about the true motivation for the passage of the Rural Land Act?

（A）The legislators who voted for the Rural Land Act owned land in rural area.

（B）The majority of farmers who own their land did not sell their land to potential urban purchasers.

（C）The legislators who voted for Rural Land Act were heavily influenced by the bureaucrats.

（D）Farmers managed to preserve their custom and culture despite the impact of industrialization.

（E）Urban purchasers who bought a lot of plots of rural land consolidated them into huge farms.

【说明】

题干要求从逻辑上反对作者关于某法案(Act)通过的真正动机或原因(motivation)。原文作者认为，法案通过的理由是官僚(bureaucrats)可以从中受益benefit，即bureaucrats benefit → Act。要支持这一说法，只要选项能够暗示官僚的确在其中发挥了作用、得到了利益就可以。注意，由于题干是if true，选项中不必出现原文讲过的内容，即便只是提供具体的中间环节，只要能够体现官僚的利益输送，就可作为支持。

A. 立法者(legislators)拥有土地，没有提到官僚对他们有影响。

B. 多数农场主(farmers)不会卖地，没有提到官僚的影响。

C. 正确。投票支持法案的立法者受到官僚的严重影响，这提供了中间环节：bureaucrats → legislators → Act。

D. 农场主设法保留风俗和文化，没有提到官僚的利益或中间环节。

E. 城市购买者整合农地为大农场，没有提到他们受到官僚影响。

1.4.1.3 假设、调和差异、完成推理

除了逻辑支持与反对，逻辑题也许会问原文论证或理论的假设(assumption)。假设，按其定义，指的是如其不成立，则原推理不成立的条件，这时，答案要提供一个桥梁，连接推理的两端，好比bridge the gap。另一种考法是，原文的两个命题之间存在语言上的矛盾，比如，A句说某事物增，B句说另一个相关的事物减。题干要求解释原文两个说法A与B之间的差别：explain the difference，或者，由于A、B在这种情况下彼此似乎冲突，题干就问如何调节这种差异或冲突：reconcile the discrepancy，或者解决或消除这种冲突或矛盾：resolve the paradox。这时的答案不能重复A或B，而是提供中间环节X，使得A → X → B。最后，原文给出一个推理

小段落，其中一句、往往是最后一句以类似"because _____"的形式空出，问哪个选项可以complete the paragraph，或者complete the argument。这时，解法与假设、调和差异提供中间环节没有实质分别，都是将推理的中间环节给出，使得推理可以完备。

题干：assumption / explain the difference / reconcile the discrepancy, resolve the paradox, complete the paragraph / complete the argument

解法：找出论证的条件或中间环节

▶ 例 13 ◀

Because of the recent booming of internet advertising, most traditional media companies have experienced a severe decrease in advertising revenue. At the same time, however, more people are reading news than ever before, and some traditional media companies have generated record high revenues in the recent years.

Which one of the following, if true, most helps to resolve the apparent discrepancy in the information above?

（A）While traditional media companies rely on advertising for their revenue which registers severe decline, some companies succeed in cutting management and marketing cost to compensate the market share loss in advertising.

（B）Radio advertising has gained a pronounced growth rate and contributed a large share of revenue to these traditional media companies.

（C）A dramatically increasing number of people have begun to read news via internet rather than traditional paper magazines or newspapers.

（D）Several traditional media companies have bought some very successful internet advertising companies and directed their resources into these companies.

（E）Several traditional media companies adjusted their advertizing contents to cater for the new demand of consumers.

【说明】

消除差异：resolve the apparent discrepancy。原文有2句，第1句的主干说，多数传统媒体公司的广告收入下滑；however引出的第2句则说一些公司却获得创纪录的高收入（record high revenues）。在互联网广告的影响下，传统媒体公司应该都会受损，结果多数公司的确弱，但还有少数强，这是一个明显的差异。要解释这个差异，可以说，那些强的传统公司改进了方法，或者与新的互联网公司联合，等等。这时答案并不是唯一的，是相对开放的。题干有most help，也许会对选项分辨有作用。

A. 一些传统媒体公司能够削减成本，从而弥补损失。这样，它们会比一般公司好一点，但原文第2句讲到创纪录的高收入。不是特别合理，但可以作为候选。

B. 电台广告取得增长，似乎可以帮助取得新收入，但却是针对所有公司的，题干要求的是解释少数与多数公司的差别。

C. 通过互联网而非传统媒体阅读新闻的人剧烈增加，没有帮助解释差异，其实是在支持原文的部分内容：more people are reading news。

D. 正确。一些传统媒体公司购买了运营十分成功的互联网广告公司，多数公司没有，这可以解释后来的收入差别。

E. 干扰选项。一些传统媒体公司调整广告，迎合新的需求，这也许对收入有一定帮助，但不足以获得创纪录的收入，因为互联网广告公司在与他们争夺业务。

► 例 14 ◄

A study finds that, other things being equal, the weight of mice is heavily influenced by their ingestion of carbohydrates. The more regular carbohydrate in a diet, the more stable the weight. Thus one can conclude from study that when an adult mouse has had a very irregular eating schedule, its weight will increase significantly relative to the weight of those mice with a regular eating schedule.

Which one of the following is an assumption on which the reasoning depends?

(A) The weight of mice can be reliably measured so that the fluctuation of weight in an ordinary day can be considered as negligible.

(B) A regular eating schedule involves regular ingestion of carbohydrate.

(C) A regular eating schedule dictates the number of eatings and the time period of each eating in an ordinary day.

(D) The regular ingestion of carbohydrate obviates the necessity of ingestion of protein.

(E) The stability of weight in mice is determined by many factors.

【说明】

假设：assumption。原文有3句话，第1句老鼠体重受到碳水化合物的影响，第2句the more regular ... the more stable的比例关系表明正**相关性**（positive correlation）：碳水化合物摄入越有规律，则体重越稳定，即 regular carbohydrate → stable weight。第3句有thus，必须重视，老鼠如果饮食不规律，其体重相对那些饮食规律的老鼠会显著增加：irregular eating → weight increases。怎么从第2句到第3句的？中间有什么论证缺口？这个缺口在于，carbohydrate和eating。吃东西并不意味着吃碳水化合物。但原文从第2句到第3句的推理如要成立，却必须要假设这一点，否则推理无从进行。除此以外，没有他因影响这两组老鼠的行为，也可以是一个必要的假设，other things being equal，这样才能得出第3句thus的结论。

A. 体重的测量问题不是假设。

B. 正确。有规律的饮食包括有规律的摄入碳水化合物，这就把第2和3句的两个概念用involve关联起来了。

C. 有规律的饮食规定了吃多少次、每次吃多少时间，这只是针对一个概念eating进行分析，没有把它与另一个概念碳水化合物联系起来。

D. 规则的碳水化合物摄取排除了（obviate）摄入蛋白质（protein）的必要性。无关选项。

E. 体重的稳定由许多因素决定。这不构成假设。因为如果取非之，只有一个因素决定，也不影响原文推理。

► 例 15 ◄

The varroa mite, which parasitizes honey bees and transmits bee viruses, has caused devastating losses to honey bee populations throughout the United States.

Which of the following most logically completes the argument?

(A) the stocks that are not genetically resistant to the mites succumb to the viral epidemics

(B) the varroa mites can parasitize some relative stocks of these bee stocks

These mites have developed resistance to pesticides, with control failures well documented. To combat this problem, varroa mite-resistant strains of honey bees have been developed; however, resistant stocks have not yet been widely adopted because _____.

(C) researchers have found the mite-resistant strains can produce more offspring than other normal strains

(D) these stocks have some other characteristics that are detrimental to the survival of the resistant bee population

(E) a severe epidemic sweeps the bee populations that few wild strains of bees can escape

【说明】

　　完成推理：complete the argument。原文中最后一句有because从句不完整，需要补足论证的缺失环节。第1句讲v（=varroa）螨虫，导致蜂群损失。第2句讲这种螨虫有抗药性。第3句讲为了解决这个问题，培育了一些抵抗v螨虫的蜜蜂种，但是，这些有螨虫抵抗力的蜜蜂却没有被广泛采用。最后一句的because最重要；它提供中间环节，让我们可以合理地解释，为什么抗螨虫蜜蜂已经被培育出来，但却没有被广泛使用。这与调和差异（reconcile discrepancy）题目一致；那些题的前后半句或前后两句往往出现字面上冲突或矛盾的命题A vs. B，两个命题之间有时直接用语义显示，比如，一个量increase，结果另一个量却decrease；有时用对比关联词显示，如这里的however。答案只要提供中间环节就够了，答案本身是开放的，可以有很多种可能情况，只要导致这种蜜蜂不能使用就行。

A. 对这些螨虫没有遗传抵抗力的蜜蜂，会死于病毒流行病，与最后一句resistant stocks无关。这里，epidemics：流行病；succumb to：死于。

B. v螨虫会寄生于这些蜜蜂种类的亲缘物种，这不能说明为什么就不广泛采用这些抗螨虫的蜜蜂。

C. 研究者发现抗螨虫的种类产生的后代（offspring）比正常种类多。这是好事，无法推出为何不广泛采用。

D. **正确**。这些抗螨虫的种类有一些别的特征，会对蜂群的生存有损害，这就指出了反面的副效果，构成不采用的可能理由。

E. 严重的流行病横扫蜂群，很少野生蜂种能够逃脱。无关选项。

● 1.4.2 类比题

　　在极少数情况下，考题会针对原文的一个命题问与其类似的情况。在目前看到的题目里，都没有单独的类比题。

　　题干：analogous to, similar to, parallel, comparable to。平行（parallel），也可以表示相似。

　　解法：抽掉具体名词，保留关系与态度，主要是v. adj. 抽象名词。一个句子最能反映关系的是动词；而形容词，特别是那些有褒贬色彩的，也特别重要。抽象名词，如individual, development, lack等，是关系的重要组成部分；具体名词，尤其是具体的物种名字，如seal, scrub jay, walruse，都是次要的，可以抽去。

▶ 例 16 ◀

　　Paradoxically, Robert Rogers concludes by expressing reserved approval for the emergence theory in a

Rogers's pronounced position with regard to the emergence theory is most similar to which one of the following?

(A) A literary historian who is trained in the classical literature now turns to the study of popular fiction.

recent literature review in which he adamantly rejects the possibility of its application to any significant research areas.

（B）An activist who is a devotee of environmental protection recently recants and decides that economic development should be prioritized in the poorest areas.

（C）A principal who admits the weakness of the teaching of the school while publicizing its success in strengthening the critical thinking of children.

（D）A manager who was highly regarded by the staff has been defeated by an otherwise ambiguous manager in the competition.

（E）A team member remains loyal to the team leader despite the grand failure of the team.

【说明】

类比。题干问similar to，要找与原文相似的立场。原文说的R（=Rogers）的立场是有赞成，reserved approval，同时也有反对，adamantly reject。由于题干问的直接，定位原文也可以很轻松，只要找态度就够了，不需要找任何其他信息。我们找出对一个事物有反对、有支持的选项，就可以作为正确答案。至于这个事物的内容是什么，对于类比关系的考查来说，无关紧要。

A. 文学历史学家，以前研究古典文学，现在转为研究通俗小说。没有对同一个事物既支持又反对的态度。

B. 环保活动家大转弯（recant: 放弃以前信仰），断定经济发展要先行。没有同时持有的正负两种态度。

C. **正确**。校长principal承认本校教学有缺点，但又说学校在某个方面很成功，对本校教学同时有赞同和批评，与原文的混合评价的立场一致。

D. 一个经理，以前被员工看得很高，结果却被原本名不见经传的经理打败。打败属于事实陈述，无混合态度。

E. 队员在失败时依然忠于队伍带头人，没有同时存在的正负评价。

<小结>

以上是对10类题型的分析，建议考生分类训练。在做完一些文章和题目以后，将已经做过的比如50道题做一个题型归类，然后集中30-60分钟左右集中只看比如作用题、选择句子题、取非题，再集中2-3个小时集中看已经做过的逻辑支持、反对、假设等题目。这样就能对解法更加熟悉。

我们这里所列的题型也许不能涵盖所有GRE阅读的题目。但是，这么多年以来的考题，无论新G老G，题型都是相对稳定的，从上面的经验归纳，我们仍然可以得到一个相对完整的分析框架。

第二节　定位和选项

要做好题目，又快又准，除了熟悉题型和解法以外，还需要熟练掌握定位技巧和选项的甄别方法。

2.1　定位技巧

定位通常是从题干定位，而不是从选项定位。在做题时，看了题干，就应马上回原文自己寻找答案，不要先读选项，更不必拿着每个选项中的内容回原文找对应，那样太花时间。回文定位时，找到相应句子，大概明白答案中有什么中心词，然后再看选项，有的就保留、候选，没有的就先排除，每个选项都要看一眼，但不必每个选项的每个单词都看。看到题干就回原文定位，找到答案中心词，这就要求我们熟悉：题型（了解题干问的重点和解法）、结构（帮助定位文章具体模块）、常考内容（针对什么来考题，帮助预测正确答案，比如考核心、态度、因果、对比、让步等内容）。因此，解题速度的提高与多个因素有关，而不只是、有时甚至完全不是读文章的速度、仔细程度。在按照第2章所讲的框架，对10–20篇GRE文章进行多层分析以后，我们会容易明白文章的结构、常考的重点，定位时依据这两点寻找句子，这样速度才能快。速度快的练习不在自己的想法，我想快点就快点，而是在想法之外的扎实的、细致的、分层的模式训练。定位既是一个记忆问题，更是一个结构问题。当然，现在新GRE考试的文章多数都是短文章，定位相对容易一些；但对于长文章而言，定位还是需要训练的。还需要补充的是，对于信息题，不能从题干定位，而是要从核心出发，直接看选项来判断或定位。以下分类说明定位技巧，供考生训练时参考。（在本小节中，箭头 → 表示定位方向。）

1. 核心题
   主题题 → 新老观点对立的文章找新观点/KWn或转折句however句；其他类型一般找首段或首句。
   结构题 → 长文：各段首句；短文：各句关系
   态度题 → 态度句，多为负评价句aw- = however句
2. 已有定位提示（一些题目在题干出来以后，屏幕左边的文章处会把所问的单词或句子的内容刷黑）
   → i). 细节题：直接找该句，有时可找上下句顺承的内容。ii). in order to，找逻辑上一层的内容。
3. 信息题（无法从题干定位，题干只有文章主题词或直接问文章信息可以回答什么问题）
   → 从选项找线索，带核心去排除（错误选项常与发问的段落或全文的主题、态度相反或无关，直接排除，不必每个选项都定位。仅仅定位那些需要细节确认的选项。）
4. 题干仅有某个论点的核心词KW → 找到相应论点及其论据的全部内容
   题干仅有细节名词 → 通过首句判断段落；或从选项找线索
5. 题干有态度词AW → 态度句
   这时可能考 i) 态度句的内容；ii) would/might/could + AW+：态度取非题，答案需将态度的证据取非
6. 题干中可优先定位的内容：大写、人名、时间、数字，这些内容在文章中都很醒目，容易看出。

为了能够掌握以上内容，建议考生花2-3个小时时间，**集中看50-60道题题干**，不看选项，只看题干什么题型、什么解法、如何定位。任何技能，经过专业的集中训练之后，都可以再精进一步。

2.2 选项分析

看到某个选项之后，怎样就知道它是对是错？提高选项甄别的速度，当然是有用的。考试即赛场，在赛场上，每一秒钟都宝贵。从本章给出的16个题目例子，我们也许感觉到选项的设置有一些规则。正确的答案有文字对应，错误的选项也有一些特征。利用多年研究的经验，我们在经验的基础上归纳一些模式，供考生复习参考。

● 2.2.1 正确选项

原则：文字一一对应

3＋2 原则： 5个选项，3个排除，2个对照。

i） 改写：照抄部分　同义改写　词性变化　否定词＋反义词　抽象改写

　　例如：**disruptions** and *interventions* = *interferences* and **disturbances**（同义改写）

　　　　　neuronal structures ∈ physiological（抽象改写）

ii） 取非：题干中有would, might等，取非是GRE阅读做题唯一允许的推理。

　　A vs. B.　　A? = ~B　原文对比，问A，答案取非B。

　　A > B　　　= B < A　原文给出A > B，答案给出B < A。这个逻辑变换也可以称为广义取非。

　　A — B　　　~A － ~B （aw- if X: would aw+ if: ~x）

　　　　　　　　　　　原文中有两个概念相关，题干故意让一个变化，答案让另一个变化。这一点对态度及其证据尤其适用。

　　例如：**increasing**...coincided with the *growing...decentralizing* =

　　　　　would have declined if...*toward a single center*

　　又如，**cannot be viewed** as...for the group because...*depends on the genetic relatedness* =

　　　　　might be more convincing if...*regardless of genetic relatedness*

● 2.2.2 错误选项

原则：与核心或定位内容相反或无关或不尽符合；部分对应、其他地方对应不到，多数时候都是错误选项。

i） 典型陷阱：名词替换、kw相反、kw拼凑、加态度、态度相反

ii） that/which/because 从句中名词替换。相对隐蔽，不易发现。

iii） 新否定，新比较（易错词汇：similar, same, equal; most only first, the least;（all）other; new），新原因

　　例如：affected by the geographical and geological changes in the area ≠

　　　　　reflected a change in the surface of earth rather than a stable climatic history

iv） 数量词错。时间错误也可归入此类。例如，原文没有讲到大小，答案给large, small之类；原文没有比例概念，选项给出percentage, proportion等。程度错误也可以属于广义的数量错误。

v） 极端词汇。

　　程度：completely, entirely, always, primarily, exclusively, never

　　态度的程度：complete, absolute, unmitigated vs. 易对程度词partial, qualified, guarded

为了提高对选项的认知，我们建议考生花3个小时左右，**集中看50-60道题的200-300个选项**。选项所在的题目都是已经做过的，但做完题了还需要反复练习，才能烂熟于心，考试时达到自动反应的程度。

如果没有所有疯狂，哪里有值得回忆的青春？如果你曾疯狂，别为结局悲伤，而要感谢曾经有人无意之中触发了你的灵魂，从此你开始面对自己内心的力量。但同时，青春总要挥别，无人永远留守。如果青春只是停留于幼稚与疯狂，如何承担自己的责任？请将青春的冲动与疯狂，锐化成持久的搏斗。

GRE 阅读模拟练习题

　　本章有6套阅读模拟练习，文章从专业的期刊、杂志、著作改编而来，题目则为作者自己开发。所有内容，无论文章题材、结构和句子的复杂程度，还是题干和选项，都尽可能模仿实际考试的情况，供读者进行高度仿真、扎扎实实的训练。建议每个练习做3-4遍。做第一遍时，请计时。1个Exercise的做题时间，如果是刚刚开始GRE阅读训练，可控制在25-30分钟；如果已经训练GRE阅读100小时以上，则可控制在16-18分钟。每次可以连续做2个练习，做完以后对答案，自己琢磨一下，然后看下一章的文章和题目**解析**。彻底弄懂以后，自己独立地写出文章的结构（每个段落的core, function），在原文中标出每个题目所对应的句子，分析总结考试位置的共同特征。然后，再做新的2个练习，按同样的程序进行。这样，也许可以达到最佳的训练效果。**不要一口气将所有练习1遍做完**！训练很辛苦，但谁说成功的获得是容易的？训练吧！

	Time	Error (/10)
Exe 1		
Exe 2		
Exe 3		
Exe 4		
Exe 5		
Exe 6		

第一节　Exercise 1

Strengthened by a memory of the spiritual dignity of man, Lowell writes in *Land of Unlikeness* as an avowed Christian, with Eliot and Hopkins as his conscious models. Reviewing Eliot's *Four Quartets* in 1943, he argued that union with God is somewhere in sight in all poetry. A 1944 "Note" on Hopkins shows Lowell interested in the way Hopkins' unique personality and holiness flowered in poetry.

Certainly, much of the turbulence of Lowell's early poetry comes from his conscious struggle to approach Christian perfection. His effort to perfect his verse was analogous to the discipline of contemplation, the achieved aesthetic experience of a poem analogous to spiritual illumination. But Lowell's way with poetry would be neither Hopkins' nor Eliot's. In the American romantic tradition, he not only merged poetry with religion but equated both with culture, and thus attempted to be oratorical and satirical, exalted and apocalyptic, visionary and prophetic. Yearning for a civilization in which men bear a likeness to God, he finds in the modern world only capitalism, war and secularized consciousness.

1. The passage is primarily concerned with

   (A) discussing the religious theme in the poetry of Lowell

   (B) explaining the aesthetic motivation of Lowell's poems

   (C) comparing and contrasting the writing styles of Lowell and Eliot and Hopkins

   (D) focusing on the romantic and spiritual message in the poetry of Lowell

   (E) pointing out the importance of religious dimension for Lowell's critique of capitalism

2. According to the passage, Lowell's approach to poetry differs from that of Hopkins and Eliot in that he

   (A) presents poetic theme as entangled with spiritual revelation

   (B) reinvents a form of poetry that is both religious and secular

   (C) produces a form of poetry that is integrated with religion and identified with culture

   (D) mixes different genres of surrealism and representationalism in the poetry

   (E) underscores the role of speculation and contemplation in the poetry

3. Which of the following characterizations of the relationship between Lowell and Eliot and Hopkins can be inferred from the passage?

   (A) They all share common concerns about the religious and realistic elements to be explored in the poetry.

   (B) They all share the same sociopolitical agenda implicitly developed in their poems.

   (C) They disagree over the extent to which secular factors should be involved in the production of poetry.

   (D) Whereas Lowell emphasizes the power of political mobilization of poetry, Eliot and Hopkins only concern the contemplative, spiritual message of poetry.

   (E) Although they share a religious vision in thematic expression, Lowell and Eliot and Hopkins part in their ways to poetry.

A survey finds that the percentage of young employees in a company in the last three years varies with the percentage of young applicants who have grown up in the same city as the company resides. Since young applicants of the company are usually either from the same city or from the other cities, it can be concluded that the percentage of young employees in the company is highly influenced by the recruitment rate for the company's young applicants growing up in the same city.

4. Which one of the following statements, if true, most weakens the conclusion?

（A） Human resource department of the company is dominated by local employees.

（B） A high number of young employees from the other cities have joined in the company in the last three years.

（C） The percentage of young applicants from the other cities increases dramatically in the last three years.

（D） The percentage of young employees in the company increases slightly in the last three years.

（E） The young people from the same city favor working at home town to working at the other city.

[*This page intentionally left blank*]

It is widely agreed that modifiable neuronal ensembles support cognition. Therefore, alterations in these networks could be responsible for the behavioral impairments observed with ageing. Advances in multiple single unit recording methods have allowed the dynamics of hippocampal cell populations to be investigated in behaving rats, and studies using these methods have shown that certain properties of these networks are compromised during ageing. Interestingly, many of the age-related changes that have been discovered can be linked to plasticity deficits, as blockade of NMDA (N-methyl-d-aspartate) receptors in young rats results in ensemble dynamics that resemble those of aged rats.

Neuronal recordings from the hippocampus of adult rats reveal that when a rat explores an environment, pyramidal and granule cells show patterned neural activity that is highly correlated with a rat's position in space. Between 30% and 50% of pyramidal cells in CA1 region of the hippocampus show place-specific firing in a given environment, which has earned these neurons the name 'place cells'. When the firing patterns of many hippocampal neurons are recorded simultaneously, it is possible to reconstruct the position of a rat in an environment from the place cell firing patterns alone. The composite cell activity is 'map-like' and, in different environments, hippocampal place maps change markedly. Although these maps can be driven by external environmental features, internal events are also important and a new map might be generated in the same environment if the demands of the task change.

In young rats, CA1 place fields expand asymmetrically during repeated route following, which results in a shift in the centre of mass of place fields in the direction opposite to the rat's trajectory. This observation is consistent with neural network models dating back to Hebb's 1949 concept of the 'phase sequence' of cell assemblies, which suggested that an associative, temporally asymmetric synaptic plasticity mechanism could serve to encode sequences or episodes of experience. The magnitude of this place field expansion, however, significantly decreases in aged rats. It is likely that this age-associated reduction in experience-dependent plasticity is due to some specific plasticity deficits, as it does not occur when CPP, a selective and competitive antagonist of NMDA-type receptors, is administered to young rats.

In addition, the maintenance of place maps also differs between young and old animals. In normal young rats, a place map for a given environment can remain stable and retrievable for months. A similar stability of CA1 place maps in aged rats is observed within and between episodes of behavior in the same environment. Occasionally, however, if the old rat is removed from the environment and returned later, the original place map is not retrieved and an independent population of place cells may be activated even in a familiar room. Such map retrieval failures might be attributed to specific defective plasticity in aged rats.

5. It can be inferred from the passage that the author would draw which of the following conclusions if they had <u>not</u> found that young rats administered with CPP show no reduction in experience-dependent plasticity?

(A) The extent of place field expansion does not decrease in aged rats.

(B) The extent of place field expansion does not affect the experience-dependent plasticity.

(C) The reduction in experience-dependent plasticity does not vary with age.

(D) CPP cannot be used to inhibit the effect of NMDA-type receptors.

(E) The reduction in experience-dependent plasticity in aged rats does not correlate with certain plasticity deficits.

6. Which of the following statements about the relationship between young and old rats are true, based on the information in the passage?

(A) They invoke different neural machineries in the maintenance of place maps according to the time length of different tasks.

(B) They share the same machinery in the formation and retrieval of original place map which then is replaced by the reinvented place map in CA1 area.

(C) They differ in the rates of retrieval of original place map when they experience temporary displacement from their original environment.

(D) They differ in the success of retrieval of original place map since the aged rats fail to retrieve it if they experience temporary displacement from their original environment.

(E) They differ in the success of retrieval of original place map if the original environments they are exposed to are different.

7. Which of the following claims about the place cells are supported by the information in the passage?

(A) They track different environments in which the rats find themselves.

(B) They remain in the same firing pattern regardless of the environmental change.

(C) They form the same firing pattern whenever external environmental features remain the same.

(D) They can be reconstructed only if the task change induces intense internal events.

(E) They correlate with the map the researchers show to the rats.

8. The author mentions Hebb's concept of the 'phase sequence' of cell assemblies in the third paragraph most probably in order to

(A) contrast Hebbian neural network models and the model proposed here

(B) offer the conceptual foundations of the neural network models to explain the phenomenon of place field asymmetric expansion.

(C) anticipate the objections that reduction in the place field expansion in aged rats

(D) show that the place field expansion in aged rats might have increased

(E) suggest that the age-associated reduction in experience-dependent plasticity is the result of specific plasticity deficits

Many people behave like strong reciprocators. In a ten-round public goods experiment, each subject grouped with three other subjects under conditions of strict anonymity is given "points", divided between a "common account" and the subject's "private account''. Each private account will be added by 40% of the total amount of points contributed to the common account. Clearly, full free riding is a dominant strategy, but the experiment shows that many subjects begin by contributing on average about half of their endowment to the public account. However, the level of contributions decays gradually, until in the final rounds most players behave in a self-interested manner. Presumably, cooperative subjects retaliated against free-riding low contributors in the only way available to them — by lowering their own contributions. This interpretation is confirmed in a 25-round game.

9. It can be inferred from the passage that a successful and consistent cooperative and reciprocal strategy in a population composed of contributors and free-riders would depend at least partly on

(A) credible punishment against free-riding low contributors

(B) careful assessment of cost and benefit of all possible situations and the corresponding strategies

(C) serious fining of free-riding low contributors by enforcing them to pay a fee

(D) reasonable retaliation against self-interested players by ceasing their contributions

(E) correct evaluation of different payoff matrix for each and every game players

The fact that so many things in life conform to a bell curve pattern of data points suggests that it's much easier to be ordinary than to be outstanding. Inspirational public television always features children dreaming of being great successes. Yet normal distribution theory reveals that values cluster around midpoints and mediocrity loves company. Another relentless power implied in the bell curve is regression to the mean: the extraordinary tends to lose its edge over time. An athlete often goes into decline after appearing on the cover of best sport magazine. This might result from the pressures of fame, or a superstition subsumed into self-fulfilling prophecy, but the fact is, after doing extraordinarily well for a long period of time, the athlete is simply not able to maintain outlier status for much longer, but rather starts regressing, however slightly, back toward the mean.

For the following question, consider each of the choices separately and select all that apply.

10. The passage provides information to support the following statements EXCEPT?

（A）An athlete who keeps staying away from media when achieving the high performance can maintain that status much longer.

（B）To stay somewhere within the normal distribution is to be ordinary.

（C）Managing an even reasonably long time of extraordinary performance is a challenge that any eminent sportsmen cannot meet, regardless of their talent, diligence, and perseverance.

第二节　Exercise 2

What was causing the periodic advance and retreat of the glaciers? Milankovitch correlated glacier cycle with the variations in the amount of solar radiation (insolation) reaching the Earth. In the short, cool summers of the high polar latitudes, insolation may not be enough to melt back snow and ice accumulated in the winter. The small changes in insolation could change the delicate balance of glacial stability to one of advance. Once the advance starts, the increased reflectivity of the ice surface, as compared to sea or land cover, cools the local atmosphere further and causes a self-feeding process of glacial growth.

However, the variations in insolation are not enough to drive the enormous shift in climate which a glacial onset represents. Some climatologists have attempted to find other factors. The most popular theory today proposes that shifts in the thermohaline circulation, the global ocean current which circulates cold water from the north Atlantic around the cape of Africa to the northeastern Pacific, may be the trigger for the sudden changes which bring on the Ice Ages.

1. The passage is primarily concerned with

   (A) discussing the important role of insolation in the advance and retreat of the glaciers

   (B) criticizing the insolation theory proposed by Milankovitch to explain the glacier cycles

   (C) comparing and contrasting the variety of hypotheses concerning periodicity of glaciers

   (D) explaining how insolation brings about the self-feeding process of glacial growth

   (E) exploring the factors of cyclic advance and retreat of the glaciers

2. Which of the following statements about sea or land cover can be inferred from the passage?

   (A) The reflectivity of sea or land cover can cause the decline of the temperature of the local atmosphere and to the self-feeding process of glacial growth.

   (B) The reflectivity of sea or land cover can be interpreted as related to the reflectivity of the ice surface which impinges upon the delicate balance of glacial stability.

   (C) When the local atmosphere cools, the reflectivity of the ice surface increases whereas the reflectivity of sea and land cover decreases.

   (D) When the advance of the glaciers begins, the reflectivity of sea and land cover does not increase relative to the reflectivity of the ice surface.

   (E) The reflectivity of sea and land cover differs from that of the ice surface in that the former can cause fundamental temperature change in a way that the latter cannot.

3. The author considers the explanation put forward by Milankovitch for the periodic retreat and advance of the glaciers to be

   (A) misleading and unfocused

   (B) seminal but speculative and ambiguous

   (C) accurate but incomplete

   (D) plausible but yet to be confirmed

   (E) credible but generally undervalued

[This page intentionally left blank]

Early feminist literary critics believed that the traditional concept of domesticity as manifested in the distinction between a masculinized public sphere and a privatized feminine one has become 'misleading' and oversimplified as a framework for understanding the construction of social space for women even in the nineteenth century. In their reformist view, domesticity was not simply confining for women but a source of agency or 'sentimental power': the public-private distinction was treated as the basis for creating an alternative feminine culture. For instance, Nancy Hartsock argues that resistant forms of feminist consciousness spring from women's immersion into housework or child-rearing, a world more complete than men's, which then transforms women's domesticity into a critical position.

In contrast, a second wave of feminist work on domesticity envisions the idea of 'home' as a specific racial and class position for white, middle-class women, and therefore as an extension or even a supplement to the capitalist marketplace, not an alternative to it. This second-wave critique emphasizes how casting domesticity as a countercultural movement, based on its exclusion from dominant economic formations, obscures the way domesticity reproduces other kinds of power relations. In this second reading, it is precisely the reformist impulse privileged by earlier feminist critics as an unrecognized form of women's historical agency that is now understood as fueling a kind of expansionist or missionary project, characterized by rhetoric of expanding woman's sphere and of social or enlarged housekeeping, which often translated into projects of class socialization and the imposition of middle-class norms.

However, these second-wave critiques of domesticity also depend upon spatial metaphors, to the extent that they present domesticity as a bounded position occupied by a specific race and class of women. Furthermore, they underestimate the extent to which the representation of domesticity as able to travel beyond the walls of the middle-class home had the ideological function of mystifying or suppressing the internal contradictions within the feminine sphere of domestic responsibilities.

Such contradictions in the representations of domesticity, I argue, only started to become obvious in the modernist period. Modernist women's writing anticipates a notion of "homelessness at home", in which home figures a claim to a gendered identity, while homelessness echoes the writer's consciousness that this identity is neither completely determined nor inherently spatialized in the ways that the ideology of separate spheres represents women as being. But this metaphorical phrase does not entirely reject the spatial figuration of femininity; in fact, the implication is that an alternate conception of space might empower a new feminist politics, as in Audre Lorde's poem 'School Note', where the speaker refers to herself as being 'at home' anywhere because no place 'is' home.

4. Which one of the following best expresses the main idea of the passage?

(A) There is not yet a satisfactory understanding of domesticity in feminist literary criticism, whether for earlier feminist literary criticism or for second-wave critiques.

(B) Both earlier and second wave of feminist literary criticism fail to understand the implications of domesticity, a concept that is better interpreted only in modern period.

(C) Early literary criticism has a misleading effect on later critiques of domesticity and modernist alternatives as well.

(D) Both earlier and later feminist literary criticism contribute to modern understanding of domesticity.

(E) Earlier and later and modern feminist literary criticisms have equal value in our understanding the concept of domesticity.

5. The author's mention of Nancy Hartsock's study serves primarily to

(A) illustrate the reformist view of domesticity as an empowering and critical force

(B) illustrate the reformist view of domesticity as a supplementary force to marketplace

(C) demonstrate that women's world is more complete than men's world

(D) demonstrate that housework and child-rearing are among the prevailing jobs for women

(E) demonstrate that the private-public dichotomy confines the role of women to housekeeping

6. The second-wave feminist critique of domesticity differs from earlier feminist criticism in that the second-wave critique

(A) abandons the concept of domesticity altogether

(B) denies any negative role of the ideology of domesticity in women's social life and self-image

(C) advocates the critical thrust of the concept of domesticity

(D) deems as important to the interpretation of domesticity the traditional dichotomy of public and private spheres for men and women respectively

(E) views household as a supplementary or extensive power to society

7. The passage suggests that the second-wave critiques would have been more illuminating if they could do which of the following?

(A) Highlight more assuredly the function of class socialization and middle-class mores in casting the image of women

(B) Abandon more quickly the spatial allegory to embrace its literal, physical meaning

(C) Recognize more clearly the contradictions in the conception of domesticity in modern period

(D) Assess more appropriately the role of domesticity in mythologizing and repressing the inner conflict endemic to women's duty of domesticity

(E) Reject more vehemently the early feminist interpretation of domesticity

The proposal that reelin, a large protein regulating neuronal migration and positioning, is the chief cause of schizophrenia was questioned when human reelers were discovered in two separate families in Saudi Arabia and England. In both these families cousins had married each other and the marriage had brought together faulty versions of the reelin gene, causing a disorder called lissencephaly with cerebellar hypoplasia （LCH）. If inherited reelin deficiency is the cause of schizophrenia, one would expect that some of the apparently unaffected relatives of these unfortunate children would be schizophrenic, because they are carrying the mutation in one of their genes. But so far there is no history of schizophrenia in either family, though the Arab family has not been studied in detail.

8. Which of the following would be true if most of the relatives with inherited reelin deficiency in both families turned out to be schizophrenic rather than normal as they are today?

（A） The lack of reelin may be highly associated with the schizophrenia.

（B） The lack of reelin may be unrelated to the schizophrenia.

（C） Lissencephaly with cerebellar hypoplasia （LCH） might also be fatal during the adulthood.

（D） Lissencephaly with cerebellar hypoplasia （LCH） would be treated by genetic therapy in the immediate future.

（E） Cousins in those families would finally give up marrying each other.

In his new study, Anderson outlines what is special about human language: syntax. Our vocabularies are dramatically larger than those of other animals, and our sound systems are more complex, but the essential design property of human language is syntax — the way we use combinations of words to convey meaning. This concept is alien to the communication systems of other species. It is true that what animals learn is impressive and their cognitive abilities may be remarkable, but they never master anything like a human language and seem incapable of doing so: the complexity of their grammar is not remotely comparable to ours.

For the following question, consider each of the choices separately and select all that apply.

9. According to the information in the passage, which of the following features is essentially <u>unique</u> to human language and accompanying human cognitive powers?

（A） Extraordinary complexity of grammar

（B） Combinatory ways to express meaning

（C） Remarkable cognitive abilities

Companies who expect that they cannot find a high quality project to invest usually wait and keep a huge amount of capital. Yet the percentage of invested capital in the last year increased significantly from that in the previous year. This is convincing evidence that the Enterprise Association founded two years ago to facilitate the investment has gradually assisted the member companies to invest residual capital.

10. Which one of the following most seriously weakens the argument?

（A） Those companies which did not join the Association in the previous year have begun to reconsider their earlier decision.

（B） A significant economy recovery that spurred intensive capital investment has begun to take shape since the last year.

（C） The reserved capital in the companies still far more exceeds the invested capital in total for this year.

（D） The entrepreneurship confidence index indicates that entrepreneurs of most companies are optimistic about the economy in the next two years.

（E） The reserved capital in the companies is disproportionately lower than the invested capital in total for this year.

第三节 Exercise 3

Deferring reproduction presumably increases reproductive gains later in life through improved competitive ability by increased body size. This should be true for young fallow deer males, which attain physiological maturity at two years old but continue to grow until six. In our results, two-year-old males refrained from fighting. Three-year-old males appear to be equivocal: they act as adults when given the opportunity, but act as juveniles by refraining from groaning when competition is high. By contrast, four- and five-year-old males are willing to take part but are outcompeted by older males. They then resort to alternative strategies, such as intruding on territories and chasing females away from territory holders, the strategies occasionally successful because up to twenty percent of estrous females that were chased by young males in an experiment mated with them.

1. Which of the following statements, if true, would cast most doubt on the author's claim that alternative strategies undertaken by four- and five-year-old males sometimes could be successful?

   (A) Some estrous females that were chased by young males mated with older males.

   (B) Most estrous females that were chased by young males mated with them.

   (C) Only sporadic mating took place between young males and estrous females they chased.

   (D) The number of mating between young males and estrous females they chased was lower than that between older males and estrous females.

   (E) More estrous females chased by young males mated with them than the estrous females expelled from the territories of older males by the same young males.

2. The author's exemplification of intruding on territories of older males by younger males serves which one of the following functions in the passage?

   (A) It helps distinguish the behavior of intruding on territories from that of chasing females away from territory holders.

   (B) It illustrates the crucial difference between two different strategies taken by younger males under fierce competition with older males.

   (C) It clarifies the otherwise ambiguous and equivocal intentions implicit in the putative strategies taken by younger males.

   (D) It gives an example of a strategy other than normal mating strategies, taken by younger males under fierce competition with older males.

   (E) It proves that the alternative strategies taken by younger males sometimes outperform the normal mating strategies taken by older males.

The orientation to sociopolitical issues and racial identity in the poems of Claude McKay contrasts sharply with the tradition represented by Braithwaite. While McKay explicitly weaved racial-political markers into his poems that unequivocally indicate the author's racial identity and lamented that the failure of black leadership was rooted in a socioeconomic and intellectual chasm between the black masses and the intelligentsia, Braithwaite preferred to camouflage racial identity under his pen and barely touched the issue of race in America in his own poems.

McKay's disagreement with Braithwaite's advice to write aracial poetry reflected his broader skepticism regarding the background and motives of the black intelligentsia. This does not mean that all the black intellectuals McKay encountered would have agreed with Braithwaite. Indeed, Locke, White, and Du Bois had committed themselves to genres of African American literature that to an extent "betrayed" racial identities as African descendants. But they also have mutual identification with a community notorious for its cultural and socioeconomic exclusivity and its detachment from a large black population, which was in conflict with Mckay's preference for radical society that was unpalatable and abominable for Black elites.

3. The primary objective of the first paragraph of the passage is to

(A)   discuss the different approaches of McKay and Braithwaite to literature

(B)   emphasize McKay's approach to literature over Braithwaite's for its focusing on racial issues

(C)   explain why McKay's approach to literature differs from Braithwaite's conservatism

(D)   advocate McKay's approach to literature while deploring Braithwaite's as timid

(E)   discuss the main theme of McKay's genre of literature in its sociopolitical orientation

4. It can be inferred from the passage that McKay would have found Braithwaite's writing more acceptable if which of the following had happened?

(A)   Braithwaite would embrace and reinforce the idea common in the black elites of pursuing universal public audience.

(B)   Braithwaite would recognize as deleterious the cultural discrepancy between the black population and the elite.

(C)   Braithwaite would cease to conceal his racial identity in the writings and explicitly express his views about racial issues.

(D)   Braithwaite would collaborate with his contemporary poets to promote the social status of Black writers in the White America.

(E)   Braithwaite would denounce the snobbish and self-centered mentality implicitly present in other writer's poems.

5. The author's discussion of the genres of African American literature practiced by Locke, White, and Du Bois in explaining McKay's skepticism toward the motives of the black intelligentsia is probably intended to

(A)   correct the misconception that Braithwaite and Locke, White, and Du Bois share the same intellectual and cultural views

(B)   underline the difference between Braithwaite and McKay in their preferences for the ideal form of society

(C)   strengthen the preceding claim that the orientation and motivations of the black intelligentsia have much in common

(D)   explain the divergence of Locke, White, and Du Bois's approach to literature from Braithwaite's and precludes a possible misinterpretation of the previous claim

(E)   emphasize the nonconservative element of Locke, Walter White, and Du Bois's writings and contrast it with that of McKay's

6. In the second paragraph, the author is primarily concerned with

(A)   contrasting two approaches to literature and offering a compromise

(B)   presenting the disagreement of one approach to literature with the other approach shared by the authors who still differ to a certain extent

(C)   examining three different approaches to literature and endorsing one over the other two

(D)   questioning one traditional approach to literature and advocating another different one

(E)   discussing a specific theme common to several authors in the different literary traditions

The assessment of the degree of admixture of a given population has traditionally relied on the comparison of gene frequencies between two potential parental populations and a putative hybrid population. Recently, these methods have been improved by incorporating information on the molecular diversity present in the admixed and in parental populations or by explicitly taking into account the genetic drift since the admixture event. However, the accuracy of the estimation of the contribution of the parental populations to the hybrid depends highly on the extent of differentiation between parental populations and the time elapsed since the admixture event. No single method was found to date superior to others in all circumstances.

7. It can be inferred from the passage that the traditional and recent methods in the assessment of the degree of admixture of a given population differed in which of the following respects?

(A) The accuracy of the estimation of the contribution of the parental populations to the hybrid

(B) The universality of the estimation method in most circumstances

(C) The degree of reception among evolutionary biologists and molecular geneticists

(D) Whether factoring in molecular diversity and genetic drift or not

(E) Whether comparing gene frequencies between parental populations and a hybrid population or not

Why a country like England that had suffered from a lengthy period of political instability before 1688 suddenly underwent a transition to stable representative government with a limited monarchy? Olson suggested that democracy results from accidents of history that leave a balance of power or stalemate, making it impossible for any one leader or group to overpower all of the others or create a new autocracy. But one group did eventually establish full control in England: after 1715 the Whigs had command of all government institutions, retaining this control for a considerable period of time. Weingast adds a new dimension by demonstrating that democratic stability depends on the two groups successfully committing to a strategy of opposing any attempts to tread upon the basic rights of any citizens. The Bill of Rights of 1689 in England might be seen as just such an "elite pact". However, this suggestion may be inaccurate. During the period of partisan conflict between 1690 and 1715, it was common for those who found themselves in the opposition to be thrown in prison on dubious legal grounds.

8. Which of the following, if true, would strengthen the challenge to Weingast's hypothesis as presented in the passage?

(A) The Bill of Rights broke important constitutional ground by making it illegal for the monarchy to pass laws, levy taxes, or maintain a standing army without consent of Parliament.

(B) The Act of Settlement passed in 1701 by the Parliament is a written commitment between different groups to respect constitutional ground rules.

(C) Through the Act of Settlement passed in 1701, leaders of different groups reaffirmed that they committed themselves to respect basic constitutional principles.

(D). Historical evidence suggests that the cross-cutting character of political cleavages provided the room for politicians to propose moderate policies that can minimize incentives for radical opponents to revolt.

(E) A government in 1701 dominated by one party put several leaders of the opposition party on trial on concocted charges.

9. Select the sentence that merely provides support for a hypothesis.

The diet rich in fruits and vegetables resulted in mild reductions in blood pressure, lowering the systolic pressure by 2.8 mmHg and the diastolic by 1.1 mmHg. A combination diet rich in fruits, vegetables, and dairy products more than doubled those numbers in individuals with normal blood pressure. Thus, calcium does play a crucial role in blood pressure regulation since the level of consumption of dairy products, with their high calcium content, was the biggest difference between the combination diet and the other diet.

10. Which one of the following, if true, most strongly supports the argument?

（A） The combination diet resulted in mild reductions in blood pressure as the diet rich in fruits and vegetables did.

（B） The combination diet was lower in saturated fat than the other one, and included two servings of low-fat dairy products as well as almost 10 of fruits and vegetables.

（C） Another major difference between the combination diet and the other diet lies in the degree of concentration of minerals.

（D） In people with mild high blood pressure, the reductions caused by the combination diet were 11.4 mmHg in systolic and 5.5 in diastolic.

（E） Some other diet with the same level of consumption of dairy products as the combination diet proved to be no more effective in lowering blood pressure than the other diets.

第四节　Exercise 4

In a laboratory study, when bees are made to fly through tunnels with visual patterns on the walls, the distance they indicate in their dance corresponds to the complexity of the pattern to which they have been exposed. The researchers hypothesize that the dance reflects the bee's subjective experience, rather than a map of the external world and that the bees' perception of distance is largely a function of differences in their visual, subjective experience.

1. Which of the following, if true, most seriously undermines the researcher's hypothesis?

（A） Bees as subjects flying through the tunnels with pictures on the wall indicate the amount of distance by their various forms of dances.

（B） Bees as subjects flying through the tunnels with pictures on the wall do not vary their indications of the distance with different visual patterns.

（C） Bees in the experiment fail to respond to the directions of the visual images on the wall since those images are too perplexing and, in some cases, ambiguous.

（D） Bees in the experiment stumble upon the wall when the map shows there is light on the striking point.

（E） Bees in the other experiment show a certain similar behavior pattern but, to researchers' dismay, they stop flying whenever external intervention is withdrawn.

The high mobility of nineteenth-century Americans generally, and especially those under thirty years of age is well documented. The most common way to vary one's work was to move, if the youths did not want to see their fate sealed by their proficiency on one particular portion of the work. Those unacquainted with factory populations said that they possess as roving a disposition as the Tartars. But few remove because they are fond of changing their locations, though they go where they can get the best employment and the best wages. Hareven's thorough analysis of the payrolls of the Amoskeag Mills showed that the typical worker's career was short and frequently interrupted. Those whose years at Amoskeag were unbroken by any departure from the mills usually did not stay there long. The reasons for leaving were many: discharge, desire to try another job, pregnancy, an attempt to get a raise in pay, or anger at an overseer. In general, however, men left to search for better jobs; women left to care for other members of their families.

For the following question, consider each of the choices separately and select all that apply.

2. It can be inferred from the passage that the author would be likely to agree with which of the following are the factors for the transience of workers in the nineteenth-century America?

   (A) Desire to get a better job and a better payment

   (B) Disposition to wander around different factories

   (C) Care for the family members

3. The author of the passage mentions Hareven's study of the payrolls of the Amoskeag Mills in order to

   (A) emphasize Hareven's insightful observation that the career of average workers there did not last long and confronted intervention

   (B) suggest that young workers left a factory for a variety of reasons

   (C) anticipate the objection that the workers moved around the different factories for different reasons

   (D) indicate that young worker moved not because of their migrant proclivities but because of other reasons

   (E) blame the employers for removing the young workers repeatedly

4. The main purpose of the passage is to

   (A) document the high mobility of nineteenth-century Americans

   (B) explain the high transience of young workers in the nineteenth-century America

   (C) highlight the difference between male workers and female workers

   (D) refute the suggestion that young workers move because they have an innate disposition to do so

   (E) discuss the fate of workers in the nineteenth-century America

Philopatry, the behavior returning to an individual's birthplace, has several advantages. The presence of kin in the natal area makes easier to receive help from related individuals; the level of aggression might be lower among kin than among unrelated individuals; breeding close to kin can also increase breeding success, as in the case of microtine rodents. However, this behavior may also result in an elevated probability of incestuous pairings. The fact that close inbreeding is rarely observed even in highly philopatric species suggests that animals have developed mechanisms to avoid breeding with close relatives and can discriminate between kin and non-kin via recognition.

One proposed mechanism by which animals can recognize unfamiliar relatives is phenotype matching, which involves learning the phenotype of familiar relatives, or of oneself, thereby forming a phenotypic template against which the phenotypes of unfamiliar individuals can be compared. Some animals might be using some form of phenotype matching: mice have been shown to use MHC odor type to avoid breeding with close relatives; olfactory cues also seem to be used by Arizona tiger salamanders and rainbow fish seem to use both visual and chemical cues to detect shoals of related individuals. Many studies, however, have found that individuals only recognize familiar kin.

A problem in investigating the behavior of settling close to kin is to exclude the possibility that they are philopatric because of benefits of settling in the natal area, rather than because of benefits of settling close to kin. The study of dispersal of relatives in colonially breeding seabirds and waterfowl is of particular interest in this context because virtually all species in this group share characteristics that are generally believed to promote the evolution of cooperation. Nonrandom dispersal within colonies of seabirds and waterfowl has been reported but is usually explained by philopatry to the natal nest site rather than by attraction to kin.

A recent study shows that the settling pattern of barnacle geese Branta leucopsis females returning to their natal colony is nonrandom with respect to the nest sites of their parents and sisters. Because breeding birds rarely changed nest sites between years, this natal philopatry could be caused by an attraction to the natal nest site itself or to the parents nesting there. However, females that settled on a different island than where their parents bred still settled close to their sisters. This clearly demonstrates that sisters' nesting close to each other is not a by-product of either extreme natal philopatry or a preference to nest close to parents, but results from a genuine preference for nesting close to kin. In addition, that females only nested close to sisters born in the same year (i.e., sisters that they had been in close contact with) also suggests that the clustering of female kin in barnacle geese does not result from phenotype matching.

5. The author might have to revise the conclusion that sisters' nesting close to each other is a result of a preference for nesting close to kin if which of the following might happen?

   (A) Females that settled on an island other than where they were born still nest close to each other.

   (B) Females that settled on an island other than where their parents bred build their nesting sites in a scattered pattern.

   (C) Females that settled on a different island than where they were born cooperate to defend their territory, though separated.

   (D) All females that settled on an island other than where they were born change the site of breeding in some year.

   (E) Some females that settled on an island other than where they were born change the nesting sites, while others not.

6. The author mentions which of the following as the benefits of philopatry EXCEPT

   (A) help from relatives

   (B) reproductive success

   (C) close inbreeding

   (D) reduced antagonism

   (E) nice neighbor

7. The author mentions the MHC odor type of mice probably in order to

   (A) contrast with the olfactory cues used by Arizona tiger salamanders and the visual and chemical cues used by rainbow fish

   (B) highlight the difficulty the phenotype matching hypothesis confronts

   (C) stress the pressure of kin recognition of mice

   (D) indicate the advantage of philopatry to mice

   (E) provide partial support for phenotype matching hypothesis

8. Which of the following, if true, would support the phenotype matching hypothesis?

   (A) Seabirds and waterfowl tend to cooperate in their breeding season.

   (B) Barnacle geese females settle close to their sisters born in any years.

   (C) Rainbow fish use MHC odor type to avoid breeding with their kin.

   (D) Mice using MHC odor type reproduce more successfully than their relatives not using the same odor.

   (E) Mice using MHC odor type still have other ways to prevent them from breeding with their relatives.

Why researchers have difficulties in uncovering ancient moneys has much to do with the practice of archeology and the nature of money itself. Archeologists spend their careers sifting through the trash of the past, ingeniously reconstructing vanished lives from broken pots and dented knives. But like us, ancient Mesopotamians and Phoenicians seldom made the error of tossing out cash, and only rarely did they bury their most precious liquid assets in the ground. Even when archeologists have found buried cash, though, they have trouble recognizing it for what it was. Money doesn't always come in the form of dimes and sawbucks. It assumes many forms, from debit cards and checks to credit cards and mutual funds. The forms it took in the past have been, to say the least, elusive.

9. The passage contains information that would support which of the following statements about the money studied by the archeologists?

(A) It assumed a variety of forms that are completely different from today's forms.

(B) In the ancient societies, only wealthy citizens were flaunting money.

(C) In the past, it greased the wheels of Mesopotamian commerce, spurred the development of mathematics, and helped officials and kings rake in taxes and impose fines.

(D) It was often buried in the ground by the ancient rich people who accumulated the wealth by hoarding the precious noble metal.

(E) Because of its elusive forms, it was not easy for archeologists to uncover and recognize.

The concentration of atmospheric methane is projected to increase significantly given the large pools of carbon stored in permafrost that can be converted to methane upon thaw, the susceptibility of methane hydrates to release from the ocean floor with rising seawater temperature and the acceleration of methane-producing anthropogenic activities. A recent study examines one particular source of atmospheric methane that may be significantly larger than previously recognized: ebullition (bubbling) from northern lakes. Careful measurements of the spatial and temporal patchiness of ebullition in Siberian thermokarst lakes revealed that total emissions from lakes were five times greater than earlier estimates. Furthermore, thaw of permafrost along lake margins releases labile organic matter previously sequestered in permafrost for centuries to millennia into anaerobic lake sediments, enhancing methane production and ebullition emission and serving as a positive feedback to climate warming.

10. The passage mentions which of the following are possible factors for increased concentration of atmospheric methane EXCEPT

(A) the thawing of permafrost that may convert stored carbon to methane

(B) ebullition in Siberian thermokarst lakes and emission from other northern lakes

(C) the deflationary effect of feedback mechanism on climate warming

(D) human-engineered carbon emission that enhances methane production

(E) the mounting seawater temperature that triggers methane compounds to release from the ocean floor

第五节　Exercise 5

The direct detection of extrasolar planets is extraordinarily difficult, because of the enormous difference in luminosity between a star, which shines with its own light, and orbiting planets, which are not only much smaller and very close to the star, as seen from Earth, but shine by reflected light. The situation is akin to trying to identify a firefly buzzing around an intensely bright searchlight—from a great distance. At optical wavelengths, a star might be several billion times brighter than a large planet. However, at infrared wavelengths, where the planet emits its own thermal radiation, the contrast is only a factor of a million. Astronomers' best hopes of imaging an extrasolar planet are to "mask" the bright star, and hope to detect a faint infrared blip off to the side—another world. One method of masking is to insert an occulting disk in the telescope, which blocks the light from the central star. This method resulted in the telescope near-infrared images, where rings of dust have been discovered orbiting a particular star.

1. The author uses the analogue of identifying a firefly to

   (A) emphasize the distinguishing feature of finding a firefly around an intensely bright light source

   (B) compare the reflected light of planets and self-generating light of stars

   (C) underscore the importance of infrared wavelength radiation for the detection of extrasolar planets

   (D) illustrate the difficulty of identifying an extrasolar planet around a highly luminous star from an enormous distance

   (E) give an example of the difficulty of detecting an extrasolar planet with current technology

2. Which of the following statements about the relationship between stars and extrasolar planets is supported by information given in the passage?

   (A) They shine by different types of light, though emitting the same thermal radiation.

   (B) They differ in luminosity because their lights are derived from different extraterrestrial bodies.

   (C) They differ in luminosity because stars emit self-generated light while planets shine by borrowed light.

   (D) Reflected light at optical wavelengths radiated from planets is entirely obscured by the light emitted from stars, so as to be invisible.

   (E) An occulting disk in the telescope can help block out the central star, making it possible to detect visible light at the optical wavelength emitted by an extrasolar planet.

[This page intentionally left blank]

Critics of Jean-Luc Godard's celebrated film *Breathless* wondered if its protagonist's weak acting and the film's general roughness are meant to be parodies of conventional acting and filmmaking. But such a diagnosis doesn't fit. Parody suggests consistent mockery in the service of a specific goal, usually that of puncturing pretension, with the immediate aim of getting a laugh. But *Breathless* is more pretentious in its low-key way than any film-noir production that it could be said to parody. It doesn't ramp up but brings down and scatters conventional elements. Although there are several scenes that some viewers might find humorous, this humor is of the whimsical not the parodic variety.

Critics today are also inclined to see this French film as an example of reality cinema. The insouciant attitude that *Breathless* takes toward its audience may encourage impressionable viewers to mistake it for realism, but there is nothing about the characters' talk or behavior that corresponds to the way people actually talk or behave, even in France.

The best way to understand *Breathless* is to reconsider its genre—that is, to approach it primarily as a work of ideas rather than as a work of art. The British critic Matthew Arnold, in his 1864 essay "The Function of Criticism in the Present Time," noted that art and criticism are distinct but mutually supportive genres, and that the relative merit of each may vary in different eras and in different cultures. The French, he argued, tend to be drawn to ideas, while the English distrust them, with the result that English art is often less intellectually informed than one would wish (even the great Wordsworth, he added, would have done well to read more books). A corollary, which Arnold doesn't pursue, is that French art tends to be overladen with ideas, to be more like criticism than art—an assumption that pertains well to *Breathless*.

The sequence of shifting signifiers used in the film also corresponds to ideas about meaning that the linguistic philosopher Jacques Derrida was developing, under the name of deconstruction, during the same period. In deconstructionist terms, then, the film's sloppiness becomes a value, a way of exposing both the arbitrary *constructedness* of past meaning and the opportunities for making new meaning in the future. The former constitutes the political dimension of the film insofar as it critiques what has been done in the name of cinema, society, capitalism, or whatever. The latter is the theoretical dimension, the film's way of demonstrating what is possible if one lets loose from old constraints and assumptions. Godard's film can be viewed as the critical antecedent to a new era in which movies were freed from the constraints of classic Hollywood cinema.

3. Based on the information in the passage, which of the following statements about the perspective of deconstruction in the interpretation of the film could be true?

(A) From deconstructionist perspective, the film's shifting scenes could be a reflection of transitory and nihilistic character of established tradition and culture.

(B) From deconstructionist perspective, the film's unsystematic or casual arrangement could be a valuable way of exposing the autocratic and whimsical characters of constructed establishment in politics and theory.

(C) A deconstructionist interpretation could liberate the film from its confined and stilted scenes and reveal its promising implication in the sociopolitical arena.

(D) A deconstructionist interpretation betrays the ideal of Jacques Derrida who advocates a valuable combination of theoretical critique and political reflection in the criticism of classic Hollywood cinema.

(E) Free from the conventional constraints and assumptions, the film could be envisioned as anticipating a new era in which movies are created from a random patchwork piecing together diverse, heterogeneous elements haphazardly.

4. The author discusses Matthew Arnold's essay "The Function of Criticism in the Present Time" in the third paragraph primarily in order to do which of the following?

(A) Prove that art and criticism are different but mutually supportive genres

(B) Argue that the relative merit of art and criticism may vary in different time periods and in different cultures

(C) Highlight the crucial divergence between English art and French art

(D) Indicate that the film *Breathless*, as a French art, is awash with ideas, closer to criticism than art

(E) Criticize Arnold for failing to draw from his ideas an important conclusion

For the following question, consider each of the choices separately and select all that apply.

5. The information provided in the passage indicates that parody of traditional acting and filmmaking might include which of the following as its features?

(A) Consistent mockery

(B) Whimsical humor

(C) Aim to trigger a laugh

6. Which of the following best describes the organization of the passage as a whole?

(A) Two views are devalued, an alternative view is presented and substantiated.

(B) A hypothesis is presented, a better alternative partly based on the hypothesis is discussed, and the new hypothesis is evaluated in light of new evidence.

(C) Two views are compared and contrasted, evidence that undercuts these two views is then presented, and a new view that may better interpret the subject is discussed.

(D) A tentative view is refuted, a revised view is presented and challenged, and a third view that combines previous two views is suggested and yet to be confirmed.

(E) Two views are questioned, a relatively new view is introduced, but then supplanted by a more recent view.

Historians have devised different methods to estimate the levels of immigration in the eighteenth-century America. Using tenuous fertility and mortality data compiled by other historians, Gemery calculates net migration as a residual, with the results being a plausible range of 278,400 to 485,300 white immigrants for the period 1700 to 1780. An alternative method, however, relies on an improved surname analysis of the 1790 census as a check for the increasing expertise of ethnic group historians who rely on actual immigration data from ship and passenger lists. Despite some gaps, this method produces enlightening results for most ethnic groups during the period − 585,800 immigrants（278,400 blacks and 307,400 whites）, roughly consistent with Gemery's finding.

7. According to the passage, the residual method used by Gemery differs from the alternative method in that it

（A） relies on the fertility and mortality data about immigrants that have previously been inaccessible

（B） produces a total number far larger than the total number generated by the alternative method

（C） yields a more accurate estimate than the alternative method

（D） eschews the sketchy fertility and mortality data that the alternative method draws on

（E） does not exploit the immigration data of ethnic groups from ship and passenger lists

A new class of insecticides known as neonicotinoids is broadly and commonly used in most cropping systems and on turf and forest pests. But one of the compounds in this class, imidacloprid, was banned in France, because it is acutely toxic to bees and because sub-lethal doses have been shown to impair honey bee short-term memory.

8. Which of the following, if true, most strongly supports the French policy about imidacloprid?

（A）　Short-term memory is critical to bee's navigational abilities necessary for foraging flights and for returning to the hive.

（B）　Short-term memory is an essential part of bee's cognitive repertoire as is long-term memory.

（C）　Short-term memory and long-term memory function simultaneously when bees fly and navigate.

（D）　Environmentalists oppose the widespread use of imidacloprid for fearing its unintended consequences for the turf and forest pests.

（E）　Government policy-makers have not yet reached a final rejection of imidacloprid since its effects have not been extensively investigated.

Some factors have been suggested as causal mechanisms of bee colony collapse disorder (CCD), for example, the use of genetically modified (GMO) crops. However, large bee die-offs have also occurred in Europe, where GMO crops are not widely grown. Also, in the United States, the patterns of CCD-affected colonies do not appear to correlate with the distribution of GMO-crops such as Bt-corn. Other hypotheses are even less likely. For example, the public has become concerned that cell phone use may be causing bee die-offs; however, exposure of bees to high levels of electromagnetic fields is unlikely. Similarly, shifts in the Earth's magnetic field, which could conceivably affect bee navigation, have not been correlated with bee die-off episodes, but cannot be completely ruled out at this time.

9. Which of the following best describes the main idea of the passage?

(A) Several factors, such as GMO crops, cell phone use and change in the magnetic field, cannot explain why bee colony collapses in disorder.

(B) Scientists have dismissed several theories of bee colony collapse disorder because of their lack of strong experimental evidence and solid theoretical framework.

(C) Scientists failed to explain the collapse of bee colony because they cannot easily measure the impact of cell phone use on the alteration of electromagnetic fields.

(D) The use of GMO crops did not bring about large bee die-offs more than the shifts in the Earth's magnetic field.

(E) The reason that proposed hypotheses cannot explain large bee die-offs is that they cannot establish the correlation between the pattern of colony collapse and the putative factors.

10. It can be inferred from the passage that the GMO-crops hypothesis would have been more convincing if researchers had been able to

(A) prove that exposure of bees to high levels of electromagnetic fields does not correlate with large bee die-offs in Europe

(B) demonstrate that the changes in the Earth's magnetic field, though affecting bee navigation, do not vary with the periods of bee die-offs

(C) demonstrate that the pattern of bee colony collapse correspond to the demographical mode of genetically modified crops

(D) dismiss the hypotheses that explain the bee colony collapse disorder by invoking the non-European evidence

(E) make extensive laboratory and field testing to indicate a lack of acute and sub-lethal effects on bees exposed to GMO-pollen

第六节 Exercise 6

Diffusible compounds released by algae may mediate coral mortality via microbial activity. Algae can release excess photosynthate in the form of polysaccharides, or dissolved organic carbon, that can fuel microbial activity and accelerate microbial growth. The microbial community growing on or near the coral surface may then exhibit explosive growth, eventually creating a zone of hypoxia on the surface of the live coral tissue. In this study, all corals exposed to but not in direct contact with algae bleached and were physiologically compromised within 2–4 days. Clearly, some algae may release chemical compounds that may be toxic to other organisms. But here, coral mortality could be completely prevented with the addition of antibiotics, thus supporting the hypothesis that the microbial community was the agent of coral death.

For the following question, consider each of the choices separately and select all that apply.

1. Given the information given in the passage, it can be inferred that which of the following statements is true of the zone of hypoxia on the surface of the live coral tissue?

   （A） The live corals in the zone of hypoxia would be physiologically suffered within several days.

   （B） The zone of hypoxia is awash in chemical compounds released by algae that are directly harmful to corals.

   （C） The deleterious effect on corals of hypoxia area generated by a microbial community can be counterbalanced by the addition of antibiotics.

2. Which of the following, if true, would most weaken the hypothesis proposed in the passage?

   （A） Corals generally show significant declines in health when placed next to algae without antibiotics.

   （B） Not all coral species are equally susceptible to algal mediated mortality and not all algae have deleterious effects on corals.

   （C） A significant input of dissolved organic carbon that facilitates the growth of microbes comes either from the algae themselves or from anthropogenic sources （e.g. waste water）.

   （D） On healthy reefs, corals are the dominant, habitat forming organisms and algae are kept at low levels of standing biomass via intense grazing.

   （E） A new experiment discovers that increased organic carbon loading directly kill corals and that coral mortality caused by organic carbon loading is negatively correlated with an increase in microbial activity.

Unlike the traditional qualitative approaches to acculturation, Padilla presented a multidimensional and quantitative model of acculturation that relied on cultural awareness, i.e., implicit knowledge that individuals have of their cultures of origin and of their host cultures. If individuals show more knowledge of their heritage cultures than they do of the new contact cultures, they are less acculturated, and vice versa. But like those major theories of acculturation, this model did not take into consideration individual differences and personality characteristics that facilitate or retard acculturation. Certainly, Padilla's emphasis on the preference of individuals for the dominant or heritage cultures is an important advance. But the model falls short of explaining how individuals from the same socioeconomic, generational, and familial backgrounds differ on willingness and competence to acculturate.

3. Select the sentence in the passage in which the author qualifies the disapproval of Padilla's model in explaining how individual differences and personality characteristics influence the rate of acculturation.

For the following question, consider each of the choices separately and select all that apply.

4. It can be inferred from the passage that which of the following descriptions would be true of conventional approaches to acculturation?

（A） The traditional theories of acculturation would argue that if the persons possess more knowledge of the host cultures, then they are less acculturated.

（B） The traditional theories of acculturation have not provided the quantitative hypothesis of how acculturation takes place.

（C） The traditional theories of acculturation have yet to appreciate and explain individual differences within the demands of cultural and sociopolitical contexts.

Carbohydrate causes the elevation of transmitter serotonin in the brain, which can fuel neuron activity and stimulate behavior. Scientists propose reducing carbohydrate in the diet for patients of neuronal oversensitivity and increasing protein, which can suppress the production and release of transmitter serotonin. However, the low level of serotonin might induce a strong craving for carbohydrate and finally minimize the effect of high protein diet. Thus the scientists' proposal does not work.

5. Which one of the following, if true, most supports the scientists' proposal?

（A） Some patients who crave for carbohydrate reported they feel sleepy after a diet containing mostly carbohydrate.

（B） Some patients who do not crave for carbohydrate reported they feel refreshed after a diet containing mostly protein.

（C） The consumption of protein indirectly decreases blood concentration of tryptophan which is the only precursor of serotonin in the brain.

（D） The high level of serotonin in the brain can facilitate neuronal activity and produce strong emotional and behavioral responses.

（E） A high protein diet, though benefiting physical health, turns out to have other detrimental effects on mental health.

The cooling rate of a magma determines the texture of the final rock. As a magma cools, the specific cations and anions that ultimately form solid crystals must initially bond with one another to form very small crystal nuclei. Scientists have determined the general relationship between cooling rate and the total number of crystal nuclei. Slow cooling rates generally form only a small number of crystal nuclei, and, with abundant time for crystal growth, lead to a coarse grained rock dominated by large crystals. As the cooling rate increases, so does the number of crystal nuclei; the result is a fine grained rock that contains numerous small crystals. Finally, very fast cooling rates can lead to a situation where no crystals grow. Not remaining liquid, the magma solidifies to a dark-colored solid — volcanic glass. It is analogous to the man-made glass; the only difference is that man-made glass is formed from compositionally "simple" magma whereas volcanic glass is derived from a compositionally complex natural magma.

6. The passage is primarily concerned with discussing

（A） the different roles of crystal nucleus and cooling rate in the formation of the final rock

（B） the difference and similarity between and among three types of crystal nuclei

（C） the difference and similarity between and among three kinds of textures of rocks

（D） the general relationship between cooling rate of magma and the texture of the final rock

（E） the particular chemical composition in a magma and its effect on the texture of the final rock

7. Given the information in the passage, which of the following statements is true of volcanic glass?

（A） It is completely different from man-made glass in that it includes crystals within itself.

（B） It is a simple magma because of its simple chemical composition.

（C） It forms at a specific rate at which the magma cools.

（D） It defies the general relationship between cooling rate and the number of small crystal nuclei.

（E） It verges on the phase boundary of liquid and solid before it evolves into a critical state.

When 1,000 people who have not smoked or smoked only in a short time are tested for lung cancer, only 10 show early signs of lung cancer. By contrast, of every 1,000 people who have smoked frequently 750 show early signs of lung cancer. Thus, for a randomly chosen group of people, the majority of those who show early signs of lung cancer will be people who have smoked frequently.

8. A reasoning error in the argument is that the argument

(A) identifies the group who have smoked frequently with the group who have shown early signs of lung cancer

(B) fails to take into account what proportion of the population have smoked frequently

(C) ignores the fact that some people who smoked frequently have not shown early signs of cancer

(D) attributes early signs of lung cancer to smoking

(E) attempts to infer a strong conclusion from a shaky premise

A sudden intense surge in anxiety is characterized by arousal of the sympathetic branch of the autonomic nervous system as expressed in elevated heart and breathing rates, blood pressure, sweating, and other signs. This led to the expectation that N (neuroticism) personality or trait anxiety would be related to measures of these indicators. Research has failed to support this correlational hypothesis. Longitudal research has shown that N is a personality precursor of anxiety and mood disorders, so why does N not show relationships with some of the same biological indicators that characterize these disorders? There may be a threshold effect so that the dysregulation of neurotransmitter systems characteristic of the disorders only emerges at some critical level of persistent stress that is not reproducible in controlled laboratory studies.

9. Which of the following statements best describes the organization of the passage as a whole?

(A) A situation is described and explained, and a new hypothesis is provided to supplant the previous one.

(B) An assertion is made and several arguments are provided to strengthen it and dismissed.

(C) A theory is discussed and then ways in which it has been revised are described.

(D) A fact is stated, a hypothesis is suggested and fails to be proved, and its failure is explained.

(E) A controversial theory is discussed and then arguments both against and for it are described.

10. It can be inferred from the passage that the necessity of threshold effect hypothesis stated in the last sentence would need to be reassessed if researchers found that which of the following were true?

(A) The dysregulation of neurotransmitter systems characteristic of the anxiety and mood disorders does not emerge below a certain critical level of persistent stress simulated in laboratory studies.

(B) The study attempting to find a biological basis for the anxiety and mood disorders obtains the positive results in experimental research with animals and with humans that suffer from anxiety and mood disorders.

(C) N shows the negative relationship with some of the same biological indicators that characterize anxiety and mood disorders.

(D) N shows the positive relationship with some biological indicators that are not typical of anxiety and mood disorders.

(E) N is demonstrated to be related to measures of these indicators in reaction to persistent stress in a masterfully designed laboratory study.

很多事不能太犹豫，不要等目标清晰才行动；人生苦短，不要等到对的人和事才开始，要先行动，然后在冲动和摸索中清楚目标。《奥德赛》的名句："对人来说，没有什么比漫无目的地徘徊更令人无法忍受的了"（Nothing is more evil than homelessness for mortals）。

六套阅读练习题解析

本章对6套练习题做详细的解析，解析分为文章分析与题目分析。

文章分析的内容包括：

【*cues*, function & **core**】与"Paragraph段落：Examples 段落结构练习"一样，在左边的文章正文中，段落核心词以及证据重现论点核心的词（**core**）以**黑体**表示，结构和逻辑的提示词（*cues*）以斜体表示，少数提示词可兼任核心词，以***斜黑体***表示。在右边的结构图中，最重要的是function与core。其中，在function一栏中，以符号形式写出文章每一句的功能作用，标志着我们对文章结构的理解有了一个外在的、摆在眼前的客观指标，而不是停留在自己头脑里的自以为自己懂了的主观幻觉。在core一栏中，则只有kw的核心词，那些中间证据中重现的核心词，虽然在左边文章中会标识（方便在阅读时做同义对应或逻辑等价），但就现场记忆来说，只要记住论点与论据的任意一个核心词，往往是论点的核心就可以了，所以，在下面的图表中，我们只把核心句或kw句中的核心内容表示为**黑体**，那些重现核心的词则以正常字体出现，它们当然比没有被标识出来的词汇重要。建议读者在看完结构图表和结构分析以后，将*cues* function & **core**自己画一遍，尤其是其中的function & **core**部分，这是扎实训练不可或缺的步骤。

Cues	Function	**Core**
1.	1.	1.
2.	2.	2.
3.	3.	3.

通常我们认为，在阅读时应注意*cues*，想到句子function，抓出**core**，核心词就是我们在现场阅读时在当前意识的词。读者可特别留意，我们在文中标出的黑体核心词是不是句子里的生词、难词；句子的生词、难词是不是核心词（通常不是）。

【结构分析】相对详细地说明结构图表的含义。从一个句子与上下句的关系来判断它的作用和核心词汇，并讨论各个论点与论据的关系。如果读者熟悉了本书使用的结构分析术语和它们所代表的含义，就能通过结构图表（*cues*, function & **core**）直接把握文章思路，有时可以略去结构分析。

【词汇】按字母顺序列出文章以及题目里相对难的词汇。当然，并不一定需要掌握所有单词才能理解文章的主要意思和逻辑关系，虽然多学一些动词、形容词、抽象名词是必需的。

题目分析的部分针对每一道题进行详细解析，包括两个部分：【解法】和【选项分析】。

【解法】逐一说明每道题的题型、题干定位的思路。

【选项】逐一说明每个选项为何对，为何错，指出正确答案的文字对应和错误答案的错处。

【考位分析】对于多个题目的文章，常会说明所有题目及对应原文的考点位置。通常，**各段首末句、转折句或态度句、对比、因果、让步转折、句子功能作用是考点。**

第一节 Exercise 1 解析

1.1 Lowell's poetry

【*cues*, function & **core**】

Strengthened by a memory of the spiritual dignity of man, **L**owell writes in *Land of Unlikeness* as an avowed **Christian**, with **E**liot and **H**opkins as his conscious *models*. Reviewing Eliot's *Four Quartets in 1943*, he argued that union with **God** is somewhere in sight in all poetry. A *1944* "Note" on Hopkins shows Lowell interested in the way Hopkins' unique personality and **holiness** flowered in poetry.

Certainly, much of the turbulence of Lowell's early poetry comes from his conscious struggle to approach **Christian** perfection. His effort to perfect his verse was *analogous to* the discipline of **contemplation**, the achieved aesthetic experience of a poem *analogous to* **spiritual** illumination. **But** Lowell's way with poetry would be *neither* **H**opkins' *nor* **E**liot's. *In* the American romantic tradition, he *not only* merged poetry with religion *but* equated both with **culture**, and thus attempted to be oratorical and satirical, exalted and apocalyptic, visionary and prophetic. Yearning for a civilization in which men bear a likeness to God, *he finds* in the modern world **only** capitalism, war and **secularized** consciousness. （174 words）

Cues	Function	Core
1. L: 人名及书名	1. TW: kw1	1. **L = E.H.: Christian**
（*2. in 1943*	2. a.	2. E: God = Christian
3. 1944）	3. b.	3. H: holiness
1. Certainly	1. kw$_1$ = ~kw$_2$	1. **L: Christian**
（*2. analogous to*）	2. x$_{1, 2}$	2. = contemplation
3. But neither...nor	3. vs. kw2	3. **L ≠ H. E.**
（*4. In..., not only, but also*	4. m	4. **culture** = religion = satirical, visionary
5. he finds...）	5. n	5. only secularized = capitalism = war

【结构分析】

◆ 第一段

第1句：主题及论点。首句大写人名 + 斜体书名，而且是文艺作品，典型的评述对象 = 主题词TW。评述型文章，后文会展开说明，基本的结构预期是：TW. kw1. a. b. kw2. x. y。从内容上看，本句的主干是L（owell）writes as an avowed Christian（L写作品时公开声称自己是基督徒）。这已经是一个判断句，可以作为文章的主题句TS；后面的with介词结构里还出现了model一词，文科讲对比，如果我们对此敏感，则可

以感觉到，这是一个小重点，于是得到L = E.H.，即第一个小论点kw1。所有人名都取了首字母，不需要知道这些人物的背景知识。

2：证据。此句有时间1943，**中间时间、地点、大写、数量 = 证据**。证据重现首句论点核心，此句讲到L主张与神统一，可见于所有诗歌；很明显，神的概念是基督教的。God = Christian。

3：证据。继续写另一个时间1944，L的兴趣在于H的人格和神圣气息，证据重现论点核心，holiness = Christian。通常，**证据略读**，不必深究其含义。

◆ 第二段

第1句：让步。段首句让步的情况少见。本句讲到L的早期诗歌的激流涌动（turbulence），来自他追求基督教的完善。此让步的内容与上段首句相同，因此后面的转折一定出现与此不同的新内容，即kw2。

2：让步的证据。本句无转折，是上句让步的证据和细节。证据重现论点核心，contemplation, spiritual = Christian。他的一些方面类似于宗教沉思，审美的经验又类似于精神的启示。

3：转折，给出新的观点。But引出的转折句指出：L的方式不同于H或E，这就与第1段首句的model所表示的相同形成对比。本句只是过渡，并没有直接给出L处理诗歌的方式是什么。后面的证据会说明。

4：第二个观点的证据。以in引导的介词短语，通常表示证据与细节，次要。本句说，L不仅融合诗歌与宗教，而且将这两者等同于文化，在此语境下，merge = equate，即他认为poetry与culture相关。not only...but的内容，以but为重点，故culture为该句中心。一般地，**新词为核心**。后半句thus从内容上看并非总结，仅为顺承，指出L试图做到演说、讽刺等兼备，宾语内容是连续的形容词短语并列，**句内并列成分次要**。如要找词，可找比如visionary，作为culture的广义同义词或逻辑等价词。

5：证据。上一句以L为主语，L merged, equated，本句也如此，L finds...；这些平行的写作结构属于典型的并列。本句的大意是：L渴望文明社会，人如神，结果他在现代世界仅发现资本主义、战争与世俗意识，没有发现神性。宾语的"，and"**并列次要**，可抓住only和secularized。资本主义或经济政治、战争等问题，都属于世俗范畴，不在精神层面，最后一句说明L以宗教气质的文化来评判现实社会。于是：religion: Christian, God, holiness, contemplation, spiritual *vs.* capitalism, war, secularized consciousness，宗教与世俗、精神与物质、宗教文化与社会政治对比。

◆ 全文

首句给主题词，并讲第一个方面，L与H、E的相同之处。2–3句给证据。第二段1–2句是让步及其证据，第3句是反驳观点，指出不同之处。最后2句是证据。这是典型的**评述型**文章，包括主题及2个分论点。重点在1–2段首句：**TW: kw1**. a. b. ~kw2. x1,2. **kw2**. m. n.

【词汇】

apocalyptic	*adj.* =prophetic, 预言的，预示灾难的	
avowed	*adj.* =declared, 公开宣称的，明显的	
exalted	*adj.* 兴奋的，情绪高涨的；ex-=out + alt-(high) → exalt *v.* 激励；推崇	
contemplation	*n.* 思索，沉思；contemplate (*v.*)	
illumination	*n.* -lumin-, 流明，亮 → 启示，启发	
merge	*v.* 融合，合并	
oratorical	*adj.* 演说的；oration *n.* 演说	

satirical	*adj.* =sarcastic, ironic, 讽刺的；satire *v.* 嘲弄，讽刺
secularized	*adj.* 世俗化的；secular = sociopolitical, social, material, economic *vs.* religious, spiritual, metaphysical
turbulence	*n.* 波动，动荡；湍流，激流
visionary	*adj.* 有远见的，有想象力的
yearn for	(=long for), 渴望

【题目分析】

1. The passage is primarily concerned with

   (A) discussing the religious theme in the poetry of Lowell

   (B) explaining the aesthetic motivation of Lowell's poems

   (C) comparing and contrasting the writing styles of Lowell and Eliot and Hopkins

   (D) focusing on the romantic and spiritual message in the poetry of Lowell

   (E) pointing out the importance of religious dimension for Lowell's critique of capitalism

【解法】主题题。本题问is primarily concerned with，直接定位主题句，文章的主题词在首句：人名及书名，但作者给出的判断却不只第1段第1句，还有第2段的转折句。要同时考虑这两个内容。

【选项】

A. **正确**。第1段讨论L诗歌的宗教主题，与另外两人相同；第2段让步转折以后提到文化，但并不否定宗教，而与宗教等同，只是说L诗歌中的宗教处理与两人不同。

B. 审美动机（aesthetic motivation）不是文章主题。

C. **干扰选项**。文章比较了L.E.H，但不是文章主题，文章是通过对比来说明L的诗歌方法。对比是途径，不是目标。而且写作风格一词，也不太准确。

D. L的诗歌里的浪漫主义与精神启示，浪漫主义非重点。

E. L从宗教层面对资本主义进行批判在末句或有所体现，但不是文章主题。

2. According to the passage, Lowell's approach to poetry differs from that of Hopkins and Eliot in that he

（A）presents poetic theme as entangled with spiritual revelation

（B）reinvents a form of poetry that is both religious and secular

（C）produces a form of poetry that is integrated with religion and identified with culture

（D）mixes different genres of surrealism and representationalism in the poetry

（E）underscores the role of speculation and contemplation in the poetry

【解法】（对比）核心题，differ from H. E.只在第2段But句出现，定位到该句，neither H nor E，只给出对比关系，没讲内容。But之后的句子讲到内容，重点在poetry = religion = culture。

【选项】

A. 对诗歌主题的体现与精神启示缠绕（entangled）在一起。没有谈到文化。

B. 重新发明(reinvent)，原文无，遇错即停，不必再看。

C. 正确。创造了一种艺术形式，整合宗教与认同文化，与but句之后的证据句子构成对应：is **integrated with** religion and *identified with* culture = **merged** poetry **with** religion ... *equated* both *with* culture

D. 混合超现实主义与表征主义的不同风格（genres），这些概念都未出现。

E. 强调思辨(speculation)和沉思(contemplation)的作用，未在But之后的内容中出现。

3. Which of the following characterizations of the relationship between Lowell and Eliot and Hopkins can be inferred from the passage?

（A）They all share common concerns about the religious and realistic elements to be explored in the poetry.

（B）They all share the same sociopolitical agenda implicitly developed in their poems.

（C）They disagree over the extent to which secular factors should be involved in the production of poetry.

（D）Whereas Lowell emphasizes the power of political mobilization of poetry, Eliot and Hopkins only concern the contemplative, spiritual message of poetry.

（E）Although they share a religious vision in thematic expression, Lowell and Eliot and Hopkins part in their ways to poetry.

【解法】（段落）核心题。L.E.H的关系在1段首句、2段But句都有提到，定位这两句。基本的关系是既相同、又不同。

【选项】

A. 他们在探索诗歌中宗教和现实主义的要素方面都相同，这是错误的，因为But句之后谈到L以文化批判现实，realistic不是E.H.的做法。

B. 他们有同样的社会政治议程，错误；原文只提到L对世俗意识表示批判，E.H.与此不同。

C. 他们在诗歌中应该涉及多少世俗因素的看法上有分歧，原文并没有提到L.E.H.对此的看法，只说L与他们不同，用文化来评判社会。

D. L强调诗歌的政治动因，原文没有提到。遇错即停。

E. 正确。虽然他们都有宗教视野，但却在处理诗歌的路径上分离（part...way...）。they **share** a religious vision in thematic expression = 首段首句 with Eliot and Hopkins as his conscious **models**；**part their ways** to poetry = But Lowell's **way** with poetry would be **neither** Hopkins' **nor** Eliot's。

【考位分析】

Q1：**首句与2段转折句**；Q2：**2段But**句及证据；Q3：**首句与2段转折句**。首段2、3句证据未考。2段1、2句让步内容未考。

※ 逻辑题

A survey finds that the percentage of young employees in a company in the last three years **varies with** the percentage of young applicants who have grown up in the same city as the company resides. **Since** young applicants of the company are usually either from the same city or from the other cities, **it can be concluded** that the percentage of young employees in the company **is highly influenced by** the recruitment rate for the company's young applicants growing up in the same city.

4. Which one of the following statements, if true, most weakens the conclusion?

   （A） Human resource department of the company is dominated by local employees.

   （B） A high number of young employees from the other cities have joined in the company in the last three years.

   （C） The percentage of young applicants from the other cities increases dramatically in the last three years.

   （D） The percentage of young employees in the company increases slightly in the last three years.

   （E） The young people from the same city favor working at home town to working at the other city.

【解法】逻辑反对。题干问most weakens。原文大意为：调查发现过去3年公司年轻员工百分比与本地年轻申请人的百分比相关；因为公司的年轻申请人要么来自本地，要么来自其他城市，所以推出结论，即公司年轻员工百分比受到公司本地年轻申请人的招聘率的影响。第1句讲percentage of young employees – percentage of young applicants growing up in the same city，第2句讲percentage of young employees – recruitment rate for young applicants growing up in the same city。论证的缺口是招聘率，这涉及其他城市的年轻申请人占整个年轻申请人的百分比。

【选项】

A. 人力资源部门主要是本地员工。没有提到百分比问题。不构成反对。

B. 很多来自其他城市的年轻员工加入公司，绝对数字，不是相对数字的百分比。

C. 正确。来自其他城市的年轻申请人的百分比在过去3年来显著增加，则即便招聘率不变，绝对数字也会上升，从而影响公司年轻员工的百分比，这样，本地年轻申请人的招聘率不一定对年轻员工百分比有显著影响。

D. 公司年轻员工百分比增加，未涉及申请人百分比，无关。

E. 本地年轻人的工作偏好，无关。

1.2 Neuronal ensembles

【*cues*, function & core】&【结构分析】

It is *widely agreed* that modifiable **neuronal ensembles** *support* cognition. *Therefore*, **alterations** in these networks *could be responsible for* the **behavioral** impairments observed with **ageing**. *Advances* in multiple single unit *recording methods have allowed* the dynamics of hippocampal cell populations *to be investigated* in behaving rats, and *studies using these methods have shown that* certain properties of these networks are compromised during ageing. Interestingly, many of the age-related changes that have been discovered can be *linked to* **plasticity deficits**, as **blockade** of NMDA (*N*-methyl-d-aspartate) receptors in young rats **results in** ensemble dynamics that resemble those of aged rats.

Cues	Function	Core
1. *widely agreed*	1. i.	1. **neuronal** → cognition
2. *responsible for*	2. j.	2. n (euron) network → behavior
3. *studies ...shown*	3. k.	3. ...
4. *linked to*	4. **TS**	4. **change ← plasticity deficits**

第1句：背景/introduction。首句老观点或常见观点的用法有2种：1）铺垫背景，已知理论；2）作为反驳对象。本句表背景。神经集群支持认知：n（euron）→ c（ognition）。

2：推论。Therefore顺承上句，神经网络改变，年老行为受损，behavioral 属于cognition。

3：证据。研究表明年老时神经网络受损（compromised）。

4：结果 = TS。神经变化与可塑性缺陷有关。理科讲因果/link。as从句从反面讲年幼老鼠的NMDA受体受阻也会有同样效果，证明NMDA受体影响神经以至可塑性。

Neuronal *recordings* from the hippocampus of adult rats *reveal that* when a rat explores an environment, pyramidal and granule cells show **patterned neural** activity that is *highly correlated with* a rat's **position** in space. Between 30% and 50% of pyramidal cells in CA1 region of the hippocampus *show* **place-specific firing** in a given environment, which has earned these neurons the name '**place cells**'. When the firing patterns of many hippocampal neurons are recorded simultaneously, it is possible to *reconstruct* the **position** of a rat in an environment *from* the place cell **firing patterns** alone. The composite cell activity is 'map-like' and, in *different* **environments**, hippocampal **place maps** *change markedly*. *Although* these maps can be driven by **external environmental** features, **internal** events are *also* important and a new map might be generated in the same environment if the demands of the task change.

Cues	Function	Core
1. *highly correlate*	1.kw1	1. **position → *n*. pattern**
2. *show*	2. a	2. place cell (neuron)
3. *reconstruct ... from*	3. b	3. pattern – position
4. *different ... change*	4. c	4. environ → cell maps
5. *Although, ... also*	5. d	5. external + internal

第1句：论点。理科讲因果，correlate with前后重要：spatial position → neural patterns。其他专业名词次要。

2：证据。**中间数量=证据**：30–50%。神经元有place-specific/地方特异性。

3：证据。从A重构B，提示相关：cell patterns – position in the environment，对应首句。

4：证据。首句论点说position → patterns，可推出position变化，神经模式变化；本句说环境即位置不同，则神经细胞的位置地图即神经模式也不同。

5：让步转折。外部环境固然重要，但内部事件也有影响。转折内容提出internal events的影响。强调不可片面强调外部环境的作用，限制本段观点的适用范围。

In young rats, CA1 place fields **expand asymmetrically** during repeated route following, which results in a shift in the centre of mass of place fields in the direction opposite to the rat's trajectory. This observation *is consistent with* neural network models dating back to **Hebb**'s 1949 concept of the '**phase sequence**' of cell assemblies, *which suggested that* an associative, temporally **asymmetric** synaptic plasticity mechanism could *serve to encode* sequences or episodes of **experience**. The magnitude of this place field expansion, *however*, significantly **decreases** *in aged* rats. It is likely that this **age-associated reduction in** experience-dependent **plasticity** *is due to* some specific **plasticity deficits**, as it does *not occur when* CPP, a selective and competitive antagonist of NMDA-type receptors, is administered to young rats.

Cues	Function	Core
1. In young ...,	1. kw2.1	1. **young**: ↑ **asymmetrically**
2. consistent with, serve to encode ...	2. x	2. = **H**.: asymmetric → experience
3. however, in aged	3. vs. kw2.2	3. vs. **aged**: ↓
4. is due to, as ... not occur when ...	4. ← TS'	4. **plasticity deficits** → ↓

第1句：实验证据为本段核心。"In结构"讲年幼老鼠的情况，神经位置区不对称扩张，which从句为事实，次要。

2：证据与解释。This observation指出上句属于事实，该观察与H的"阶段序列"概念一致；which suggests说明这一概念，serve to encode提示因果关系：asymmetric → experience，即不对称的可塑机制编码经验序列，可看做解释的一部分，与首段主题句一致。

3：对比证据。年老老鼠的位置区域的扩展程度减小。

4：解释。本段**先实验再解释**，is due to表因果：可塑性缺陷导致经验可塑性的减小；as从句从反面证明，年幼老鼠注射与NMDA受体竞争的CPP，可塑性不会减少。

In addition, the maintenance of place maps *also differs* between **young and old** animals. *In normal young* rats, a place map for a given environment can remain **stable** and **retrievable** for months. A *similar* **stability** of CA1 place maps *in aged* rats is observed within and between episodes of behavior in the same environment. *Occasionally, however, if the old* rat is removed from the environment and returned later, the original place map is **not retrieved** and an independent population of place cells may be activated even in a familiar room. Such map **retrieval failures** *might be attributed to* specific **defective plasticity** in aged rats. (469 words)

Cues	Function	Core
1. In addition, differ	1.kw3	1. **maintain**: **young** ≠ **old**
2. In normal young	2. m1.	2. young: retrievable
3. similar, in aged	3. m2.	3. = aged: stable
4. however, if ... old	4. n.	4. **vs. later, not retrieve**
5. be attributed to	5. n'/cs.	5. ← **defective plasticity**

第1句：本段论点，以对比内容支持首段主题。与上段对比证据并列，指出年老年幼动物位置地图维持方面有差别。

2：证据。说明正常幼鼠情况，位置地图稳定，可获取。

3：证据。年老老鼠在同一环境下也类似。

4：对比证据。令年老老鼠脱离环境，之后返回，则无法获取。对比找反义：retrievable vs. not retrieved。

5：解释。与第3段一样，**先证据再解释，先实验再假说**，解释与首段末句主题一致，确认可塑性缺陷的影响。

全文：论点说明文章，1段总，2-3-4段分。第1段引出主题句。第2段给出一个方面论据，为小论点。第3、4段讲两个对比论据。

【词汇】

administer	v. 给予；实施、执行；行政管理
antagonist	n. 对抗药；敌手、对手
assemblies	集会；组合、装配，本文中 = ensembles
asymmetric	adj. 不对称的：a-=not + symmetric
attributed to	due to 归因于；attribute v. 归因于 n. 属性
cognition	n. 认知；从信息加工角度研究大脑
compromise	v. = impair, 损害 n. 妥协，折中
correlate with	与…相关；常表相关关系，很重要
dynamics	n. 动力学 vs. statics n. 静力学
encode	v. en-：动词前缀 + code密码：编码

ensemble	n. 整体；合唱；文中 = assembly
episode	n. 连续过程中的一段；美剧的一集
firing	n. 发动、激发；文中表示神经元激活
impairment	损害，伤害；来自 impair v. =harm, damage
marked	adj. = pronounced, significant，明显的
plasticity	n. 可塑性；来自plastic adj. 塑料的，可塑的
reconstruct	v. 重构
retrieve	v. 提取，获取
synaptic	adj. 突触的；synapse 突触，神经元的接触处

【题目分析】

5. It can be inferred from the passage that the author would draw which of the following conclusions if they had <u>not</u> found that young rats administered with CPP show no reduction in experience-dependent plasticity?

   (A) The extent of place field expansion does not decrease in aged rats.

   (B) The extent of place field expansion does not affect the experience-dependent plasticity.

   (C) The reduction in experience-dependent plasticity does not vary with age.

   (D) CPP cannot be used to inhibit the effect of NMDA-type receptors.

   (E) The reduction in experience-dependent plasticity in aged rats does not correlate with certain plasticity deficits.

【解法】取非题。题干infer不重要；重要的是would ... if ... had not的虚拟语气所暗示的取非。定位所取非的内容。题干中**大写优先定位**，CPP仅第3段末句提到，该句有as引导的原因从句，因为有CPP实验的事实，所以得出experience-dependent plasticity is due to plasticity deficits。题干问如果没发现该事实会如何。答案将此结论取非，可塑性减少不是因为可塑性缺陷。

【选项】

A. 位置区域扩张不会减少，无关。

B. 部分对应。位置区域扩张不会影响可塑性，答案应是可塑性缺陷不会影响。

C. 可塑性减少不随年龄而变化，age不是答案中心词。

D. CPP被用来抑制某受体的效果。这是as从句里的when从句的内容，题干已将该部分取非，答案应是将与as大从句相对的主句的内容取非。本选项答非所问。

E. **正确**。可塑性减少不会与可塑性缺陷相关。对应：
not found that **young rats administered** with CPP show **no reduction** + the reduction in experience-dependent plasticity in aged rats does <u>*not correlate with* certain plasticity deficits</u> = reduction in experience-dependent plasticity *is due to* some specific plasticity deficits, as **it [reduction] does not occur** when **CPP is administered to young rats**.

6. Which of the following statements about the relationship between young and old rats are true, based on the information in the passage?

   (A) They invoke different neural machineries in the maintenance of place maps according to the time length of different tasks.

   (B) They share the same machinery in the formation and retrieval of original place map which then is replaced by the reinvented place map in CA1 area.

   (C) They differ in the rates of retrieval of original place map when they experience temporary displacement from their original environment.

   (D) They differ in the success of retrieval of original place map since the aged rats fail to retrieve it if they experience temporary displacement from their original environment.

   (E) They differ in the success of retrieval of original place map if the original environments they are exposed to are different.

【解法】（对比）核心题。题干问年幼与年老老鼠的关系，原文第3-4段讲了2组对比关系。对比关系常考。按照第3段however句，差别在于不对称扩张的增减；按照第4段however句，差别在于一段时间以后是否可提取位置信息。答案也有可能考两者的相同之处，但原文没有涉及。

【选项】

A. 它们援用（invoke）不同的神经机制来维持位置地图，原文未提。

B. 它们的位置地图的形成与提取机制相同，也未提。

C. 它们的提取速度有差别，rate非中心词，第4段对比的核心在retrievable, stable。

D. 正确。它们的提取成功度有差别，成功度即是否可提取；since从句讲，年老老鼠无法提取，与原文相符。对应是：the *aged rats* **fail to retrieve** it if they experience temporary displacement from their original environment = if the *old rat* is removed from the environment and returned later, the original place map **is not retrieved**

E. 干扰选项。主句与D选项的主句相同，但if从句说最初的暴露或接触环境不同，无对应；而原文说的是一个维持几个月，一个维持不了多久，重点在维持时间，不在暴露环境。

7. Which of the following claims about the place cells are supported by the information in the passage?

   (A) They track different environments in which the rats find themselves.

   (B) They remain in the same firing pattern regardless of the environmental change.

   (C) They form the same firing pattern whenever external environmental features remain the same.

   (D) They can be reconstructed only if the task change induces intense internal events.

   (E) They correlate with the map the researchers show to the rats.

【解法】（段落）信息题。题干about/regarding/concerning/of后为发问对象，place cells原文第2段多次提到，无法精确定位某句。**从选项找线索，带核心去排除，**通常会有2-3个选项与place cells所在第2段的核心相反或无关。第2段核心是place cells的模式与老鼠所在空间位置密切相关。

【选项】

A. 正确。它们追踪老鼠所位于（find themselves）的不同环境，They [*place cells*] **track different environments** = patterned *neural* activity that **is highly correlated with** a rat's **position in space**。考到2段首句。

B. 不管环境变化，维持相同激发模式，与原文完全相反。

C. 只要外部环境相同，它们就保持相同模式，这属于支持论据。但不幸的，第2段末句让步转折句指出，internal实践可在外部环境不变时影响模式。矛盾。

D. 仅当任务改变引起内部事件才可重构，only if错误，原文没有。而且原文所说重构针对的是位置，而非神经细胞。

E. 干扰选项。它们与研究者给老鼠看的地图相关。研究者给老鼠看的地图，并非老鼠所处的空间环境。

8. The author mentions Hebb's concept of the 'phase sequence' of cell assemblies in the third paragraph most probably in order to

（A） contrast Hebbian neural network models and the model proposed here

（B） offer the conceptual foundations of the neural network models to explain the phenomenon of place field asymmetric expansion.

（C） anticipate the objections that reduction in the place field expansion in aged rats

（D） show that the place field expansion in aged rats might have increased

（E） suggest that the age-associated reduction in experience-dependent plasticity is the result of specific plasticity deficits

【解法】作用题/in order to题。题干问作者提到H的概念是为了做什么，定位第3段大写人名，找逻辑上一层。第3段第2句提到H的概念，是第二句is consistent with之后的宾语，宾语成分的逻辑上一层是整个句子。此句的主干说第1句的观察与H的观念一致，在其后的which suggested that从句又指出这个观念的内容，即不对称的神经可塑机制，目的在于编码经验。句子成分可找句子主干或大意作为上一层。

【选项】

A. 对比H的模型与本文提出的模型，但文章无对比。

B. 正确。提供神经网络模型的概念基础，以解释不对称扩张现象。这些内容刚好涉及第1–2句的重点。

C. 预期反对（anticipate objection）表示让步，而原文结构词consistent with表示并列，无让步。

D. 年老老鼠的位置区域扩张也许增加，这是对原文下一句however内容的取非，不对。如果问问到第1句的目的时可以以此为答案，因为对比要素的目的在对比另一要素，或者突出另一要素，但这里考查的不是提到H的概念的作用。

E. 经验依赖的可塑性减少是因为可塑性缺陷，这是第2段末句内容，与此句的作用无关。作用题不要找逻辑的上上上一层，只需找上一层。

【考位分析】

Q5: 考3段末句取非；Q6: 4段对比核心；Q7: 2段首句核心；Q8: 3段细节作用。可见，均考各段首末句、对比核心和句子功能作用。

1.3 Strong reciprocator

【*cues*, function & **core**】&【结构分析】

Many people ***behave*** like **strong reciprocators**. *In a* ten-round public goods *experiment*, each subject grouped with three other subjects under conditions of strict anonymity is given "points", divided between a "common account" and the subject's "private account''. Each private account will be added by *40%* of the total amount of points contributed to the common account. *Clearly*, full **free riding** is a dominant strategy, *but* the experiment shows that many subjects begin by **contributing** on average about half of their endowment to the public account. *However*, the level of **contributions decays** gradually, until in the final rounds most players behave in a self-interested manner. *Presumably*, cooperative subjects **retaliated against free-riding** low contributors in the only way available to them — by lowering their own contributions. *This interpretation is* **confirmed** in a 25-round game.（133 words）

Cues	Function	Core
1. *behave like*	1. kw	1. **strong reciprocator**
2. *In a ... experiment*	2. a.	2. common – private
3. *40%*	3. b.	3. ...
4. *Clearly, but*	4. ~kw, kw	4. **free riding** *vs.* **contribute 50%**
5. *However*	5. x.	5. **contribution decay**
6. *Presumably*	6. kw'	6. **retaliate**
7. *confirmed*	7. aw+	7. **confirmed**

第1句：作者判断/论点。多数人行为像强互惠者。

2： 实验证据。叙述实验内容，分共同账户与私人账户。

3： 证据。40%为**中间数量 = 细节**。

4： 让步转折。搭便车是占优策略，但依然有人贡献一半。

5： 对比。本句仅指出与上一句不同的情况：贡献在逐渐减少。

6： 解释。有些合作者报复和惩罚（retaliate）搭便车者。惩罚搭便车本身也是合作行为的体现。该解释并未与首句强互惠对立，至少文章没明确这样说，因此是kw'。

7． 正评价。解释最后被一个实验证实。末句给出正评价。

【题目分析】

9. It can be inferred from the passage that a successful and consistent cooperative and reciprocal strategy in a population composed of contributors and free-riders would depend at least partly on

(A) credible punishment against free-riding low contributors

(B) careful assessment of cost and benefit of all possible situations and the corresponding strategies

(C) serious fining of free-riding low contributors by enforcing them to pay a fee

(D) reasonable retaliation against self-interested players by ceasing their contributions

(E) correct evaluation of different payoff matrix for each and every game players

【解法】（观点）核心题。题干infer基本无用；问成功的、持续的合作策略依赖于什么？原文however句讲到贡献会减少，下一句的解释讲合作者惩罚搭便车者，可见搭便车是主要威胁，惩罚低贡献的搭便车者是关键。

【选项】

A. **正确**。可信的惩罚，抵制搭便车的低贡献者。

B. 仔细评估所有可能情况及相应策略的成本收益，原文未讲到成本收益问题。互惠者没有考虑这个问题。

C. 严厉处罚（fining）搭便车者，要求他们交费。原文说的是有人出来惩罚搭便车者，没说让他们交钱。

D. 停止做出贡献，合理报复自利玩家。"停止"语气太强，原文为减少。

E. 正确评估每个游戏玩家的不同的支付矩阵（payoff matrix），没有提到支付矩阵问题。

1.4 Normal distribution

【*cues*, function & **core**】& 【结构分析】

The fact that so many things in life conform to a **bell curve** pattern of data points *suggests that* it's much **easier to be ordinary** than to be outstanding. Inspirational public television always features children dreaming of being great successes. *Yet* normal distribution theory reveals that values cluster around midpoints and **mediocrity** loves company. *Another* relentless power implied in the bell curve is **regression to the mean**: the extraordinary tends to lose its edge over time. An athlete often goes into decline after appearing on the cover of best sport magazine. This *might result from* the pressures of fame, or a superstition subsumed into self-fulfilling prophecy, *but* the fact is, after doing extraordinarily well for a long period of time, the athlete is simply **not** able to maintain **outlier** status for much longer, but rather starts **regressing**, however slightly, back **toward the mean**. (143 words)

Cues	Function	**Core**
1. fact ... suggests	1. TW: kw1	1. **bell curve: ordinary**
2. ...	2. ~a	2. children
3. Yet	3. a	3. mediocrity
4. Another	4. kw2	4. **regression to mean**
5. ...	5. x	5. athlete
6. might ...	6. ~kw2	6. **pressures**
but	vs. kw2	***vs. regressing***

第1句：论点。事实表明论点：the fact suggests that KW。文章主题词是钟形曲线（bell curve），它的一个含义是：普通比出色易达到。

2：让步。励志电视节目总是讲些怀有很大抱负的孩子。

3：转折。但是，正态分布/normal distribution = bell curve 表明，多数值都聚集在中间点，平庸的伙伴最多。

4：并列论点。钟形曲线隐含的另一个无情的（relentless）观点是回归平均：那不同寻常的，总会失去锋芒。

5：举例。运动员上了最好的体育杂志封面后，就会陷入光芒黯淡之时。这是典型的封面诅咒。

6：让步转折。也许这是因为为名所累或是迷信，但其实在长时间的优异表现以后，运动员无法再维持突出地位（outlier）更长时间，只能回归平均。

【题目分析】

For the following question, consider each of the choices separately and select all that apply.

10. The passage provides information to support the following statements EXCEPT?

   (A) An athlete who keeps staying away from media when achieving the high performance can maintain that status much longer.

   (B) To stay somewhere within the normal distribution is to be ordinary.

   (C) Managing an even reasonably long time of extraordinary performance is a challenge that any eminent sportsmen cannot meet, regardless of their talent, diligence, and perseverance.

【解法】（多选）信息题。3个选项是可多选的题，题干 information ... EXCEPT，信息题，无法直接定位，且问 EXCEPT，答案可找核心相反或无关的内容。核心是一切都会回归平均，普通比优秀容易。

【选项】

A. 正确。运动员如果远离媒体，就能将高水平发挥更长时间。第5句只是说，运动员被媒体曝光以后会走下坡路，但没说远离媒体可避免这种结果。可选。

B. 保持在正态分布之内，就是普通和平凡的状态。原文有此说法，不能选，因题干问EXCEPT。

C. 正确。维持哪怕合理的一段长时间，都是任何杰出运动员无法做到的，程度过强，末句说，after doing extraordinarily well for a long period of time，可推出，一段时间的优秀还是有希望的，只不过不能永远如此。

第二节　Exercise 2　解析

2.1　Glacier cycle

【*cues*, function & **core**】

What was causing the periodic advance and retreat of the **glaciers**? Milankovitch *correlated* glacier cycle with the variations in the amount of **solar radiation**（insolation）reaching the Earth. *In* the short, cool *summers* of the high polar latitudes, **insolation** may *not be enough to melt back* snow and ice accumulated in the winter. The small changes in insolation *could change* the delicate balance of glacial stability to one of advance. *Once* the advance *starts*, the increased reflectivity of the ice surface, as *compared to* sea or land cover, *cools* the local atmosphere further and *causes* a **self-feeding** *process* **of glacial growth**.

However, the variations in insolation are ***not enough*** to drive the enormous shift in climate which a glacial onset represents. *Some climatologists have attempted to find* **other factors**. *The most popular theory today proposes that* shifts in the **t**hermohaline **circulation**, the global ocean current which circulates cold water from the north Atlantic around the cape of Africa to the northeastern Pacific, may be the *trigger* for the sudden changes which *bring on* the Ice Ages.（178 words）

Cues	Function	Core
1. what ... causing...?	1. tw/fact	1. **glaciers?**
2. correlated with	2. kw1	2. **M: insolation →** **cycle**
(3. in summers, not melt	3. x →	3. **insolation**
4. change	4. y	4. **→**
5. Once started, cool, cause)	5. $z_{1\to2}$	5. **→ → glacial**
1. However, not enough	1. aw-	1. **not enough**
2. other factors	2. kw2'	2. other factors
3. popular theory today, trigger	3. kw2	3. **t. circulation → ice**

【结构分析】

◆ 第一段

第1句：主题。给出事实并追问原因。对于现象解释，通常会有2-3个解释，前负后正: tw. kw1. aw-. kw2.

2：解释1=kw1。人物常有观点，且correlate表示相关。理科讲因果: insolation → glacier cycle。后文如讲证据，通常以平行或序列因果展开。如无，也可能出现评价。

3：证据。具体时间summers暗示细节，insolation不足以融化冰雪。

4：证据。insolation的变化可以改变平衡。

5：证据。Once...starts为明确时间词，确认3-5句为连续动作的序列因果 = 机制，机制找末句，不必记住所有内容，只需抓住最后环节: → → → glacial growth。句内还有compared to比较，为常考特殊语言。

◆ **第二段**

第1句：负评价转折句。第一个理论不足以解释部分事实。典型的部分否定。其后给出证据或新解释。

2：过渡句。有人试图找出其他因素，本句尚未给出新的解释是什么，以kw2'表示kw2的引导句或重述句。

3：解释2=kw2。给出今天最流行的理论，trigger表因果关系。该理论认为一种全球洋流t. circulation造成突然变化，从而引起冰河时代。

◆ **全文**

典型的现象解释文章，首句给出现象，然后提出第1个解释：连续因果或机制证据，然后2段首句给出负评价，再给其他解释。**有事实就有解释（先事实后假说），有解释就有证据（先假说后验证）或评价。**

【题目分析】

1. The passage is primarily concerned with

   (A) discussing the important role of insolation in the advance and retreat of the glaciers

   (B) criticizing the insolation theory proposed by Milankovitch to explain the glacier cycles

   (C) comparing and contrasting the variety of hypotheses concerning periodicity of glaciers

   (D) explaining how insolation brings about the self-feeding process of glacial growth

   (E) exploring the factors of cyclic advance and retreat of the glaciers

【解法】主题题。主题不在各个分论点解释，而在首句现象，文章的所有内容都是为了解释这个现象。定位首句。

【选项】

A. 片面。insolation仅为第1个解释。

B. 片面。第2段首句有负评价批判M的理论，但仅是文章结构的一部分，非整篇文章主题。

C. 文章并无明显的对比内容，虽然可以认为2个理论（或解释）的内容不同，但这只是文章的副产品，并非核心。

D. 片面。只有第1个解释的insolation。

E. 正确。exploring the **factors** of *cyclic* advance and retreat of the glaciers = What was **causing** the *periodic* advance and retreat of the glaciers?

2. Which of the following statements about sea or land cover can be inferred from the passage?

   (A) The reflectivity of sea or land cover can cause the decline of the temperature of the local atmosphere and to the self-feeding process of glacial growth.

   (B) The reflectivity of sea or land cover can be interpreted as related to the reflectivity of the ice surface which impinges upon the delicate balance of glacial stability.

   (C) When the local atmosphere cools, the reflectivity of the ice surface increases whereas the reflectivity of sea and land cover decreases.

   (D) When the advance of the glaciers begins, the reflectivity of sea and land cover does not increase relative to the reflectivity of the ice surface.

   (E) The reflectivity of sea and land cover differs from that of the ice surface in that the former can cause fundamental temperature change in a way that the latter cannot.

【解法】细节题。问有关sea or land cover，属于原文细节；infer没用。定位时直接按照句子顺序寻找，如果对考点敏感，可优先定位句内的特殊语言，如中间大写、对比比较、让步转折。定位在1段末句的compared to，对比A≠B，问B？答案取非A，则答案很可能为ice surface性质的反面：no increased reflectivity。

【选项】

A. 相反。原文说冰的表面反射度增强会有反射效果，海水表面或陆地表面应该没有。

B. 干扰选项。原文仅讲两者不同，没说它们之间有因果关系related to；impinge upon：influence，impact。

C. 原文说局部大气变冷，冰表面的反射度也许增加，但没说海表和地表反射度会相应减小；not increase不等于要减少。维持不变也是可以的。

D. 正确。冰河时代开始，海表和地表相对于冰表的反射度不会增加。

E. 错误。两者的不同在于海表和地表可以影响根本的温度变化，而冰表不能。定位句没说这个差别，事实上，冰表的反射度可能影响温度变化。

3. The author considers the explanation put forward by Milankovitch for the periodic retreat and advance of the glaciers to be

- （A）misleading and unfocused
- （B）seminal but speculative and ambiguous
- **（C）accurate but incomplete**
- （D）plausible but yet to be confirmed
- （E）credible but generally undervalued

【解法】态度题。选项为态度词，题干也有提示：the author considers...to be...，评价的对象是M的理论，因此定位在第2段首句however负评价句，该句有not enough，为不完全否定或部分否定。需注意选项中态度词的程度。（可参考第二章第四节 "Words & Phrases 单词与短语 特殊词汇：态度词"的讨论）。

【选项】

A. 误导的、没有重点的，态度是完全否定的。错误。

B. 有潜在影响的，但却是推测的、模糊的。但其实，作者态度绝不模糊。

C. 正确但是不完整；incomplete = not enough；不完整就意味着部分内容也正确：not enough = incomplete = accurate but incomplete。

D. 合理的但尚未得到确认。也是部分否定，但内容没有C选项直接。尚未确认不等于不足以解释事实。

E. 可信但一般被低估。没有提到人们低估这一理论。

【考位分析】

　　Q1：主题 → 首句；Q2：对比细节 → 1段末句；Q3：态度 → 2段首句/however句。1段3-5句证据未考；2段末句内的细节未考。

2.2 Feminist literary critics

【*cues*, function & **core**】&【结构分析】

Early feminist literary *critics believed* that the *traditional* concept of **domesticity** as manifested in the distinction between a masculinized public sphere and a privatized feminine one has become '*misleading*' *and oversimplified* as a framework for understanding the construction of social space for women even in the nineteenth century. *In their* **reformist** *view*, domesticity was **not** simply **confining** for women but a source of **agency** or 'sentimental **power**': the public-private distinction was treated as the basis for creating an alternative feminine culture. *For instance*, Nancy **Hartsock** argues that resistant forms of feminist consciousness spring from women's immersion into **housework** or child-rearing, a world **more complete** than men's, which then transforms women's domesticity into a **critical position**.

Cues	Function	Core
1. Early critics traditional: misleading	1. kw1'	1. **early: traditional domesticity: misleading**
2. in their ... view	2. kw1	2. **reformist: power** vs. confining
3. For instance, N.H.	3. e.	3. **H**: housework: critical

第1句：观点1。早期女权文学批评家认为传统的家庭活动（domesticity）概念有误导性且过度简化。早期观点认为过去传统的概念错误，而不是说早期观点错误。

2：观点1。正面讲早期观点，not...but对比，对比找反义，confining vs. agency=power；他们认为家庭活动其实不是限制，而是力量。

3：举例。例子（example=e）内容次要，抓住中间**人名最后大写字母**：H。**例子重现论点核心**，则housework = domesticity; critical position = power。

In contrast, a second wave of feminist *work* on domesticity envisions the idea of 'home' as a specific **racial and class position** for white, middle-class women, and therefore as an **extension** or even a supplement to the capitalist marketplace, not an alternative to it. *This second-wave critique emphasizes* how casting domesticity as a countercultural movement, based on its exclusion from dominant economic formations, *obscures* the way domesticity reproduces **other kinds of power** relations. *In this second reading*, it is precisely the reformist impulse privileged by *earlier* feminist critics as an unrecognized form of women's historical agency that is *now understood as* fueling a kind of **expansionist** or missionary project, characterized by rhetoric of expanding woman's sphere and of social or enlarged housekeeping, which often translated into projects of **class socialization** and the imposition of **middle-class norms**.

Cues	Function	Core
1. In contrast, second	1. kw2	1. **racial, class: extension**
2. emphasize, obscure	2. x:~kw1	2. other power
3. in this reading, earlier vs. now	3. y: kw1 vs. kw2	3. agency **vs. expansion** class socialization

第1句：观点2。第二波女权研究认为家的观念是白人中产女性的种族和阶层的地位的体现，是在延伸或增补资本主义市场，而非取代，取代论（alternative）属第1段。

2：证据。以前的看法掩盖了家庭活动其实可以复制其他权力关系，此句主要在批评1段观点，countercultural = alternative = reformist = agency or power。

3：证据。Earlier... now的时间对比：以前认为是具有力量的，现在则被认为是扩展或负有使命的计划。分别对应2个观点核心的逻辑等价词：earlier: reformist, agency, countercultural，alternative = **power** vs. now: **expansionist** = extension, class socialization, class norms= **class position**。

However, these second-wave critiques of domesticity *also depend upon* **spatial metaphors**, to the extent that they present domesticity as a **bounded position** occupied by a specific race and class of women. *Furthermore, they underestimate* the extent to which the representation of domesticity as able to travel beyond the walls of the middle-class home had the **ideological** function of mystifying or **suppressing** the internal **contradictions** within the feminine sphere of domestic responsibilities.

Cues	Function	**Core**
1. however, also	1. aw-: m	1. -: **spatial, bounded**
2. Furthermore, underestimate	2. n	2. -: **ideological**: suppress contradictions

第1句：负评价。上段的观点2也被给出负评价，说它依赖空间比喻，因为 to the extent that = because 他们认为家庭活动是女性阶级所占据的有限制的位置。

2: 并列负评价。他们也低估家庭活动的某种表征，具有意识形态的功能，神秘化或抑制内部的矛盾。

Such **contradictions** in the representations of domesticity, *I argue, only* started to become obvious in the *modernist period*. *Modernist* women's writing anticipates a notion of "**homelessness at home**", in which home figures a claim to a gendered identity, *while* homelessness echoes the writer's consciousness that this identity is neither completely determined nor inherently spatialized in the ways that the ideology of separate spheres represents women as being. But this metaphorical phrase does *not entirely* reject the spatial figuration of femininity; *in fact*, the implication is that an **alternate conception of space** might empower a new feminist politics, *as in* Audre Lorde's poem 'School Note', where the speaker refers to herself as being 'at home' anywhere because no place 'is' home. (444 words)

Cues	Function	**Core**
1. I argue, only in modernist period	1. kw3'	1. **modern: contradiction**
2. Modernist ... while	2. kw3: i vs. j.	2. **home vs. homeless**
3. But does not; in fact, A.L.	3. k1, k2.	3. spatial vs. **alternative L**

第1句：观点3。I argue 提示作者本人看法，说出第2个观点所忽视的矛盾只有在现代时期才变得明显。

2: 观点3。在家却无家即 homeless at home。后面的 in which、while 从句说明具体内容，home = gender identity *vs.* homeless = not determined, not spatialized。

3: 证据。But 表示转换，作者不会自己否定自己；this ... does not 在表否定陈述，后半句 in fact 给出肯定陈述。这种比喻的说法似乎不完全拒绝空间图象，而是暗示一种替代的空间观念。再举出 L 的诗歌，这种新空间观念下，到处都是家，因为本来没有固定的家。

全文：观点对比或新老对比类型，一共讲了3个观点。第1段 kw1 认为家庭活动是力量来源；第2段反驳说其实只是补充和延伸，是扩展已有阶层地位；第3段反驳，用并列证据指出不足；第4段给出作者观点，真正好的想法只在现代批判中才出现，正视矛盾，在家即无家。

【词汇】

cast...as...	将…塑造为
confine	*v.* 约束，限制
domesticity	家庭活动；来自 domestic *adj.* 国内的；家里的
fuel	*n.* 燃料 *v.* 加燃料；加速；加油
immersion	*n.* 沉浸，融入

masculine	*adj.* 雄性的，男性的 *vs.* feminine *adj.* 女性的；masculinize *v.* 使男性化
metaphor	*n.* 比喻
privilege	*v.* 给予…特权
suppress	*v.* = repress, inhibit, block，抑制，压制

【题目分析】

4. Which one of the following best expresses the main idea of the passage?

   (A) There is not yet a satisfactory understanding of domesticity in feminist literary criticism, whether for earlier feminist literary criticism or for second-wave critiques.

   (B) Both earlier and second wave of feminist literary criticism fail to understand the implications of domesticity, a concept that is better interpreted only in modern period.

   (C) Early literary criticism has a misleading effect on later critiques of domesticity and modernist alternatives as well.

   (D) Both earlier and later feminist literary criticism contribute to modern understanding of domesticity.

   (E) Earlier and later and modern feminist literary criticisms have equal value in our understanding the concept of domesticity.

【解法】主题题。题干问main idea。本文为观点对比，有3个观点，不能以老观点作为主题，重点应关注3–4段首句作者的看法，同时也可找涉及对1–2段观点的批评的选项。宗旨就是，定位各段首句、尤其3–4段首句做题。

【选项】

A. 迄今还没有满意的理解，这个说法错误，第4段首句作者提出了自己的主张和看法。

B. 正确。 早期和第二波的女性主义文学批评都没能理解家庭活动的含义，这个概念只在现代时期才得到更好的阐释。这个选项很完美地综合了1–4段首句的内容。

C. 早期的批评误导了以后的批评和现代的批评，很明显是错的。

D. 早期和后来的批评都促进了现代的理解。错误，原文并没有提到关于促进或贡献（contribute to）的评价。

E. 早期、后来以及现代的批评都有同等价值。原文没有提到equal value的概念，属于**数量词错误**。

5. The author's mention of Nancy Hartsock's study serves primarily to

   (A) illustrate the reformist view of domesticity as an empowering and critical force

   (B) illustrate the reformist view of domesticity as an supplementary force to marketplace

   (C) demonstrate that women's world is more complete than men's world

   (D) demonstrate that housework and child-rearing are among the prevailing jobs for women

   (E) demonstrate that the private-public dichotomy confines the role of women to housekeeping

【解法】作用题/in order to。题干问作者提到N.H.的研究是出于什么目的，serve to = in order to，找逻辑上一层作为答案。NH的研究在1段末句，该句为举例，不需要读其中内容，直接找上一层，恰好是上一句。于是，答案中心词是第2句的power, agency。

【选项】

A. 正确。 具体说明改良论观点，认为家庭活动是一种赋权的、批判的力量，empowering force = power, critical与例子末尾的critical position的总结对应。

B. 观点错误。家庭活动是市场的一种增补力量，这不是改良论的观点，而是第2段的观点。

C. 干扰选项。 证明女性的世界比男性的更完整，more complete这个说法的确在例子中出现，但这不是例子的作用，而是例子的内容，没有找逻辑上一层。

D. 例子内容，错误。证明家庭工作和孩子抚养属于女性的主要工作，暗示例子说法，没有提到力量。

E. 相反。第2句否定confining，但选项说私人–公共领域的两分（dichotomy）将女性的角色局限于家务劳动。

6. The second-wave feminist critique of domesticity differs from earlier feminist criticism in that the second-wave critique

   (A) abandons the concept of domesticity altogether

   (B) denies any negative role of the ideology of domesticity in women's social life and self-image

   (C) advocates the critical thrust of the concept of domesticity

   (D) deems as important to the interpretation of domesticity the traditional dichotomy of public and private spheres for men and women respectively

   (E) views household as a supplementary or extensive power to society

【解法】（对比）核心题。问第二波批判不同于早期的地方，定位2段首句contrast。1段核心是power，2段核心是extension。

【选项】

A. 第二波批判完全放弃家庭活动概念，显然不对。第3段首句负评价明确提到，他们依然依赖这个概念。

B. 否认家庭活动这个意识形态在女性社会和自我形象中有任何否定作用。**程度错**。第3段第2句提到他们低估，但没说他们完全否认。

C. 主张家庭活动的概念具有批判的力量（thrust），这是第1段末句的早期观点，不是第二波批判的观点。

D. 认为传统的公共和私人领域的两分（dichotomy），对家庭活动概念的解读很重要；但第2段重点在于阶层。

E. 正确。第二波批判认为家庭是社会的增补或延伸力量，直接给出2段首句作为答案。

7. The passage suggests that the second-wave critiques would have been more illuminating if they could do which of the following?

   (A) Highlight more assuredly the function of class socialization and middle-class mores in casting the image of women

   (B) Abandon more quickly the spatial allegory to embrace its literal, physical meaning

   (C) Recognize more clearly the contradictions in the conception of domesticity in modern period

   (D) Assess more appropriately the role of domesticity in mythologizing and repressing the inner conflict endemic to women's duty of domesticity

   (E) Reject more vehemently the early feminist interpretation of domesticity

【解法】取非题。题干有 would have been more illuminating，针对第二波批判的观点以虚拟语气给出正评价，则应定位相反态度。于是我们可以找到3段负评价两个：1个是依赖空间比喻，1个是低估家庭活动的意识形态压制矛盾。将任意一个取非，即为答案。

【选项】

A. 更加明确地强调阶级社会化和中产阶级道德风俗的功能，这些内容在2段末句出现过，是细节，不是取非。

B. 干扰选项。更快放弃空间比喻，依赖空间比喻的取非是放弃，但不是更快；即便这可以对，to embrace之后讲拥护家庭的字面和物理含义，并非取非内容。

C. 干扰选项。更清楚地认识到家庭活动观念在现代时期的矛盾。未取非。

D. 正确。更恰当地评估家庭观念的作用，它把女性的家庭义务固有的内部冲突神秘化和压制了，取非3段第2句：the role of domesticity in *mythologizing and repressing the inner conflict* endemic to women's duty of domesticity. = the representation of domesticity...had the ideological function of *mystifying or suppressing the internal contradictions* within the feminine sphere of domestic responsibilities.

E. 更猛烈地拒绝早期的女性主义关于家庭活动的解释。从2段首句contrast来看，他们已经这样做了。

2.3 Reelin

【*cues*, function & **core**】

The proposal that **r**eelin, a large protein regulating neuronal migration and positioning, is the *chief cause* of schizophrenia *was questioned* when human reelers were discovered in two separate families in Saudi Arabia and England. *In both these* families cousins had married each other and the marriage had brought together **faulty versions of the r**eelin gene, *causing* a disorder called lissencephaly with cerebellar hypoplasia（**LCH**）. *If* inherited **r**eelin **deficiency** is *the cause of* **s**chizophrenia, *one would expect* that some of the apparently **unaffected** relatives of these unfortunate children would be schizophrenic, because they are carrying the mutation in one of their genes. *But so far* there **is no history of** schizophrenia in either family, though the Arab family has not been studied in detail.（123 words）

Cues	Function	**Core**
1. proposal... cause... questioned	1. aw-	1. **r**(eelin) → **s**(chizo-): **questioned**
2. In...causing	2. x	2. faulty r → L
3. If...would expect	3. y	3. r → s; **unaffected: s**
4. But so far	4. ~y/aw-	4. **no history**

【结构分析】

第1句：负评价主题句。首句即对一个说法给出质疑，该说法认为R是S(chizophrenia)的原因。专业名词均取首字母。

2：证据。In结构具体给出两个家庭的情况，他们带有r的错误基因，导致一种疾病：L(CH)。

3：推理。如果R的缺失造成S，则我们会推测，目前未受影响的亲属会有S，因为这些亲属也同样有R缺失的问题。

4：反驳。结果没有发现两个家庭里有S的病史。

全文：首句给出负评价观点，然后2-4句给出支持负评价的证据和推理。

【题目分析】

8. Which of the following would be true if most of the relatives with inherited reelin deficiency in both families turned out to be schizophrenic rather than normal as they are today?

（A）The lack of reelin may be highly associated with the schizophrenia.

（B）The lack of reelin may be unrelated to the schizophrenia.

（C）Lissencephaly with cerebellar hypoplasia（LCH）might also be fatal during the adulthood.

（D）Lissencephaly with cerebellar hypoplasia（LCH）would be treated by genetic therapy in the immediate future.

（E）Cousins in those families would finally give up marrying each other.

【解法】取非题。题干问would be true if...，如果两个家庭里面有R缺失问题的亲属都是S而不是今天发现的正常情况，那么可以推出下面哪个选项的内容。这个if后面的虚拟语气取非了原文最后一句话的内容：没有S的病史。因为没有S病史的例子在R缺失的家族中被发现，所以，作者才在第一句中说，R(的缺失)导致S的说法受到质疑。现在题干假设发现了病史，则不必质疑R是S的原因。

【选项】

A. 正确。R的缺失也许与S高度相关，高度关联即是原因。

B. 相反。本选项说，两者也许无关(unrelated)。

C. LCH也许是在成年人中是致命的，与问题无关。

D. LCH将来可以用基因疗法治疗，与问题无关。

E. 这些家庭的亲戚可能最终放弃近亲结婚，与问题无关。

2.4 Syntax

[*cues*, function & **core]**

In his *new study*, Anderson outlines what is *special* about human language: **syntax**. Our vocabularies are dramatically larger than those of other animals, and our sound systems are more complex, *but* the essential design property of human language is **syntax** — the way we use combinations of words to convey meaning. This concept *is alien to* the communication systems of other species. *It is true that* what animals learn is impressive and their cognitive abilities may be remarkable, *but* they *never* master anything *like* a human language and seem incapable of doing so: the complexity of their grammar is *not remotely comparable to* ours. (103 words)

Cues	Function	**Core**
1. *new study, special*	1. TW: kw	1. **human: syntax**
2. *but*	2. $a_{1,2}$, b	2. syntax
3. *alien to*	3. vs. x	3. vs. other species
4. *It is true that., but*	4. x'	4. animals vs. human

【结构分析】

第1句：主题。新研究（new study）表示文章主题，A提出人类语言的独特之处在句法。独特（special）一词暗示对比，人类与其他物种有差别。

2：证据。人类的词汇大、声音系统复杂，但最重要的是句法。

3：对比。这些是其他物种没有的。

4：让步转折。动物也能学习，也有认知能力，但永远不会拥有类似人类语言的交流方式。

全文：一个观点及其对比证据。相对简单。通常GRE文章不会只有一个观点。

【题目分析】

For the following question, consider each of the choices separately and select all that apply.

9. According to the information in the passage, which of the following features is essentially <u>unique</u> to human language and accompanying human cognitive powers?

   （A） Extraordinary complexity of grammar

   （B） Combinatory ways to express meaning

   （C） Remarkable cognitive abilities

【解法】 信息题。题干问人类语言与人类认知能力的独特之处，unique = special，也就是在问主题词，答案可在全文任意一句寻找。问法为多选，要求选出所有正确的说法。信息题的做法是，**从选项找线索，带核心去排除**。

【选项】

A. 正确。语法非常复杂；原文末句说动物语言的语法复杂度无法与人类相比，可推出人类的语法极度复杂。

B. 正确。直接对应第2句：the way we use **combinations** of words to *convey meaning* = **combinatory** ways to *express meaning*。

C. 显著的认知能力。在末句让步中提到动物也有这样的能力，全文都没有提到人与动物认知能力的根本差异。

※ 逻辑题

Companies who expect that they cannot find a high quality project to invest usually wait and keep a huge amount of capital. Yet the percentage of invested capital in the last year increased significantly from that in the previous year. *This is convincing evidence* that the Enterprise Association founded two years ago to facilitate the investment has gradually assisted the member companies to invest residual capital.

10. Which one of the following most seriously weakens the argument?

 （A） Those companies which did not join the Association in the previous year have begun to reconsider their earlier decision.

 （B） A significant economy recovery that spurred intensive capital investment has begun to take shape since the last year.

 （C） The reserved capital in the companies still far more exceeds the invested capital in total for this year.

 （D） The entrepreneurship confidence index indicates that entrepreneurs of most companies are optimistic about the economy in the next two years.

 （E） The reserved capital in the companies is disproportionately lower than the invested capital in total for this year.

【解法】逻辑反对。原文说，公司如果找不到高品质项目投资就会持币等待。然而，去年投资的百分比相比以前有显著增加。这说明，两年前成立的企业协会正在逐渐帮助成员公司投资剩余资本。原文是从证据到解释，要推理这个推理，只要说明其实企业协会没有起到作用，或者有其他原因就可以。

【选项】

A. 那些从前没有加入协会的公司现在也开始重新考虑了；既不质疑也不反对。

B. 正确。 从去年开始经济就开始显著复苏，这刺激了密集的资本投资。这暗示了他因，经济复苏促使企业投资，而不一定是企业协会的作用。

C. 这些公司保留的资本依然超过投资资本。与问题无关。

D. 企业信心指数表明多数公司的企业家对未来两年经济表示乐观。与问题无关。

E. 这些公司保留的资本在比例上远远低于投资的资本。与C一样，与问题无关，既不支持，也不反对。

第三节　Exercise 3　解析

3.1　Deer

【*cues*, function & **core**】

　　Deferring reproduction presumably *increases* **reproductive gains** later in life through improved competitive ability by increased body size. This should *be true for* young fallow deer males, which attain physiological maturity at two years old but continue to grow until six. *In our results, two-year-old* males **refrained from** fighting. *Three-year-old* males appear to be **equivocal**: they act as adults when given the opportunity, but act as juveniles by refraining from groaning when competition is high. *By contrast, four- and five-year*-old males are willing to **take part** but are **outcompeted** by older males. They then resort to *alternative* strategies, *such as* intruding on territories and chasing females away from territory holders, the strategies occasionally *successful* because up to twenty percent of estrous females that were chased by young males in an experiment mated with them. (133 words)

Cues	Function	Core
1. ... *increase gains*	1. kw/ts	1. **defer →** **reproductive**
2. *be true for*	2. e	2. deer
3. *In our results, two-year*	3. a	3. 2: refrain
4. *three-year*	4. b	4. **3: equivocal**
5. *By contrast, 4-5*	5. c	5. **vs. 4-5: take part**
6. *alternative successful*	6. c'	6. **alternative:** **successful**

【结构分析】

第1句：论点。不是他人或过去的观点，也非单纯的现象或事实，而是两个事物之间的关系的判断，是作者的观点：推迟繁殖也许可以增加以后的繁殖收益。

2：举例。这种观点对于年幼的雄鹿是成立的，它们2岁已经达到生理成熟，但一直会长到6岁。

3：证据。2岁雄性一般不参加繁殖打斗，refrain = defer。

4：证据。3岁雄性的态度则模棱两可（ambiguous）：有时

参与，有时不参与，refrain = defer，重现首句核心。

5：对比证据。4-5岁雄性则愿意参与，但竞争不过年龄更大的。

6：顺承证据。于是它们就采用替代策略，这些策略奏效。

全文：论点说明。一个论点举例，分3个方面证据来支持。结构十分清晰，相对简单。

【词汇】

ambiguous	*adj.* =unclear, vague，模糊的，不清楚的	juvenile	*adj.* 年幼的 *vs.* senior, old
chase	*v.* 追逐	outcompete	*v.* 胜过；out + *v.* 常表超出
equivocal	*adj.* 模棱两可的；有歧义的	presumably	*adv.* =perhaps 或许
estrous	*adj.* 发情的；文中可取首字母	refrain from	忍住不做，克制
fallow	*adj.* 浅棕黄色的；休耕的；文中可取首字母	resort to	=rely on, depend on，诉诸
fierce	*adj.* 惨烈的，野蛮的	sporadic	*adj.* 零星的，少量的
intrude	*v.* 闯入		

【题目分析】

1. Which of the following statements, if true, would cast most doubt on the author's claim that alternative strategies undertaken by four- and five-year-old males sometimes could be successful?

    （A） Some estrous females that were chased by young males mated with older males.

    （B） Most estrous females that were chased by young males mated with them.

    （C） Only sporadic mating took place between young males and estrous females they chased.

    （D） The number of mating between young males and estrous females they chased was lower than that between older males and estrous females.

    （E） More estrous females chased by young males mated with them than the estrous females expelled from the territories of older males by the same young males.

【解法】逻辑反对或态度取非。题干有if true, would cast doubt on, 反对作者所说4-5岁采取的替代策略有时会成功的说法。可以定位到末句。原句含有because从句，既然题干反对成功，则答案可取非原因。末句原因说，高达20-30%的雌性会与雄性交配，答案取非后应说，不到20-30%，只有极少或根本没有雌性会与之交配。

【选项】

A. 年轻雄鹿追逐的一些发情雌性还是与年纪更大的雄性交配。Some表示依然有，答案要求将相对数字减少，some还不足以否定20-30%的百分比。

B. 年轻雄鹿追逐的多数发情雌性，都与它们交配。支持和加强原命题，未反对。

C. 正确。 年轻雄鹿和它们所追逐的雌性只会有很少的情况会进行交配。sporadic说明很少，与20-30%相对不少的比例不同。

D. 年轻雄鹿与它们所追逐的雌性的交配数目低于年老雄鹿与雌性的。低但不等于少或没有，未反对。

E. 年轻雄鹿追逐的雌性与之交配的比例，高于同一批年轻雄鹿从年长雄鹿地盘赶出的雌性与之交配的比例。无关比较。

2. The author's exemplification of intruding on territories of older males by younger males serves which one of the following functions in the passage?

    （A） It helps distinguish the behavior of intruding on territories from that of chasing females away from territory holders.

    （B） It illustrates the crucial difference between two different strategies taken by younger males under fierce competition with older males.

    （C） It clarifies the otherwise ambiguous and equivocal intentions implicit in the putative strategies taken by younger males.

    （D） It gives an example of a strategy other than normal mating strategies, taken by younger males under fierce competition with older males.

    （E） It proves that the alternative strategies taken by younger males sometimes outperform the normal mating strategies taken by older males.

【解法】作用题/in order to。题干问年轻雄性闯入年长雄性地盘的例子，服务于什么功能，serve...function = in order to, 可定位例子的逻辑上一层。该例子在末句由such as引出，例子内容次要，它作为句子成分，上一层即句子主干，答案中心词应有alternative strategies的同义词。

【选项】

A. 它帮助区分闯入地盘的行为与追逐雌性的行为。以例子本身内容作为答案，错误。

B. 它说明年轻雄性在与年长雄性惨烈(fierce)竞争中所采取的两种不同策略的关键差别，是例子本身内容。

C. 它阐明年轻雄性采取的可能策略中所包含的原本模棱两可的意图。4-5岁雄性的意图并非equivocal, 这是对比之前3岁雄性行为的特点。

D. 正确。 它举例说明与正常求偶策略不同的策略，other than normal = alternative, competition = （out）compete。

E. 干扰选项。 它证明年轻雄性采取的替代策略有时比年长雄性采取的正常求偶策略表现更好（outperform），原文仅说替代策略取得一定成功，并没有说它比正常策略更好。这种比较是多余的。

3.2　Poems of McKay

【*cues*, function & **core**】

The orientation to **sociopolitical** issues and **racial** identity in the poems of Claude **M**cKay *contrasts sharply with* the tradition represented by **B**raithwaite. *While* McKay explicitly weaved **racial-political** markers into his poems that unequivocally indicate the author's **racial identity** and lamented that the failure of black leadership was rooted in a **socioeconomic** and intellectual chasm between the black masses and the intelligentsia, Braithwaite preferred to **camouflage racial identity** under his pen and barely touched the issue of race in America in his own poems.

McKay's *disagreement with* Braithwaite's advice to write **aracial** poetry *reflected* his *broader skepticism* regarding the background and motives of the black intelligentsia. *This does **not** mean that all* the black intellectuals McKay encountered would have *agreed with* Braithwaite. *Indeed*, **L**ocke, **W**hite, and **D**u **B**ois had committed themselves to genres of African American literature that to an extent "betrayed" **racial** identities as African descendants. *But* they also have ***mutual*** identification with a community notorious for its cultural and **socioeconomic exclusivity** and its **detachment** from a large black population, which was *in conflict with* McKay's preference for radical society that was unpalatable and abominable for Black elites.
（188 words）

Cues	Function	Core
1. contrast with	1. kw1	1. **M: racial, political vs. B**
2. While	2. a₁ ᵥₛ. ₂	2. **M: economic, racial vs.B: aracial**
1. reflect broader	1. kw2	1. **M (≠B) vs. intelligentsia**
2. does not mean... all agree	2. x	2. not: all = B
3. Indeed	3. x'	3. **L.W.DB: racial**
4. But mutual, in conflict with	4. y/kw2	4. **=detachment vs. M**

【结构分析】

◆ 第一段

第1句：对比论点。M的诗歌中有明确的社会政治论题和种族身份倾向，与B所代表的传统形成鲜明对比。首句对比，后文展开模式预测：kw: A≠B.（a1. a2. vs. b1. b2.）

2：证据。复杂长句，重点**是对比找反义、反义在宾语**。M是racial-political；B则camouflage racial identity（隐藏种族身份）。全句：M明显会把种族–政治的标记谱入他的诗歌，确定无疑地表现作者的种族身份，他还哀叹黑人领导的失败根源于黑人大众与知识界之间在社会经济与理智上的分裂；而B则倾向于将种族身份藏于文字，很少在诗歌中触及美国的种族问题。

◆ 第二段

第1句：论点。M与B的分歧，反映出他对整个黑人知识界的怀疑。M的质疑不只针对B个人，而是针对更广大的（broader）知识界。

2: 否定性证据。这当然不是说，M遇到的所有知识分子都同意B。应该也有不同意的，而愿意触及种族问题。

3: 续写证据。Indeed表顺承，3个人都会在作品中显露自己的种族身份。

4: 肯定性证据。但是，这些人依然与黑人知识界有相同点，在文化上和社会经济上排斥和疏远黑人大众，这就与M的偏好形成冲突，in conflict with 重现首句 skepticism。

【词汇】

abominable	*adj.* = detestable，可恨的，厌恶的	descendant	*n.* 后裔，后代
betray	*v.* 显露，泄露；背叛	detachment	*n.* 脱离，超脱
camouflage	*v.* = conceal，掩饰，掩盖	discrepancy	*n.* 距离；差异、分歧；冲突
chasm	*n.* 分歧，巨大差异；裂缝	lament	*v.* = wail, mourn，哀叹
collaborate	*v.* 合作	represent	*v.* 代表 *n.* representation
deleterious	*adj.* = harmful, pernicious，有害的	snobbish	*adj.* 势利的，趋炎附势的
denounce	*v.* 谴责，批评	unequivocally	*adv.* 毫不含糊地，清楚地
deplore	*v.* 哀叹，贬低	unpalatable	*adj.* 不合口味的，令人厌恶的

【题目分析】

3. The primary objective of the first paragraph of the passage is to

(A) discuss the different approaches of McKay and Braithwaite to literature

(B) emphasize McKay's approach to literature over Braithwaite's for its focusing on racial issues

(C) explain why McKay's approach to literature differs from Braithwaite's conservatism

(D) advocate McKay's approach to literature while deploring Braithwaite's as timid

(E) discuss the main theme of McKay's genre of literature in its sociopolitical orientation

【解法】（段落）主题题。题干问主要目的（primary objective），定位1段首句，谈的是M与B的差别：M谈 sociopolitical = racial，而B则避而不谈，力图在诗歌中掩饰种族或非种族化（aracial）。一般地，本文的种族与非种族对比，反映了更广意义的宗教与世俗、精神与物质、理论与实践之间的对比：religious, sacred *vs.* secular, worldly; spiritual, metaphysical, transcendental *vs.* material, economic, sociopolitical, racial, ethnic; theoretical, ideal *vs.* practical。比较Exe1.1（Exercise 1 第1篇文章）。

【选项】

A. 正确。 讨论M与B在文学上的不同方法，different = contrast。

B. 干扰选项。 强调M在文学上的处理方法，压低B的方法，因为M的方法聚焦种族问题。Emphasize...over... 有对比含义，而且有态度，而原文是纯对比，作者并无抬高或压低其中一方的意思。

C. 解释为什么M的方法与B的保守做法不同。第1段仅指出这种不同，没有解释为什么（explain why），错误。

D. 倡导M的方法，而哀叹B的方法，指其怯懦（timid）。作者没有给出这种态度。

E. 讨论M的文学风格的主题。第1段旨在对比，不是直接讨论M的方法。

4. It can be inferred from the passage that McKay would have found Braithwaite's writing more acceptable if which of the following had happened?

 （A） Braithwaite would embrace and reinforce the idea common in the black elites of pursuing universal public audience.

 （B） Braithwaite would recognize as deleterious the cultural discrepancy between the black population and the elite.

 (C) Braithwaite would cease to conceal his racial identity in the writings and explicitly express his views about racial issues.

 （D） Braithwaite would collaborate with his contemporary poets to promote the social status of Black writers in the White America.

 （E） Braithwaite would denounce the snobbish and self-centered mentality implicitly present in other writer's poems.

【解法】取非题。题干问M会觉得B的作品would ... more acceptable if ... had，这是虚拟语气的正评价，暗示原文M对B持负评价，将造成这种评价的内容取非，即可得到答案。M之所以质疑B，就是因为后者掩饰、避谈种族问题。答案中心词是B不再掩饰、开始谈论种族以及社会政治问题。

【选项】

A. B拥护和强化黑人精英共有的理念，追求广泛的读者群。没有包含正确答案的中心词。

B. B承认文化差异有害。无关内容。

C. 正确。B停止在其著作中掩盖其种族身份，明确表达他对种族问题的观点，正好将1段第2句B的内容取非。

D. B与他的同代诗人合作，促进黑人作家的社会地位。合作一词不是答案中心。

E. B谴责其他作家的诗歌所表现的一种势利的、以自我为中心的心智状态。无关内容。

5. The author's discussion of the genres of African American literature practiced by Locke, White, and Du Bois in explaining McKay's skepticism toward the motives of the black intelligentsia is probably intended to

 （A） correct the misconception that Braithwaite and Locke, White, and Du Bois share the same intellectual and cultural views

 （B） underline the difference between Braithwaite and McKay in their preferences for the ideal form of society

 （C） strengthen the preceding claim that the orientation and motivations of the black intelligentsia have much in common

 (D) explain the divergence of Locke, White, and Du Bois's approach to literature from Braithwaite's and precludes a possible misinterpretation of the previous claim

 （E） emphasize the nonconservative element of Locke, Walter White, and Du Bois's writings and contrast it with that of McKay's

【解法】作用题/in order to。题干问作者在解释M对黑人知识界的动机的怀疑时，讨论了L.W.DB等人的文学风格，其主要意图是什么。M怀疑知识界，是2段首句主题，定位2段，再用大写人名找到2段第3句，回答此句的作用，需要找逻辑上一层。该句以indeed开始，顺承上一句即2段第2句，且与之等价，该句This does not mean that为否定结构，其作用在于防止读者对前一句的误解，误以为所有黑人知识分子都与B一样，避谈种族身份和社会政治问题。一般地，否定肯定结构所在的段落的整个结构，可以表示为kw. not a. but b/kw。问：not a的作用；答：防止人们误把kw等价于a，或者指出kw不是a。

【选项】

A. 纠正错误观念，以为B与L.W.DB等人都有相同的理智和文化观点。原句的意思在于说明L.W.DB与B其实有不同之处，以防止人们认为所有人都完全与B相同。A选项刚好说反了，与原句内容抵触。

B. 强调B与M在偏好上的差异。这应该是第1段的内容，不是第2段，第2段重点在说明M与整个知识界的分离。

C. 加强前面的主张，认为黑人知识界的倾向与动机有很多共同点。上一句只是在说知识界不是每个人都与B一样，并没有说知识界因此就有特别多的相同点。

D. 正确。解释L.W.DB与B的方法的分离或差别（divergence），排除对前面主张可能存在的误解。L.W.DB所在句的与之等价的上一句的确在说有些人还是与B不同，not ... that all ... agreed with B = divergence ... from B；而作为否定陈述does not mean that = precludes a possible misinterpretation，防止误解。

E. 强调L.W.DB作品不太保守的方面，将之与M对比。此句目的主要是说这三人与B不同，而非与M不同。

6. In the second paragraph, the author is primarily concerned with

（A） contrasting two approaches to literature and offering a compromise

（**B**） presenting the disagreement of one approach to literature with the other approach shared by the authors who still differ to a certain extent

（C） examining three different approaches to literature and endorsing one over the other two

（D） questioning one traditional approach to literature and advocating another different one

（E） discussing a specific theme common to several authors in the different literary traditions

【解法】（段落）主题题。定位2段首句。中心词是M质疑黑人知识界。

【选项】

A. 对比两种方法，提供折中方法（compromise）。原文没有涉及此内容。

B. 正确。提出一种文学方法与多位作者采取的另一种方法不同，而后者在一定程度上也有所差别。2段讲到M与黑人知识界的方法有别，一个重社会政治与种族，一个远离；但同时在黑人知识界内部，又有B与L.W.DB的差别。2段是对比套对比，比较难。

C. 考查3种文学方法，赞成一个，反对另外两个。作者本身无赞同，只是陈述差别而已。态度endorse错误。

D. 质疑一种传统方法，主张另外一种不同的方法。表示态度的词语"advocate, question"皆错。原文只讲M质疑，没说作者质疑。

E. 讨论延续不同文学传统的一些作者所共有的一个主题。第2段没有谈到不同文学传统这么宽泛的主题。

3.3 Hybrid populations

【*cues*, function & **core**】

The assessment of the degree of **admixture** of a given population has *traditionally* relied on the comparison of **gene frequencies** between two potential parental populations and a putative hybrid population. *Recently*, these methods have been *improved* by incorporating information on the **molecular diversity** present in the admixed and in parental populations or by explicitly taking into account the **genetic drift** since the admixture event. *However*, the **accuracy** of the estimation of the contribution of the parental populations to the hybrid depends highly on the extent of differentiation between parental populations and the time elapsed since the admixture event. *No single method was found* to date **superior** to others in all circumstances. （111 words）

Cues	Function	**Core**
1. traditionally	1. kw1	1. **gene frequencies**
2. recently, improve	2. kw2	2. **+ diversity, drift**
3. however	3. aw-	3. **accuracy?**
4. No...superior	4. aw-/cs	4. **no...superior**

【结构分析】

第1句：老观点。传统上评估种族的混合度靠比较基因频率。

2：新观点。现在这些做法有改进，因为纳入了分子多样性和基因漂移。新观点并未推翻老观点，因为动词 improve 表示改善以前做法：kw2 + kw1，而非kw2 vs. kw1。老观点可以作为反驳对象，也可作为已知背景。

3：负评价。指出新做法也有不足，因为其精确性高度依赖亲本种群的差异以及自混合事件发生以来流逝的时间。

4：负评价或结论。没有哪种方法在所有情况下都优于其他方法。每个方法都有缺憾。

全文：新老观点文章，重点在新观点。文章苦短，各个观点或态度都没有给证据展开。

【题目分析】

7. It can be inferred from the passage that the traditional and recent methods in the assessment of the degree of admixture of a given population differed in which of the following respects?

（A） The accuracy of the estimation of the contribution of the parental populations to the hybrid

（B） The universality of the estimation method in most circumstances

（C） The degree of reception among evolutionary biologists and molecular geneticists

（**D**） Whether factoring in molecular diversity and genetic drift or not

（E） Whether comparing gene frequencies between parental populations and a hybrid population or not

【解法】（对比）细节题。题干问传统方法与近期方法的差别（differ），对应原文在第1-2句，不涉及第3句however句，后者是对现行方法的负评价。抓住对比核心。第1句是 comparison of gene frequencies，第2句用 improved 说明，与通常新老对比不同，这里的新观点并未推翻老观点，而是补充它。第2句的重心是吸收分子多样性（molecular diversity）信息以及考虑基因漂移或漂变。

【选项】

A. 精确性是however句的内容，与第1-2句对比无关。

B. 普遍性在第1-2句未提及。末句提到任何方法在所有情况下的优越程度比较问题，但与题干所问无关。

C. 错误。接受度在第1-2句未提及，整篇文章也没有。

D. 正确。新做法比传统做法好的原因在于考虑了分子多样性和基因漂移。factoring in = incorporating, taking into account；专业词汇 molecular diversity 和 genetic drift 来自原文。

E. 干扰选项。传统做法是比较基因频率（gene frequencies），新做法是在此之外还加上了其他做法。因此重点不在于比不比较基因频率，而在于有没有基因漂移和分子多样性的信息。1-2句不是非此即彼的对立关系，而是第2句补充和改善第1句的做法。

3.4 Democratic stability

【 cues, function & core 】

Why a country like England that had suffered from a lengthy period of political instability before 1688 *suddenly* underwent a **transition to stable** representative government with a limited monarchy? **O**lson *suggested* that democracy *results from* **accidents** of history that leave a **balance of power** or stalemate, making it impossible for any one leader or group to overpower all of the others or create a new autocracy. *But* **one group** did eventually establish full control in England: after 1715 the Whigs had command of all government institutions, retaining this control for a considerable period of time. **W**eingast *adds a new dimension by demonstrating that* democratic stability *depends on* the two groups successfully committing to **a strategy** of opposing any attempts to tread upon the basic **rights** of any citizens. The **B**ill of **R**ights of *1689 in England* might be seen as just such an "**elite pact**". *However*, *this suggestion may be* **inaccurate**. *During the period* of partisan conflict between 1690 and 1715, it was common for those who found themselves in the opposition to be thrown in prison on **dubious legal** grounds.（181 words）

Cues	Function	Core
1. why...suddenly	1. tw/fact	1. **stable?**
2. O. suggested, result from	2. kw1	2. **O: balance of power** → stable
3. But	3. aw-	3. **vs. one group control**
4. W. adds...new... depend on	4. kw2	4. **W: strategy: rights** → stability
5. 1689 in England	5. x	5. BR
6 However, inaccurate	6. aw-	6. **inaccurate**
7. During the period...	7. m	7. dubious legal

【结构分析】

第1句：主题。追问事情原因。英格兰在经历长期政治不稳定以后为何突然转变成有限君主制的稳定代议政府？

2： 观点1。**人物常有观点**，O. 提出这是因为历史偶然，当时处于权力平衡或僵局状态，不可能一派独大或个人专权。

3： 负评价。用事实来反驳。当时有一个群体最终获得全部控制权：W党派掌握了政府所有机构。

4： 观点2。**人物常有观点**。W. 指出稳定性依赖于两个群体成功地坚持一个策略：反对任何践踏公民基本权利的做法。

5： 证据。**中间时间、地点或大写 = 细节**。证据重现论点**核心**，（elite）pact = strategy。

6： 负评价。这种说法不精确。非常简短的负评价。

7： 负评价的证据。**中间时间 = 细节**。当时，反对派的人经常会因为不可靠的法律依据被抓进牢房。

全文：现象解释。首句现象，后文连续2个解释，都被给出负评价。文章很短，但解释和态度很多，因此它们各自的证据较少。重点是抓出各自观点和态度。

【词汇】

autocracy	*n.* 独裁统治，专制政治	
cleavage	*n.* 裂缝；分离	
concoct	*v.* =fabricate，捏造，伪造	
cross-cutting	*adj.* 交叉的；锯齿状的	
demonstrate	*v.* 证明，表明	
elite	*n.* 精英	
incentive	*n.* 激励，动机	

levy	*v.* 征（税）	
monarchy	*n.* 君主制度	
pact	*n.* 协议，条约	
partisan	*n.* 党徒，党派分子	
stalemate	*n.* 僵局	
tread upon	踩上去，践踏	
undergo	*v.* 经受，经历	

【题目分析】

8. Which of the following, if true, would strengthen the challenge to Weingast's hypothesis as presented in the passage?

   （A） The Bill of Rights broke important constitutional ground by making it illegal for the monarchy to pass laws, levy taxes, or maintain a standing army without consent of Parliament.

   （B） The Act of Settlement passed in 1701 by the Parliament is a written commitment between different groups to respect constitutional ground rules.

   （C） Through the Act of Settlement passed in 1701, leaders of different groups reaffirmed that they committed themselves to respect basic constitutional principles.

   （D） Historical evidence suggests that the cross-cutting character of political cleavages provided the room for politicians to propose moderate policies that can minimize incentives for radical opponents to revolt.

   （E） A government in 1701 dominated by one party put several leaders of the opposition party on trial on concocted charges.

【解法】逻辑支持。题干问if true, would strengthen文中对W的假说的挑战。题干不是问如何支持W，而是要支持对W的挑战，其实就是如何反对W。要反对W，就要定位原文负评价的证据，然后再举一例或重复反驳的内容就可以。最后1~2句是对W的负评价及证据。证据的中心是当时有人被丢进楼房，但于法不合，法律依据可疑。答案可重复这些中心词。

【选项】

A. BR奠定了重要的制度基础，从此以后，君主在未经议会同意的情况下，不得立法、征税、维持常备军。这与对W的挑战无关。事实上，是在支持W的看法。

B. AS是不同群体之间的一个书面承诺，尊重体制的基本规则。依然是支持而非反对W。

C. 通过AS，不同群体的领导者重新确认他们一定会尊重基本的宪政原则。同样是支持W的观点而不是支持挑战W。

D. 历史证据表明政治裂缝的锯齿状特点为政治家提供了空间，他们可以提出温和的政策，减弱极端分子暴动的动机。无关选项。

E. 正确。1701年，一个党派主宰的政府审判反对党的若干领导人，其指控为捏造，concocted charges = dubious legal grounds。

9. Select the sentence that merely provides support for a hypothesis.

【解法】选择句子。常考句子的功能作用，题干问为一个假说提供支持的句子，假说是观点，提供支持是证据。原文虽有两个观点，但文章结构紧凑，不是每个观点都提供证据。第2句开始的O的观点就没有证据，直接被第3句的负评价所反驳。第4句为W的假说，其证据即在第5句。因此所选句子的开头就是："The Bill of Rights of 1689..."。

※逻辑题

The diet rich in fruits and vegetables resulted in mild reductions in blood pressure, lowering the systolic pressure by 2.8 mmHg and the diastolic by 1.1 mmHg. A combination diet rich in fruits, vegetables, and dairy products more than doubled those numbers in individuals with normal blood pressure. *Thus*, calcium *does play a crucial role* in blood pressure regulation *since* the level of consumption of dairy products, with their high calcium content, was the biggest difference between the combination diet and the other diet.

10. Which one of the following, if true, most strongly supports the argument?

（A） The combination diet resulted in mild reductions in blood pressure as the diet rich in fruits and vegetables did.

（B） The combination diet was lower in saturated fat than the other one, and included two servings of low-fat dairy products as well as almost 10 of fruits and vegetables.

（C） Another major difference between the combination diet and the other diet lies in the degree of concentration of minerals.

（D） In people with mild high blood pressure, the reductions caused by the combination diet were 11.4 mmHg in systolic and 5.5 in diastolic.

（E） Some other diet with the same level of consumption of dairy products as the combination diet proved to be no more effective in lowering blood pressure than the other diets.

【解法】逻辑支持。题干问if true...support, 原文有一个论证，最重要的词汇是末句thus和since。第1句讲蔬菜和水果饮食导致血压一定程度降低，s（ystolic）下降2.8，d（iastolic）下降1.1；有牛奶的组合饮食则是这些数字的2倍——一定要注意！这表示降低得更厉害，而不是说增加。末句说，因此，c（alcium）一定有很大作用，因为两种饮食的唯一差别是有牛奶的组合饮食c含量高。要支持c导致血压降低，可以说没有他因，也可以举例或重复该观点。

【选项】

A. 组合饮食导致血压有一定程度的降低，与水果蔬菜的饮食一样。不能支持c（alcium）导致血压降低。

B. 组合饮食饱和脂肪低，与c降低血压无关。

C. 组合饮食与其他饮食还有一个差异。这是削弱末句的since，逻辑反对，不是支持。

D. 正确。对轻微高血压群体，组合饮食引起的血压减少是s：11.4；d：5.5，提到了减少，同时量也比第1句的大，至少是2倍，与第2句中正常血压的人能降低1倍的说法一致。对c降低血压的观点起到加强作用。

E. 一些其他饮食，牛奶含量与这里的组合饮食一样，但降低血压的效果不比别的饮食好。这说明牛奶也许不是主要原因，逻辑反对，而非支持。

第四节　Exercise 4　解析

※ 逻辑题

In a laboratory study, when bees are made to fly through tunnels with visual patterns on the walls, the distance they indicate in their dance *corresponds to* the complexity of the pattern to which they have been exposed. The researchers hypothesize that the dance *reflects* the bees' subjective experience, rather than a map of the external world and that the bees' perception of distance is largely *a function of* differences in their visual, subjective experience.

1. Which of the following, if true, most seriously undermines the researcher's hypothesis?

(A) Bees as subjects flying through the tunnels with pictures on the wall indicate the amount of distance by their various forms of dances.

(B) Bees as subjects flying through the tunnels with pictures on the wall do not vary their indications of the distance with different visual patterns.

(C) Bees in the experiment fail to respond to the directions of the visual images on the wall since those images are too perplexing and, in some cases, ambiguous.

(D) Bees in the experiment stumble upon the wall when the map shows there is light on the striking point.

(E) Bees in the other experiment show a certain similar behavior pattern but, to researchers' dismay, they stop flying whenever external intervention is withdrawn.

【解法】逻辑反对。题干问if true, seriously undermine。原文第1句的大意是：研究者让蜜蜂在隧道中飞行，结果蜜蜂舞蹈所表示的距离与蜜蜂所看到的模式的复杂程度对应，correspond to属于广义的相关关系。第2句的大意是：研究者于是假设，蜜蜂舞蹈反映了蜜蜂的主观经验，而不是外部世界的地图；蜜蜂对距离的感知主要是其视觉主观经验差异的函数。在这里，"reflect, a function of"都表示广义的因果关系。要反对这个因果关系，就要说有他因，或者直接反对说，舞蹈其实不表示主观经验。

【选项】

A. 蜜蜂飞过隧道，墙上有画，可见蜜蜂是用不同的舞蹈来指示不同的距离。这个不能反对原文观点：蜜蜂舞蹈反映主观经验。

B. 正确。蜜蜂飞过隧道，墙上有画，结果这些蜜蜂不会按照不同的视觉模式来改变它们对距离的指示，本句not vary...with直接否定了视觉模式与表示距离的舞蹈之间的关系。

C. 蜜蜂没有对墙上的视觉图像做出反应，因为那些图像太复杂，有时还很模糊。因为图像复杂而模糊导致蜜蜂无法反应，这只说明了蜜蜂能力的高低，不能否定它们会对所感知的信息做出反应。

D. 地图上有光时，蜜蜂撞到墙上。无关选项。

E. 在其他实验里，蜜蜂有某种类似的行为模式，但它们却在外部干扰被撤销后停止飞行。这也许说明外部环境信息是它们飞行的原因，但这个外部干扰与原文所说的主观经验之间的关系不清楚。

4.1 Transience of workers

【*cues*, function & **core**】

The high **mobility** of nineteenth-century Americans generally, and especially those under thirty years of age *is well documented*. The *most common way* to **vary one's work** was to **move**, if the youths did not want to see their fate sealed by their proficiency on one particular portion of the work. *Those* unacquainted with factory populations *said that* they possess as roving a **disposition** as the Tartars. *But few* remove because they are **fond of changing** their locations, though they go where they can get the best employment and the best wages. Hareven's *thorough analysis* of the payrolls of the Amoskeag Mills showed that the typical worker's career was short and frequently **interrupted**. Those whose years at Amoskeag were unbroken by any departure from the mills usually did **not stay** there long. The *reasons* for leaving were *many*: discharge, desire to try another job, pregnancy, an attempt to get a raise in pay, or anger at an overseer. *In general, however*, men left to search for **better jobs**; women left to care for other members of their **families**. (177 words)

Cues	Function	Core
1. well documented	1. tw	1. **mobility**
2. common way...	2. e.	2. move
3. those said that...	3. kw1	3. **disposition**
4. But few	4. aw-	4. **vs. few fond**
5. H. thorough analysis	5. kw2: x	5. **H, +: interrupted**
6. ...	6. y	6. not stayed long
7. reasons: many	7. y'	7. many reasons
8. general, however	8. $y_{1,2}$	8. **jobs vs. family**

【结构分析】

第1句：主题词/TW。19世纪，30岁以下的美国人流动性高。文章接下来也许会提出证据支持这一判断，或者给出解释。

2: 顺承说明。改变工作最快的方式就是移动。继续说明主题。

3: 观点1。一些不熟悉工厂劳工群体的人说这是因为工人有盲目游荡的秉性(disposition)。以性格解释行为。

4: 负评价。但很少人离开是因为他们喜欢改变地方，该句也有让步，说他们当然也会因为就业好和工资高而离开。

5: 新研究及证据。H的分析表明，一般工人的职业期都很短，而且经常被打断。不是他们自己喜欢改变，而是被改变。

6: 证据。那些没被打断的，也不会呆很长时间。

7: 原因。离开的理由很多，并列列举4–5个，位置>内容。

8: 对比原因。特别强调男性与女性的原因不同，需重视。

全文：现象解释。首句给出高流动性的事实，然后给出第1个解释，反驳之后给出第2个解释，再用证据展开之。

【词汇】

departure	*n.* 离开；离境；migration *n.* 迁移
discharge	*n.* 解除职务，解雇
disposition	*n.* 性情，倾向，禀赋
document	*v.* 记录，证实
interrupt	*v.* 打断，干扰
mills	*n.* 作坊
mobility	*n.* =transience, move，移动
proclivity	*n.* 倾向，癖性
remove	*v.* 移动，离开；排除，消除
rove	*v.* =roam, wander，游荡
unacquainted	*adj.* 不熟悉的，不了解的

【题目分析】

For the following question, consider each of the choices separately and select all that apply.

2. It can be inferred from the passage that the author would be likely to agree with which of the following are the factors for the transience of workers in the nineteenth-century America?

   （A）Desire to get a better job and a better payment

   （B）Disposition to wander around different factories

   （C）Care for the family members

【解法】（多选）信息题。题干infer无用，重点在factors for the transience，transience = mobility，转变、变动，这是文章的主题词。题干问TW，则为信息题。从选项找线索、带核心去排除：有些选项与核心相反或无关，直接排除，其他选项定位原文某句。

【选项】

A. 正确。 得到更好的工作和薪酬，是第4句But句里的让步语气though后面的内容，让步也是作者认可的事实。

B. 错误。工人的游荡性格是一些人的观点，遭到反对。

C. 正确。 关心家庭成员是女性流动的原因，在末句。

3. The author of the passage mentions Hareven's study of the payrolls of the Amoskeag Mills in order to

   （A）emphasize Hareven's insightful observation that the career of average workers there did not last long and confronted intervention

   （B）suggest that young workers left a factory for a variety of reasons

   （C）anticipate the objection that the workers moved around the different factories for different reasons

   （D）indicate that young worker moved not because of their migrant proclivities but because of other reasons

   （E）blame the employers for removing the young workers repeatedly

【解法】作用题/in order to。题干问提到H关于AM的工资账单的研究是为了干什么，找逻辑上一层。定位中间大写，容易找到是在But之后的句子，第5句。该句提出新观点，上一层就是首句；或者，它在But之后，在一定程度上可看做负评价的证据。故答案中心词应该是反对工人的性情、提出新的理由。

【选项】

A. 强调H的观察很有洞见，他看到，工人的职业生涯不会持续很长。这是后文细节，不是它的目的。

B. 指出年轻工人离开工厂的理由有多种。这也是下一句的内容，不是提到H研究的理由。

C. 预见反对（anticipate objections），属于让步。这里没有。

D. 正确。 指出年轻工人跑来跑去，不是因为有移动的癖性proclivity = disposition，而是因为其他理由。

E. 指责雇主反复解雇年轻工人。原文没有指责的态度。

4. The main purpose of the passage is to

   （A）document the high mobility of nineteenth-century Americans

   （B）explain the high transience of young workers in the nineteenth-century America

   （C）highlight the difference between male workers and female workers

   （D）refute the suggestion that young workers move because they have an innate disposition to do so

   （E）discuss the fate of workers in the nineteenth-century America

【解法】主题题。考查文章目的，定位首句，要解释工人为何流动。

【选项】

A. 记录和证实高流动性。完全重复首句，但没有解释。

B. 正确。 解释年轻工人的高流动性。比A好。

C. 突出男性和女性工人的差异。这是末句细节。

D. 反驳年轻工人流动是因为性格因素。这是文章的部分内容，非主题。

E. 讨论工人的命运（fate），这个词太宽泛了。

4.2 Philopatry

【*cues*, function & **core**】&【结构分析】

Philopatry, *the behavior* returning to an individual's birthplace, has *several **advantages***. The presence of kin in the natal area makes **easier** to receive **help from related** individuals; the level of **aggression** might be **lower** among kin than among unrelated individuals; breeding close to kin can *also* increase **breeding success**, as in the case of microtine rodents. *However*, this behavior may *also* result in an **elevated** probability of **incestuous** pairings. *The fact* that close inbreeding is rarely observed even in highly philopatric species *suggests that* animals have developed mechanisms to **avoid** breeding with close relatives and can discriminate between kin and non-kin via **recognition**.

Cues	Function	Core
1. *behavior, several advantages*	1. tw	1. **P: advantages**
2. *; ; also*	2. a; b; c	2. help; low aggression; success
3. *However, also*	3. d'	3. **incest**
4. *suggest that*	4. d''/ tw'	4. **avoid: recognize**

第1句：主题。行为P是现象，有许多优势，后面并列展开。

2: 并列证据。3个分号并列出现，位置>内容。多次重现核心：help, low aggression, success = advantages。

3: 转换。However仅在别人观点之后才是反驳，这里仅在事实之后，所以不是反驳。本句提到P的劣势：近亲配对的概率高。

4: 相关主题。避免incest；这说明有识别亲属与非亲属的方法。末句给出1段另一重点：P需要recognition。

One proposed mechanism by which animals can **recognize** unfamiliar relatives is **phenotype matching**, which involves learning the phenotype of familiar relatives, or of oneself, thereby forming a phenotypic template against which the phenotypes of unfamiliar individuals can be compared. *Some animals might be using* some form of phenotype matching: mice have been shown to use **MHC** odor type to avoid breeding with close relatives; olfactory cues also seem to be used by Arizona tiger salamanders and rainbow fish seem to use both visual and chemical cues to detect shoals of related individuals. *Many studies, however, have found* that individuals **only** recognize **familiar kin**.

Cues	Function	Core
1. *one mechanism*	1. kw1	1. **phenotype matching**
2. *some...using: mice; A. tiger*	2. x: $x_{1,2}$	2. mice; A. tiger
3. *however, found*	3. aw-	3. **only familiar kin**

第1句：观点。一种识别方法是表型匹配（phenotype matching）。句子后半段有which, thereby forming, against which等多层修饰，次要。也可以认为这是P的原因，表型匹配，所以才重返出生地。

2: 证据。一些动物就是使用这种方法，列举老鼠和一种老虎作为证据。

3: 负评价。非作者观点之后的however句表反驳，动物只能认出熟悉的亲属，only表示限定范围，观点适用范围有限，就是负评价了。期待后文讲出更好的方法。

A problem in investigating the behavior of settling **close to kin** is *to exclude the possibility* that they are philopatric *because of* benefits of settling in the **natal** area, *rather than* because of benefits of settling **close to kin**. *The study of* dispersal of relatives in colonially breeding seabirds and waterfowl *is of particular interest in this context* because virtually all species in this group share characteristics that are generally believed to promote the evolution of cooperation. **Nonrandom** dispersal within colonies of seabirds and waterfowl has been reported but *is usually explained by* philopatry to the **natal** nest site rather than by attraction to kin.

Cues	Function	Core
1. problem, because of... rather than...	1. kw2 vs. kw3	1. **natal** **vs. close to kin?**
2. study, interest	2. i	2. s.w.
3. is explained by	3. kw2	3. **nonrandom: natal**

第1句：引出观点。讲到研究P = settling close to kin的困难。要区分P的原因是要住在出生地，还是要靠近亲属？可能性（possibility）就在暗示alternative theories。如果是因为住在出生地才重返的，那就不需要识别亲属与非亲属。

2：证据。对海鸟和水禽的研究特别有用，因为一般认为它们生活在一起的目的是要合作。

3：观点2。海鸟与水禽的非随机分布，不是随便住，而是跟出生地有关，这通常是因为出生地本身而不是亲属。

A recent study shows that the settling pattern of barnacle geese *Branta leucopsis* females returning to their natal colony is **nonrandom** with respect to the nest sites of their parents and sisters. Because breeding birds rarely changed nest sites between years, this natal philopatry *could be caused by* an attraction to the natal nest site itself or to the parents nesting there. *However*, females that settled on a **different island** than where their parents bred still settled close to their sisters. *This clearly demonstrates that* sisters' nesting close to each other is *not a by-product of* either extreme natal philopatry or a preference to nest close to parents, *but results from* a genuine preference for nesting **close to kin**. *In addition, that* females only nested close to sisters **born in the same year** (i.e., sisters that they had been in close contact with) *also suggests that* the clustering of female kin in barnacle geese does **not** result from **phenotype matching**. (471 words)

Cues	Function	Core
1. recent study	1. m	1. **b: nonrandom**
2. could be caused	2. kw2,2'	2. **natal or parents**
3. However	3. aw-	3. **vs. different island**
4. This demonstrate...not..but...	4. kw3	4. **close to kin** → close to sisters = P
5. In addition	5. kw1: -	5. same year: **not P matching**

第1句：证据。新研究发现非随机行为，不是随便住，而是靠近父母或姐妹。这能用3段的出生地本身偏好来解释吗？

2：可能的理论，或让步。可能解释是靠近出生地本身或靠近父母，kw2, kw2'。其中natal site与3段末句呼应。

3：反驳/转折。不在出生地的也会靠近姐妹，反驳第2句理论。

4：新观点。先事实后假说，本句提出这是因为靠近亲属。

5：反驳另一观点。只会住在同年出生的姐妹周围，这也说明b的做法，不是因为第2段所说的表型匹配/kw1。本段反驳了3种解释，确认了一种解释，相当复杂。

全文：现象解释。1段给出行为P，指出其优势以及问题；2段给出kw1，表型匹配，末句负评价；3段引出其他解释，对出生地偏好，给出海鸟与水禽的证据；4段再有B鹅的新研究，表明出生地偏好及表型匹配理论皆错，亲属偏好为正确解释。2段与3段的衔接较薄弱，关系隐蔽，其实都是P行为的不同解释。

【题目分析】

5. The author might have to revise the conclusion that sisters' nesting close to each other is a result of a preference for nesting close to kin if which of the following might happen?

（A）Females that settled on an island other than where they were born still nest close to each other.

（**B**）Females that settled on an island other than where their parents bred build their nesting sites in a scattered pattern.

（C）Females that settled on a different island than where they were born cooperate to defend their territory, though separated.

（D）All females that settled on an island other than where they were born change the site of breeding in some year.

（E）Some females that settled on an island other than where they were born change the nesting sites, while others not.

【解法】取非题。题干 might...revise the conclusion...if... might happen，故意将原文某句内容反过来。题干中要修改结论：姐妹住得较近，是因为住在亲属附近的偏好。这个观点是4段所肯定的。既然要修改这一结论，答案可以取非得到这个结论的证据。4段是先证据后解释，第4句为该结论，第3句为其证据，将之取非之后得到：females that settled on a different island than where their parents bred DID NOT settle close to their sisters.（住在与父母抚养地不同的岛上的个体不会住在姐妹附近。）

【选项】

A. 住在与出生地不同的岛上的雌性依然会住得很近。未取非，重复原文内容。

B. 正确。住在与父母抚养地/出生地不同的岛上的雌性，会以分散模式居住，也就是说不是非随机的、居住在姐妹附近，scattered = random，取非了close to their sisters = nonrandom。

C. 住在与出生地不同岛上的雌性会合作来捍卫地盘，即便分开住着。合作捍卫地盘说明还是会靠近亲属。

D. 住在与出生地不同的岛上的雌性会在某年改变繁殖地点。与问题无关。

E. 住在与出生地不同的岛上的一些雌性会改变筑巢地，另一些则不会。与问题无关。

6. The author mentions which of the following as the benefits of philopatry EXCEPT

（A）help from relatives

（B）reproductive success

（**C**）close inbreeding

（D）reduced antagonism

（E）nice neighbor

【解法】列举题。题干问P的好处，benefits = 1段首句advantages。主要考1段2句内部并列。题干EXCEPT，可找确定没有的；对已有的，只要模糊确认即可，不必仔细定位。

【选项】

A. 有。

B. 有。

C. 正确。正好是however句劣势的内容，在第4句有同义重复词汇close inbreeding = incest。

D. 有，reduced = lower。

E. 有。

7. The author mentions the MHC odor type of mice probably in order to

　（A）　contrast with the olfactory cues used by Arizona tiger salamanders and the visual and chemical cues used by rainbow fish

　（B）　highlight the difficulty the phenotype matching hypothesis confronts

　（C）　stress the pressure of kin recognition of mice

　（D）　indicate the advantage of philopatry to mice

　（E）　provide partial support for phenotype matching hypothesis

【解法】作用题/in order to。题干问提到老鼠的MHC气味有什么用途。定位到2段该大写词所在的第2句，它在句子冒号之后出现，是与老虎并列的证据，找逻辑上一层，就是该句的主干。答案中心词应有Some animals might be using some form of phenotype matching的对应内容。本题相对容易。

【选项】

A. 对比老虎的情况。老鼠与老虎在原文中是并列。

B. 突出表型匹配理论所面临的困难。本句恰好是支持性的证据。

C. 强调老鼠的亲属识别的压力。pressure一词与问题无关。

D. 指出p对于老鼠的好处，1段主题，与本问题无关。

E. 正确。为表型匹配假说提供部分支持。

8. Which of the following, if true, would support the phenotype matching hypothesis?

　（A）　Seabirds and waterfowl tend to cooperate in their breeding season.

　（B）　Barnacle geese females settle close to their sisters born in any years.

　（C）　Rainbow fish use MHC odor type to avoid breeding with their kin.

　（D）　Mice using MHC odor type reproduce more successfully than their relatives not using the same odor.

　（E）　Mice using MHC odor type still have other ways to prevent them from breeding with their relatives.

【解法】逻辑支持。题干问if true, would support，要支持表型匹配。该观点在第2段被反驳，可将2段末句反驳证据取非，即为NOT found that individuals only recognize familiar kin；或者，4段末句也有反驳，将此句的that从句的反驳证据取非，即为that females DID NOT only nest close to sisters born in the same year。

【选项】

A. 海鸟和水禽常常在繁殖季节合作。无关。

B. 正确。B鹅的雌性会与出生在任何年份的姐妹为邻。刚好是取非了同一年出生。

C. 彩虹鱼使用M气味，这是证据里老鼠的做法。无关。

D. 干扰选项。用M气味的老鼠，比那些不用的老鼠繁殖更成功。表型匹配的理论的目的在于解释如何避免近亲婚配，avoid breeding with close relatives，而不只是繁殖成功，中心词错。

E. 使用M气味的老鼠还有其他方法可以组织近亲婚配，这没有支持表型匹配理论，反而削弱了它。

【考位分析】

　　Q5：4段however之后的推理；Q6：1段中的连续并列；Q7：2段句内并列成分与句子主干；Q8：4段末句负评价。

4.3 Concept of money

【*cues*, function & **core**】&【结构分析】

Why researchers have *difficulties* in uncovering **ancient moneys** *has much to do with* the practice of **archeology** and the nature of **money itself**. Archeologists spend their careers **sifting** through the trash of the past, ingeniously reconstructing vanished lives from broken pots and dented knives. *But* like us, ancient Mesopotamians and Phoenicians seldom made the error of tossing out cash, and only **rarely** did they **bury** their most precious liquid assets in the ground. *Even when* archeologists have found buried cash, though, they have **trouble recognizing** it for what it was. Money doesn't always come in the form of dimes and sawbucks. It assumes *many forms*, from debit cards and checks to credit cards and mutual funds. The forms it took in the past have been, to say the least, **elusive**.（130 words）

Cues	Function	Core
1. has to do with	1. kw/ts	1. **difficulty: money**
2. ...	2. a	2. **sifting**/archeology
3. But	3. b	3. **M.P.: rarely bury**
4. Even when	4. c	4. **not recognize**
5. ...	5. c1	5. ...
6. many forms	6. c2	6. many forms
7. ...	7. c2'	7. **elusive**

第1句：总论点。找出古代钱币很困难，这与考古学和古钱本身的性质有关。

2: 证据1。考古学家筛选过去的遗迹。

3: 证据2。古代的M.P.也很少乱丢钱，很少把钱埋起来。

4: 证据3。即便找到了埋起来的钱，也很难认出它们。

5: 证据3.1。形式不只10美分（dimes），10美元（sawbucks）。

6: 证据3.2。钱有多种形式。

7: 延续证据。历史中的钱的形式难以索解（elusive）。

全文：论点说明。首句给出困难的原因，2-7句并列说明各个原因。结构较为简单。

【题目分析】

9. The passage contains information that would support which of the following statements about the money studied by the archeologists?

   （A） It assumed a variety of forms that are completely different from today's forms.

   （B） In the ancient societies, only wealthy citizens were flaunting money.

   （C） In the past, it greased the wheels of Mesopotamian commerce, spurred the development of mathematics, and helped officials and kings rake in taxes and impose fines.

   （D） It was often buried in the ground by the ancient rich people who accumulated the wealth by hoarding the precious noble metal.

   （E） Because of its elusive forms, it was not easy for archeologists to uncover and recognize.

【解法】信息题。题干重点是about之后的money=TW/文章主题词，选项可涉及全文任意一句；从选项找线索，带核心去排除。

【选项】

A. 钱有多种形式，与今天不同（completely different）。错误。

B. 在古代社会，只有富人才炫耀金钱。原文没提到穷人富人的问题。flaunt v. 炫耀，夸耀。

C. 过去，钱润滑了M的商业之轮，加速了数学的发展，帮助官员和国王获得税收和施加罚金。原文没有提到这些内容。

D. 古代富人经常将钱埋在地里。与此相反，原文说的是rarely。

E. **正确**。因为钱的形式难以把握，所以不容易发掘和识别。

4.4　Methane

【*cues*, function & **core**】&【结构分析】

The concentration of atmospheric **methane** is projected to ***increase*** significantly *given* the large pools of carbon stored in permafrost that can be converted to methane upon thaw, the susceptibility of methane hydrates to release from the ocean floor with rising seawater temperature and the acceleration of methane-producing anthropogenic activities. *A recent study examines one particular source* of atmospheric methane that may be significantly *larger than previously recognized*: ebullition（bubbling）from northern lakes. *Careful measurements* of the spatial and temporal patchiness of ebullition in Siberian thermokarst lakes *revealed that* total emissions from lakes were five times **greater** than earlier estimates. *Furthermore*, thaw of permafrost along lake margins releases labile **organic matter** previously sequestered in permafrost for centuries to millennia into anaerobic lake sediments, **enhancing m**ethane production and ebullition emission and serving as a positive feedback to climate warming.（137 words）

Cues	Function	Core
1. *increase...given,*	1. kw: abc	1. **m ↑**
2. *recent study,* one source	2. kw: d	2. **e → m ↑**
3. *measurements*	3. d1	3. e > previously
4. *furthermore*	4. d2	4. thaw → organic → **m/e**

第1句：论点。大气甲烷/m的浓度预期会有显著增加，given之后有连续3个内容并列，**位置>内容**，记为kw: a b c。

2：　论点的新证据。近期研究考查新的来源：湖里冒泡。

3：　证据。S湖的测量揭示，湖里的m释放比以前预计的多5倍。

4：　并列证据。湖的某个地方融化(thaw)以后，释放不稳定的有机物质，增加m的产生量和冒泡释放，形成气候变暖的正反馈。句子内部有连续动作或机制，抓动作首尾。

全文：论点说明。首句论点，然后再讲近期证据，之后给第3~4句详细说明。结构简单，但一些句子较复杂。

【题目分析】

10. The passage mentions which of the following are possible factors for increased concentration of atmospheric methane EXCEPT

    (A) the thawing of permafrost that may convert stored carbon to methane

    (B) ebullition in Siberian thermokarst lakes and emission from other northern lakes

    (C) the deflationary effect of feedback mechanism on climate warming

    (D) human-engineered carbon emission that enhances methane production

    (E) the mounting seawater temperature that triggers methane compounds to release from the ocean floor

【解法】列举题。题干问大气甲烷增加的可能因素，这是文章核心，定位1句和2句皆可。题干问EXCEPT，找确定没有的，对那些已经有的，模糊确认就可以。

【选项】

A.　permafrost融化之后，将储存的碳变成甲烷，首句given之后第一个并列成分即是。

B.　S的冒泡和北部湖区的冒泡，都会导致甲烷增多。

C.　正确。对气候变暖会有抑制性的反馈机制效应，这是说，它有负反馈效果，直接与原文末句的正反馈对立。

D.　人类导致的碳排放，增加甲烷的产生。首句given之后并列成分的最后一个即是：human-engineered = anthropogenic 人类产生的。

E.　海水温度增加/mount = increase，引起甲烷化合物从洋底释放出来，对应首句susceptibility（易受影响）of methane hydrates to release from the ocean floor with rising seawater temperature。

第五节　Exercise 5　解析

5.1　Planet hunting

【*cues*, function & **core**】

　　The direct **detection of extrasolar planets** is extraordinarily *difficult*, *because of* the enormous **difference in luminosity** between a star, which shines with its own light, and orbiting planets, which are not only much smaller and very close to the star, as seen from Earth, but shine by reflected light. The situation *is akin to* trying to identify a firefly buzzing around an intensely bright searchlight—from a great distance. *At* optical wavelengths, a star might be several **billion times** brighter than a large planet. *However, at* infrared wavelengths, where the planet emits its own thermal radiation, the contrast is only a **factor of a million**. Astronomers' *best hopes* of imaging an extrasolar planet are to "**mask**" the bright star, and hope to detect a faint infrared blip off to the side—another world. *One method* of masking is to insert an occulting **disk** in the telescope, which blocks the light from the central star. This method resulted in the telescope near-infrared images, where rings of dust have been discovered orbiting a particular star. (173 words)

Cues	Function	**Core**
1. difficult	1. tw	1. **extrasolar: difficult luminosity**
2. is akin to	2. i	2. =firefly
3. At...	3. a	3. star, **billion** > planet
4. However, at...	4. vs. b	4. vs. **million** >
5. best hopes	5. kw	5. **mask**
6. One method	6. x	6. insert a disk
7. ...	7. y	7. → images → dust

【结构分析】

第1句：主题。探测太阳系外的行星极度困难，因为恒星和它的行星之间的亮度存在巨大差异。

2：类比。举例说明为何困难。这好比在很亮的探照灯旁找一只萤火虫，而且还是从远处。

3：证据。在可见波长（optical wavelength）范围内，恒星比行星亮billion倍，行星是恒星亮度的1/billion。

4：对比证据。与上句平行。在红外波长（infrared wavelength）范围内，行星亮度只是恒星的1/million。

5：解决方法。天文学家最大的希望是能盖住亮的恒星。

6：具体方法。其中一个遮盖做法是在望远镜中插入一个能够挡光（occulting）的圆盘。

7：结果。本句有连续动作，属于广义因果。这种方法可以让望远镜呈现接近红外的图像，天文学家发现，这里有一个围绕恒星做轨道运行的尘埃环。

全文：问题+1个解决方案，也可看做论点说明。1-4句讲困难，5-7句讲解决方案。

【词汇】

akin	*adj.* =similar, analogous，相似的	
extrasolar	*adj.* 太阳系之外的	
faint	*adj.* 微弱的	
luminosity	*n.* 亮度；luminous *adj.* 亮的	
obscure	*v.* 遮蔽、掩盖 *adj.* 不透光的，晦涩的	

occult	*v.* =obscure, block out, 挡（光），掩蔽	
	adj. =secret, concealed，神秘，隐藏的	
optical	*adj.* 光的；视觉的；optics *n.* 光学	
thermal	*adj.* 热的；thermodynamics *n.* 热动力学	
underscore	*v.* =emphasize, underline，强调	

【题目分析】

1. The author uses the analogue of identifying a firefly to

   (A) emphasize the distinguishing feature of finding a firefly around an intensely bright light source

   (B) compare the reflected light of planets and self-generating light of stars

   (C) underscore the importance of infrared wavelength radiation for the detection of extrasolar planets

   (D) illustrate the difficulty of identifying an extrasolar planet around a highly luminous star from an enormous distance

   (E) give an example of the difficulty of detecting an extrasolar planet with current technology

【解法】作用题/in order to。题干问作者引用找萤火虫的类比是为什么。定位萤火虫所在的第2句，找逻辑上一层。该类比是为了说明第1句中的探测行星的困难程度。

【选项】

A. 强调在强光源附近找出萤火虫有独特之处。题干本身内容，不是逻辑上一层。

B. 比较行星的反射光和恒星自己产生的光。细节内容本身，不是逻辑上一层。

C. **干扰选项**。强调红外波长辐射对探测行星的重要性。第1句的重点是探测困难，而不是说红外波长。

D. **正确**。具体说明从远距离找出高亮度恒星附近的行星的困难。与第1句内容对应。

E. **干扰选项**。Give an example = illustrate，与D选项相同。在本文语境下，identifying = detecting。两个选项差别在于E选项中提到的当前技术（current technology）。虽然在事实上，现代技术也许无法探测行星，但文章中并没提。除了EXCEPT题和与逻辑相关的题以外，正确答案必须与原文形成文字对应；current technology在原文无对应。

2. Which of the following statements about the relationship between stars and extrasolar planets is supported by information given in the passage?

   (A) They shine by different types of light, though emitting the same thermal radiation.

   (B) They differ in luminosity because their lights are derived from different extraterrestrial bodies.

   (C) They differ in luminosity because stars emit self-generated light while planets shine by borrowed light.

   (D) Reflected light at optical wavelengths radiated from planets is entirely obscured by the light emitted from stars, so as to be invisible.

【解法】信息题。题干about之后说恒星和行星之间的关系，是全文主题内容的一部分。从选项找线索，带核心去排除。

【选项】

A. 错误。恒星和行星发出的光的类别不同，但有相同的热辐射。原文也许承认前半句，一个是自有光，一个是反射光，但后半句的相同的热辐射，原文未提。

B. 错误。选项前半部分说亮度不同，这是对的，但because从句提到恒星和行星的光线来自不同的天体，这却是错的，或至少是不确切的。行星的反射光也来自恒星，恒星的光线当然来自自己。第1句说的不同，是指亮度不同，以及光线是来自自己还是其他，但光的来源其实都是同一颗恒星。

C. **正确**。它们亮度有别，因为恒星自己发光，行星借光。与文章第1句相符。

（E）An occulting disk in the telescope can help block out the central star, making it possible to detect visible light at the optical wavelength emitted by an extrasolar planet.

D. 程度错误。来自行星的可见波长的反射光，完全被恒星的光掩盖，以至于不可见。entirely的程度过强，原文并未说被完全遮盖，只是说亮度高几十亿倍。而且选项中的invisible，程度也太强。

E. **干扰选项**。望远镜里阻挡光线的圆盘可以挡住中间恒星的光，与末句对应；但选项后半部分说，这就可以探测行星发出的可见波长的可见光，这是错的，末句说的是探测红外线。

5.2 *Breathless*

【*cues*, function & **core**】&【结构分析】

Critics of Jean-Luc Godard's celebrated *film Breathless* wondered if its protagonist's weak acting and the film's general roughness are meant to be *parodies* of conventional acting and filmmaking. *But such a diagnosis doesn't fit*. Parody suggests consistent mockery in the service of a specific goal, usually that of puncturing pretension, with the immediate aim of getting a laugh. *But Breathless is more pretentious in its **low-key** way than any film-noir production that it could be said to parody. It doesn't ramp up but brings down and scatters conventional elements. *Although* there are several scenes that some viewers might find humorous, this humor is of the **whimsical** not the parodic variety.

Cues	Function	Core
1. critics: parody	1. kw1	1. **critics: B: parody**
2. But doesn't fit	2. aw-	2. **not fit**
3. ...	3. x	3. parody: **mockery**
4. But...more	4. vs. y	4. vs. **B: low-key**
5. ...	5. y1	5. ...
6. Although...,	6. ~y2, y2	6. whimsical humor

第1句：观点1。批评家评论Godard的电影B，认为主角的弱表演和电影的粗糙感，意在故意模仿和嘲弄传统电影。

2: 负评价。这种诊断不适合。文章会有多个观点评论同一个主题，在这里就是电影B。

3: 证据。通常parody是要持续嘲笑，以达到某一目的，引起人们开怀大笑。

4: 对比证据。但B的做法却比较低调，不像正常的parody。

5: 证据。它没有加强、只是减少和打散了传统要素。

6: 让步转折。虽然有些观众认为它幽默，但这种幽默是随意的（whimsical），与parody的不同。

Critics today are also inclined to *see* this French film *as* an example of **reality** cinema. The insouciant attitude that *Breathless* takes toward its audience *may encourage* impressionable viewers to mistake it for **realism**, *but there is **nothing*** about the characters' talk or behavior that *corresponds to* the way people *actually* talk or behave, even in France.

Cues	Function	Core
1. critics today... see...as...	1. kw2	1. **today: B: reality**
2. may encourage, but nothing	2. aw+ vs. aw-	2. realism **vs. nothing...actually**

第1句：观点2。今天的批评家认为这部法国电影是现实电影。

2: 让步转折+态度。B的一些内容的确符合这种看法，但电影中人物的言谈和行为与人们的实际情况并不相符。

*The **best** way to understand Breathless* is to reconsider its **genre**—that is, *to approach it primarily as* a work of **ideas** rather than as a work of art. The British critic Matthew Arnold, *in his 1864 essay* "The Function of Criticism in the Present Time," noted that art and **criticism** are distinct but mutually supportive genres, and that the relative merit of each may vary in different eras and in different cultures. The French, *he argued*, tend to be drawn to **ideas**, while the English distrust them, with the result that English art is often **less intellectually** informed than one would wish (even the great Wordsworth, he added, would have done well to read more books). *A corollary*, which Arnold doesn't pursue, *is that* French art tends to be **overladen with ideas**, to be more like criticism than art—an assumption that **pertains well to** *Breathless*.

Cues	Function	Core
1. best way	1. kw3.1	1. **best: B: ideas**
2. A. 1864 essay	2. p	2. A: criticism
3. he argued	3. q:	3. **F: ideas**
...while	q1 vs. q2	**vs. E: less intellect**
4. corollary is that	4. cs	4. **B: ideas** = criticism

第1句：论点3+正评价。最好的理解B的方法是重新考虑它的风格：把它作为观念而非艺术的作品。

2: 证据。A指出艺术和批判虽不同，但相互支持。

3: 证据。他认为法国人喜欢观念，而英国人则不信任观念，英国艺术的理智信息较少，在这里，ideas = intellect。

4: 结论。一个自然推论（corollary）就是，法国艺术充满观念，更像批评而非艺术，这也适合B。

The sequence of shifting signifiers used in the film *also corresponds to* **ideas** about meaning that the linguistic philosopher Jacques **D**errida was developing, under the name of **deconstruction**, during the same period. In deconstructionist terms, *then*, the film's sloppiness becomes a value, a way of **exposing** both the arbitrary *constructedness* of past meaning and the opportunities for making new meaning in the future. *The former constitutes the* **political** *dimension* of the film insofar as it critiques what has been done in the name of cinema, society, capitalism, or whatever. *The latter is the* **theoretical** *dimension*, the film's way of demonstrating what is possible if one lets loose from old constraints and assumptions. Godard's film *can be viewed as* the critical antecedent to **a new era** in which movies were freed from the constraints of classic Hollywood cinema. (451 words)

Cues	Function	Core
1. also	1. kw3.2	1. = **D: deconstruction**
corresponds		
2. then	2. u.	2. **exposing**
3. the former	3. v1.	3. political
4. the latter	4. v2.	4. theoretical
5. can be viewed	5. cs	5. **B: new era**

第1句：论点3的平行论点，以kw3.2表示。该电影中使用的一些做法，也对应着D在同时期所开创的意义观念：解构。

2: 顺承证据。按解构的说法，电影的松散拖沓（sloppiness）反而成为优点，既能揭露过往意义的被建构性，又能显示未来提出新意义的机会。专业内容无需懂得，只需抓住exposing = deconstruction，**论据重现论点核心**。

3: 证据1。前一方面构成政治维度，因它批判一切已有。

4: 证据2。后一方面构成理论维度，因它展示一旦放松旧有的约束与假设之后的可能性。

5: 本段结论。于是，G的电影可看做新时代的批判先导。

全文：观点对比型。第1段观点1，被反驳；第2段观点2，也被反驳；第3-4段观点3的两个分论点，正评价，这两段中内部论据都是并列展开。

【词汇】

antecedent	*n.* 先行者	parody	*n.* 以嘲弄和讽刺为目的的模仿
constraint	*n.* 约束	pertain to	与…切合、相关
corollary	*n.* 自然推论，直接结果	pretension	*n.* 假装
deconstruction	*n.* 解构	protagonist	*n.* 主人公，主角，主演
diagnosis	*n.* 诊断	puncturing	*adj.* 刺穿的，使之无效的
genre	*n.* 风格	pursue	*v.* 追求，探索
insouciant	*adj.* =nonchalant, 不在意的	ramp up	增加，加速，扩大
let loose	使放松	scatter	*v.* 分散，散开
mockery	*n.* 嘲弄；mock *v.*	whimsical	*adj.* 随意的；whim *n.* =caprice, 奇思怪想
mutually	*adv.* 相互地		

【题目分析】

3. Based on the information in the passage, which of the following statements about the perspective of deconstruction in the interpretation of the film could be true?

(A) From deconstructionist perspective, the film's shifting scenes could be a reflection of transitory and nihilistic character of established tradition and culture.

(B) From deconstructionist perspective, the film's unsystematic or casual arrangement could be a valuable way of exposing the autocratic and whimsical characters of constructed establishment in politics and theory.

(C) A deconstructionist interpretation could liberate the film from its confined and stilted scenes and reveal its promising implication in the sociopolitical arena.

(D) A deconstructionist interpretation betrays the ideal of Jacques Derrida who advocates a valuable combination of theoretical critique and political reflection in the criticism of classic Hollywood cinema.

(E) Free from the conventional constraints and assumptions, the film could be envisioned as anticipating a new era in which movies are created from a random patchwork piecing together diverse, heterogeneous elements haphazardly.

【解法】（段落）信息题。题干about之后才是重点，deconstruction是4段首句词汇。定位4段全段，从选项找线索，带核心去排除。

【选项】

A. 电影不断转变的场景可能反映了既有传统和文化的快速变化和虚无主义的（nihilistic）特点。虚无有点太过了，错误。

B. 正确。电影的不够系统或随意的安排也许很有价值，暴露了政治和理论领域建构的既有状态（constructed establishment）的独裁性和任意性特点。对应第2句：autocratic and whimsical = arbitrary；unsystematic and casual = sloppiness，也考虑到第3-4句的理论和政治两个维度。

C. 解构主义的解读可以解放电影，摆脱局限、僵硬的场景，揭示它在社会政治领域的潜在含义。原文第3句讲政治，但仅说要批判，并无正面的建设意义（promising implication）。内容过度。

D. 解构主义的解读显示了D的影响，他主张在评论好莱坞的经典电影时，综合理论批判和政治反思。关于好莱坞的电影，末句提到，但文章没说D主张批判好莱坞电影，只在第1句说到D的基本观念。延伸太多。

E. 摆脱传统的约束和假设，该电影被认为预示了一个新时代：电影可以通过随机拼凑各式各样、五花八门的元素产生出来。过度延伸末句，末句仅说摆脱既有，没说一切都要乱来、一切随机进行（haphazardly, random）。

4. The author discusses Matthew Arnold's essay "The Function of Criticism in the Present Time" in the third paragraph primarily in order to do which of the following?

(A) Prove that art and criticism are different but mutually supportive genres

(B) Argue that the relative merit of art and criticism may vary in different time periods and in different cultures

(C) Highlight the crucial divergence between English art and French art

(D) Indicate that the film *Breathless*, as a French art, is awash with ideas, closer to criticism than art

(E) Criticize Arnold for failing to draw from his ideas an important conclusion

【解法】作用题/in order to。题干问讨论A的文章的目的。定位第3段第2句，找逻辑上一层，提到该人物的目的是为了说明首句论点，证明观念研究角度的重要性。

【选项】

A. 证明艺术和批判不同，但互相支持。只是重复所问内容。

B. 主张艺术和批评的相对优点在不同时期和不同文化中有区别。依然重复第2句内容，与A的错误相同。

C. 突出英国和法国艺术的关键差别（divergence）。这不是提到这个人物的目的，只是他的观点的展开。

D. 正确。指出B电影作为法国艺术，充满观念，更像批评而非艺术，对应末句结论。论据的逻辑上一层也可以是末尾结论。

E. 批评A没有从他的观念推出一个重要结论。错误。

For the following question, consider each of the choices separately and select all that apply.

5. The information provided in the passage indicates that parody of traditional acting and filmmaking might include which of the following as its features?

(A) Consistent mockery

(B) Whimsical humor

(C) Aim to trigger a laugh

【解法】（多选）列举题。题干问对传统表演和电影制作的嘲弄模仿包含什么特征。parody是1段核心词之一，在1段3–4句的对比中包含这些内容，parody的特点是mockery, laugh。本题的重点还是考对比。

【选项】

A. 正确。持续嘲弄。选项内容完全照抄原文。

B. 偶然出现的幽默。末句 whimsical not the parodic variety 将这两种幽默进行明确的对比。错误。

C. 正确。aim to trigger a laugh = immediate aim of getting a laugh。

6. Which of the following best describes the organization of the passage as a whole?

(A) Two views are devalued, an alternative view is presented and substantiated.

(B) A hypothesis is presented, a better alternative partly based on the hypothesis is discussed, and the new hypothesis is evaluated in light of new evidence.

(C) Two views are compared and contrasted, evidence that undercuts these two views is then presented, and a new view that may better interpret the subject is discussed.

(D) A tentative view is refuted, a revised view is presented and challenged, and a third view that combines previous two views is suggested and yet to be confirmed.

【解法】结构题。题干问全文的organization，定位各段首句解题。本文第1–2段2个观点，均被反驳，第3–4段提出正确观点。

【选项】

A. 正确。两个观点被贬低，一个替代观点被提出然后被证实。

B. 一个假说被提出，一个更好的解释被讨论，到此已错，结构题的选项必须与原文写作顺序对应，但文章第2段没有提出更好的解释。

C. 干扰选项。两个观点被对比和比较，削弱（undercut）这两个观点的证据然后被提出，这已经错误，文章第1段不是先比较两个观点，然后才提出证据同时反驳两者。

D. 一个试验性观点被反驳，一个修改的观点被提出，然

（E）　Two views are questioned, a relatively new view is introduced, but then supplanted by a more recent view.

后被挑战，第3个观点综合前两个观点被提出，还有待确证。最后的yet to be confirmed是负评价，与第3段首句the best way不符。

E.　两个观点被质疑，一个相对新的观点被引入（introduced），但被一个更新的观点所取代。如果是这样，文章就应该有4个观点，数量错误。

【考位分析】

Q3：4段细节；Q4：3段首末句与中间证据的关系；Q5：1段对比细节；Q6：各段首句，文章逻辑结构；第1段、第4段中间的专业知识未考。专业生词不重要。

5.3　Measuring eighteenth-century migration

【*cues*, function & core】

Historians have devised ***different*** *methods* to estimate the **levels of immigration** in the eighteenth-century America. Using tenuous fertility and mortality data compiled by other historians, *Gemery calculates* net migration as a **residual**, with the results being a plausible range of 278,400 to 485,300 white immigrants for the period 1700 to 1780. An ***alternative method, however,*** relies on an improved **surname analysis** of the 1790 census as a check for the increasing expertise of ethnic group historians who rely on actual immigration data from ship and passenger lists. *Despite some* ***gaps***, *this method produces* ***enlightening*** *results* for most ethnic groups during the period — 585,800 immigrants（278,400 blacks and 307,400 whites）, roughly consistent with Gemery's finding.（115 words）

Cues	Function	Core
1. *different* methods	1. tw	1. **different methods**
2. *G. calculates*	2. kw1	2. **G: residual**
3. *alternative method*	3. vs. kw2	3. **vs. surname analysis**
4. *Despite gaps, ... enlightening*	4. aw-, +	4. **gaps; enlightening**

【结构分析】

第1句：主题。历史学家发明不同的方法来估计当时的移民水平。没有具体的观点，但提示会有不同的方法，different 暗示会有对比观点出现：kw1 *vs.* kw2。

2：观点1。G运用其他历史学家统计的不太可靠的（tenuous）生育率和死亡率的数据，从余数（residual）来计算净移民，得出一些数字。

3：观点2。替代的方法则用1790人口普查的姓氏进行分析，检查研究族群的历史学家的结果。

4：让步转折+态度。虽然这种方法也有空白和缺口，但得到的结果还是相当有启发性的，所获得的一组数字与G的发现基本一致。

全文：评述。首句给出不同的研究方法的评述对象，然后展开对比的两类方法。

【题目分析】

7. According to the passage, the residual method used by Gemery differs from the alternative method in that it

(A) relies on the fertility and mortality data about immigrants that have previously been inaccessible

(B) produces a total number far larger than the total number generated by the alternative method

(C) yields a more accurate estimate than the alternative method

(D) eschews the sketchy fertility and mortality data that the alternative method draws on

(E) does not exploit the immigration data of ethnic groups from ship and passenger lists

【解法】（对比）核心题。题干问G所用的剩余法与替代方法的差别何在。定位文章第2–4句，也就是however前后。

【选项】

A. G的方法依赖生育率和死亡率，这些数据从前无法获得（inaccessible）。后半句在原文中没有提到。

B. G的方法得出的总数比替代方法的总数大很多。与末句所说的roughly consistent矛盾。

C. G的方法产生的结果比替代方法更精确。态度错误。原文仅仅是对比，没有给G以正评价。事实上，负评价的可能性更大。

D. G的方法避免（eschew）了粗略的（sketchy）生育率和死亡率数据，而替代方法则立足于这些数据。与原文相反。

E. **正确**。G的方法没有利用来自轮船和旅客清单的族群移民数据。这种数据是替代方法用的，G的确没用。

※逻辑题

A new class of insecticides known as neonicotinoids is broadly and commonly used in most cropping systems and on turf and forest pests. *But* one of the compounds in this class, imidacloprid, was banned in France, *because* it is acutely toxic to bees and because sub-lethal doses have been shown to impair honey bee short-term memory.

8. Which of the following, if true, most strongly supports the French policy about imidacloprid?

(A) Short-term memory is critical to bee's navigational abilities necessary for foraging flights and for returning to the hive.

(B) Short-term memory is an essential part of bee's cognitive repertoire as is long-term memory.

(C) Short-term memory and long-term memory function simultaneously when bees fly and navigate.

(D) Environmentalists oppose the widespread use of imidacloprid for fearing its unintended consequences for the turf and forest pests.

(E) Government policy-makers have not yet reached a final rejection of imidacloprid since its effects have not been extensively investigated.

【解法】逻辑支持。题干问if true, support法国对i（midacloprid）的政策。原文第2句because前后的逻辑推理最重要。因为i对蜜蜂有毒，也因为不够致命的剂量的i也会伤害蜂群的短期记忆，所以法国才禁止（ban）使用它。要支持这一做法，可以举例、重复、或否定他因、或提供中间环节等。

【选项】

A. **正确**。短期记忆对蜜蜂飞行导航很关键，而导航能力又是觅食飞行和飞回蜂巢所必需的。这样来看，损害蜜蜂短期记忆，就会让蜜蜂无法回巢。这提供了推理的中间环节，进一步说明i不好。

B. 短期记忆是蜜蜂认知能力的必不可少的一部分，就如长期记忆一样。这个说法的支持力度不够强。该句没有在认知能力（cognitive repertoire）和蜜蜂生存之间建立关联。

C. 短期记忆和长期记忆在蜜蜂飞行和导航时同时起作用。与B的错误相同，没有直接说明它对蜜蜂生存的意义。

D. 环保主义者反对广泛使用i，因为害怕它对一些害虫会有意想不到的后果。没有提供推理的中间环节。

E. 政府的政策制定者迄今还没有最终拒绝i。这不是支持，反而像反对政府禁止i。

5.4 Bee colony collapse

【*cues*, function & **core**】

*Some **factors** have been suggested as causal mechanisms* of bee colony collapse **disorder**（CCD）, *for example*, the use of genetically modified（**GMO**）crops. *However*, large bee die-offs have also occurred in **Europe**, where GMO crops are **not** widely **grown**. *Also*, in the United States, the patterns of CCD-affected colonies do **not** appear to **correlate** with the distribution of GMO-crops such as Bt-corn. *Other hypotheses are even **less likely**. For example*, the public has become concerned that **cell phone** use *may be causing* bee die-offs; *however*, exposure of bees to high levels of electromagnetic fields is *unlikely*. *Similarly*, shifts in the Earth's **magnetic** field, which *could conceivably affect* bee navigation, have ***not*** been **correlated** with bee die-off episodes, *but **cannot*** be completely ***ruled out*** at this time.（126 words）

Cues	Function	Core
1. factors suggested, for example	1. tw: kw1	1. **disorder** ← GMO
2. however...not	2. aw-: x	2. **not** grown
3. also not correlate	3. y	3. **not correlate**
4. other hypotheses	4. kw'	4. **other: less likely**
5. for example; however, unlikely	5. kw2 aw-	5. cell phone: **unlikely**
6. Similarly, not correlate, but	6. kw3 aw-, +	6. **magnetic: not correlate; not out**

【结构分析】

第1句：现象与假说1。首句提出蜂群崩溃的现象，并提出一个原因，即转基因（GMO）作物的使用：GMO → disorder。

2：负评价。但是，在欧洲也有大规模的蜜蜂死亡，而欧洲没有广泛使用GMO作物。GMO ↛ die off=disorder。

3：负评价并列证据。在美国，蜂群崩溃的模式也与GMO作物的分布不相关。

4：过渡句。其他假说更不可能，暗示下面有假说，且给负评价。

5：假说2及负评价。公众担心使用手机会导致蜜蜂死掉，但是，蜜蜂不太可能暴露在高密度的电磁场中。

6：假说3及态度。地球磁场的变化，也许会影响蜜蜂导航，但却与蜜蜂死亡的事件无相关性，但目前还不能完全排除这个因素。末句的态度是混合评价，有正有负。

全文：现象解释。首句给出现象，马上给出假说1，接着负评价，然后假说2，再负评价，然后假说3，再给负评价和部分正评价。文字上无难度，主要是观点较多。

【题目分析】

9. Which of the following best describes the main idea of the passage?

   （A） Several factors, such as GMO crops, cell phone use and change in the magnetic field, cannot explain why bee colony collapses in disorder.

   （B） Scientists have dismissed several theories of bee colony collapse disorder because of their lack of strong experimental evidence and solid theoretical framework.

   （C） Scientists failed to explain the collapse of bee colony because they cannot easily measure the impact of cell phone use on the alteration of electromagnetic fields.

   （D） The use of GMO crops did not bring about large bee die-offs more than the shifts in the Earth's magnetic field.

   （E） The reason that proposed hypotheses cannot explain large bee die-offs is that they cannot establish the correlation between the pattern of colony collapse and the putative factors.

10. It can be inferred from the passage that the GMO-crops hypothesis would have been more convincing if researchers had been able to

   （A） prove that exposure of bees to high levels of electromagnetic fields does not correlate with large bee die-offs in Europe

   （B） demonstrate that the changes in the Earth's magnetic field, though affecting bee navigation, do not vary with the periods of bee die-offs

   （C） demonstrate that the pattern of bee colony collapse correspond to the demographical mode of genetically modified crops

   （D） dismiss the hypotheses that explain the bee colony collapse disorder by invoking the non-European evidence

   （E） make extensive laboratory and field testing to indicate a lack of acute and sub-lethal effects on bees exposed to GMO-pollen

【解法】主题题。题干问文章的main idea，现象解释类文章的主题就在首句中的现象。文章就是为了解释CCD或蜜蜂蜂群崩溃。

【选项】

A. 正确。选项的主语中列举了若干因素，概括了文中所提到的3个解释，谓语的cannot explain表示负评价，给出了作者态度。与原文相符。

B. 干扰选项。虽由dismiss给出负评价，而且给出了实验证据匮乏的问题，但其原因中包含了理论框架（theoretical framework）缺失一项，原文未涉及。多数地方都对，就一个词组错误，属于典型的a+b+X错误（请参见第三章题型部分关于错误选项的说明）。

C. 虽有负评价，但其原因仅涉及电话使用一项，内容片面，不足以概括全文内容。原文的负评价针对3个解释给出，有多个证据支撑。

D. 该选项将转基因作物（GMO-crops）与磁场理论（magnetic field）作比较，仅属于两个理论之间的关系，非全文主题内容，全文共讲3个理论。

E. 干扰选项。仅给出对理论负评价的原因，但主题是针对一些理论给出负评价，而不仅仅讨论负评价的原因。

【解法】（态度）取非题。题干问would have been more convincing if...had...，GMO假说要更加令人信服，需要什么条件；定位负评价，将其内容取非即可。

【选项】

A. B.这两个选项仅仅使磁场理论和电话理论不令人信服，并不直接支持转基因作物的假说。有人可能以为否定他因，本身会构成对转基因作物假说的间接支持，但题干所问并非逻辑反对，而是更令人信服的原因。

C. 正确。将第3句反对转基因作物的证据取非。

D. 干扰选项。放弃那些援引非欧洲证据来解释蜂群崩溃现象的假说。这很奇怪；将"large bee die-offs have also occurred in Europe, where GMO crops are not widely grown"取非，其结果是GMO作物的种植地区，发生了大规模的死亡。

E. 做大量的试验和检验，指出转基因作物的花粉不会对蜂类造成严重和比较致命的伤害。这不会造成蜂群崩溃，但不是原文提到的负评价证据的取非。

第六节　Exercise 6　解析

6.1　Coral mortality

【*cues*, function & **core**】

　　Diffusible compounds released by **algae** *may mediate* **coral mortality via microbial** activity. Algae can *release* excess **p**hotosynthate in the form of **p**olysaccharides, or **d**issolved **o**rganic **c**arbon, that can *fuel* microbial activity and *accelerate* microbial growth. The microbial community growing on or near the coral surface may *then exhibit* explosive growth, *eventually creating* a zone of **h**ypoxia on the surface of the live coral tissue. In this study, all corals *exposed to* but not in direct contact with algae *bleached* and were physiologically ***compromised*** within 2-4 days. *Clearly,* some algae *may* release chemical compounds that may be toxic to other organisms. *But* here, coral mortality could be completely prevented with the addition of antibiotics, *thus supporting the hypothesis that* the **microbial** community *was the **agent of coral death***. （128 words）

Cues	Function	Core
1. may mediate via	1. kw/ts	1. **algae → microbe → coral** ↓
2. release → fuel →	2. $x_{1\to2}$	2. **algae** → p,d.o.c, → micro
3. then → eventually	3. → $y_{1\to2}$	3. m↑ → h. -
4. ... compromised	4. → z	4. **coral**↓: **compromised**
5. Clearly, may	5. ~kw	5. compounds: toxic
6. But, supporting the hypothesis	6. u; cs/kw	6. antibiotics → coral↑; **micro → coral↓: death**

【结构分析】

第1句：论点。**理科讲因果**。水藻释放的可扩散化合物会通过微生物活动导致珊瑚的死亡。有3个动作环节：algae, microbe, coral；下面会用连续动作/机制展开，**机制抓首尾**。

2: 环节1。水藻释放过量的p，即poly-，或叫溶解有机碳c，它加强微生物活动，加速微生物生长：Algae → c → micro。

3: 环节2。微生物群体爆炸式地生长，最终产生h区域。

4: 环节3/结果。所有暴露于algae的珊瑚都在2-4天内变白，而且在生理上受损（compromised）。这是动作最

后一步。在此语境下，compromised≈首句mortality。

5: 让步/替代观点。也许，一些algae会释放化学化合物，对有机体有毒。也就是说，珊瑚死亡的原因不是微生物。

6: 转折/作者观点。但是，加了抗生素，珊瑚就没死亡；这说明微生物导致珊瑚死亡；用他因来质疑替代观点，最后再支持微生物是珊瑚死亡的原因，回到首句论点。

全文：论点说明。因果论点，连续动作展开，还有让步转折。全文为机制套让步。

【词汇】

agent	*n.* 作用者，因素，行为者	compound	*n.* 化合物
antibiotics	*n.* 抗生素	compromise	*v.* 损害；妥协 *n.* 折中
bleach	*v.* 变白，漂白	diffusible	*adj.* 可散开的，可扩散的

dissolved	*adj.* 溶解的；solution *n.* 溶液 dissolution *n.* 分解，溶解	mediate	*v.* =regulate，调节，间接造成
fuel	*v.* 加速，刺激 *n.* 燃料	microbe	*n.* 微生物
		mortality	*n.* 死亡；mortal *adj.* 要死的
		toxic	*adj.* 有毒的；toxin *n.* 毒素

【题目分析】

For the following question, consider each of the choices separately and select all that apply.

1. Given the information given in the passage, it can be inferred that which of the following statements is true of the zone of hypoxia on the surface of the live coral tissue?

   (A) The live corals in the zone of hypoxia would be physiologically suffered within several days.

   (B) The zone of hypoxia is awash in chemical compounds released by algae that are directly harmful to corals.

   (C) The deleterious effect on corals of hypoxia area generated by a microbial community can be counterbalanced by the addition of antibiotics.

【解法】（多选）细节题。题干true of后面的hypoxia最重要。无需知道这个专业词汇如何翻译，可从上下文推出其意思。定位第3句，微生物疯狂生长，在珊瑚周围形成h，第4句说珊瑚会变白和生理受损。可见h对珊瑚会产生负面作用。

【选项】

A. **正确**。h区域的活珊瑚也会在几天内生理受损，suffered = compromised。

B. h地区充满（awash in）化学化合物，直接对珊瑚有害，这是第5句让步句的替代观点，不是文章作者的看法。题干问的是文章的信息。

C. **正确**。微生物产生h，h对珊瑚造成有害影响，这种影响可以通过加入抗生素来反制或平衡。与末句说的加入抗生素珊瑚就没死亡对应。本题考到文章多个句子。

2. Which of the following, if true, would most weaken the hypothesis proposed in the passage?

   (A) Corals generally show significant declines in health when placed next to algae without antibiotics.

   (B) Not all coral species are equally susceptible to algal mediated mortality and not all algae have deleterious effects on corals.

   (C) A significant input of dissolved organic carbon that facilitates the growth of microbes comes either from the algae themselves or from anthropogenic sources (e.g. waste water).

   (D) On healthy reefs, corals are the dominant, habitat forming organisms and algae are kept at low levels of standing biomass via intense grazing.

   (E) A new experiment discovers that increased organic carbon loading directly kill corals and that coral mortality caused by organic carbon loading is negatively correlated with an increase in microbial activity.

【解法】逻辑反对。假说是algae造成microbe生长，最终损害coral。反对可以是直接否定、肯定他因、摧毁中间环节等。

【选项】

A. 放在靠近水藻、但没有抗生素的地方，珊瑚的健康水平通常会下降。这对应文章假说。是支持，不是削弱。

B. 不是所有珊瑚种类都会同等受到水藻间接造成的死亡影响；不是所有水藻都对珊瑚有害。但这并不反对有一些、甚至很多都会有害。

C. 一定量的溶解有机碳会加速微生物生长。重复原文的环节。支持，而非反对。

D. 在健康的礁石上，珊瑚是主要的、塑造栖息地的有机体，而水藻则会因为密集的食草行为处于低水平。说水藻较少，珊瑚较多，这支持原假说。

E. **正确**。一个新的实验发现，增加有机碳会直接杀死珊瑚，由有机碳增加所导致的珊瑚死亡，与微生物活动增加呈负相关。负相关就说明，不是因为通过中间环节即微生物导致珊瑚死亡，而是有机碳本身直接导致。这与假说所认为的"水藻 → 有机碳 → 微生物 → 珊瑚死亡"的推理步骤相违背。

6.2 Acculturation

【*cues*, function & **core**】

　　Unlike the traditional **qualitative** *approaches* to **acculturation**, **P**adilla *presented a* multidimensional and **quantitative** *model* of acculturation that relied on cultural awareness, i.e., implicit knowledge that individuals have of their cultures of origin and of their host cultures. If individuals show **more knowledge** of their heritage cultures **than** they do of the **new** contact cultures, they are **less acculturated**, and vice versa. *But like* those *major theories* of acculturation, *this model did* **not** *take into consideration* individual **differences** and personality characteristics that facilitate or retard acculturation. *Certainly*, Padilla's emphasis on the preference of individuals for the dominant or heritage cultures is *an important* **advance**. *But the model falls* **short of explaining** how individuals from the same socioeconomic, generational, and familial backgrounds **differ** on willingness and competence to acculturate. (127 words)

Cues	Function	Core
1. *unlike traditional,* P present a model	1. tw: x	1. **P: quantitative: ac-**(culturation)
2. *if..., less*	2. y	2. less new: less ac-
3. *But like major, not consider*	3. aw-	3. **not consider differences: -**
4. *Certainly, advance*	4. aw+	4. advance **+**
5. *But, short of*	5. aw-	5. **short of...differ...**

【结构分析】

第1句：主题。与传统的质的研究不同，P提出多维度和量的研究模型，研究ac-(culturation)/文化融合；that从句次要。

2： 论据。如果个体对传统文化的知识多于新接触文化，则文化融合就较少，反之亦然（vice versa）。本句数量相关。

3： 负评价。该模型与主流理论一样，没有考虑个体差异。

4： 让步。当然，P的做法也是一种重要进步。

5： 转折。但是，P的模型还是没有解释来自同一背景的个体如何会在文化融合的意愿和竞争能力上有差别。**让步找相反，转折找相似**，该转折内容与第3句负评价对应。

全文：评论型文章。先论点再证据，再负评价和让步转折。最后3句的态度是负–正–负。

【词汇】

acculturation	*n.* 文化融合；ac-: to, at		qualify	*v.* 限制；通常表示让步的作用
competence	*n.* 竞争能力，胜任资格		retard	*v.* =block, hinder, hamper, 阻碍
facilitate	*v.* =accelerate, spur, 加速，促进		short of	差一点，还未达到
host	*n.* 移入地区；主人；(寄生物)宿主		vice versa	反之亦然
multidimensional	*adj.* 多维度的；dimension *n.* 维度			

【题目分析】

3. Select the sentence in the passage in which the author qualifies the disapproval of Padilla's model in explaining how individual differences and personality characteristics influence the rate of acculturation.

【解法】选择句子。要选出一个句子，作者在该句中限制了他对P的模型的不赞成态度；in explaining后面内容都次要；找到负评价态度的让步句即可。不能只是找负评价句！选择句子题的题干通常会提供2-3个要素，要考查多个句子的关系及作用。这样，disapproval = 3句But，qualify = 4句Certainly。答案是"Certainly, Padilla's emphasis on..."。

For the following question, consider each of the choices separately and select all that apply.

4. It can be inferred from the passage that which of the following descriptions would be true of conventional approaches to acculturation?

　（A）　The traditional theories of acculturation would argue that if the persons possess more knowledge of the host cultures, then they are less acculturated.

　（B）　The traditional theories of acculturation have not provided the quantitative hypothesis of how acculturation takes place.

　（C）　The traditional theories of acculturation have yet to appreciate and explain individual differences within the demands of cultural and sociopolitical contexts.

【解法】（多选对比）细节题。题干问传统研究方法，原文1句unlike，3句like，把它与P的方法比较。定位这两句。

【选项】

A. 传统方法主张，如果人们对移入区文化有更多认识，他们的文化融合就较少。这句的反面是P的观点，在第2句；但它并非P与传统做法的不同点，故取非之后也无法确认这就是传统做法的观点。

B. 正确。传统理论没有提供量的假说。这是第1句的内容。原文首句有A vs. B，问其中一个A，则A = not B。问传统如何，就可将P的做法取非。

C. 正确。传统理论尚未评估和解释个体差异。对应第3句：与多数理论一样，P的模型也没有考虑个体差异。从该句P的情况可以推出多数理论肯定也包含传统理论的情况。

※ 逻辑题

　　Carbohydrate causes the elevation of transmitter serotonin in the brain, which can fuel neuron activity and stimulate behavior. *Scientists propose* reducing carbohydrate in the diet for patients of neuronal oversensitivity and increasing protein, which can suppress the production and release of transmitter serotonin. *However,* the low level of serotonin might induce a strong craving for carbohydrate and finally minimize the effect of high protein diet. *Thus the scientists' proposal does not work.*

5. Which one of the following, if true, most supports the scientists' proposal?

　（A）　Some patients who crave for carbohydrate reported they feel sleepy after a diet containing mostly carbohydrate.

　（B）　Some patients who do not crave for carbohydrate reported they feel refreshed after a diet containing mostly protein.

　（C）　The consumption of protein indirectly decreases blood concentration of tryptophan

【解法】逻辑支持。题干问if true, support科学家的提议。文章末句提到科学家的建议不会奏效，由thus引导，之前一句为原因。第3句由however引导，它讲s(erotonin)的浓度低，也许会导致对c(arbohydrate)的强烈需求(strong craving)，最终可能减小高蛋白p(rotein)饮食的效果：s↓：c↑。要支持科学家的提议，可将原文负评价的证据取非，则答案也许是：s低不会导致c的欲求增加：s↓：not c↑。或者，可以支持第2句科学家的说法：对神经过度敏感（即思维过度活跃、行为过度猛烈）的病人，减少饮食里的c，增加p，这样会抑制s的产生和释放：c↓：s↓；从这个负相

which is the only precursor of serotonin in the brain.

(D) The high level of serotonin in the brain can facilitate neuronal activity and produce strong emotional and behavioral responses.

(E) A high protein diet, though benefiting physical health, turns out to have other detrimental effects on mental health.

关，可以推出，c↑：s↑。逻辑支持可以是举例、重复、提供中间环节、否定他因等。

【选项】

A. 一些病人想吃c，吃完主要含有c的食物后，觉得昏昏欲睡；sleepy相当于神经活动削弱。这句等于说，吃了c，神经活动削弱。而科学家认为，吃了c，神经活动会增强。所以，该选项不是支持，而是反对。

B. 一些病人不想吃c，吃完主要含有蛋白质p(rotein)的食物后，觉得很有精神(refreshed)。这说明p导致神经活跃，与科学家的说法p会抑制s相反。

C. **正确**。吃了p会间接减小t(ryptophan)在血液中的浓度，而t是s在大脑中唯一的前驱物质(precursor)。这句说，p多，则t少，由于t是前驱物质，是t产生s，所以，s也少。于是：p↑：t↓：s↓。这就为第2句科学家的说法提供一个中间环节，更进一步证明了c少s多、p多s少的看法。

D. 大脑里的s水平高，可以加速神经活动，产生强烈的情感和行为反应。这是第1句的内容，与第2句科学家的观点没有直接关系。既不支持，也不反对。

E. 高蛋白饮食虽然会有助于生理健康，但却对心理健康有其他的负面影响。没有对科学家所提出的s.p.c之间的关系表示支持或反对。无关选项。

6.3 Crystallization of magma

【*cues*, function & **core**】

The **cooling rate** of a magma *determines* the **texture** of the final rock. *As* a magma cools, the specific cations and anions that ultimately form solid crystals must *initially* bond with one another *to form* very **small crystal nuclei**. *Scientists have determined the general relationship* between **cooling rate** and the total **number of crystal nuclei**. *Slow* cooling *rates* generally form only *a small number* of crystal nuclei, and, with abundant time for crystal growth, lead to a **coarse grained** rock dominated by **large c**rystals. As the cooling *rate increases*, *so does the number* of crystal nuclei; the result is a **fine grained** rock that contains **numerous small** crystals. *Finally, very fast* cooling *rates* can lead to a situation where **no c**rystals grow. Not remaining liquid, the magma solidifies to a dark-colored solid — **volcanic glass**. It is *analogous to*

Cues	Function	Core
1. determine	1. kw'	1. rate → texture
2. As..., initially	2. i	2. small crystal nuclei
3. Scientists relationship	3. kw	3. **rate – nuclei**
4. Slow rates, large	4. x	4. **slow: large** nuclei
5. increase, small	5. y	5. **increase: small**
6. finally, fast, no	6. z	6. **fast: no**
7. ...	7. z1	7. volcanic glass
8. analogous to; difference whereas	8. z2	8. = **glass;** **complex vs. simple**

the man-made glass; the *only difference is* that man-made glass is formed from compositionally "**simple**" magma *whereas* volcanic glass is derived from a compositionally **complex** natural magma. (166 words)

【结构分析】

第1句：引入主题。m(agma)的冷却速度决定了最终形成的岩石的质地。

2：具体说明。当m冷却时，阳离子和阴离子彼此相连，形成非常小的晶体核(crystal nuclei)。

3：真正主题。科学家确定冷却速度与晶核之间的相关性；理科讲因果，rate: nuclei。

4：证据1。冷却速度慢，只形成少数晶核，岩石为大晶体。

5：证据2。冷却速度增加，晶核数目增加，岩石为小晶体。

6：证据3。冷却速度极快，不会产生晶体。

7：顺承证据。m会固化成为黑色固体，称火山玻璃。

8：类比。这类似于人造玻璃；唯一差别在于人造玻璃来自构造简单的m；而火山玻璃来自构造复杂的m。

全文：论点说明。1–2句为引子/背景/铺垫，3句为主题 = 因果相关；然后平行因果展开。相对容易。

【题目分析】

6. The passage is primarily concerned with discussing

 (A) the different roles of crystal nucleus and cooling rate in the formation of the final rock

 (B) the difference and similarity between and among three types of crystal nuclei

 (C) the difference and similarity between and among three kinds of textures of rocks

 (D) the general relationship between cooling rate of magma and the texture of the final rock

 (E) the particular chemical composition in a magma and its effect on the texture of the final rock

【解法】主题题。相对容易。定位1–3句，主要是第3句，冷却速度与晶核的关系。

【选项】

A. 晶核与冷却速度的不同作用。不是different roles，而是它们之间的correlation。

B. 三种晶核之间的相同与不同。原文的确有涉及，但这是细节，不是主旨。

C. 三类岩石质地之间的相同与不同。也有涉及，但依然是细节。错误方式同B。

D. 正确。m的冷却速度与最终岩石的质地之间的关系。岩石质地即为晶核问题。

E. m的特定化学构成；化学元素构成不是全文重点。

7. Given the information in the passage, which of the following statements is true of volcanic glass?

 (A) It is completely different from man-made glass in that it includes crystals within itself.

 (B) It is a simple magma because of its simple chemical composition.

 (C) It forms at a specific rate at which the magma cools.

 (D) It defies the general relationship between cooling rate and the number of small crystal nuclei.

 (E) It verges on the phase boundary of liquid and solid before it evolves into a critical state.

【解法】(比较)细节题。由于文章内容简单，本题也相对容易。题干问的是火山玻璃，定位到最后2句。它与人造玻璃有相同和不同，这应该就是考点。火山玻璃的构成更复杂。

【选项】

A. 它与人造玻璃完全不同。completely程度过强，原文讲过有相同之处。

B. 它是一种简单的m，化学构成简单。错误。末句说它复杂。与末句相反。

C. 正确。在一种特定的m冷却速度下，会形成火山玻璃。原文finally句说它在very fast的冷却速度下形成。

D. 它违反了冷却速度与小晶核数目之间的关系。它没有否定任何关系，相反，它是相关性的证据之一。

E. 它介于液态和固态的边界。错误。原文说它是固体。

※ 逻辑题

When 1,000 people who have not smoked or smoked only in a short time are tested for lung cancer, only 10 show early signs of lung cancer. By contrast, of every 1,000 people who have smoked frequently 750 show early signs of lung cancer. *Thus*, for a randomly chosen group of people, the majority of those who show early signs of lung cancer will be people who have smoked frequently.

8. A reasoning error in the argument is that the argument

(A) identifies the group who have smoked frequently with the group who have shown early signs of lung cancer

(B) fails to take into account what proportion of the population have smoked frequently

(C) ignores the fact that some people who smoked frequently have not shown early signs of cancer

(D) attributes early signs of lung cancer to smoking

(E) attempts to infer a strong conclusion from a shaky premise

【解法】逻辑错误。这是逻辑题的一种问法，要求判断原文推理的缺陷，在一定程度上类似于逻辑反对。第1句，对1000个不吸烟或短暂吸烟的人作测试，只有10个有早期肺癌迹象。第2句对比，1000个经常吸烟的人，则有750个都有早期肺癌迹象。第3句，因此，对一个随机选择的群组，那些表现出早期肺癌迹象的人，其中多数都是经常吸烟的人。有什么错？第1-2句是对比的事实，不会有错。错误只在第3句。从1-2句只能推出在不常吸烟的人里，10/1000有早期肺癌迹象；在常吸烟的人里，750/1000有早期肺癌迹象；**但却不能倒过来**，推出第3句所说的，随机选择的一组人，其中有早期肺癌迹象的，多数都经常吸烟；因为这随机选择的一组的人里，不知道有多少是经常吸烟的。如果大家都吸烟，那当然可以；如果大家都不吸烟，当然就不能得到原文的结论。

【选项】

A. 该推理把一个经常吸烟的群体，等同于一个表现出早期肺癌迹象的群体。这不是问题，这是推理的结果。

B. 正确。该推理未能考虑这个群体有多少比例的人经常吸烟。

C. 该推理忽视了，一些经常吸烟的人没有表现出癌症迹象。无关。

D. 该推理把早期癌症迹象归因于吸烟。这不是第3句推理的错误，只是1-2句的自然结论。

E. 该推理试图从一个不稳定的(shaky)前提推出一个强有力的结论。

注：本练习有2道逻辑单题，少数时候会出现这种情况。通常1个语文部分，除了10道填空以外的10道阅读题中，只会有1道逻辑单题。同时，这并不排斥有些正常阅读文章中也会出逻辑题；而我们并不把这种阅读文章里的逻辑题算在逻辑单题之内。

6.4 Anxiety disorders

【*cues*, function & **core**】

A sudden *intense surge* in **anxiety** *is characterized by arousal of* the sympathetic branch of the autonomic **nervous** system as expressed in *elevated* heart and breathing rates, blood pressure, sweating, and other signs. *This led to the expectation* that N（neuroticism）personality or trait **anxiety** would be **related to** measures of **these indicators**. *Research has* **failed** *to support this* **correlational** *hypothesis*. Longitudinal *research has shown that* **N** is a personality **precursor of anxiety** and mood disorders, so *why* does N *not show relationships with* some of the **same biological indicators** that characterize these disorders? *There may be a* **threshold effect** so that the dysregulation of neurotransmitter systems characteristic of the disorders **only emerges** at some **critical level** of persistent stress that is not reproducible in controlled laboratory studies.（128 words）

Cues	Function	Core
1. characterized by	1. tw/ i	1. **anxiety ↑ : nervous ↑**
2. expectation, related to	2. kw1	2. **these indicators → N/anxiety**
3. failed to support	3. aw-	3. **fail, correlation**
4. research shown why not?	4. x	4. **N → anxiety; Not, the same indicator?**
5. may be a...effect	5. kw2	5. **threshold: critical level**

【结构分析】

第1句：事实。突然产生的强烈焦虑，其特征是自律的神经活动的觉醒，例如心脏跳动、呼吸速度、血压、出汗等升高。本句认为心理与生理有关。

2: 观点。这就引发一种预测，以为N人格或焦虑与这些生理指标的程度有关系。理科讲因果，本句确认相关性：N/anxiety: indicators。

3: 负评价。但是研究未能支持这个相关假说。

4: 问题。一些研究表明，N是焦虑和心情紊乱的前驱性格，那为什么N不会与之有相同的生物指标呢？这意思是说，一些indicators → disorders; 而N → disorders，因此N也许与disorders有相同的生理或生物指标。

5: 观点。也许存在一种阈值效应，紊乱特有的那种神经递质失调只有在持久压力的临界水平上才会出现，而这个临界点还不能在控制实验研究中复制，以此回答4句的迷惑。本句threshold = critical。

全文：现象解释。1句事实，2句相关性假说，3句负评价，4句给出事实，并追问何以没有相关性，5句给出解释。

【词汇】

anxiety	*n.* 焦虑
arousal	*n.* 觉醒，唤醒
characteristicof	=typical of, marked by, 特有的，典型的
disorder	*n.* 紊乱；dis-（表否定）+ order
dysregulation	*n.* 失调；dys-（表否定）+ regulation
elevated	*adj.* =increased, 增加的，上升的
emerge	*v.* 涌现，突现
indicator	*n.* 指示器，指标
longitudinal	*adj.* 纵向、历时的（研究）；longitude *n.* 经度

neurotransmitter	*n.* 神经递质
persistent	*adj.* 持续的，长久的
perseverant	*adj.* 坚韧不拔的，百折不挠的
precursor	*n.* 前驱物（产生后端物）；先行者
sympathetic	*adj.* 同感的，共情的；≠compassion *n.* 同情
surge	*n./v.* 涌动，浮现；突然增加
threshold	*n.* 阈值；门槛

【题目分析】

9. Which of the following statements best describes the organization of the passage as a whole?

   （A） A situation is described and explained, and a new hypothesis is provided to supplant the previous one.

   （B） An assertion is made and several arguments are provided to strengthen it and dismissed.

   （C） A theory is discussed and then ways in which it has been revised are described.

   （D） A fact is stated, a hypothesis is suggested and fails to be proved, and its failure is explained.

   （E） A controversial theory is discussed and then arguments both against and for it are described.

【解法】结构题。题干问全文的organization，可定位各个观点和态度。文章有2个观点，分别解释两个有关联的事实。结构题答案必须与原文写作顺序一致。

【选项】

A. 描述和解释一个情况，对应1-2句；提出一个新假说，以取代以前的假说。漏掉了负评价，不够精确。

B. 提出一个主张，提供若干论证，以加强前者，然后否定两者。最后的态度dismiss不对。

C. 讨论一个理论，然后描述对它的一些修改。第1句不是理论；也忽视了文章末句的第2个解释。

D. 正确。 陈述一个事实，提出一个假说，但没有被证实；解释该假说为何失败；分别对应文章第1、2、3、4-5句。

E. 讨论一个有争议的理论，然后描述反对和支持它的论据。文章有2个解释，这里只讲一个，不准确。

10. It can be inferred from the passage that the necessity of threshold effect hypothesis stated in the last sentence would need to be reassessed if researchers found that which of the following were true?

   （A） The dysregulation of neurotransmitter systems characteristic of the anxiety and mood disorders does not emerge below a certain critical level of persistent stress simulated in laboratory studies.

   （B） The study attempting to find a biological basis for the anxiety and mood disorders obtains the positive results in experimental research with animals and with humans that suffer from anxiety and mood disorders.

   （C） N shows the negative relationship with some of the same biological indicators that characterize anxiety and mood disorders.

   （D） N shows the positive relationship with some biological indicators that are not typical of anxiety and mood disorders.

   （E） N is demonstrated to be related to measures of these indicators in reaction to persistent stress in a masterfully designed laboratory study.

【解法】取非题。题干问if...true，末句的hypothesis would need to be reassessed。要重新评价末句假说，其实就是修正或反驳它。也相当于逻辑反对题。做法是否定关系、指出他因等。末句说的是有阈值效应，必须达到临界水平（critical level），才会有神经递质系统失调的情况出现。

【选项】

A. 神经递质系统失调不会在低于临界水平时出现。支持。

B. 研究试图发现焦虑和情绪紊乱的生物学基础，结果在动物和人类的实验研究中发现了肯定的结果。支持。

C. N与焦虑和情绪紊乱的典型生物学指标有负相关。原文第2句的观点是说正相关。第5句则说在临界水平下，N与这些指标没有相关性。没有反对第5句的观点2，也没有支持第2句的观点1。

D. N与焦虑和情绪紊乱的非典型生物学指标有正相关；要注意not typical of。但这并不推翻末句所说的阈值效应。N还是与典型的生物学指标没有相关性。

E. 正确。 在一项精心设计的实验室研究中，N被证明与这些指标的程度（measures）有相关性。直接挑战第3句负评价，认可N与指标的关系是存在的，同时也说实验研究可控制持久压力，与末句对立。这样，就不需要末句的阈值理论了，这就取非和削弱了末句的假说。

一切都会回归平均。优秀是困难的；没有人随随便便成功。成功没有捷径，你所知道的捷径都是陷阱。成功必有代价，这代价是持续的奋斗或是天才的缺憾。科比说，我知道洛杉矶每天早晨4点钟的样子。即便如此，还是要回归平均。明知成功会谢幕，但依然选择优秀。让优秀多飞一会吧，让生如夏花般灿烂，即使我狠狠地知道它会凋谢。

六套阅读练习题的多层分解训练

在做完练习题、看过解析以后，还需要分项集中训练，这样才能真正掌握阅读和做题所需要的各项技能。读者可将这3个步骤，应用到自己分析GRE真题或其他模拟训练题的实践中去。

Deliberate practice 分项练习

1. 集中练习文章结构

  看4–6篇长文章的各段首句及转折句、10篇多观点短文章的核心句，找出结构模式

2. 集中练习30–40个段落的结构

  并列、因果机制、对比、让步、多观点段落共5种，分类练习

3. 集中练习40个长句

4. 题干50道，训练解法和定位

5. 题型分类训练；9–10类题，每类最好5道题以上

  核心题（主题、态度、结构）、信息题、定点题（细节、列举、作用、选择句子、取非）、逻辑题

6. 80个选项集中分析

  集中看80个选项，分析正确答案为何对，错误选项为何错，尤其注意干扰选项与正确答案

  我们这里以本书所编的6套模拟题为例。读者也可以用"GRE阅读36套"等网络材料来做类似的工作。

第一节　文章结构训练

下面列出6套模拟题中长文章和多观点段落的核心句，请集中阅读，了解频繁出现的结构模式。"1–3"表示练习1的第3篇文章，其余类推，注意不包含逻辑题。

◎ 1–1

Lowell writes in *Land of Unlikeness* as an avowed Christian, with Eliot and Hopkins as his conscious models. Certainly, much of the turbulence of Lowell's early poetry comes from his conscious struggle to approach Christian perfection. ... But Lowell's way with poetry would be neither Hopkins' nor Eliot's.

TW: kw1. ~kw2. kw2

◎ 1–2

It is widely agreed that modifiable neuronal ensembles support cognition.

Neuronal recordings from the hippocampus of adult rats reveal that when a rat explores an environment, pyramidal and granule cells show patterned neural activity that is highly correlated with a rat's position in space.

In young rats, CA1 place fields expand asymmetrically during repeated route following, which results in a shift in the centre of mass of place fields in the direction opposite to the rat's trajectory.

In addition, the maintenance of place maps also differs between young and old animals.

TW'. kw1. kw2. kw3.

◎ 2–1

What was causing the periodic advance and retreat of the glaciers?

Milankovitch correlated glacier cycle with the variations in the amount of solar radiation (insolation) reaching the Earth.

However, the variations in insolation are not enough to drive the enormous shift in climate which a glacial onset represents.

Some climatologists have attempted to find other factors.

TW. kw1. aw-. kw2.

◎ 2–2

Early feminist literary critics believed that the traditional concept of domesticity as manifested in the distinction between a masculinized public sphere and a privatized feminine one has become 'misleading' and oversimplified as a framework for understanding the construction of social space for women even in the nineteenth century.

In contrast, a second wave of feminist work on domesticity envisions the idea of 'home' as a specific racial and class position for white, middle-class women, and therefore as an extension or even a supplement to the capitalist marketplace, not an alternative to it.

However, these second-wave critiques of domesticity also depend upon spatial metaphors, to the extent that they present domesticity as a bounded position occupied by a specific race and class of women.

Such contradictions in the representations of domesticity, I argue, only started to become obvious in the modernist period.

kw1. vs. kw2. aw-. kw3.

3-2

The orientation to sociopolitical issues and racial identity in the poems of Claude McKay contrasts sharply with the tradition represented by Braithwaite.

McKay's disagreement with Braithwaite's advice to write aracial poetry reflected his broader skepticism regarding the background and motives of the black intelligentsia.

TW: kw1. kw2.

3-4

Why a country like England that had suffered from a lengthy period of political instability before 1688 suddenly underwent a transition to stable representative government with a limited monarchy?

Olson suggested that democracy results from accidents of history that leave a balance of power or stalemate, making it impossible for any one leader or group to overpower all of the others or create a new autocracy.

But one group did eventually establish full control in England

Weingast adds a new dimension by demonstrating that democratic stability depends on the two groups successfully committing to a strategy of opposing any attempts to tread upon the basic rights of any citizens.

However, this suggestion may be inaccurate.

TW. kw1. aw-. kw2. aw-.

4-1

The high mobility of nineteenth-century Americans generally, and especially those under thirty years of age is well documented.

Those unacquainted with factory populations said that they possess as roving a disposition as the Tartars.

But few remove because they are fond of changing their locations

Hareven's thorough analysis of the payrolls of the Amoskeag Mills showed that the typical worker's career was short and frequently interrupted.

TW. kw1. aw-. kw2.

4-2

Philopatry, the behavior returning to an individual's birthplace, has several advantages.

One proposed mechanism by which animals can recognize unfamiliar relatives is phenotype matching

A problem in investigating the behavior of settling close to kin is to exclude the possibility that they are philopatric because of benefits of settling in the natal area, rather than because of benefits of settling close to kin.

A recent study shows that the settling pattern of barnacle geese *Branta leucopsis* females returning to their natal colony is nonrandom with respect to the nest sites of their parents and sisters.

TW. kw1. kw2 vs. kw3. m.

5–2

Critics of Jean-Luc Godard's celebrated film *Breathless* wondered if its protagonist's weak acting and the film's general roughness are meant to be parodies of conventional acting and filmmaking.

But such a diagnosis doesn't fit.

Critics today are also inclined to see this French film as an example of reality cinema.

... but there is nothing about the characters' talk or behavior that corresponds to the way people actually talk or behave, even in France.

The best way to understand *Breathless* is to reconsider its genre—that is, to approach it primarily as a work of ideas rather than as a work of art.

The sequence of shifting signifiers used in the film also corresponds to ideas about meaning that the linguistic philosopher Jacques Derrida was developing, under the name of deconstruction, during the same period.

TW: kw1. aw-. kw2, aw-. kw3.1. kw3.2.

5–3

Historians have devised different methods to estimate the levels of immigration in the eighteenth-century America.

Gemery calculates net migration as a residual

An alternative method, however, relies on an improved surname analysis of the 1790 census

TW. kw1. vs. kw2.

5–4

Some factors have been suggested as causal mechanisms of bee colony collapse disorder (CCD), for example, the use of genetically modified (GMO) crops.

However, large bee die-offs have also occurred in Europe, where GMO crops are not widely grown.

Other hypotheses are even less likely.

TW: kw1. aw-. kw2-.

6–4

A sudden intense surge in anxiety is characterized by arousal of the sympathetic branch of the autonomic nervous system as expressed in elevated heart and breathing rates, blood pressure, sweating, and other signs.

This led to the expectation that N (neuroticism) personality or trait anxiety would be related to measures of these indicators. Research has failed to support this correlational hypothesis.

There may be a threshold effect so that the dysregulation of neurotransmitter systems characteristic of the disorders only emerges at some critical level of persistent stress that is not reproducible in controlled laboratory studies.

TW. kw1. aw-. kw2.

第二节　段落结构训练

以下将6套题中的论点及其论证分类，请集中练习。读者可仿照这种方式，将GRE真题的段落做类似这样的分类练习。"2-2-1"表示第2个练习除逻辑题以外的第2篇文章的第2段，"4-3"表示第4个练习除逻辑题以外的第3篇文章；其余类推。

2.1　并列

● 1-1-1

Strengthened by a memory of the spiritual dignity of man, Lowell writes in *Land of Unlikeness* as an avowed Christian, with Eliot and Hopkins as his conscious models. Reviewing Eliot's *Four Quartets* in 1943, he argued that union with God is somewhere in sight in all poetry. A 1944 "Note" on Hopkins shows Lowell interested in the way Hopkins' unique personality and holiness flowered in poetry.

● 2-2-1（举例）

In their reformist view, domesticity was not simply confining for women but a source of agency or 'sentimental power': the public-private distinction was treated as the basis for creating an alternative feminine culture. For instance, Nancy Hartsock argues that resistant forms of feminist consciousness spring from women's immersion into housework or child-rearing, a world more complete than men's, which then transforms women's domesticity into a critical position.

● 2-2-3（态度及并列证据）

However, these second-wave critiques of domesticity also depend upon spatial metaphors, to the extent that they present domesticity as a bounded position occupied by a specific race and class of women. Furthermore, they underestimate the extent to which the representation of domesticity as able to travel beyond the walls of the middle-class home had the ideological function of mystifying or suppressing the internal contradictions within the feminine sphere of domestic responsibilities.

● 2-2-4

Such contradictions in the representations of domesticity, I argue, only started to become obvious in the modernist period. Modernist women's writing anticipates a notion of "homelessness at home", in which home figures a claim to a gendered identity, while homelessness echoes the writer's consciousness that this identity is neither completely determined nor inherently spatialized in the ways that the ideology of separate spheres represents women as being. **But** this metaphorical phrase does not entirely reject the spatial figuration of femininity; in fact, the implication is that an alternate conception of space might empower a new feminist politics, as in Audre Lorde's poem 'School Note', where the speaker refers to herself as being 'at home' anywhere because no place 'is' home.

（中间 but 转换表示另一方面，属于广义并列）

4–2–1

Philopatry, the behavior returning to an individual's birthplace, has several advantages. The presence of kin in the natal area makes easier to receive help from related individuals; the level of aggression might be lower among kin than among unrelated individuals; breeding close to kin can also increase breeding success, as in the case of microtine rodents.

4–2–2（并列举例）

One proposed mechanism by which animals can recognize unfamiliar relatives is phenotype matching, which involves learning the phenotype of familiar relatives, or of oneself, thereby forming a phenotypic template against which the phenotypes of unfamiliar individuals can be compared. Some animals might be using some form of phenotype matching: mice have been shown to use MHC odor type to avoid breeding with close relatives; olfactory cues also seem to be used by Arizona tiger salamanders and rainbow fish seem to use both visual and chemical cues to detect shoals of related individuals.

4–3

Why researchers have difficulties in uncovering ancient moneys has much to do with the practice of archeology and the nature of money itself. Archeologists spend their careers sifting through the trash of the past, ingeniously reconstructing vanished lives from broken pots and dented knives. But like us, ancient Mesopotamians and Phoenicians seldom made the error of tossing out cash, and only rarely did they bury their most precious liquid assets in the ground. Even when archeologists have found buried cash, though, they have trouble recognizing it for what it was.

5–1（类比）

The direct detection of extrasolar planets is extraordinarily difficult, because of the enormous difference in luminosity between a star, which shines with its own light, and orbiting planets, which are not only much smaller and very close to the star, as seen from Earth, but shine by reflected light. The situation is akin to trying to identify a firefly buzzing around an intensely bright searchlight—from a great distance.

5–2–4

In deconstructionist terms, then, the film's sloppiness becomes a value, a way of exposing both the arbitrary *constructedness* of past meaning and the opportunities for making new meaning in the future. The former constitutes the political dimension of the film insofar as it critiques what has been done in the name of cinema, society, capitalism, or whatever. The latter is the theoretical dimension, the film's way of demonstrating what is possible if one lets loose from old constraints and assumptions.

2.2　因果

◉ 1–2–2

Neuronal recordings from the hippocampus of adult rats reveal that when a rat explores an environment, pyramidal and granule cells show patterned neural activity that is highly correlated with a rat's position in space. Between 30% and 50% of pyramidal cells in CA1 region of the hippocampus show place–specific firing in a given environment, which has earned these neurons the name 'place cells.' When the firing patterns of many hippocampal neurons are recorded simultaneously, it is possible to reconstruct the position of a rat in an environment from the place cell firing patterns alone. The composite cell activity is 'map-like' and, in different environments, hippocampal place maps change markedly.

◉ 2–3

If inherited reelin deficiency is the cause of schizophrenia, one would expect that some of the apparently unaffected relatives of these unfortunate children would be schizophrenic, because they are carrying the mutation in one of their genes.

◉ 4–2–4

Because breeding birds rarely changed nest sites between years, this natal philopatry could be caused by an attraction to the natal nest site itself or to the parents nesting there. However, females that settled on a different island than where their parents bred still settled close to their sisters. This clearly demonstrates that sisters' nesting close to each other is not a by-product of either extreme natal philopatry or a preference to nest close to parents, but results from a genuine preference for nesting close to kin.

◉ 6–3

Scientists have determined the general relationship between cooling rate and the total number of crystal nuclei. Slow cooling rates generally form only a small number of crystal nuclei, and, with abundant time for crystal growth, lead to a coarse grained rock dominated by large crystals. As the cooling rate increases, so does the number of crystal nuclei; the result is a fine grained rock that contains numerous small crystals. Finally, very fast cooling rates can lead to a situation where no crystals grow.

2.3 机制

2–1

Milankovitch correlated glacier cycle with the variations in the amount of solar radiation (insolation) reaching the Earth. In the short, cool summers of the high polar latitudes, insolation may not be enough to melt back snow and ice accumulated in the winter. The small changes in insolation could change the delicate balance of glacial stability to one of advance. Once the advance starts, the increased reflectivity of the ice surface, as compared to sea or land cover, cools the local atmosphere further and causes a self-feeding process of glacial growth.

4–4

The concentration of atmospheric methane is projected to increase significantly given the large pools of carbon stored in permafrost that can be converted to methane upon thaw, the susceptibility of methane hydrates to release from the ocean floor with rising seawater temperature and the acceleration of methane-producing anthropogenic activities.

4–4

Furthermore, thaw of permafrost along lake margins releases labile organic matter previously sequestered in permafrost for centuries to millennia into anaerobic lake sediments, enhancing methane production and ebullition emission and serving as a positive feedback to climate warming.

6–1

Diffusible compounds released by algae may mediate coral mortality via microbial activity. Algae can release excess photosynthate in the form of polysaccharides, or dissolved organic carbon, that can fuel microbial activity and accelerate microbial growth. The microbial community growing on or near the coral surface may then exhibit explosive growth, eventually creating a zone of hypoxia on the surface of the live coral tissue. In this study, all corals exposed to but not in direct contact with algae bleached and were physiologically compromised within 2-4 days.

2.4 对比

1–2–3

In young rats, CA1 place fields expand asymmetrically during repeated route following, which results in a shift in the centre of mass of place fields in the direction opposite to the rat's trajectory. This observation is consistent with neural network models dating back to Hebb's 1949 concept of the 'phase sequence' of cell assemblies, which suggested that an associative, temporally asymmetric synaptic plasticity mechanism could serve to encode sequences or episodes of experience. The magnitude of this place field expansion, however, significantly decreases in aged rats.

1–2–4

In addition, the maintenance of place maps also differs between young and old animals. In normal young rats, a place map for a given environment can remain stable and retrievable for months. A similar stability of CA1 place maps in aged rats is observed within and between episodes of behavior in the same environment. Occasionally, however, if the old rat is removed from the environment and returned later, the original place map is not retrieved and an independent population of place cells may be activated even in a familiar room.

3–1

In our results, two-year-old males refrained from fighting. Three-year-old males appear to be equivocal: they act as adults when given the opportunity, but act as juveniles by refraining from groaning when competition is high. By contrast, four- and five-year-old males are willing to take part but are outcompeted by older males.

3–2–1

The orientation to sociopolitical issues and racial identity in the poems of Claude McKay contrasts sharply with the tradition represented by Braithwaite. While McKay explicitly weaved racial-political markers into his poems that unequivocally indicate the author's racial identity and lamented that the failure of black leadership was rooted in a socioeconomic and intellectual chasm between the black masses and the intelligentsia, Braithwaite preferred to camouflage racial identity under his pen and barely touched the issue of race in America in his own poems.

3–3

The assessment of the degree of admixture of a given population has traditionally relied on the comparison of gene frequencies between two potential parental populations and a putative hybrid population. Recently, these methods have been improved by incorporating information on the molecular diversity present in the admixed and in parental populations or by explicitly taking into account the genetic drift since the admixture event.

5–1

At optical wavelengths, a star might be several billion times brighter than a large planet. However, at infrared wavelengths, where the planet emits its own thermal radiation, the contrast is only a factor of a million.

5–2–1

Parody suggests consistent mockery in the service of a specific goal, usually that of puncturing pretension, with the immediate aim of getting a laugh. But *Breathless* is more pretentious in its low-key way than any film-noir production that it could be said to parody. It doesn't ramp up but brings down and scatters conventional elements.

5–3

Historians have devised different methods to estimate the levels of immigration in the eighteenth-century America. Using tenuous fertility and mortality data compiled by other historians, Gemery calculates net migration as a residual, with the results being a plausible range of 278,400 to 485,300 white immigrants for the period 1700 to 1780. An alternative method, however, relies on an improved surname analysis of the 1790 census as a check for the increasing expertise of ethnic group historians who rely on actual immigration data from ship and passenger lists.

2.5 让步

1–1–2

Certainly, much of the turbulence of Lowell's early poetry comes from his conscious struggle to approach Christian perfection. His effort to perfect his verse was analogous to the discipline of contemplation, the achieved aesthetic experience of a poem analogous to spiritual illumination. But Lowell's way with poetry would be neither Hopkins' nor Eliot's.

1–3

Clearly, full free riding is a dominant strategy, but the experiment shows that many subjects begin by contributing on average about half of their endowment to the public account.

1–4

Inspirational public television always features children dreaming of being great successes. Yet normal distribution theory reveals that values cluster around midpoints and mediocrity loves company.

1–4

An athlete often goes into decline after appearing on the cover of best sport magazine. This might result from the pressures of fame, or a superstition subsumed into self-fulfilling prophecy, but the fact is, after doing extraordinarily well for a long period of time, the athlete is simply not able to maintain outlier status for much longer, but rather starts regressing, however slightly, back toward the mean.

2–4

It is true that what animals learn is impressive and their cognitive abilities may be remarkable, but they never master anything like a human language and seem incapable of doing so: the complexity of their grammar is not remotely comparable to ours.

◎ 5-2-1

Although there are several scenes that some viewers might find humorous, this humor is of the whimsical not the parodic variety.

◎ 5-2-2

The insouciant attitude that *Breathless* takes toward its audience may encourage impressionable viewers to mistake it for realism, but there is nothing about the characters' talk or behavior that corresponds to the way people actually talk or behave, even in France.

◎ 6-1

Clearly, some algae may release chemical compounds that may be toxic to other organisms. But here, coral mortality could be completely prevented with the addition of antibiotics, thus supporting the hypothesis that the microbial community was the agent of coral death.

◎ 6-2

Certainly, Padilla's emphasis on the preference of individuals for the dominant or heritage cultures is an important advance. But the model falls short of explaining how individuals from the same socioeconomic, generational, and familial backgrounds differ on willingness and competence to acculturate.

2.6　补充：否定肯定结构

◎ 3-2-2

　　This does not mean that all the black intellectuals McKay encountered would have agreed with Braithwaite. Indeed, Locke, White, and Du Bois had committed themselves to genres of African American literature that to an extent "betrayed" racial identities as African descendants. But they also have mutual identification with a community notorious for its cultural and socioeconomic exclusivity and its detachment from a large black population, which was in conflict with Mckay's preference for radical society that was unpalatable and abominable for Black elites.

2.7　多观点段落

◎ 2-1-2

　　However, the variations in insolation are not enough to drive the enormous shift in climate which a glacial onset represents. Some climatologists have attempted to find other factors. The most popular theory today proposes that shifts in the thermohaline circulation, the global ocean current which circulates cold water from the north Atlantic around the cape of Africa to the northeastern Pacific, may be the trigger for the sudden changes which bring on the Ice Ages.

3–4

Why a country like England that had suffered from a lengthy period of political instability before 1688 suddenly underwent a transition to stable representative government with a limited monarchy? Olson suggested that democracy results from accidents of history that leave a balance of power or stalemate, making it impossible for any one leader or group to overpower all of the others or create a new autocracy. But one group did eventually establish full control in England: after 1715 the Whigs had command of all government institutions, retaining this control for a considerable period of time. Weingast adds a new dimension by demonstrating that democratic stability depends on the two groups successfully committing to a strategy of opposing any attempts to tread upon the basic rights of any citizens. The Bill of Rights of 1689 in England might be seen as just such an "elite pact". However, this suggestion may be inaccurate. During the period of partisan conflict between 1690 and 1715, it was common for those who found themselves in the opposition to be thrown in prison on dubious legal grounds.

4–1

The high mobility of nineteenth-century Americans generally, and especially those under thirty years of age is well documented. The most common way to vary one's work was to move, if the youths did not want to see their fate sealed by their proficiency on one particular portion of the work. Those unacquainted with factory populations said that they possess as roving a disposition as the Tartars. But few remove because they are fond of changing their locations, though they go where they can get the best employment and the best wages. Hareven's thorough analysis of the payrolls of the Amoskeag Mills showed that the typical worker's career was short and frequently interrupted.

5–4

Some factors have been suggested as causal mechanisms of bee colony collapse disorder, for example, the use of genetically modified (GMO) crops. However, large bee die-offs have also occurred in Europe, where GMO crops are not widely grown. Also, in the United States, the patterns of CCD-affected colonies do not appear to correlate with the distribution of GMO-crops such as Bt-corn. Other hypotheses are even less likely. For example, the public has become concerned that cell phone use may be causing bee die-offs; however, exposure of bees to high levels of electromagnetic fields is unlikely. Similarly, shifts in the Earth's magnetic field, which could conceivably affect bee navigation, have not been correlated with bee die-off episodes, but cannot be completely ruled out at this time.

6–4

A sudden intense surge in anxiety is characterized by arousal of the sympathetic branch of the autonomic nervous system as expressed in elevated heart and breathing rates, blood pressure, sweating, and other signs. This led to the expectation that N (neuroticism) personality or trait anxiety would be related to measures of these indicators. Research has failed to support this correlational hypothesis. Longitudal research has shown that N is a personality precursor of anxiety and mood disorders, so why does N not show relationships with some of the same biological indicators that characterize these disorders? There may be a threshold effect so that the dysregulation of neurotransmitter systems characteristic of the disorders only emerges at some critical level of persistent stress that is not reproducible in controlled laboratory studies.

第三节　长句集中训练

训练思路请参考 "第2章 Sentence 句子：Examples句子结构练习"。**黑体**表示句子核心，***斜黑体***表示广义从句(含有动词的修饰)中重复核心(逻辑等价)或反义重复的词；*斜体*表示第一层广义从句修饰引导词，<u>*划线斜体*</u>表示第二层，<u>*双划线斜体*</u>表示第三层；凡修饰内容均有斜体。此外，并列或对比的独立从句的先行词，如when, if, although, whereas，不作标识。读者也可自行收集其他长句，集中阅读，抓住主干。

1. Interestingly, many of the age-related **changes** *that* have been discovered **can be linked to plasticity deficits**, as **blockade of NMDA** （N-methyl-d-aspartate）receptors in young rats **results in ensemble dynamics** *that* resemble those of aged rats.

2. **Neuronal recordings** from the hippocampus of adult rats **reveal** *that* <u>*when*</u> a rat explores an **environment**, pyramidal and granule **cells show patterned neural activity** *that* is highly ***correlated with a rat's position*** in space.

3. This **observation is consistent with neural network models** *dating back* to Hebb's 1949 concept of the '***phase sequence***' of cell assemblies, <u>*which*</u> suggested <u>*that*</u> an associative, temporally asymmetric synaptic plasticity mechanism could serve to ***encode sequences*** or episodes of experience.

4. It is likely *that* this **age-associated reduction** in experience-dependent plasticity **is due to** some specific **plasticity deficits**, as it does ***not occur*** *when* CPP, a selective and competitive antagonist of NMDA-type receptors, is administered to ***young rats***.

5. **This might result from** the **pressures of fame**, or a superstition subsumed into self-fulfilling prophecy, but **the fact is**, after *doing* extraordinarily well for a long period of time, the **athlete** is simply **not able to maintain outlier status** for much longer, but rather **starts regressing**, however slightly, back toward the mean.

6. Once the advance starts, **the increased reflectivity** of the ice surface, *as compared to* sea or land cover, **cools** the local atmosphere further and **causes a self-feeding process** of glacial growth.

7. The **most popular theory** today **proposes** *that* **shifts in the** thermohaline circulation, the global ocean current *which* circulates cold water from the north Atlantic around the cape of Africa to the northeastern Pacific, may be the **trigger for the sudden changes** <u>*which*</u> bring on the Ice Ages.

8. **Early** feminist literary **critics believed** *that* the **traditional concept of domesticity** <u>*as manifested in*</u> the distinction between a masculinized public sphere and a privatized feminine one **has become 'misleading' and oversimplified** as a framework for understanding the construction of social space for women even in the nineteenth century.

9. For instance, Nancy **Hartsock argues** *that* **resistant forms** of feminist consciousness **spring from** women's immersion into **housework or child-rearing**, a world more complete than men's, *which* then transforms ***women's domesticity*** into a critical position.

10. This **second-wave critique emphasizes** *how* casting **domesticity as a countercultural** movement, *based on* its exclusion from dominant economic formations, **obscures the way** *domesticity reproduces* other kinds of power relations.

11. In this second reading, it is precisely **the reformist impulse** *privileged by* earlier feminist critics as an unrecognized form of women's historical agency that **is now understood as fueling** a kind of **expansionist or missionary project**, *characterized by* rhetoric of *expanding* woman's sphere and of social or *enlarged* housekeeping, *which* often translated into projects of *class socialization* and the imposition of *middle-class norms*.

12. Furthermore, **they underestimate the extent** *to which* the **representation of domesticity as able to travel beyond the walls** of the middle-class home **had the ideological function** of mystifying or suppressing the internal contradictions within the feminine sphere of domestic responsibilities.

13. **Modernist women's writing anticipates** a notion of "**homelessness at home**", *in which home* figures a claim to a *gendered identity*, while *homelessness* echoes the writer's **consciousness** *that* this identity is neither completely determined nor inherently spatialized *in the ways that* the ideology of separate spheres represents women as being.

14. But **this metaphorical phrase** does **not entirely reject the spatial** figuration of femininity; in fact, the **implication is** *that* an *alternate conception of space* might empower a new feminist politics, as in Audre Lorde's poem 'School Note', *where* the speaker refers to herself as being '*at home*' anywhere *because* **no place** '*is*' home.

15. **They** then **resort to alternative strategies**, such as intruding on territories and chasing females away from territory holders, *the strategies* occasionally **successful** *because* up to twenty percent of estrous females *that* were chased by young males in an experiment *mated with them*.

16. While **McKay** explicitly **weaved racial-political markers** into his poems *that* unequivocally indicate the *author's racial identity* and **lamented** *that* the failure of black leadership was rooted in a *socioeconomic* and intellectual chasm between the black masses and the intelligentsia, **Braithwaite** preferred to **camouflage racial identity** under his pen and **barely touched** the issue of **race** in America in his own poems.

17. But **they** also **have mutual identification with a community** notorious for its cultural and socioeconomic **exclusivity** and its **detachment** from a large black population, *which* was **in conflict with** Mckay's preference for radical society *that* was *unpalatable* and abominable *for Black elites*.

18. The **presence of kin** in the natal area **makes easier to receive help** from related individuals; the level of **aggression might be lower** among kin than among unrelated individuals; breeding close to kin can also **increase breeding success**, as in the case of microtine rodents.

19. **One proposed mechanism** *by which* animals can *recognize unfamiliar relatives* is **phenotype matching**, *which* involves learning the *phenotype* of familiar relatives, or of oneself, *thereby forming* a *phenotypic template against which* the *phenotypes* of unfamiliar individuals can be compared.

20. **Some animals** might be **using some form of phenotype matching: mice** have been shown to **use** MHC odor type to avoid breeding with close relatives; **olfactory cues** also seem to be **used by** Arizona **tiger** salamanders and **rainbow fish** seem to **use** both visual and chemical cues to detect shoals of related individuals.

21. The **study of dispersal of relatives** in colonially breeding seabirds and waterfowl **is of particular interest** in this context because virtually **all species** in this group **share characteristics** *that* are generally believed to promote the evolution of cooperation.

22. **This clearly demonstrates** *that* **sisters' nesting close** to each other **is not** a by-product of either extreme natal philopatry or a preference to nest close to parents, **but results from** a genuine **preference for nesting close to kin**.

23. In addition, *that* **females only nested close to sisters born in the same year** (i.e., sisters *that* they had been in close contact with) **also suggests** *that* the **clustering of female kin** in barnacle geese does **not result from phenotype matching**.

24. The **concentration of** atmospheric methane **is projected to increase** significantly *given* the large pools of carbon stored in permafrost *that* can be converted to methane upon thaw, the susceptibility of methane hydrates to release from the ocean floor with rising seawater temperature and the acceleration of methane-producing anthropogenic activities.

25. Furthermore, **thaw of p**ermafrost along lake margins **releases** labile **organic matter** *previously sequestered in* permafrost for centuries to millennia into anaerobic lake sediments, *enhancing* methane production and ebullition emission and *serving as* a positive feedback to climate warming.

26. The **insouciant attitude** *that* Breathless takes toward its audience **may encourage** impressionable viewers **to mistake it for realism**, but there is **nothing** about the characters' **talk or behavior** *that corresponds to* the way people *actually talk or behave*, even in France.

27. **There may be a threshold effect** so that the **dysregulation** of neurotransmitter systems characteristic of the disorders **only emerges at some critical level** of persistent stress *that* is not reproducible in controlled laboratory studies.

第四节　题型、题干、选项集中训练

4.1　题型分类训练

　　这里将6套模拟题的60道题分类总结，然后可集中分类看任何一类题型。尤其请集中看最常考的主题/结构题、功能作用题、取非题、对比比较题、逻辑单题等。读者可依照这里的方法，将GRE真题的10–15个练习的题目分类，然后集中训练，这样，才能提高对题干的敏感度，在考场上自动反应。 在下表中，"2.10"表示第2个练习的第10道题，其余类推。标有星号的是混合题型，或从选项内容角度来看可归入多类的。

主题/结构	态度	段落核心/首末句	功能作用	选择句子	取非	对比比较：核心/细节	列举	信息/多句细节	单句细节	逻辑支持反对	类比	逻辑单题
1.1		13, 1.7* 1.9	1.8		1.5	12, 1.3* 1.6	1.10*	1.7 1.10				1.4
2.1 2.4	2.3	2.6*	2.5		2.7 2.8	2.2* 2.6	2.9		2.2 2.9*			2.10
3.3 3.6		3.7* 3.4*	3.2 3.5	3.9	3.1 3.4	3.4* 3.7				3.8		3.10
4.4	4.8*		4.3 4.7		4.5		4.6 4.10	4.2 4.9		4.8		4.1
5.6 5.9	5.10*	5.7*	5.1 5.4		5.10	5.2* 5.7	5.5	5.2 5.3*	5.3			5.8
6.6 6.9			6.3		6.10	6.4* 6.7			6.4	6.1	6.2	6.5 6.8

4.2　题干集中训练

　　集中看6套模拟题的所有题干，想想它们是什么题型、什么解法、如何定位。

Exe 1

1. The passage is primarily concerned with

2. According to the passage, Lowell's approach to poetry differs from that of Hopkins and Eliot in that he

3. Which of the following characterizations of the relationship between Lowell and Eliot and Hopkins can be inferred from the passage?

4. Which one of the following statements, if true, most weakens the conclusion?

5. It can be inferred from the passage that the author would draw which of the following conclusions if they had not found that young rats administered with CPP show no reduction in experience-dependent plasticity?

6. Which of the following statements about the relationship between young and old rats are true, based on the information in the passage?

7. Which of the following claims about the place cells are supported by the information in the passage?

8. The author mentions Hebb's concept of the 'phase sequence' of cell assemblies in the third paragraph most probably in order to

9. It can be inferred from the passage that a successful and consistent cooperative and reciprocal strategy in a population composed of contributors and free-riders would depend at least partly on

10. The passage provides information to support which of the following statements EXCEPT?

Exe 2

1. The passage is primarily concerned with

2. Which of the following statements about sea or land cover can be inferred from the passage?

3. The author considers the explanation put forward by Milankovitch for the periodic retreat and advance of the glaciers to be

4. Which one of the following best expresses the main idea of the passage?

5. The author's mention of Nancy Hartsock's study serves primarily to

6. The second-wave feminist critique of domesticity differs from earlier feminist criticism in that the second-wave critique

7. The passage suggests that the second-wave critiques would have been more illuminating if they could do which of the following?

8. Which of the following would be true if most of the relatives with inherited reelin deficiency in both families turned out to be schizophrenic rather than normal as they are today?

9. According to the information in the passage, which of the following features is essentially unique to human language and accompanying human cognitive powers?

10. Which one of the following most seriously weakens the argument?

Exe 3

1. Which of the following statements, if true, would cast most doubt on the author's claim that alternative strategies undertaken by four- and five-year-old males sometimes could be successful?

2. The author's exemplification of intruding on territories of older males by younger males serves which one of the following functions in the passage?

3. The primary objective of the first paragraph of the passage is to

4. It can be inferred from the passage that McKay would have found Braithwaite's writing more acceptable if which of the following had happened?

5. The author's discussion of the genres of African American literature practiced by Locke, White, and Du Bois in explaining McKay's skepticism toward the motives of the black intelligentsia is probably intended to

6. In the second paragraph, the author is primarily concerned with

7. It can be inferred from the passage that the traditional and recent methods in the assessment of the degree of admixture of a given population differed in which of the following respects?

8. Which of the following, if true, would strengthen the challenge to Weingast's hypothesis as presented in the passage?

9. Select the sentence that merely provides support for a hypothesis.

10. Which one of the following, if true, most strongly supports the argument?

Exe 4

1. Which of the following, if true, most seriously undermines the researcher's hypothesis?

2. It can be inferred from the passage that the author would be likely to agree with which of the following are the factors for the transience of workers in the nineteenth-century America?

3. The author of the passage mentions Hareven's study of the payrolls of the Amoskeag Mills in order to

4. The main purpose of the passage is to

5. The author might have to revise the conclusion that sisters' nesting close to each other is a result of a preference for nesting close to kin if which of the following might happen?

6. The author mentions which of the following as the benefits of philopatry EXCEPT

7. The author mentions the MHC odor type of mice probably in order to

8. Which of the following, if true, would support the phenotype matching hypothesis?

9. The passage contains information that would support which of the following statements about the money studied by the archeologists?

10. The passage mentions which of the following are possible factors for increased concentration of atmospheric methane EXCEPT

Exe 5

1. The author uses the analogue of identifying a firefly to

2. Which of the following statements about the relationship between stars and extrasolar planets is supported by information given in the passage?

3. Based on the information in the passage, which of the following statements about the perspective of deconstruction in the interpretation of the film could be true?

4. The author discusses Matthew Arnold's essay "The Function of Criticism in the Present Time" in the third paragraph primarily in order to do which of the following?

5. The information provided in the passage indicates that parody of traditional acting and filmmaking might include which of the following as its features?

6. Which of the following best describes the organization of the passage as a whole?

7. According to the passage, the residual method used by Gemery differs from the alternative method in that it

8. Which of the following, if true, most strongly supports the French policy about imidacloprid?

9. Which of the following best describes the main idea of the passage?

10. It can be inferred from the passage that the GMO-crops hypothesis would have been more convincing if researchers had been able to

Exe 6

1. Given the information given in the passage, it can be inferred that which of the following statements is true of the zone of hypoxia on the surface of the live coral tissue?

2. Which of the following, if true, would most weaken the hypothesis proposed in the passage?

3. Select the sentence in the passage in which the author qualifies the disapproval of Padilla's model in explaining how individual differences and personality characteristics influence the rate of acculturation.

4. It can be inferred from the passage that which of the following descriptions would be true of conventional approaches to acculturation?

5. Which one of the following, if true, most supports the scientists' proposal?

6. The passage is primarily concerned with discussing

7. Given the information in the passage, which of the following statements is true of volcanic glass?

8. A reasoning error in the argument is that the argument

9. Which of the following statements best describes the organization of the passage as a whole?

10. It can be inferred from the passage that the necessity of threshold effect hypothesis stated in the last sentence would need to be reassessed if researchers found that which of the following were true?

4.3 选项集中训练

请读者集中看6套模拟题的所有选项，尤其是那些自己做错或蒙对的选项，想想这些选项，为何对，为何错。

我们都在努力超出现在的自我，在这个意义上，你就是另一个我。我们是走在同一条奋斗之路上。在这条路上，有辛苦，有兴奋，有冲动，有疯狂，有百转千回，有望远天际；唯一没有的，就是自傲和浮夸。卡夫卡的《变形记》里的小白领，为了突破现有，敢于变成甲壳虫，以脆弱与敏感的新身，活着。脆弱的个体，伟大的勇气。残雪写下《灵魂的城堡》，将这一切不断取非当下自我的冲动，化成稳定的叙事，令我们想到如果2-3年自己都没有奋斗没有进步，一定会痛哭。最大的责任是自己。建设好自己，就能带出你最想给的，给你想给的人。空想与哀怨，都是停留在伤感的过去，是萎缩的自我，是空洞的安慰。让我们不断取非当下的自我，向优秀的人聚集、靠拢，与他们一起奔跑，而未来，会有人跟随你奔跑。

结构方法的延伸

通过以上各章，我们已经大致了解GRE的浓缩学术文章应该如何读、如何分析、如何训练。是否可以把这里的结构化阅读方法推广到其他体裁呢？我们知道，英文主要是学术英文、媒体英文、文学与日常英文（Academic English, Media English, Literature, Ordinary English）。结构化的方法主要适用于学术和分析类体裁。许多大学英文的训练书籍，往往将这四类英文一锅烩，不顾它们之间的分别，要求读者以精读或泛读的方式统一处理。这样的传统阅读书籍或阅读方法瞄准的对象太大了。一个方法，竟要分析所有体裁的文本。这假定了所有体裁的文本遵循同一套表层语言结构。但很不幸，这假设不成立。另外一个困难是，这类传统方法集中于最底层的语法分析（grammar analysis），而不是论点与论据的关系。即便有语篇分析，也是以对话开始，而很少考虑专业的学术英文，很少讨论论点与论据的关系。一些作文书会讨论论点与论据，但却把它与修辞和句法并举，重视程度不够。语法分析是必要的，但意义绝不只在语法，而更多的是在单词、短语之外。学术英文的体裁，当然是要用不同的方法去处理。这里的问题是，这种方法是否可以推广到非学术类的体裁？

第一节　对话、文学、媒体、学术文章

本节将简要叙述人类语言创造的自然史，同时提出各个阶段的文本分析的解决方案。人类最早的语言是口语和对话。**对话**能否进行逻辑分析？人类的对话包含了自然演化和社会风俗的全部秘密，斑驳纠缠，是极难分析的。人工智能的困难，不是解决深度逻辑推理问题，而是模仿和重构人类的日常行为，包括对话。学术分析的对象不是我们每天眼睛看见、耳朵听到的事！诚然，这些是要分析的，但难度超乎想象；它们是演化的奇迹和最终结果，很难进行逆向工程式的还原分析。什么样的语言现象是可以分析的呢？这是要碰巧的。学术研究需要一些运气，恰好有了这个和那个理论，组合起来，恰好可以解释一些现象，然后才可以解释了。20世纪50年代，Noam Chomsky用数理的方法来研究人类的语言，提出以句法（syntax）为中心的普遍语法学说，才为语言学奠定了一个基本框架。但这只是语言分析的开始，而不是结束。人类如何说出一句话？所指为何？这是十分困难的问题！Ray Jackendoff在他的伟大著作*Foundations of Language*中，用演化的理论来改造普遍语法学说，提出语音、句法、语义、空间的4层结构分析，才分析了一句话是如何被人类的大脑说出、被人理解的。这些分析早就不是普通的英语学习的范畴，而是属于认知科学、演化论、科学导向的语言学。本书第2章的多层结构分析，可以看做该书第12章第7节所说的语篇、对话、叙事（discourse, conversation, narrative）的意义分析向着段落和文章层次的延伸。研究语言与学习语言不同。在科学家还没有弄清楚人类的对话之前，人类能否讲话呢？我们已经讲了几万年了！对那些自然和社会演化的奇迹般的产品，模仿是比还原分析更快的逼近方法。对于对话，我们只需要在自造的或自然的英语环境下进行大量的、高强度的模仿训练就可以。如果要先懂得对话的理论，再来学习对话，那学会估计是下几辈子的事了。通过研究对话的原理来学说话，好比通过研究生理学来学走路和吃饭，效率是非常低的。要青少年通过学语法来学对话，效果差是可以预期的。大量背诵才是学习日常对话和生活英文的王道。

日常**对话**是有结构的吗？人类的对话内容稳定，但稳定在何处？或者，向何处收敛？按照Robin Dunbar关于语言的研究（*Grooming, Gossip and the Evolution of Language*），人类的对话向人际关系收敛；这些对话，多数不是讨论逻辑与理性，而是gossip，闲聊一些人际关系的事。而这些人际关系的内容也有模式，但这些模式不是来自语言本身，而是来自人的生存需求。语言是为生存服务的，从演化论来看这几乎是必然的结论。人类对话里讨论的多数都是：你身体怎么样、天气如何（适不适合外出）、衣服怎么样、谁对我好、谁骗过我、谁可以信任、做什么事、跟谁一起去做。亲人、朋友、对手、陌生人，是几乎人类所有对话里最常出现的字眼。分析这些问题，只知道语法是不够的。重要的是研究人类演化的共有天性，John Tooby 和Leda Cosmides倡导的演化心理学（Evolutionary Psychology）对此提供了一个很好的指引。

对话的下一步发展就是**故事和短文**。有些对话本身就是故事，人类通过这些故事来评估自己在人际交往中应该采取的角色和应该认同的价值观。人类的语言创造了丰富的社交信息环境，它反过来又强化了人类的语言，说出更复杂、更摄人心魄的故事，这样一步步训练了人类的心智。语言的力量不只在于沟通，而且在于将特殊的事情变成普遍的概念，故事里的人是特殊的、具体的，但通过语言表达出来之后，却能成为一类人认同的典范和榜样。这样，偶然创造的事件，就有机会形成共同叙事，在群体中传承下来。在故事的世代传递中，那些能够吸引人的或者有用的情节和说辞，就逐渐保留下来，变成越来越复杂的叙事，故事的情节日益丰富，有时也越来越有层次，慢慢就有了有韵律的诗歌，还有无韵律的小说。听故事是人类的天性。小孩特别喜欢听故事，通过故事里的人物、情节来了解社会规则、表述自我、排练自己的社会角色。听故事的目的不是为了获得道德训诫，而是为了在社会中生存。也有成人收集、整理各种故事，写成各种短文，于是有了《鹅妈妈童谣》、《一千零一夜》、《格林童话》。而且，在文明发轫时，故事不仅属于儿童，而且是成人认知世界的主要方式。通过故事，成年人可以了解部落、家族、群体的历史和文明，了解社会风俗和行为规范。

故事的聚合可以构成更长更复杂的**诗歌、戏剧和小说**，民间故事可以变成有组织的文化创造。一些故事经过有心人的收集、改编，变成了诗歌，如《荷马史诗》；有的则是各种短篇故事集，如《山海经》、《圣经》。一些人将民间故事整理、再加上自己增加的情节，创造出戏剧、话本、传奇、甚至小说，如埃斯库罗斯的《悲剧》、但丁的《神曲》、莎士比亚的戏剧、《福尔摩斯探案集》，又如《三国演义》、《水浒》、《红楼梦》，又如《雾都孤儿》、《简爱》、《傲慢与偏见》、《复活》、《白痴》、《了不起的盖茨比》、《老人与海》。诗歌、戏剧和小说不只是日常对话，日常对话处理的是小范围的熟人社会关系；相反，它们往往涉及大范围的社会互动，已经超出人类天性所能掌握的范围，涉及陌生人群居社会的文化。如何分析这些相对系统的戏剧、诗歌和小说呢？它们是有结构的，这些结构就是情节，而这些情节所暗示的社会运行规则，往往各不相同。情节结构与社会规则的差异，就是不同社会的文化差异。在普遍的人类天性或心智倾向的基础上，人类的各个语言群体和文化圈在不同的文化演化道路上，逐渐累积了许多差异。如何解释这些差异？这需要一般的文化理论。目前比较有价值的文化理论是弥母学（memetics），它的首创者是Richard Dawkins，他在*The Selfish Gene*中提出，除了基因以外，这个世界还有一种能够自我复制的东西，meme/弥母，它是任何可以在人类大脑或其他媒介中传播的最小文化单位，并不完全受人的控制，也摆脱了基因的限制。Daniel Dennett应用这个理论研究了人类的意识（*Consciousness Explained*）和宗教（*Breaking the Spell*）。虽然它仍然欠缺定量的研究，但弥母学特别适合于讨论文化的差异和快速变化，例如新词汇的演变、时尚的流行、互联网时代快速传播的文化等等。一般地，弥母学探讨的是，观念或文化如何基于人的天性、并因具体的社会条件而聚合、演化、累积成形。所以，它所提供的分析框架，也许可以帮助我们研究诗歌、戏剧和小说的模式和内容。一些文艺作品只是诉诸天性，其情节聚焦于人际关系和人在社会中的行为，这时主要用演化心理学。许多文艺作品则讨论特定社会的特定事件，这时就需要弥母学，通过它来研究某些特定的语言聚合体，例如典故、桥段，如何出现和演化。当然，也有少数伟大的文学作品，已经超脱人的演化天性或社会环境的边界，从世俗事件中脱离，专门讨论信念和抽象价值观这样的精神层面的问题，例如卡夫卡的小说，这时就需要系统的逻辑解读，比如残雪的《灵魂的城堡》。但总的来看，多数诗歌、戏剧、小说，主要还是靠事件本身的进程来驱动，它们的句子和句子构成的片段，往往经过精心组织，以吸引着有着特定心智倾向的读者和听众。所以，可以认为，文艺作品是一连串有组织的事件；阅读文艺作品，就是理解一连串的事件。在这个方面，本书所讨论的逻辑总分、对比、因果等结构还是不容易派上用场的。我们需要掌握的是演化心理学、弥母学、文学的传统模式，有时也要一点社会风俗的常识。

可以通过语法研究学习如何写诗、写小说吗？当然不能。伟大的作品使用的单词也许与受过教育的人一样多，但这些单词是通过特定的方式聚合，不由得你不感动、不由得你不钦佩，说明它们有着奇妙的设计。这些奇妙的聚合就是一个非常成功的语言设计，要从语法上逆向工程几乎是不可能发现其中的奥妙的，这就像你很难通过肌肉分析来发现一个网球运动员的优美动作和神奇能力。组合爆炸是搜索成功的设计所要克服的主要问题。假设一部小说用到的词汇为5000个，写了100000字，考虑这个问题：从这5000字的词汇库里挑词，构造一个100000字的文本，词汇可以重复，则有多少种可能情况？答案：5000^{100000}！这也许比整个宇宙的粒子还要多。这就是组合爆炸：要素（在此例中就是词汇）越多，可用的位置（文章总字数）越多，则可能的设计空间就越大，可以大到无法想象；一般地，假定要素为m个，可用的位置有n个，则可能的设计结果有m^n个。对写作而言，即便加上语法约束，这个数字也不会降低到我们可以操作的程度。所以，从词汇、甚至合乎语法的句型出发，自己制造好作品，其概率可以小到忽略不计。

换个角度，如果我们已经有了一部好作品，那么，模仿它，就能让我们快速地接近优秀作品的设计空间，写出相对可取的作品。即便这似乎没有什么创造性，但写得似模似样就很了不起了，因为君不见，那些教导你要有创造性的人，似乎从来没有写过什么伟大的作品，做过什么有创造性的事，他们是怎么知道创造性是怎么回事的？他们也许连判断创造性的标准都没有！他们也许误把与众不同当做创造性了！但天可怜见，100000字的文本，每个地方都用同一个词，这样的文本也是很与众不同的！重要的不是与众不同，因为设计空间是如此如此如此如此的巨大，你总会与众不同的。在与众不同这一点上，大家都是相同的；你的这篇文章，几乎永远不可能再有人跟你写得一样，包括你自己在内。事实上，这正是判断抄袭的重要原理：两个极其相似的文本，完全巧合引起相似的概率远远低于拷贝导致相似的概率。那么，重要的是看作品为什么优秀，但这一点也是很难确定的。如果你已经懂得什么叫优秀，那么你已经区分了优秀与平庸，那说明你已经超越平庸了。但一个人通过自己摸索，写出的文章是平庸的机会多点，还是优秀的机会多点呢？在如此巨大的一个语言空间里搜索，要找到好的山坡都是困难的，更不用说山顶。所以，辨别优秀的设计，本身就需要多年训练的眼光，通常不是只凭天分或是忽然感悟，就可以有此能力。优秀，不是那些平庸的、浅尝辄止的心智所能鉴赏的。那么，如果我现在不优秀，如果我现在的语言能力薄弱，怎么办？找到万人传诵的作品，找到众人敬仰的精英，先模仿吧！我们总是从模仿优秀的运动员的动作开始，来学习如何打球，我们甚至都不必、也不能研究他们在打球时肌肉是怎么运动的。更难以下咽的一个事实是，面对优秀的人和事，我们可能还不知道他们优秀在哪里。所以合适的做法是，先模仿优秀的人的作为、思想、价值观，都不要问为什么——就像不要通过研究运动员的肌肉运动来学习如何像他们那样打球，这样反而可以提升学习的效率和成功的概率。模仿得多一点，就会与优秀人才的设计空间更近一点。应用到语言学习上，背诵和练习，是学习如何写作好的诗歌、戏剧、小说和其他优质文本的主要方法。要学习写好英文吗？看着人类已有的好不容易出现的经典，背诵吧！练习吧！希望缪斯女神垂青吧！即便弥母学提供了一个分析语言设计的框架，它目前也不能教你如何写出最一流的作品。当然，研究模式可以提高效率。通过研究一流的脚本，更有希望写出相对正常的或说平庸的剧本。例如，利用一些已经研究清楚的桥段，加上已知的人类基本情感诉求和世俗追求，如家庭、爱情、权力斗争之类，你也可以写出让人吐血的肥皂剧，例如都市情感剧。这当然还不够。如果能够把从各种一流文本学来的技巧和模式，调整、组合、重新编织，应用到新的语境，也许就有更大的希望创造出比较精彩的作品。伟大的作品呢？这是要靠运气的。没有人知道怎么创造出伟大作品；这计划不来，这指导不来，甚至，连作者也只是在写出来之后，才战战兢兢地觉得，自己的作品也许是伟大的。我们要写好的作品，第一步就是模仿已经很好的作品。

对话、故事、小说并非人类创造的全部语言体裁，人类也发明了**逻辑论述**。在古希腊时代，贸易频繁，无数的生意人从各地赶来，聚居在同一个城邦，也许是为了制定清晰的契约的需要，语言的精密性的要求提高；同时，古希腊在偶然情况下发展出的民主决策的社会组织体制，也要求人用自己的演说和文字，说服非亲族的公民。逻辑与修辞的学问由此产生出来，并在特定的社会环境下，获得极大的推动。伟大的思想家将人类讨论自然和社会的语言整理、发挥、创造，写出了伟大的逻辑文章，比如柏拉图的对话、亚里士多德的论文式的作品。在东方，也有陌生人聚居的社会出现，在面对和理解这种社会时，理性的思考也会时不时闪现，于是有哲人的对话录，如论语，或者哲理诗篇，如《道德经》、庄子的《逍遥游》。

与中国古代的散文以及世界各地其他文化的书面文字通常聚焦于家、国、神，向人际关系、社会关系、人–神关系收敛不同，古希腊的推理文字抽离社会和人际关系，纯粹地讨论自然、社会、以及说话的一般规则，从这里开始，有了非常系统的**假说演绎的推理系统**，也就是总分展开的思维模式，尤其是有了因果关系的严密讨论。虽然在其他民族的文化中这些推理也有所体现，例如中国古代的屈原的"天问"、或贾谊的"过秦论"，但是，系统的逻辑思维，也就是假说演绎的思想架构，主要是古希腊人创立的（Russell在*A History of Western Philosophy*中的重要观点，见Russell, 1946）。有了演绎逻辑的思路以后，人类开始超越普遍的家族和神灵的心理天性、超出国家与社会的特定文化圈的认同，探索一些抽象的、所有人都可以理解的推理模式。语言从产生以来，终于表现出它超出人类基因的魔力，通过逻辑推理，为人类打开了新的精神空间。这些逻辑推理的基本形态是，围绕一个一般性的论点或公理，展开一系列的论述，推出各种各样的命题，这些命题最后再与人类的现象观察、行为实践对接。中间论证都向论点收敛；小论点向大论点收敛。所有的推理步骤尽量是所有人，无论种族、教育水平、文化背景，都可共享的、认可的。这样的系统的逻辑推理反映在各式各样的文本中，例如亚里士多德的《形而上学》、塞涅卡的《道德书简》、马基雅维利的《君王论》、斯宾诺莎的《伦理学》、洛克的《政府论》。这样的作品都可以用结构化分析的方法，找出主题、论点、论据、态度、结论，理出文章的主要逻辑线索。当然，它们的篇幅通常较长，不适合作为GRE学习的阅读材料！不过，即便如此，在考完GRE以后，完全是可以用结构化的方法去阅读，把长篇大论分解为章节，每个章节再化解为几个部分，每个部分约等于GRE式的3–4段，一一分析各段首句及中间论据的展开方式，再把各个部分彼此串联，考查它们之间的关系，然后再把章节的重点抓出，然后再掌握章节与章节之间的关系，这样，就能逐层分析伟大的推理作品的逻辑思路、把握其中的主要思想。

除了学术圈内流传的系统推理以外，还有**面向大众的分析性文字**。在欧洲印刷术发明、工商业和消费社会兴起以后，大众媒体开始出现，报纸媒体或报道事实，或评论社会，分析性的文字在社会中普遍传播。现代的媒体英文，往往以一个小故事开始，然后展示事件各方的立场，有时还提供深度分析，分析相关各方的利益、目标和策略的起源、发展、结果、优劣等。本书倡导的结构化阅读方法不能适用于其中的故事部分，但是完全可以用来分析其中的评论部分。但是，要学习逻辑推理，是否要从媒体英文开始呢？学英文和了解英美社会，最好的入口也许是媒体英文，但学习逻辑推理却无此必要，因为媒体里的英文的逻辑相对简单，而且任何一方的立场往往介绍和展开得不够充分，不能充分展示逻辑推理的深度。不过，今天的一些媒体，如*Economist, New Yorker, Atlantic Monthly, New Republic*，常有非常好的分析文字，值得多读，而且用本书讨论的逻辑结构方法去读，也能很快找出核心的意义。相比之下，基于单词和语法的精读和泛读的方法，也许就不是那么有效了。当然，只是结构分析的方法也不够；许多媒体文章预设了读者对特定社会的基本常识。懂得关于社会体制、文化习惯的常识，对于深入阅读媒体文章也是必要的。

结构化阅读方法最适用的对象还是**现代学术文章**。现代学术英文，比之传统的系统学术推理，结构更清晰，总分结构更明显，这也许是因为参与学术讨论的人来自全球和社会各个阶层，在反复的学术沟通中，最清晰的结构被保留下来了，成为学术界的通用规范。本书讲的总分、对比等结构，对分析这类论文和专著，非常适用。另一方面，一些学术文章，即便推理和逻辑结构都很清楚，但依然不能被普遍接受的。这是为什么呢？逻辑严密并不保证观点正确；逻辑推理的确可以让人的思想飞翔，摆脱特殊因素的限制，走向普遍的概念思考，但同时，如果没有自我约束，逻辑推理也可能虚无缥缈、高深莫测、让人误入歧途。找到和应用逻辑推理的自我检验法则的文章，是**科学文章**。对于科学文章，结构化的阅读方法、尤其其中的因果关系展开的思维，就更有用了。科学论述的特点是假说演绎的逻辑推理和数理实证。早在古希腊，欧几里德就通过假说演绎的方法，应用于可量度的数学对象，创造了古典几何学。伽利略借鉴这种方法，将它应用于非数学的物质对象，创立了现代科学方法和古典物理学；他要求每个推理所用的概念，都用定量和数学公式去描述，而不只是作为一个推理环节而已。与学术推理通常只是给出公理、演绎推导不同，科学方法是先观察现象，然后构思假说，将其中的概念量化，再找自然实验或做人工实验，验证该假说对某种预测的可量化或可观察的情况是否也成立。与普通人所以为的不同，科学假说并不一定是观察现象之后归纳的结果，而是思想家自己发明的，其来源可以是归纳、可以是意识形态、或者文化习惯等等。在科学中，重要的不是假说怎么来的，而是假说是否在原则上可证伪，并在当前得到验证。卡尔·波普在他的伟大著作《猜想与反驳》(Karl Popper, *Conjectures and Refutations*) 总结了这种方法的精髓。这样，科学的文章比逻辑推理的文字更进了一步，它把概念量化，而不只是提出概念系统。科学将概念系统的对比和并列都变成一个连续的量的序列的各点之间的关系，也将总分结构变成一个概念与它自身的量的展开的关系，比如，电磁场与它的各种电磁波段，又比如，环境压力下的自然选择与特定的某个环境下的某种行为或性状的选择。

本书讨论的结构化阅读方法，现象解释的观点之间的关系、以及因果论点的展开结构，对于阅读科学论文应该很有作用。读者如果能够在读完本书的基础之上，再看1-2本Critical Thinking, Scientific Method方面的书（如Moore and Parker 2008, Popper 1963），那就更好了，因为基本的批判思维和科学方法在国内的大学课程较少讲授，但却是研读科学论文所必需，自己补课是必要的；GRE的科学文章在此方面也能帮上忙。在分析以科学论文为代表的学术文章时，首先，我们可以把3-4段作为一个小部分，看它们之间的关系以及各自内部的论证模式，这与GRE的长短文章的分析方法完全相似。而学术论文1节的内容往往有10-20段，就相当于3-5篇连续的GRE长文章。一篇论文有4-5节，第1节通常提出研究话题，第2节文献综述，评论以前的各派研究，然后第3节提出作者的方法，第4节给出实验数据，最后1节是讨论、分析和结论。这样就可以层层分析，从段、到节、到整篇论文；或者，在了解了这种组织结构以后，从论文主题、到节、到段。需要注意的是，在段落的内部论证方面，GRE文章多为先论点后论据、先观点后阐述、先假说后实验；而在学术文章中，除了这种情况以外，也会经常出现先实验后解释，先数据后假说。但一旦假说或解释提出以后，还是会以因果机制、对比等方式来展开更多的论据，支持这个理论。当然，除了最基本的逻辑把握以外，要理解学术文章的内容，还需要该学科的理论知识。显然，结构化阅读的方法，只是一种逻辑识别方法，并非是学问本身；学问是一整套的逻辑推理系统，一篇特定的论文往往预设读者熟悉其中许多基本定律、假说、理论，所以要彻底弄懂文章，自然需要掌握学科常识。但这些学科的常识本身，也是按照逻辑来构造的，并非只是一些事实描述而已，所以，读学术教科书，也可以用结构化的方法。相比之下，科普读物并不预设读者知道该学科的理论常识，写得更加清晰，用结构化方法去阅读，快速而有效。

如果写作学术文章、尤其科学论文呢？与戏剧、诗歌、小说等虚构类作品不同，非虚构类作品、更不用说科学论文，写作模式往往固定，甚至，如上一段所说，连模块的顺序都是相对统一的。它们的句子和段落，不是按照故事情节、以文化传统接受的方式来推进，而是按照学术研究的固定步骤来组织。由于这些组织方式高度一致，于是，学写科学论文和学术文章，是相对容易的。依然按照上文所说的模仿优秀作品的思路，读者如要训练，可以先找10篇自己学科的专业英文论文，仔细地分析论文主题、各个小节的核心、各段的首句和转折句核心、段落内部的论证方法等内容，再加上自己所学的专业知识，例如如何做适合，如何分析数据等，就知道可以怎么写学术文章了。这个工作辛苦而有趣，是值得努力尝试的。

我们可以将4类阅读体裁的分析内容和分析方法总结如下：

体裁	分析内容；分析工具
日常对话、闲聊 Conversation, Gossip	对话分析；演化心理学/evolutionary psychology
故事、文学 Stories, Literature	情节与桥段；文学传统 + 演化心理学 + 弥母学/memetics
分析性、事实性文字，媒体 Nonfiction, Media	小段叙事、评论推理；结构化阅读 + 社会常识
学术文字 Academic writings	复杂逻辑；结构化阅读 + 科学方法 + 各门学科的理论常识

学习了结构化的阅读思路，可以让人的思维更连贯、更清晰，但并不保证可以获得正确的、可用于实践的理论。那么怎么获得正确和有效的理论呢？人类的自然智能已经就人际之间的关系进行推理，我们不需要刻意练习，也能大致明白如何与人沟通、采取何种策略、理性评估成本与收益，等等。后来，古希腊人把这种人际关系中所蕴含的推理，提炼成普遍的命题形式，推广到非人际的社会和自然领域，如用逻辑方式来研究正义、真理、自然等问题，这就是逻辑推理的起源。之后的思想者常以构造逻辑前提和推理系统为乐。人们甚至被此能力诱骗，以为任何逻辑自洽的概念和命题系统都是真的，都是有用的，如德国和法国的许多思想家的作品。我们说过，逻辑没有自我批判的检验机制，也会制造陷阱，很多人就是被自己的逻辑推理所困，但从不知道可以如何检验这些命题。但是，自伽利略的科学验证方法出现以来，至少在科学界，只有那些以可量度或可操作的概念为元素进行的推理才可能是有效的。所以，推理演化有3个阶段：自然选择的人际推理、普遍的逻辑推理、数理实证的逻辑推理。人类的自然思维向人际关系收敛，偏向站队、情绪宣泄、立场表达、群体认同；自然选择塑造了人的这些特定的情绪和决策行为集合，以保证它在社会是有效的。人类后天的逻辑思维向论点收敛，保持论调的前后一致，说话的内容清晰可传达。但逻辑严密不等于有效和正确，科学方法要求论点与论据的关系成为可量度、因而可验证的关系；所以，科学的推理向论点数理收敛。

此外，还有一些听起来特别悦耳、公众特别认可的观念，比如关于人生而平等、人有的权利我都具有的普遍人权等观念，也是特别强大的文化观念，为多数人类社会所认可。这些观念本身也是一个公理系统，可从中推出各种关于社会政策的理论命题，希望付诸实践。又比如，市场是分散决策的，发展经济并不需要一个中央计划者，就如语言的繁荣只需要每个个体说来说去，并不需要一个中央语言委员会一样。这个理论很难量化，但它在实践中非常有用。虽然这些命题还不是在可验证的可量度的意义上有效，但属于人类社会的生存智慧或者文化共识，而鉴于多数人在多数时候其实不会是错的，这些观念也值得我们去跟踪、效仿和研究。

　　逻辑分析：假说演绎 = 公理系统 = 总分结构
　　科学实证：假说演绎的总分结构 + 概念的量的分解
　　社会文化：公认的观念，如人权、平等的公理，市场的分散决策系统

最后，一些中文的文章也以逻辑的总分结构来展现和论证自己的论点，所以，我们这里的方法不仅适用于英文学术文章，当然也适用于中文学术类文章以及分析类的作品。

第二节　商业与社会应用

逻辑是与陌生人沟通的方法之一。本书分析的学术文章中的逻辑，可以应用到更广的商业和社会领域。首先，公文与媒体的阅读和写作都可以用逻辑的方法来处理。面向公众的文字，常常诉诸情感、文化认同、社会的价值观等，这是获取注意力的好方法。但同时，除了情感诉求以外，还需要有逻辑来支撑，才能让不同的人也信服。工商业迅速或高度发展的社会，人越来越多样化，形成一个异质陌生人大规模聚居的社会，情感、偏好、利益虽然不至于激烈冲突，但也不会完全相同，而是和而不同、彼此相容。在这种情况下，只能诉诸不同个体和群体之间的最大公约数，这些公约数除了共同的利益交集和普遍的人类情感天性以外，就是人类后天发明的逻辑了。逻辑推理是从一个前提或公理出发，经过一系列推理步骤，得到一些结论。发表在公开媒体和面向社会公众的公文，是可以写得于情于理都令人接受的。于情，是调动和诉诸社会各个异质群体的最大公约数，往往就是人类的普遍天性；于理，则是诉诸逻辑，按照总分结构的框架，逐步地展示自己的论点，既不拖泥带水，也不前后矛盾。一些在中国工作的媒体记者，模仿和学习Economist以及其他优秀杂志的写作方式，极大地提升了媒体文字的逻辑水准。

其次，逻辑思维也可以在商业文案甚至ppt文档中反映。先写出一个总的结构图，大标题大论点、小标题小论点。然后每个论点都用事实、数据、调查结果、证据等来支撑。在与客户、消费者进行沟通时，一份前后自洽、论点清晰的文案或文档，会极大地减少沟通的信息成本。了解各自的预设、论据、理由，能够帮助我们有效地说服对方或与对方有效沟通。麦肯锡的明托（Minto）曾专门以总分结构的思维，写出一本《金字塔原理》的名作，阐述在商业文案中怎样写得清晰、明确、合理。该书也许是进入职场、甚至写作论文的必读之作！

最后，数理验证的科学逻辑，对于分辨、判断和评估一些商业计划的作用，也是有效的。科学验证不必以研发部门的实验室为限。有论者专门以假说验证的角度来分析7-11百货店的员工和经理如何按照天气、店铺周边的人群特点，来判断是否应该多做关东煮、多放凉品等等。这本书是《巷口商学院》，可以帮助我们认识到科学方法在商业世界的应用。另外一本通常被认为是经典的商业中的科学书籍，是Eliyahu M. Goldratt and Jeff Cox 写的Goal，该书以小说体的形式写成，但内容是商业的科学教育，十分值得一读。在企业与社会方面，数理实证相对困难，但也有对比的案例，相当于自然的控制实验，可供参考；另外，科学思维的重要部分，概率与统计的思维，对于观察企业成功和社会兴衰，通常相当有用。冯仑的《理想丰满》一书，应用概率思维和对照实验的思路，分析企业成败、社会体制，非常有启发性。Hubbard的杰作How to Measure Anything，甚至主张将这种量度的方法应用于一切看似不可量度的问题。由于概率和统计的思维不属于人的天生能力，所以，了解这些知识，掌握其中的逻辑，对于职业选择、企业运作、投资管理、社会认识，也许都是十分重要的。Nassim Taleb的两本伟大著作，The Black Swan, Fooled by Randomness，对此做了杰出的论述。读这些书，既可以应用本书所分析的结构化的方法，也可以学到逻辑推理的知识，还可以知道它如何应用，可以说是一举数得！

以上种种，充分说明，逻辑的方法，无论是基本的总分结构，还是科学的假说验证和概率思维，不仅在学术中有效，而且在商业和社会中也适用。在一定程度上，阅读的结构方法同时也是内容的逻辑，两者高度统一。练习逻辑思维的好处，并不限于GRE。诚然，掌握逻辑思维决不等于拥有一切，你掌握了运动规律并不一定就是运动达人，你懂得社会的原理并不意味着自己已经获得权力和地位，也就是说，逻辑也有它的力量的边界，生活是斑驳的组合，需要各种层次的能力和实力。但是，逻辑依然重要，它可以让我们理解这些生活和社会目标，让我们在自己的约束条件下，更有效率地达到它们。这种能力在异质人群大规模聚居的现代社会尤其重要，因为这个社会超出了人类的天性和直觉所能自动把握的范围，通过逻辑和系统的知识，更有可能更快地把握社会的运转规则，以强大的精神姿态面对不确定的未来和不断变化的社会。一个人年轻的时候，总要学点硬知识；学好逻辑思维，应该不算坏吧！通过GRE的文章来学逻辑，你会很快乐！将来把这种思维应用于自己的学习和工作，更会受益良多。

在起步的时候，没有什么比向精英学习更快的成功方法了。 如果成功是一套算法，则搜到这个算法实在太困难，自己独自搜索找到的概率接近于零。先向多个精英学习，优秀的概率才会大一点点。如果有人已经到达附近山顶，我们可以先模仿他们爬山的步骤和方法，结果也许爬不到山顶，但半山腰也不错，比在山谷反复徘徊好很多。成功的最大敌人是概率，不是模仿。在人生的设计空间里搜索，多数步骤都通向平庸；有人教你保持平常心、有人请你处之泰然。他们在走向普通人的道路上，一步都没有走错。请敢于与普通人不同，请勇于向优秀的人学习。谁是优秀的人？优秀的人就是与优秀的人在一起的人。

附录(一) 参考资料

1. 给考生

Kane, Thomas S (1988). *Oxford: Essential Guide to Writing*. Oxford University Press. 尤其是Part III.

Moore, Brooke Noel & Richard Parker (2008). *Critical Thinking*. 9 edition, McGraw-Hill. 尤其是Ch2, 11.

Rosenwasser, David & Jill Stephen (2008). *Writing Analytically* /罗森瓦塞尔和史蒂芬:分析性写作. 北京大学出版社.

Silentwings, "爱一个美女好难", 网络文章, URL: http://wenku.baidu.com/view/594e4a85bceb19e8b8f6ba99.html

2. 给教员

Chalker, Sylvia (1996, 2001). *Linking Words*. Max Hueber Verlag /雀卡: 连词. 北京: 外文出版社.
（该书讨论英文关联词, 属于Collins系列。与中文不同, 英文高度重视关联词的用法, 以确定逻辑关系。）

马焱俊. "从ETS角度看GRE阅读文章来源". 上海新东方《教学研究》(第二期).
URL: http://sh.xdf.cn/publish/portal25/tab17597/info78639.htm

Miller, George A. (1956). "The magical number seven, plus or minus two: some limits on our capacity for processing information". Psychological Review 63 (2): 81-97.
URL: http://www.musanim.com/miller1956/

Passonneau *et al.*, (2002)."Electronic Sources as Input to GRE Reading Comprehension Item Development: SourceFinder Prototype Evaluation", published by Educational Testing Service (ETS).
URL: www.ets.org/Media/Research/pdf/RR-02-12-Passonneau.pdf（必读文章, 分析GRE阅读文章的来源）

Russell, Bertrand (1946, 1961). *A History of Western Philosophy*. George Allen & Unwin Ltd.
（该书以逻辑的假说演绎方法分析西方历史上的思想家, 可从中看到逻辑推理的历史发展, 同时也可以用结构化阅读的方法去阅读。）

3. 本书其他参考资料

Dennett, Daniel (1995). *Darwin's Dangerous Idea*. Simon & Schuster.
（该书的设计空间、反对贪婪还原主义、主张多层还原的思维, 对本书的多层分析方法有巨大启发。）

Jackendoff, Ray (2002). *Foundations of Language: Brain, Meaning, Grammar, Evolution*. Oxford: Oxford University Press.
（语言学的巨著。本书的多层分析思维, 可以看做是该书方法在段落和文章层次的一次应用。）

Pinker, Steven (1994). *The Language Instinct*. New York: W. Morrow and Co.
（文笔优美, 将乔姆斯基的普遍语法理论与演化理论结合, 提出语言是人的本能。）
(1997). *How the Mind Works*. Norton. （一本杰作, 以新达尔文主义的适应理论, 讨论人类心智的各种演化模块。）
(1999). *Words and Rules*. Basic Books. （语言是组合空间里的子集, 儿童过度推广动词规则, 说明天生规则存在。）

Popper, Karl (1963, 2003). *Conjectures and Refutations*. Routledge.（盖世杰作! 对科学方法的讨论令人震撼。）

赵南元(2002). 认知科学揭秘. 北京: 清华大学出版社.
（在认知领域应用多层分析和广义进化论, 非常深刻的著作。）

附录(二)　参考答案

Exe 1

1. A	2. C	3. E	4. C.	5. E
6. D	7. A	8. B	9. A	10. AC

Exe 4

1. B	2. AC	3. D	4. B	5. B
6. C	7. E	8. B	9. E	10. C

Exe 2

1. E	2. D	3. C	4. B	5. A
6. E	7. D	8. A	9. AB	10. B

Exe 5

1. D	2. C	3. B	4. D	5. AC
6. A	7. E	8. A	9. A	10. C

Exe 3

1. C	2. D	3. A	4. C	5. D
6. B	7. D	8. E		
9. "The Bill of Rights of 1689..."			10. D	

Exe 6

1. AC	2. E			
3. "Certainly, Padilla's emphasis on..."			4. BC	
5. C	6. D	7. C	8. B	9. D
10. E				

《GRE考试官方指南》（第2版）（附CD-ROM）

美国教育考试服务中心（ETS）编著

◎ ETS官方独家授权版本，权威解析GRE考试

◎ 提供样题范例，帮助考生了解各题型的命题形式和要求

◎ 内含完整的全真试题，并配CD-ROM 1张，带给考生真实的考场体验

定价：108元　开本：16开　页码：576页

《GRE词汇精选》（最新版）

俞敏洪 编著

◎ 自1993年首版以来先后修订9次，收录迄今为止GRE考试的全部重要词汇，并给出精准释义

◎ 提供大量经典例句，结合语境加深对单词的理解与记忆

◎ 以"词根+联想"记忆法为主，辅以组合词、单词拆分、谐音等多种记忆方法，配以插图，轻松记忆

◎ 给出丰富的同义词，归纳常考搭配

◎ 提供返记菜单，便于查找定位

定价：58元　开本：16开　页码：488页

《GRE词汇精选：乱序版》

俞敏洪 编著

◎ "乱序"编排，提供科学的单词记忆方法

◎ 给出丰富的同义词，归纳常考搭配

定价：59.8元　开本：16开　页码：512页

《GRE词汇精选：便携版》

俞敏洪 编著

◎ 浓缩《GRE词汇精选》之精华，收词全面

◎ 提供"词根+联想"记忆法，实用有趣，轻松记忆

◎ 开本小巧，便于携带，方便考生随时随地记忆单词

定价：25元　开本：32开　页码：448页

《GRE词汇逆序记忆小词典》

俞敏洪 黄颀 编著

◎ 《GRE词汇精选》（最新版）的姊妹篇

◎ 采用逆序编排体例，巧学助记

◎ 增添GRE考试最新词汇

◎ 附正序词汇索引，方便检测记忆效果

◎ 本书自1999年问世以来，畅销不衰

定价：15元　开本：32开　页码：308页

《GRE考试官方指南词汇必备》（附MP3）

余仁唐 编著

◎ 页码为序，合理编排方便查找

◎ 选词科学，根据语境精准释义

◎ 重点单词，循环出现加深记忆

◎ 一书多用，全面攻克GRE词汇

定价：25元　开本：32开　页码：264页

《GRE核心词汇考法精析》

陈琦 周书林 主编

◎ 11年实战经验沉淀，精炼3000必考词汇

◎ 直击GRE同反考法，星号标注最新词汇

◎ 权威韦氏英文解释，辅以经典英文例句

◎ 高分学员励志推荐，GRE考试高分必备

定价：55元　开本：16开　页码：464页

《新GRE高频词汇：句子填空》

杜昶旭 侯宇轩 编著

定价：48元　开本：16开 页码：384页

《新GRE高频词汇：阅读理解》

杜昶旭 侯宇轩 编著

定价：59元　开本：16开 页码：568页

◎ 科学统计20年GRE考试句子填空与阅读理解真题词汇

◎ 按照单词在考试中出现的频次从高到低排序

◎ 提供单词在GRE考试中考到的中、英文释义

◎ 提供与真题难度相当的例句及高质量中文翻译

《GRE阅读必备专业词汇》

包凡一 编著

◎ 真题为准，重点难点专业词汇一网打尽

◎ 直击考点，有的放矢掌握高频易考单词

◎ 话题分类，按照学科全面罗列各科词汇

◎ 小巧便携，方便随时随地复习与记忆

定价：15元　开本：32开　页码：280页

《词以类记：GRE词汇》

张红岩 编著

◎ 词以类记，按学科和意群精心归纳57个Word List

◎ 收词新、全，收集整理最新GRE重要词汇8400多个

◎ 多重记忆法综合运用，提高了有序储存的效率

◎ 听觉辅助记忆，1000分钟超长录音，另含词汇讲座内容

定价：55元　开本：16开　页码：528页

《GRE备考策略与模拟试题》（附CD-ROM）

[美] Sharon Weiner Green, M.A., and Ira K. Wolf, Ph.D. 编著

◎ 根据新GRE考试趋势编写，全面展现新GRE考试特点

◎ 内含1套与考试难度相符的诊断试题，帮助考生定位
  薄弱环节

◎ 所有练习及模拟试题均附参考答案及详解

◎ CD-ROM内含2套机考模拟题

定价：78元 开本：16开 页码：536页

《GRE 8套题》（附CD-ROM）

[美] 杜兰 编著

◎ 提供8套高仿真模拟试题，并附有答案与详解

◎ 针对GRE写作、语文和数学讲解考试重点，分析备考策略

◎ 为GRE国际考生提供考试相关的重要信息

定价：78元 开本：16开 页码：500页

《GRE 6套题》

[美] 扎勒，[美] 托马斯 编著

◎ 提供6套GRE模拟测试题，体现新GRE考试趋势与特点

◎ 所有试题均附有参考答案和详细的解析

◎ 针对12道分析性写作题目，提供12篇高分写作范文

定价：65元 开本：16开 页码：408页

《GRE语文与写作》

[美] 扎勒，[美] 安林 编著

◎ 深度介绍了新GRE考试语文和分析性写作各题型

◎ 提供各题型的解题技巧和写作指导以及大量自测练习

◎ 附写作高分范文

定价：45元 开本：16开 页码：236页

《GRE数学》

[美] 莫耶 编著

◎ 介绍了新GRE考试所涉及的数学概念，包括算术、代数和几何
  知识

◎ 涵盖新GRE数学全部题型及考查内容，针对每一类问题提供解
  答策略

◎ 提供大量练习题供考生进行自测，有助于考生领会解题关键，
  掌握高分技巧

定价：48元 开本：16开 页码：332页

《GRE官方题库范文精讲》

[美] Mark Alan Stewart，J.D. 编著

◎ 提供200多道GRE作文真题及其范文

◎ 精讲其中的近100篇

◎ 分析、总结了Issue和Argument高分写作技巧

定价：48元　开本：16开　页码：408页

《GRE写作论证论据素材大全》

韦晓亮 编著

◎ 全面涵盖英文论证和论据素材

◎ 中西方文化大荟萃

◎ 精选权威刊物文章

◎ 汇集数年教学经验，指导考生有效备考

定价：35元　开本：32开　页码：424页

《GRE作文大讲堂——方法、素材、题目剖析》

韦晓亮 编著

◎ 详细阐述Issue和Argument写作策略与步骤

◎ 完整收录GRE写作题库，剖析题目要求

◎ 提供丰富的论证、论据素材，拓展思路

◎ 浓缩多年教学精华，指导考生高效备考

定价：48元　开本：16开　页码：388页

《GRE数学高分快速突破》

陈向东 编著

◎ 详尽归纳数学考点，全面总结数学术语、解题窍门

◎ 强化训练GRE数学考题，帮助考生考前突破，高效备考

定价：40元　开本：16开　页码：300页

《GRE&GMAT阅读难句教程》

杨鹏 编著

◎ 精选GRE、GMAT历年考题中的阅读难句

◎ 以结构分析法，采用各种特定标识，剖析每段难句

◎ 以实战要求为目的，利用语法，学练结合，以练为主

定价：32元　开本：16开　页码：272页